GREAT BATTLES OF WORLD WAR II

A VISUAL HISTORY OF VICTORY, DEFEAT —— AND GLORY ——

DEALERFIELD

This edition specially printed for
Dealerfield Ltd in 1995 by
Marshall Cavendish Books
(a division of Marshall Cavendish Partworks Ltd),
119 Wardour Street, London W1V 3TD

ISBN 1 85927 056 5

Printed and bound in Italy

Some of this material has previously appeared in the Marshall Cavendish partwork
IMAGES OF WAR

CONTENTS

BATTLE OF BRITAIN

BATTLE DIARY

JULY
10	First day's bombing
11	Attacks on Portsmouth
24	RAF lose 5 aircraft
	Luftwaffe lose 15 aircraft
25	Luftwaffe lose 19 aircraft

AUGUST
8	Weymouth convoy attacked
11	Eagle Day set
13	Eagle Day
30	RAF lose 35 aircraft
	Luftwaffe lose 76 aircraft
31	RAF lose 41 aircraft
	Luftwaffe lose 39 aircraft

SEPTEMBER
15	Battle of Britain Day
27	Day planned to smash the RAF

OCTOBER
7	RAF lose 17 aircraft
	Luftwaffe lose 19 aircraft
15	RAF lose 15 aircraft
29	Luftwaffe lose 16 aircraft
31	Battle ends – TOTAL LOSSES

RAF		1,023 aircraft
Luftwaffe		1,887 aircraft

BOMBS OVER BRITAIN

Bildarchiv Preussischer Kulturbesitz

The Battle of Britain has begun, 10 July 1940. The Luftwaffe is set to smash the RAF. Only the RAF's determination to control the skies can save the land from Nazi invasion.

▲ **The target is Britain. The objective is to destroy the RAF, its air bases and aircraft factories. A twin-engined Heinkel He-III sets out, three manually aimed guns and one 2,200 lb (1,000 kg) bomb load at the ready**

During ten tense weeks in the summer of 1940, thousands of anxious British eyes peered upwards towards the weaving vapour trails and flashes of metal that criss-crossed the sun-drenched blue sky. The fate of over fifty million citizens rested on the outcome of countless, swirling dog-fights between anonymous dots manoeuvring frantically high above.

As the last small ships had limped home to English ports with troops lifted off the bullet-marked sands of Dunkirk, on 5 June 1940, the French hastily improvised a defence line on the Aisne and Somme rivers, hoping the Maginot Line along the eastern frontier would hold. But this was blitz warfare. Within a week, German forces had crossed the Marne River and, moving south behind it, panzers outflanked the Maginot Line. Declared an open city, Paris soon fell without resistance, and on 22 June, France formally surrendered.

Hitler could now concentrate on Britain and mount the invasion of England, code-named Sealion. But the narrow

Poppertoto. Inset: Bundesarchiv—Koblenz

▲ Mustering of the German workforce. An assembly line mass produces Junkers Ju 88 bombers. Inset: anyone can serve in the Luftwaffe part-time, with or without experience, of any age. There is good pay and free child-minding for those who join the Luftwaffe on the ground.

radar chain and co-ordinated command structure.

Hitler planned to launch Sealion on 15 September. On 1 August he ordered the Luftwaffe 'to overcome the British air force with all means at its disposal, and as soon as possible'.

SOFTENING-UP ATTACKS

From early June, coastal areas and convoys had been sporadically attacked, followed a month later by a systematic attempt to destroy shipping in the Channel and to smash the south-coast ports. Portsmouth was bombed for the first time on 11 July, and on 8 August 257 enemy aircraft in relays raided a Weymouth-bound convoy, sinking seven ships.

During these softening-up attacks, losses on both sides were heavy. Between 10 July and 10 August, the Germans lost 217 planes to Fighter Command's 96. This loss of RAF aircraft in the run-up to the main conflict was of great concern to Fighter Command.

Things were so bad that at one stage No. 54 Squadron could muster only eight aircraft and thirteen pilots. Moreover, compelled to fly up to 600 sorties a day, Fighter Command risked tiring its surviving pilots (and ground crews) before the real day of reckoning.

EAGLE DAY

German air fleets (Luftlotte 2 in the Low Countries and north-east France, 3 in north-west France and 5 in Scandinavia) were to begin the elimination of the RAF on 'Eagle Day', set for 11 August. As the victors of Poland and France smelt fresh blood, Reichsmarschall Hermann Göring assured Hitler of swift, glorious success. According to his reckoning, four days would suffice to clear southern England, and a mere four weeks would be

strip of water over which the battered remnants of the BEF withdrew so dramatically, remained the major obstacle to his plans for conquest.

Air power was the key. Unless the RAF could be driven from the skies, German landing craft could not cross the Channel in safety.

For their aerial assault, the German forces deployed 2,820 aircraft (about one-third fighters, the remainder twin-engined bombers, fighter-bombers or single-engined Stukas). In defence of Britain, Air Chief Marshal Sir Hugh Dowding deployed 591 Spitfires, Hurricanes and two-seater Defiants in four Groups: No. 10 covering south-west England; No. 11 the south-east; No. 12 the east and Midlands; and No. 13 the north.

The front-line squadrons were supported by anti-aircraft units, barrage balloons, Observer Corps posts with listening and visual identification equipment, a coastal

RAF Museum, Hendon. Inset: Keystone Collection

▲ Not even dry after processing, German aerial reconnaissance photos come under scrutiny to plan the next attack.

◄ Talking anxiously at the airfield, pilots of No. 19 Squadron await the next Luftwaffe visit.

Der Kämpfer im Luftschutz hat so viel Verantwortung und so viel Ehre wie jeder Soldat an der Front!

Keystone Collection. Inset: Bundesarchiv—Koblenz

◄ **The Luftwaffe's mighty figurehead, answerable only to Hitler, Hermann Göring. His early prowess as a World War I pilot behind him, his obsession is the creation of an invincible Luftwaffe – and the annihilation of the Royal Air Force.**

LUFTWAFFE'S LEADER

On the eve of the Battle of Britain Reichsmarschall Hermann Göring was Commander-in-Chief of the largest air force in the world—the Luftwaffe. He had been in charge of a fighter squadron at the age of 24, and became one of Hitler's earliest supporters. Ambitious and vain, but with great intelligence and ability, he rose fast in the Nazi hierarchy, apparently unhindered by his addiction to morphine.

Early Luftwaffe successes led him to promise Hitler a speedy annihilation of the RAF—and a clear way for Operation Sealion to go ahead. The rout of the Luftwaffe, and subsequent defeats on the Russian front, led to his virtual retirement by the last years of the war—a loss of power from which even his aristocratic friends could not save him.

enough to crush the whole force. As bombers devastated ground installations, fighters would deal with aerial opponents.

At the appointed hour, however, low cloud and poor visibility spoiled the afternoon. Although numerous dogfights occurred in the morning, no coastal attacks were possible. The following day, 12 August, proved little better, though German bombers did manage to inflict damage on several airfields in Kent and knock out the radar station at Ventnor on the Isle of Wight. On that day, the RAF lost 22 aircraft to 31 of the enemy.

Eagle Day at last became a reality on 13 August. Although communication failures meant that some German squadrons set off piecemeal in the morning, the main assault in the afternoon was impressive. Aircraft from the Low Countries attacked Kent and the Thames Estuary; those from France swooped on areas around Southampton Water.

THE BATTLE BEGINS

The opening day of the Battle of Britain proper saw 1,485 Luftwaffe sorties for the loss of 46 planes. Encouragingly for Fighter Command, the RAF lost only 13 (six pilots being saved). But the Germans were satisfied, and the process of self-delusion and gross exaggeration thereafter quickened. Göring believed that 30 airfields and factories had been put out of action, with 300 British fighters destroyed.

The following day, 14 August, the Luftwaffe flew 500 sorties, and 15 August saw a major effort with seven massed attacks. First, 40 Ju-87 Stukas hit Kent, then 65 Heinkel He-111s—escorted by 35 Messerschmitt Bf-110 fighter-bombers from Norway—struck northern England, followed independently by 50 Junkers Ju-88s.

Further south, East Anglia suffered, with Kent receiving more punishment later in the day; and in the early evening, 80 bombers struck airfields in the south. That day, the Luftwaffe flew 520 bomber and 1,270

fighter sorties, losing 75 aircraft to 34 British, though the RAF claimed 180 destroyed and 472 damaged.

The 16th witnessed 1,700 sorties, devastating a number of airfields, including Tangmere, for the loss of 45 Luftwaffe planes to 21 of the RAF.

LUFTWAFFE FAILURE

As the German aircraft returned to their bases at the end of 17 August, the sixth day after 'Eagle Day', it was clear that the RAF had not been subdued, despite German intelligence estimates that only 300 British fighters remained operational. (In fact, there were twice that number—with more rolling off the production lines.)

A concentrated Luftwaffe assault on southern airfields

War Stories

One pilot recalled advice given him by First World War Ace Taffy Jones, who stuttered. 'There's going to be a wwwwar, and yyyou chaps are going tttto be in it. When you gggget in ccccombat, you'll be very ffffrightened. Just rremember, the chchchap in the other cccock-pit is twice as ffffrightened as you'. That same pilot, encountering his first 109, thought 'Poor chap – **he** must be **really** terrified' and put him out of his misery by shooting him straight down.

▼ **A plea for help in dire straits. As the struggle for air supremacy is on and more RAF pilots perish, the need to recruit and train more fliers is increasingly urgent.**

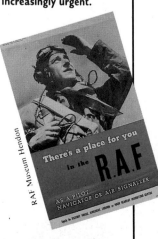

RAF Museum Hendon

There's a place for you in the R.A.F

AS A PILOT NAVIGATOR OR AIR SIGNALLER

▶ A formation of Heinkel He-III bombers prepares to take its toll on British targets. These light aircraft are armed with three manually aimed machine guns and carry a bomb load of 2,200 lb (1000 kg) in the central fuselage.

▲ The Nazi Party staffs up for the fray. From left to right, Generalfeldmarschalls Milch and Sperrle, Hitler himself, Reichsmarschall Göring and Generalfeldmarschall Kesselring, holding ceremonial batons denoting Army rank.

THE FEW

Although it was a majority of British pilots who fought during the Battle of Britain, many airmen of different nationalities gave their services, and almost a hundred their lives, in the British cause.

	Men who took part	Men killed
United Kingdom	2543	418
Polish	147	30
New Zealand	101	14
Canadian	94	20
Czech	87	8
Belgian	29	6
South Africa	22	9
Australian	22	9
Free French	14	Nil
Irish	10	Nil
United States	7	1
Southern Rhodesian	2	Nil
Jamaican	1	Nil
Palestinian	1	Nil
Total	3080	515

single-engined fighters needed to escort the more vulnerable bombers, and also capable of being hit by the short-range Ju-87 Stukas.

The first phase of the Battle of Britain had gone in Dowding's favour. A total of 363 German aircraft had been destroyed, against 181 British fighters in the air and a further 30 on the ground. The Stukas had been shot out of the sky by the more manoeuvrable Spitfires and Hurricanes and the RAF airfields were still operational.

Nevertheless, Fighter Command was facing serious difficulties. Only 170 replacement aircraft had been received, and a mere 63 new pilots replaced the 154 lost in action. Nor were all losses due to the enemy. A laconic entry in No. 111 Squadron's records was typical: 'Shot down by Kenley A A (anti-aircraft), pilot killed'.

THE BIG GAMBLE

Although not accurately aware of the RAF's predicament, the Germans reasoned that by attacking the airfields of No. 11 Group in the south-east, they could force the RAF to expose its total remaining strength in unavoidable defence. This plan was a gamble. Greater inland penetration to achieve their aim meant shorter time in the battle area for the fighters. But a large number of defending fighters with the German bombers might entice what was left of the RAF to aerial destruction.

Between 24 August and 6 September, the Luftwaffe mounted 33 major raids. Besides the loss of 286 aircraft in that period, Fighter Command lost 103 pilots killed and 128 wounded from a total strength of just over 1,000. Dowding was in acute danger of losing the initiative, if not the whole battle.

IMMINENT INVASION

For a while, the new German approach seemed promising. However, time was fast running out. At the end of August, Sealion had been postponed from 15 until 21 September, for which the executive order to proceed had to be issued by 11 September. Nevertheless, the Germans were preparing for invasion. Photographic reconnaissance revealed to the British a concentration of barges and landing craft in ports across the Channel.

on 18 August cost another 71 planes to 27 British. Göring was furious. German ace, Galland, recalled: 'He came to inspect us and stayed to insult us for over an hour'.

At this moment the Luftwaffe began, ever so slightly, to doubt its strategy. Despite the complete destruction of the installation at Ventnor—fortunately not fully appreciated by Göring—the Germans believed that the radar stations were difficult to locate and immobilise. So they began to concentrate on southern airfields and factory targets, which were well within the range of the

A POKER-FACED TACTICIAN

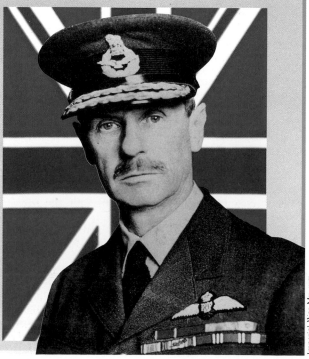

Air Chief Marshal Sir Hugh (later Lord) Dowding, nicknamed 'Stuffy' due to his reserved and undeniably crusty manner, did more than any other single man to bring the RAF victorious through the Battle of Britain.

A veteran of World War I, who had also seen service in the Middle East, Dowding became a member of the Air Council for Supply and Research from 1930 to 1936. In this post, he prophetically advocated the development of new and faster aircraft, such as the Spitfire, and research

into radar—both of which were vital in the RAF's Battle of Britain victory.

From 1936 to late 1940, Dowding was Air Officer Commanding-in-Chief, RAF Fighter Command, and led the RAF to victory in summer 1940.

In spite of his uncompromising, single-minded devotion to British air supremacy and his immense skill and experience, he was abruptly replaced soon after Hitler finally called off Operation Sealion.

▶ Dowding: crusty, humourless author of the RAF's Battle of Britain victory.

▲ Reginald J Mitchell, creator of the Spitfire. By August 1940, Fighter Command has 19 Spitfire squadrons in its ranks with which to face the Luftwaffe.

▲ No 92 Squadron of Spitfires – the 362 mph miracle aircraft which changed the face of aerial combat. Over 1200 Spitfires were delivered to the RAF before the Battle of Britain.

Imperial War Museum

JOIN THE ATS

ASK FOR INFORMATION AT THE NEAREST EMPLOYMENT EXCHANGE OR AT ANY ARMY OR ATS RECRUITING CENTRE

SERVE IN THE WAAF WITH THE MEN WHO FLY

◄ Too glamorous to be true. This ATS recruitment poster is rejected as being too slinky. A more workmanlike approach is favoured, as in the WAAF poster, inset. No new recruit is misled into the idea that a life in uniform is one of glamour.

On 6 September, British defences were warned to expect invasion within the next three days and, as the blitz on London opened, the following night forces were brought to immediate readiness.

Although the expected invasion did not materialise, the Battle of Britain was by no means over, with daylight attacks still to be countered. As the Germans flew deeper inland from the south-east, No 12 Group had the range actively to intervene. On 9 September, it claimed to have downed 28 German planes for the loss of 4. Poor visibility early in September to some extent restricted the weight and frequency of the daylight raids, but Göring remained confident that the executive order for Sealion could still be issued as planned. The weather—and RAF stubbornness—deemed otherwise.

Ten days were required between order and invasion, and Hitler now set 27 September as the date for Sealion—the last feasible one before the onset of autumn storms. So, by 17 September, Göring must finish off the RAF—a task doomed to failure.

RAF TRIUMPH

On 20 August Prime Minister Winston Churchill paid tribute to Dowding's men: ' . . . undaunted by odds, unwearied in their constant challenge and mortal danger, [British airmen] are turning the tide of world war by their prowess and devotion. Never in the field of human conflict was so much owed by so many to so few.'

Those 'few' were about to underline the trust that Winston Churchill placed in them. The day of 15 September would provide the triumphant finale to the Battle of Britain. Two days later, Hitler postponed Sealion indefinitely. Fighter Command had bought valuable time for reorganisation and recuperation after the débâcle in Flanders and the 'miracle' of Dunkirk. The RAF had retained command of the air and saved Britain from invasion.

RAF'S FINEST HOUR

Battle of Britain Day, 15 September, dawned. For the depleted RAF it was make or break. For the Luftwaffe, assembled across the Channel, it was all-or-nothing mass assault.

▲ An RAF pilot's wings.

◀ Dog fights trace vapour trails above St Paul's Cathedral, London. Inset: a newsvendor's 'scoreboard' reassures the watchers on the ground.

A t dawn on Sunday 15 September 1940, mist covered much of southern England. By 8 am, however, visibility had cleared with light cloud at 3,000 ft. And, although some local showers developed later, the day remained sunny with a light westerly wind during the afternoon and evening.

Only a few German bombers had attacked London the previous night, and Fighter Command anticipated that the Luftwaffe was gathering for a large-scale onslaught. Across the Channel an increase in enemy coastal convoys in the past week had heightened fears of invasion—so a determined, last-ditch effort by the Luftwaffe to obliterate the RAF could soon be expected.

WOULD THEY COME?

At Bentley Priory, near Stanmore, Fighter Command Headquarters staff waited tensely. Anxious group and sector controllers were in position. In Observer posts and radar stations, experienced watchers looked for signs of enemy activity. Balloon and anti-aircraft units stood by. Every squadron was alert.

From first light, Nos 10, 11 and 12 Groups put up standing patrols from Harwich to Land's End, and each sector station kept one squadron at Readiness state. For two hours, as the mists gradually thinned and the clouds drifted higher, nothing was

▲ September 1940, a formation of Supermarine Spitfires banks steeply in a 300 mph turn as they patrol above the evening clouds.

reported. Perhaps the enemy would not show up after all?

Then towards 9 am, reconnaissance planes began to appear in the Strait of Dover, over the Thames Estuary and Kent. At 10.50, Rye radar station reported enemy formations south-east of Boulogne.

Five minutes later, No. 11 Group warned the other two groups and Air Vice-Marshal Keith Park, Commander of No. 11 Group, ordered all his squadrons to readiness. As Nos. 72 and 92

Squadrons from Biggin Hill scrambled at 11.03 to patrol between Canterbury and Dungeness, Spitfires already airborne were brought back to base to refuel.

FIRST WAVES

At 11.35, the first wave of 100 bombers, with a strong fighter escort, was met by 20 Spitfires as it crossed the coast near Dungeness. Shortly afterwards, another 150 Do-17s and He-111s protected by Bf-109s cleared Ramsgate and Folkestone at 15,000 – 26,000 ft.

In all, five Spitfire squadrons attacked these two waves in the Canterbury-Dover-Dungeness area, with eleven Hurricane squadrons joining in around Maidstone and Tunbridge Wells.

The sky was etched with white vapour trails, the dirty smoke and flames of stricken aircraft plunging earthwards, while the main Luftwaffe force still pressed on relentlessly towards London.

The Germans did not adopt a uniform pattern of formation. Flying at different heights, usually the bombers flew in a V-shape of five to seven aircraft, the same number in line abreast or in a diamond shape.

However, groups of nine in

▲ Standby for a dawn raid on England. Messerschmitt Bf 109 fighters of Jagdgeschwader 53 run up their engines at a captured French airfield on the Channel coast.

Imperial War Museum. Inset: Bildarchiv Preussischer Kulturbesitz

▲ The emblem of Jagdgeschwader 53. Number III fighter wing was led by German ace Hauptmann Werner Mölders in May 1940.

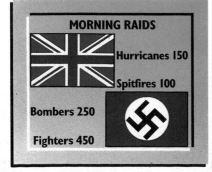

BATTLE LINE-UP

MORNING RAIDS		AFTERNOON RAIDS	
Hurricanes 150		Hurricanes 150	
Spitfires 100		Spitfires 100	
Bombers 250		Bombers 150	
Fighters 450		Fighters 240	

◀ The RAF and the Luftwaffe, relative strengths 15 September 1940.

▲ The RAF Observer badge.

▼ Target Southampton. German bomber pilots work out the night's mission – to flatten the port and factories – using a scale model of the town.

Popperfoto. Inset: Crown Copyright

Imperial War Museum

▼ 'Released', fighter pilots revert to conversing in the King's English.

RAF Museum, Hendon

PILOTS' JARGON

In the years before the outbreak of war, the pilots of Biggin Hill developed a flyer's jargon, which, with only slight modification, exists to this day.

Stages of operational commitment:

Released Not required for operational duty until a specific time

Available Combat ready to take off within 15 or 30 minutes

Readiness Combat ready to take off within 5 minutes

Standby Pilot sitting up in cockpit, awaiting start-up and scramble instructions

Identification was vital, both visually and on radar:

Flash your weapon Turn on your IFF. Identify friend or foe

Sorry, my weapon is bent My IFF signal is not working

Use of a signal in the plane would show on the radar screen as a bright tail to the moving dot—this would identify the plane as a friend.

Once in action, pilots communicate in their own special language:

Scramble Take off immediately

Vector Turn on to a specified course

Angels Height at which to fly in thousands of feet

Orbit Circle over specified area

Tally-ho Target sighted

Bogey Unidentified target

Bandit Identified enemy aircraft

Pancake Land immediately

Shiners Barrage balloons

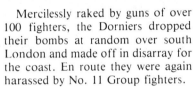

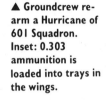

threes—'like a sergeant's stripes'—were also seen, protected by nine Bf-110s in close support and Bf-109s above. Generally, the single-engined escorts shepherded the bombers from a higher altitude, seeking to dive on attacking RAF fighters.

Although the British pilots took off in threes, once battle was joined individual pilots sought their own enemy targets and a maze of dogfights was soon strung out across the heavens.

DOGFIGHTER DANGER

The pace was furious. One Spitfire pilot described diving out of the sun to destroy a Bf-109 with his first burst, only to discover another on his own tail firing furiously at him. Managing to throw the German off, he got the Bf-109 in his sights. Two quick bursts and a second kill had been achieved in a few minutes. Returning to base, he was immediately warned of more bombers crossing the airfield at 14,000 ft. Climbing rapidly, he soon accounted for a Do-17.

As midday approached the first wave of German bombers glimpsed London—and simultaneously suffered heavy attack. As two Spitfire and three Hurricane squadrons from the Duxford Wing (led by Squadron Leader Douglas Bader, and all attacking together) appeared on the flank to burst through the close escort, four Hurricane squadrons hit the enemy head on.

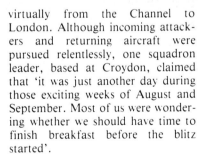

▲ Groundcrew re-arm a Hurricane of 601 Squadron. Inset: 0.303 ammunition is loaded into trays in the wings.

▼ Maintenance for an RAF fighter. A fitter checks a Hurricane's engine while another, on the wing, refuels ready for the next scramble.

Mercilessly raked by guns of over 100 fighters, the Dorniers dropped their bombs at random over south London and made off in disarray for the coast. En route they were again harassed by No. 11 Group fighters.

In central London, two unexploded bombs had fallen in the grounds of Buckingham Palace, and several funeral pyres close by bore witness to the bombers' haphazard attentions.

In one aerial encounter, Sgt. R T Holmes of No. 504 Squadron destroyed a Dornier which crashed into the forecourt of Victoria Station as its crew parachuted on to the Oval cricket ground. Holmes had a less comfortable return to earth: he baled out and landed unceremoniously in a dustbin in Chelsea.

Between 11.30 and 12.30 the action was continuous and spread out

virtually from the Channel to London. Although incoming attackers and returning aircraft were pursued relentlessly, one squadron leader, based at Croydon, claimed that 'it was just another day during those exciting weeks of August and September. Most of us were wondering whether we should have time to finish breakfast before the blitz started'.

He was able to consume his cornflakes and, once airborne, his squadron saw 30 He-111s at 15,000 ft protected by 20 Bf-110s, with another 50 Bf-109s 4,000 ft above. Manoeuvring to port, the RAF pilots got 'up sun' behind the enemy. As one flight of Hurricanes attacked from the Germans' left, the Bf-110s opened cannon fire from 1,000 yds, 'two seconds too late to engage our fighters, as two Heinkels wheeled out of formation'.

When a second flight prepared to dive on the bombers, 'the Heinkels did the unbelievable thing. They turned south, into the sun, into the

▲ A visit from the Führer. Hitler and his staff inspect progress on the French coast.

▶ The hawk's head, personal emblem of Werner Mölders, Kommodore of Jagdgeschwader 51, which appeared on the Bf-109F he flew during late 1940.

▲ The battle is on. A formation of Dornier Do-17 bombers makes its menacing appearance over the Channel, vapour trails streaming in its wake.

▲ Bandits sighted – RAF pilots 'scramble' to their waiting aircraft, ready to confront the enemy.

fighters'. With his opening burst the flight leader 'destroyed the leading bomber with such force that it knocked a wing off the left-hand bomber.' He then accounted for a third Heinkel and 'before returning home he knocked down a Bf-109'.

All over the sky similar individual and group combats were taking place. One Spitfire squadron stayed together twice to pass through an enemy bomber formation from the beam. Utterly confused by this tactic, several enemy planes collided.

Typical of individual combat was the Spitfire pilot who attacked a Bf-109, which dived almost vertically in an attempt to escape. The British pilot followed it down, recalling that 'by this time I was going faster than the enemy and I continued firing until I had to pull away to the right to avoid a collision'.

The stricken German fighter fell through the low cloud and, after recovering from his evasive action, the Spitfire pilot 'saw the wreckage of the enemy aircraft burning furiously. I climbed up through the cloud and narrowly missed colliding with a Ju-88 which was on fire and being attacked by numerous Hurricanes'.

German fighters usually attacked in pairs in line astern, getting to close range, though even without cannon sometimes opening fire up to 800 yds away. If caught without fighter protection, most German bombers (like those attacked near Buckingham Palace) dumped their loads and fled.

Twenty Do-17s found flying unescorted in a diamond formation over the London docks behaved in this way, but were chased by angry fighters and torn to pieces.

At 12.15 to the west of London, near Hammersmith, the Duxford Wing caught another collection of unescorted bombers with devastating effect. In another part of the battle, a Hurricane pilot found himself approaching a formation of 12 yellow-nosed Bf-109s. Diving under them, he shot the rear one down from below, climbed, half-rolled at the top of his loop and destroyed another from the rear before breaking away undamaged.

RESPITE – AND ATTACK!

By lunchtime, the enemy had been scattered. The Prime Minister, watching the RAF's performance from the No. 11 Group's Operations Centre at Uxbridge, clenched an unlighted cigar between his teeth, engrossed in the action. At a critical point, he asked Air Vice-Marshal Park what reserves were available, receiving the blunt but honest reply: 'None'.

A welcome respite between raids gave bomb-weary citizens time to wash their lunch dishes before returning to their air-raid shelters; tired fighter pilots snatched tea and sandwiches as ground crews worked.

War Stories

Pilots' waking hours were so hectic that their rest time was vital. A pilot recalled: 'One morning, the batman took down the blackout screens and shook me awake. 'Did you take cover last night?' he asked. I asked why and he simply said 'Look out of the window'. There was a string of craters down the garden, but they'd missed the mess building. The anti-aircraft guns had been going, bombs dropping – but I heard nothing. What an irony if I'd been bombed and killed in my bed!'

'ADOLF' IN THE RAF

Squadron Leader (later Group Captain) Adolphus G 'Sailor' Malan was a former South African merchant seaman who was to shoot down a total of 35 German aircraft during the war. A complete wipeout of the enemy plane was a success, but as he once said, 'A badly damaged enemy bomber that got home with a cargo of dead and dying had a greater effect on Luftwaffe morale'.

He joined No 74 Squadron of Spitfires on 1 July 1940, gained command of it on 8 August and during the Battle of Britain accounted for four Bf-109, one Do-17 and one Ju-88 aircraft.

His attention to proper procedures and impeccable flying became an example to fighter pilots throughout the RAF. Large posters of his watchpoints for pilots were pasted up in orders rooms all over the country.

He later became Station Commander of Biggin Hill—the most bombed air base in Fighter Command.

Imperial War Museum

▶ Adolphus or 'Sailor' Malan in the cockpit of his Spitfire.

Then, shortly after 2 pm, the enemy returned in force. Three waves of 150 He-111s and Do-17s, escorted principally by Bf-109s of Adolf Galland's and Hannes Trautloft's experienced commands, were upon them.

Orders to scramble went out between 1.30 and 2.30 pm. With a gallant effort the ground crews patched up damaged planes, allowing all three Groups to send up two flights per squadron.

The practised and co-ordinated defence organisation was able to send fighters to likely points of interception, resulting in a high degree of success. Over Kent, 170 Spitfires and Hurricanes met the enemy; those that eluded No. 11 Group were met nearer London by five squadrons of the Duxford Wing, two from No. 10 Group and another six from No. 11 Group.

Haphazardly ejecting their bombs over Hackney, Erith and Penge, the bombers sped for home as the hard-pressed fighter escorts tried to protect them—a thankless task now that their charges were hopelessly dispersed. Hunted eagerly by sweat-

▶ Ideal positioning, up-sun and over the target. A flight of Spitfires peels off and dives through light cloud towards the enemy.

Süddeutscher Verlag. Inset: Imperial War Museum

◀ A Spitfire overshoots in combat and is photographed by a crewman in a marauding Heinkel III bomber. Inset: WAAF plotters in the Operations Room at Uxbridge chart the movements of their colleagues in the sky on their map.

Suddeutscher Verlag. Inset: Imperial War Museum

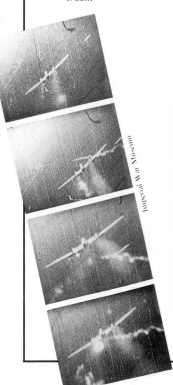

Imperial War Museum

Barnaby's Picture Library

▲ Dover's coastal defences. Radar towers stand above the white cliffs, under the protection of barrage balloons. In the distance, a pall of smoke hangs over Canterbury as German bombers take their toll. Inset: Reichsmarschall Göring, fifth from the right, and his staff survey the Channel towards Dover from the coast of Calais.
▶ The searing blaze of a German fighter plummeting earthwards in a trail of smoke.

▼ A Messerschmitt Bf-110 goes down, hit by the guns of a Spitfire. Its descent is captured on film before its explosive crash.

SEALION CANCELLED

TURNING POINT

The aim of the Luftwaffe's campaign against Britain from 13 August 1940 was to destroy the nation's air defences and to prepare the way for Operation *Seelöwe* (Sealion), the landing of three massive German armies on the south coast of England.

Hitler set the day for 15 September, but set this back six days, assembling the invasion fleet from 1 September. Final preparations needed ten days' notice, so the RAF would have to be destroyed by 11 September.

RAF resistance evaporated Hitler's dream of victory. Sealion was put back to 27 September, so the Luftwaffe had to gain air control by 17 September. The RAF's massive defeat of the Luftwaffe on 15 September forced Hitler to postpone Sealion indefinitely. The invasion was off.

Bundesarchiv.

▶ Sealion rehearsals. German troops on an invasion barge and in a dinghy.

soaked—but jubilant—RAF pilots, many bombers did not survive. And, short of fuel, the Bf-109s often had to glide across the Channel to save themselves. The rout was complete.

Pilots' reports showed how varied the many attacks were. 'We sighted a strong formation of enemy aircraft and carried out a head-on attack. The enemy scattered, jettisoned their bombs and turned for home' . . . 'The whole nose, including the pilot's cockpit, was shot away'.

Group Captain S F Vincent, station commander at Northolt and flying a Hurricane, suddenly came across eight Dorniers in formation. Looking for assistance, he decided to attack alone. Approaching head-on, he opened fire at 600 yds, then closed to 200 to break up the enemy formation.

'I made further attacks on the retreating bombers, each attack from a climbing beam . . . One Dornier left formation and lost height. With no ammunition left, I could not finish it off. I last saw the bomber at 3,000 feet dropping slowly'. Vincent was amazed at the enemy's lack of fight.

Not all the defenders escaped damage. 'Aircraft became uncontrollable, I baled out, coming down with left arm paralyzed', reported one lucky pilot.

BRILLIANT VICTORY

In just 20 minutes, the German crews encountered over 300 RAF fighters, cruelly exposing the German propaganda boast of 'the last fifty Spitfires' that the Luftwaffe would encounter. Shortly after 3.30, two small formations of fresh Bf-109s and Bf-110s flew over the coast to protect the retreating bombers. Their impact on the scene of aerial destruction that greeted them was practically non-existent.

As the threat to London receded, 27 He-111s attacking Portland were hit by six Spitfires from RAF Warmell, with the loss of one bomber and another damaged. Then, at 5 pm, Ventnor radar station reported another raid developing, which was to be the last of that event-packed day. Six squadrons went up to frustrate 18 Bf-110s from hitting their factory target at Southampton.

Emerging from Bethnal Green underground station the following evening, young railway worker Denys Childs looked at the newspaper placards proclaiming '185 enemy aircraft shot down'. 'I knew then that we had won,' he later recalled. (The actual figure was 60.)

Later on 15 September, Winston Churchill congratulated Dowding: 'The Royal Air Force cut to rags and tatters separate waves of murderous assault upon the civilian population of their native land'. Afterwards, in the House of Commons, he described the day as 'the most brilliant and fruitful of any fought upon a large scale up to that date by the fighters of the Royal Air Service'.

Enemy daylight raids continued until the end of October, but never again in such force. That sunlit Sunday, the Battle of Britain had been won. In years to come, 15 September would rightly be commemorated and revered as 'Battle of Britain Day.'

▲ The emblem of Jagdgeschwader 54 of the Channel Front.

▼ The Spitfire of Sergeant Robinson of No. 152 Squadron. It crash landed after battle damage just west of Swanage, Dorset, 8 August 1940.

▼ End of a Bf-109, washed up on a French beach on its return.

Suddeutscher Verlag. Insets: Andy Saunders

▼ Inset: a British pilot, his parachute still billowing after baling out over the Channel, is lucky – rescue has arrived just as he entered the water.

BARBAROSSA

BATTLE DIARY

JUNE 1941

22	Beginning of Operation Barbarossa
29	Minsk pocket closed

JULY

1	Fall of Riga
5	German forces reach River Dnieper
9	Rivers Dvina and Dnieper crossed, Smolensk threatened
12	First Luftwaffe bombing raid on Moscow
14	German forces reach River Luga
17	Dnieper crossed at Mogilev
27	Smolensk pocket closed
31	Army Group North reaches Lake Ilmen

AUGUST

1	Russian counter-attack begins from the Pripet Marshes
7–8	First Russian air raid on Berlin
12	Army Group Centre splits to send Panzers north and south
29	Finnish army captures Viipuri

SEPTEMBER

12	Kiev pocket closed
15	Leningrad cut off from the rest of the USSR
25	Start of the siege of Sevastopol
26	Kiev pocket eliminated – Germans now only 200 miles (320km) from Moscow

TITANIC CONFRONTATION

Keystone Collection

The spectre of Bolshevik domination had haunted Adolf Hitler since 1917. Now he was about to attempt the ultimate conquest – the destruction of the mighty Russian bear within its own lair.

▲ Finnish horsedrawn transport rattles past a column of tanks, Karelia. Throughout the war on the Eastern Front, horses were a more common sight than mechanised vehicles.

The genesis of Operation Barbarossa (codenamed after the great twelfth-century German emperor Frederick Barbarossa)—Hitler's invasion of the Soviet Union—can be traced back to the battlefields of the Western Front in 1917-18.

The young infantryman Adolf Hitler conceived a pathological hatred for Bolshevism after talking to some of the troops who had returned from the Eastern Front when Lenin and his followers overthrew the Tsar and negotiated a separate peace with Germany. During the 1920s Hitler and the National Socialist German Workers' Party (NSDAP) were in the forefront of anti-Communist demonstrations and street fights throughout a Germany torn spiritually apart by the swingeing provisions of the Treaty of Versailles which the victorious Allies had imposed in 1919.

In 1923 Hitler was jailed for his part in an attempt to overthrow the government of Bavaria (the so-called 'Beer Hall Putsch') and while in prison set out his racial and ideological fantasies in *Mein Kampf*. After he was elected Chancellor in 1933, Hitler blamed the Reichstag fire on the Communists—as the excuse for seizing absolute power and turning Germany into a one-party dictatorship.

PRELUDE TO SLAUGHTER

His hatred, moreover, was not just directed against Communists—it was directed against the Russian people themselves, whom Hitler regarded as *Untermenschen*— sub humans. For the first time, Hitler's army represented the beginnings of what Dr Joseph Göbbels' propaganda would trumpet as a true 'European' force, which would ultimately number Finns and Frenchmen, Danes and Dutchmen, Belgians and Bulgarians, Hungarians, Italians, Rumanians and others all united in a common cause—the total destruction of Communism.

Hitler had discussed the Soviet threat with his generals in January 1940 and begun thinking seriously about an invasion of Russia as early as July, buoyed up by the sweeping successes of the German divisions in Norway, Denmark, Holland, Belgium and France over the previous two months. However, it was not until 18 December that he put his concept on paper in *Führer Directive No 21*. This said that 'The bulk of the Russian army stationed in western Russia will be destroyed by daring operations led by deeply penetrating armoured spearheads. Russian forces still capable of giving battle will be prevented from withdrawing into the depths of Russia.

'The enemy will then be energetically pursued and a line will be reached from which the Russian air force can no longer attack German territory. The final objective of the

▼ General Ewald von Kleist, leader of the German 1st Panzer Group, in Army Group South.

Keystone Collection

War Stories

The enormous scope for error in locating, identifying and then dealing with targets in an appropriate way was common to all sides. The arrival of aircraft overhead was always cause for concern, be they friend or foe. A young Panzer trooper in Russia spotted low-flying aircraft and shouted, 'Hooray! Look —they're ours! To his surprise, his commander, a more seasoned campaigner, dragged him into a ditch. For him there was no doubt—patriotic fervour takes second place to self-preservation in situations such as this!

operation is to erect a barrier against Asiatic Russia on the general line Volga-Archangel. The last surviving industrial areas of Russia in the Urals can then, if necessary, be eliminated by the Luftwaffe.' However, in the wake of the Battle of Britain, more than one German officer privately expressed his doubts at the Luftwaffe's capability.

RUSSIANS UNPREPARED

In 1940, or even 1941, the Russian army was totally unprepared for war. In 1937, fearing an army coup to depose him, Stalin had used the secret police, the dreaded NKVD, to arrest and execute scores of high-ranking officers and hundreds of their subordinates, from

COMMISSAR ORDER

In March 1941, at a conference of senior officers, Hitler shocked many by declaring: 'This struggle is one of ideologies and racial differences and will have to be conducted with unprecedented, unmerciful and unrelenting harshness. All officers will have to rid themselves of obsolete ideologies. The commissars are the bearers of ideologies directly opposed to National Socialism. Therefore the commissars will be liquidated. German soldiers guilty of breaking international law . . . will be excused. Russia has not participated in the Hague Convention and therefore has no rights to it.'

This order, which was totally against German military tradition, was not obeyed by all. Some, like General Erich von Manstein, said it was 'against the honour of a soldier' and refused to implement it point-blank. Others had fewer scruples and hundreds of thousands of Russian soldiers and civilians—not just Commissars— were murdered without compunction. The Russians retaliated in exactly the same fashion and prisoners in SS uniform could expect no mercy from their captors.

Süddeutscher Verlag

Popperfoto: Inset: Imperial War Museum

Marshal Tukachevsky, his leading exponent of modern armoured warfare, downwards.

This purge left the Red Army bereft of many of its most skilled and experienced officers, whereas the German officer corps included some of the most talented soldiers of the twentieth century. Moreover, in 1940 the Russian army's new heavy KV1 and medium T-34 tanks were not yet in production, while the older designs would have been no match for the German Panzer IIIs and IVs, despite their numerical superiority.

On top of this, Russian fighter aircraft were obsolescent compared with the German Messerschmitt Bf 109, their most modern design being the Polikarpov I-16 'Rata' of 1934 vintage, which had already shown its inadequacies when faced over Spain by the fighter pilots of the German Condor Legion.

RED ARMY ROUT

The Germans had other advantages which contributed towards Hitler's confidence that an invasion of Russia would be over in a matter of weeks. As they had shown in the campaigns of 1939-40, German command, control and communication systems were superior to those of the Western Allies, and they were immeasurably superior to those of the Red Army.

▲ Soviet infantry march through Red Square in Moscow prior to the German attack. Their helmets, of a pattern more usually associated with the French, are distinctively pre-Barbarossa in style.

◀ Soviet propaganda urged the Russian people to smash the Fascist beast to pieces.

Roger-Viollet, Paris

◄ A dumpy Polikarpov I-16 lies wrecked on a forward airstrip. In the background, a German Junkers Ju-52 transport and Fieseler Storch light aircraft.

Russian communications were predominantly by field telephone, radios being in very short supply and those that existed being extremely unreliable. In 1941 only company commanders in the Soviet tank regiments had radios, having to communicate their orders to the other vehicles by means of semaphore flags! The poor state of the Russian army had been revealed during the Winter War of 1940-41, when the Russians invaded Karelia and tiny Finland gave them a bloody nose and held them to a negotiated settlement.

UNEASY ALLIANCE

Despite these shortcomings in the Soviet forces, it had never been Hitler's intention to wage a war on two fronts—even a former corporal realised that this was a natural recipe for catastrophe. He had not believed initially that France and Britain would honour their guarantees and go to war, however belatedly, over Poland. But they did, and Germany won the campaign in the West even though the English Channel proved too great an obstacle for it be brought to its logical conclusion.

Then Mussolini, Hitler's Italian ally—who was rapidly proving more of an encumbrance than a help—involved the German army first in a campaign in North Africa, then in Greece and Yugoslavia. Hitler had hoped that Spain would join the Axis and lay siege to Gibraltar, thereby denying the Royal Navy access to the western Mediterranean, but Spanish leader General Franco did not wish to get embroiled in battle with Britain so soon after the civil war which had devastated his country, and finally backed down at the beginning of December 1940.

So, plans for the invasion of Russia were laid with an unsubdued enemy on the back doorstep, meaning that 60 divisions of troops were, in effect, wasted in maintaining the security of Norway, France and the Low Countries, Greece, and Yugoslavia, while one of Germany's most capable generals, Erwin Rommel, was stuck at the end of an overstretched and inadequate supply line in Africa with his two elite divisions.

Moreover, Hitler, having to pull Mussolini's chestnuts out of the fire in Greece and then deciding to invade Crete, delayed the start of Operation Barbarossa by five or six weeks. This delay was to produce disastrous results when 'General Winter' clamped down on unprepared German troops who had largely believed their leader's propaganda that the campaign would be another short one, comparable to the sweep through France.

MILLIONS MASSED IN SECRET

The Germans built up their forces in great secrecy, explaining away the volume of troop movements by saying they were simply transferring older personnel from front line to reserve formations. In fact, by the middle of June 1941 they had assembled 128 front-line divisions in the east, 17 of them armoured plus a number of security divisions. Field Marshal Ritter von Leeb's Army Group North was the weakest of the three groups assembled for the invasion. It had seven infantry divisions, three of them motorised, and three Panzer divisions in General Erich Höpner's 4th Panzer Group.

Aerial support was provided by General Koller's 1st Air Fleet. Their objective was Leningrad. Field Marshal Fedor von Bock's Army Group Centre, targeted on Moscow, comprised 41 infantry, one cavalry and six motorised divisions, plus nine Panzer divisions divided into General Heinz Guderian's 2nd and General Hermann

BATTLE DIARY
BARBAROSSA

JUNE 1941
22 Beginning of Operation Barbarossa
29 Minsk pocket closed

JULY
1 Fall of Riga
5 German forces reach River Dnieper
9 Rivers Dvina and Dnieper crossed, Smolensk threatened
12 First Luftwaffe bombing raid on Moscow
14 German forces reach River Luga
17 Dnieper crossed at Mogilev
27 Smolensk pocket closed
31 Army Group North reaches Lake Ilmen

AUGUST
1 Russian counter-attack from the Pripet Marshes
7/8 First Russian air raid on Berlin
12 Army Group Centre splits to send Panzers north and south
23 Guderian heading rapidly towards Kleist
29 Finnish army captures Viipuri

SEPTEMBER
12 Kiev pocket closed
15 Leningrad cut off from the rest of the USSR
25 Start of the siege of Sevastopol
26 Kiev pocket eliminated – Germans now only 200 miles (320 km) from Moscow

Bildarchiv Preussischer Kulturbesitz; Inset: Süddeutscher Verlag

◄ Fit and confident German infantrymen march through a Russian village in June 1941. Their ordeal by fire is yet to come.

◄◄ The face of defeat: a Soviet NCO, shocked by the speed and impact of the German advance, contemplates his prospects as a prisoner of war. He is unlikely to have survived.

Hoth's 3rd Panzer Groups. In the air, support came from Field Marshal Albert Kesselring's 2nd Air Fleet.

Field Marshal Gerd von Rundstedt's Army Group South was the strongest of the three prongs, for the greatest opposition was expected to be encountered in the south. It had 52 infantry divisions, including four motorised and four mountain formations, 15 Rumanian, two Hungarian and two Italian divisions, plus General Ewald von Kleist's 1st Panzer Group, five divisions strong. General Lohr's 4th Air Fleet provided cover.

Their objectives were Kiev, Odessa, the Crimea and to force a crossing of the River Dnieper, opening the path to Rostov and ultimately Stalingrad and the Caucasus.

RUSSIAN RESOURCES

Opposing these forces the Russians had 160-plus infantry divisions to deploy, 30 cavalry divisions and some 35 armoured and motorised brigades. Overall commander in the north was Marshal Kliment Voroshilov, the armour being commanded by General Nikolai Kuznetsov. Marshal Semën Timoshenko commanded in ·the centre, his tank leader being General Dimitry Pavlov, while in the south Marshal Semën Budenny's armoured units were commanded by the very able General Mikhail Kirponos.

One factor the Germans had not taken into account, though, was the speed with which Russia was able to mobilise its reserves so that, in spite of enormous losses, the Red Army was able to muster 400 divisions by the end of 1941—some 12 million men.

The clash of titans was about to begin.

CRUSH THE SOVIETS

As the Panzers thundered eastwards across the vast

expanses of European Russia – their goal the legendary

cities of Kiev, Leningrad and Moscow – they

spearheaded the mightiest field army ever assembled.

Silhouetted against a burning village, a Soviet T-34/76 tank edges forward to give battle.

▲ Marshal Semën Budenny, commander of the South Western Front (Army Group) in 1941. A pre-war friend of Stalin, he owed his position more to influence than competence, and his command was virtually wiped out as the Germans advanced during Barbarossa.

The party of men slipped easily across the Polish border in the pre-dawn darkness. Over their field grey uniforms they wore the drab brown of a Russian infantry regiment. They were, in fact, members of the legendary Brandenburg Regiment and only one of several such groups tasked with capturing bridges over the rivers Niemen, Bug and Prut which were immediate obstacles to the German advance.

As they neared their objective, the western sky erupted in flame and a crescendo of sound as thousands of guns opened a massive artillery barrage all along the thousand-mile front from the Baltic to the Black Sea. It was 3.15 in the morning of 22 June 1941 and the German invasion of Soviet Russia was underway.

Reaching their objective un-detected, the men crept up behind the Russian sentries who were gazing towards the west in shock and dismay. They were quickly silenced and the men threw off their disguises and cocked their sub-machine guns. It was their task to hold the bridge and prevent the Russians from destroying it until the advancing Panzers reached it an hour later. Then, as the sky gradually lightened, the Brandenburgers watched while a huge aerial armada of Heinkels, Dorniers and the terrifying Stuka dive-bombers passed overhead, their targets Russian airfields—for an essential part of Operation Barbarossa was the destruction of the Soviet air force on the ground.

RAPID ADVANCE

During the opening days of the Russian campaign, Brandenburgers were responsible for many similar feats of daring, capturing numerous bridges and other tactical targets vital to the speed of the German advance. Speed, as in the invasions of Poland and the West, was the key to the success or failure of Operation Barbarossa, and to begin with it did indeed seem as though the campaign would be over in a few weeks.

As the Panzer divisions surged forward the Italian journalist Curzio Malaparte, who was travelling with Army Group South, wrote: 'The exhausts of the Panzers belch out blue tongues of smoke. The air is filled

8.000   2.770

24.000   3.300

BATTLE LINE-UP

12m   3m

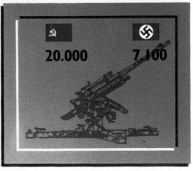

20.000   7.100

Top of article: Soviet Army general's hat band insignia.
◄ Comparison of Soviet and German forces engaged in Operation Barbarossa.

25

War Stories

Russian bravery became almost legendary. A Red Army Infantry corps leader recalled seeing a wounded Russian being tended—his teeth were clenched and there were tears in his eyes. Eager not to be misunderstood on his deathbed, the man explained he was crying, not from pain, but because he'd promised himself not to die until he'd killed five fascists. Quickly, the medical orderly protested, 'You killed at least 50 with your machine gun—I saw them falling!' Suddenly restored, the man stopped crying and died, at peace with himself at last.

▼ The Russian city of Vitebsk as the Germans found it—destroyed to hinder their relentless advance.

with a pungent, bluish vapour that mingles with the damp green of the grass and with the golden reflection of the corn. Beneath the screaming arch of Stukas the mobile columns of tanks resemble thin lines drawn with a pencil on the vast green slate of the Moldavian plain.'

RED TANKS SMASHED

In the far north the Finnish army, now allied to Germany, pushed cautiously forward into the tundra, while sweeping up through the Baltic states of Lithuania, Latvia and Estonia came Army Group North, spearheaded by Höpner's two Panzer corps, Manstein's LVI and Reinhardt's XLI.

They had a difficult task because the terrain was sandy, heavily forested and with narrow roads hardly conducive to the passage of tanks. While Manstein was ordered forward as fast as possible towards Daugavpils (Dvinsk), the critical town lying astride the River Dvina,

Reinhardt's corps engaged two opposing Soviet armoured corps, the III and the XII. Despite the fact that their KV1 and KV2 tanks were better armed and more heavily armoured than Reinhardt's Panzers, he fought them off, destroying over 100.

Meanwhile, 220 miles (354 km) from the German start line, members of the Brandenburg Regiment had captured the bridge at Daugavpils and Manstein's tanks were soon pouring across, beating back a counter-attack by the Russian XXI Mechanised Corps. Here, however, Hitler ordered a halt to allow Reinhardt's corps, on his left flank, to catch up, and the advance did not resume until the beginning of July.

In the centre, von Bock's immediate objective was the Belorussian capital, Minsk. His two Panzer groups, Hoth's 3rd striking from East Prussia just north of Grodno, and Guderian's 2nd from occupied Poland south of the fortress city of Brest-Litovsk, achieved the

◄ 22 June 1941—the first day of Operation Barbarossa: German infantry, armed with 7.92 mm Mauser 98K rifles, move cautiously into a burning village.

▼ German infantry, smoke billowing behind them, advance along a railway track during the early stages of Operation Barbarossa, June 1941.

same tactical surprise as in the north.

One immediate obstacle in Guderian's path was the River Bug, but this had been thought of. Specially modified Panzer IIIs of the 18th Panzer division, fitted with schnorkels and exhaust vents enabling them to wade to a depth of 13ft (4 m), crossed the river bed and established a bridgehead behind which sappers were soon erecting pontoons to allow the following columns of vehicles to cross. Brest-Litovsk was bypassed and left for the slower-moving infantry divisions to capture.

HUGE GERMAN 'BAG'

There was pandemonium on the Russian side of the river. German signallers intercepted one frantic radio message: 'We are being fired on. What shall we do?' Back came the answer: 'You must be insane. And why is your signal not in code?' Hoth and Guderian pressed on with such speed that infantry, despite herculean forced marches of up to 25 miles (40 km) a day, were rapidly left behind the advancing tanks.

The two armoured pincers then swung part of their strength south and north, respectively closing in behind the retreating Russian forces in the vicinity of Bialystok and Slonim, while the remainder headed on eastwards to complete a second encirclement around Minsk by 27 June.

Many Russian soldiers succeeded in slipping through the net because the distances involved were so great it was impossible to close every gap, but by 3 July, when this first phase of operations was finished, the German 'bag' was some 300,000 prisoners and 3,000 tanks captured or destroyed. Stalin had the unfortunate General Pavlov executed as a result.

Although the German advance was rapid, the Russians fought back in places with ferocity born of desperation, and localised fighting was extremely tough. Guderian himself had a narrow escape at one point. He had stopped on the outskirts of Slonim to confer with the commander of the 17th Panzer division when, suddenly, out of the clouds of smoke

Süddeutscher Verlag

▲ Blitzkrieg gathers momentum as German infantry prepare to clear a Soviet-occupied village in what had been eastern Poland, June 1941. They are waiting for an artillery bombardment to lift before advancing.

from burning buildings emerged two Russian tanks. Spotting the group of German officers, they immediately opened fire and 'we were immediately subjected to a rain of shells which, fired at such extremely close range, both deafened and blinded us for a few moments'. The men flung themselves to the ground and Panzer IVs quickly drove the Russian tanks away, but not before two officers had been wounded, one of them fatally.

WIDENING BATTLEFRONT

Army Group South, advancing south-east from southern Poland and directly east from Rumania, had a tougher time of things. General von Kleist's 1st Panzer Group was opposed by no fewer than six Soviet mechanised corps, IV, VIII, IX, XV, XIX and XXII, which were commanded by the very capable General Mikhail Kirponos.

The two forces clashed on 25 June near Brody and a sprawling tank battle, the largest of the war up to that point, swayed backwards and forwards across the steppes for four days. Superior German tactical handling and communications, plus their use of 88 mm guns, eventually won the day, however, and Kirponos was forced to retreat eastwards towards Kiev.

In the north, Höpner's Panzer

Group resumed its advance at the beginning of July and Reinhardt took Ostrov on the 4th while Manstein pressed on towards Novorshev in the direction of Lake Ilmen, but Russian resistance was stiffening. Around Novorshev, Manstein ran headlong into the XXI Mechanised Corps and his advance was checked in the swamps and woods.

He sent his 3rd Motorised Division north-east in pursuit of Reinhardt's forces, while 8th Panzer Division pushed through the swamps and the SS 'Totenkopf' Division bypassed them to the south, breaking through the Stalin Line around Zebesh and Opochka. Then, while Reinhardt was forcing a breakthrough at Pskov, on

the southern shore of Lake Peipus, Manstein headed towards Novgorod, reaching Porkhov on 10 July and Stoltsy on the 15th. Here, the Soviet I Mechanised Corps surrounded and isolated the LVI Panzer corps for three days before Manstein achieved a breakout.

FATAL DECISION

Reinhardt, meanwhile, had reached Pskov and was pushing into Estonia. Now Höpner took a bold decision and switched the direction of Manstein's advance northwards to

▼ Sheltering from Soviet fire, a German infantry section waits for an opportunity to advance, August 1941.

STALIN'S ORGAN

The Germans first encountered this extremely effective Russian weapon in July 1941—and gave it the wry musical nickname because of the terrifying screech of its missiles. The Russian name of 'Katyusha' ('Little Katy'), taken from a popular song of the time, was a good deal more affectionate. In its M-8 version, the 'Katyusha' was a standard GAZ or ZIS one and a half or two and half ton truck on which were mounted launching rails for the 36 free-flight 82 mm rockets. These fin-stabilised missiles had a range of up to 6,000 yards (6.5 km) and could lay down a saturation barrage of high explosive which was devastating against infantry in the open or convoys of vehicles. So dreadful were the results on the Germans that they promised to execute on the spot any Russian caught using the 'Katyusha'. The M-13 was similar but had rails for 16 larger rockets of 132 mm calibre. These had a range in excess of 9,000 yards (9.6 km). From a tactical point of view 'Katy' was very useful, but had one drawback in that the dense clouds of smoke emitted when the rockets were launched invariably drew artillery fire on unarmoured trucks.

Often as it appeared in propaganda films in action at the front, the Russians actually used it with great secrecy—crews were not Regular Army but Military Police.

▶ **The 'Katyusha'—capable of launching 36 freeflight rockets.**

outflank the Russian forces opposing the XLI Panzer Corps. The ploy succeeded and Manstein was in Luga on the 17th while Reinhardt pressed towards Narva, on the Baltic coast.

At this point, however, Hitler got frightened at the distance by which the Panzers had outstripped the infantry and called a halt to their advance. They were to be delayed for a fatal three weeks which gave the defenders of Leningrad time to prepare.

In the centre, Hoth's 3rd and Guderian's 2nd Panzer groups resumed their advance from Minsk towards Smolensk, the two forces co-operating in another huge pincer movement. The trap snapped shut despite ferocious Russian opposition on 16 July, a further 300,000 men and some 3,000 tanks had been lost in the Smolensk pocket between then and 5 August. Another encirclement around Gomel and Roslavl up to the 24th of the month netted a further 120,000 prisoners. At the beginning of August, though, it seemed, back in Berlin, that the Red Army must surely be finished, and Hitler took a decision which was to prove ultimately fatal, and deny the German army the prize of Moscow.

DEFENCE OF KIEV

In the north, von Leeb had been calling for armoured reinforcements in order to complete his drive on Leningrad. Similarly, in the south von Rundstedt had been making the same request.

Having successfully completed an

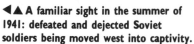

S.I.R.P.A./E.C.P.A. France; Inset: Suddeutscher Verlag

◀▲ A familiar sight in the summer of 1941: defeated and dejected Soviet soldiers being moved west into captivity.

encirclement of some 20 Russian divisions totalling about 100,000 men, around Pervomaisk by 8 August, and laid siege to the port of Odessa, von Rundstedt realised that von Kleist's Panzers could not on their own entrap the bulk of Marshal Budenny's enormous force assembled for the defence of Kiev, which Stalin had ordered held at all costs.

COUNTER-ATTACK

Kleist had very nearly run into extremely serious trouble in the middle of July, when the Soviet Fifth Army, reinforced by three mechanised corps, had come racing unexpectedly south out of the Pripet Marshes and cut off his lines of communication and supply. By a supreme effort Field Marshal Walther von Reichenau brought up the following infantry to fight the menace off.

Thus, on 4 August Hitler ordered Hoth's 3rd Panzer Group to aid von Leeb in the north and Guderian's 2nd to assist von Kleist in the south. The rewards were to be enormous, but the price was high. Fighting off another Russian counter-attack, von Kleist resumed his advance on 17 August while Guderian's Panzers were moving south to his assistance. He reached the River Dnieper on the 19th and attacked across the Zaporozhye dam, but was repulsed.

A week later, however, he succeeded in capturing an intact Russian pontoon bridge at Dnepropetrovsk and established a

TITANS CLASH

TURNING POINT

As the guns roared out their message of hate on 22 June 1941, World War II entered a new phase of ideological violence. For nearly two years, Hitler had confined his aggression to central and western Europe, biding his time and preparing for what he saw as an inevitable clash with the communism of the east. Now, that clash had begun, on a scale that dwarfed the earlier campaigns. From the start, it was obvious that this was a war to the death—Hitler would not rest until communism had been eradicated from the map of Europe; Stalin and the Russian people would fight to the bitter end to eject the invaders and destroy the very heart of Nazism. It was a clash of titans, the outcome of which could only be decided on the blood-soaked battlefields of Russia. It was the beginning of a total war.

Süddeutscher Verlag

bridgehead on the eastern bank of the river. The Russians threw everything they could into clearing the bridge-head, and only the timely arrival of the 4th Panzer Corps under General Eberhard von Mackensen saved the day after a fierce three-day battle.

By the end of August the bridge-head was being expanded rapidly into the Donets Basin and on 11 September von Kleist achieved a breakout northwards. Three Panzer divisions, the 9th, 14th and 16th, roared at full speed towards Romny, much to Budenny's consternation, for Guderian was making similarly good progress southwards in the same direction. Three days later the 16th Panzer Division linked up with Guderian's 3rd Panzer Division, completing the largest battle of encirclement of the war.

The Soviet troops in and around Kiev, 130 miles (209 km) to the west, fought fanatically but, denied any chance of escape by Stalin's order, eventually succumbed on the 26th when they were virtually out of ammunition. The Germans captured 667,000 prisoners. But, even though the whole Ukraine now lay open, vital weeks had been lost and when the advance on Moscow resumed, it came too late.

▶ **Caught in the middle, civilians emerge from their shelter to face the new reality of life under Nazi rule.**

Süddeutscher Verlag

PEARL HARBOR

BATTLE DIARY

7 DECEMBER 194.

06.00	Japanese First Air Fleet begins to fly off strike
06.37	US destroyer *Ward* depth-charges unidentified submarine
07.02	US radar unit detects incoming Japanese strike
07.49	Japanese strike deploys over Pearl Harbor
07.56	Attack on airfields begins
07.56	Attack on fleet begins
08.40	Second wave of attack
08.50	Attack ends
10.00	Japanese aircraft begin to land back on carriers
13.00	Vice-Admiral Nagumo decides against a repeat attack

DAY OF INFAMY

For the Japanese, the time for talking with the American superpower is over. Now they must strike the enemy with Samurai-like suddenness and ferocity.

Topham Picture Library

◀ Previous page: Japanese propaganda shows the might of a nation of Samurai allied with the German Nazis in the struggle against the British and Americans.

▼ Under the banner of the Rising Sun, Japanese troops, armed with rifles, mortars, machine-guns and swords, pose for a warlike propaganda shot in 1937.

At 7.50 am on 7 December 1941, a deadly swarm of Japanese aircraft thundered over Pearl Harbor, since 1940 the main base of the United States Navy in the Pacific, on Oahu Island in Hawaii. The leader of this first wave of the Japanese sneak attack, Commander Mitsuo Fuchida, signalled to the anxiously waiting Admiral Chuichi Nagumo on the *Akagi,* flagship of the Japanese carrier strike force, 'Tora, Tora, Tora', signifying that total surprise had been achieved. A typical tropical Sunday morning was about to be rudely disturbed by the shock of war.

As the Japanese formation peeled off in groups to hit the main airfields and anchorage by Ford Island (called Mokuumeume by the islanders), morning colours were about to be raised over the slumbering American fleet. Many who observed the beginning of the attack could not believe the shocking evidence of their own eyes and assumed that it was an exceptionally realistic drill by the United States Army Air Force.

The explosion of bombs and torpedoes as they crashed on to the defenceless ships and airfields interrupted the leisurely preparations for the start of another routine peacetime day. Rising columns of smoke and flame from shattered ships and aircraft indicated that World War II

had at last come to the Pacific with a vengeance.

Although the attack on Pearl Harbor came as as a bolt from the blue, tensions between the United States and Japan had been building for some time. Since the opening of Japan to Western influence in the 1850s, and the defeat of China and Russia at the turn of the century, Japan had built itself from a backward feudal nation into a formidable regional power, her dominance of East Asia confirmed by the Washington treaties of 1922 which gave her naval supremacy in the Far East.

FORCE OF ARMS

Initially, Japan's expansion in the 1920s was limited to peaceful commercial penetration of the Chinese mainland. However, with the world depression, following the Wall Street Crash of 1929, and its catastrophic impact upon the economy of Japan, this expansion accelerated and was pursued by force of arms.

Underlying Japan's aggressive policy in the 1930s were several factors. The first was the increasing power of the military over the politicians, until by 1936 the army dominated Japanese politics. Second, there was the question of Japan's ultimate goal. All Japanese were agreed on the necessity for expansion from their crowded islands but there was some dispute over the direction in which Japan's destiny lay.

The army believed that Japan's interests would be best served by expansion on the mainland of Asia, but it was open to question whether Soviet Russia as well as China should be the target. The navy, on the other hand, felt that all Japan's needs could be satisfied by a policy of southern expansion into the mineral and oil-rich areas of South East Asia and the islands of the south-west Pacific.

GEARING UP FOR WAR

In August 1936, in a disastrous compromise, it was agreed that Japan should seek to expand eastwards and southwards at the same time, a course that would ultimately lead to war with the Western powers. Initially the army continued its aggression in China, which culminated in July 1937 in a full-blown war which dragged on — despite Japan's supremacy — until 1945.

▼ A halt during training for a group of Japanese soldiers to allow them to clean their weapons and prepare food. Strong discipline made the Japanese a formidable enemy.

▲ President Franklin D Roosevelt (left), photographed in 1940 during his election campaign which would give him a third successive term of office in the USA.

However, Germany's success in the defeat of France and the Netherlands and the preoccupation of Great Britain with the Battle of Britain and events in the Middle East provided the opportunity that the Imperial Japanese Navy had been waiting for. The colonies of the Western powers in the Far East seemed to be ripe for the picking. Moreover, the Japanese army argued that a strike south would solve the long-running China problem by cutting it off from outside support.

In July 1940 the military reconstructed the government, putting Prince Fumimaro Konoye in as Prime Minister and Matsuoka as Foreign Minister. Both these men were little more than tools of the military, who began to construct a diplomatic base for the drive south. In September 1940 the Vichy authorities in French Indochina were pressured into giving the Japanese base rights in the north of the country. Simultaneously, in Berlin and Moscow, negotiations began for alliances that would give Japan a free hand to escalate its military expansion in South East Asia and the south-west Pacific.

AMERICA ENTERS THE SCENE

The only power that stood in Japan's way was the United States. But although both President Franklin D. Roosevelt and Secretary of State Cordell Hull were opposed to Japanese activities on the Chinese mainland, they were reluctant to do anything to provoke a Japanese response that might involve the US in war.

As Japan's ambitions in the south became clearer, Roosevelt gradually began to put pressure on Tokyo to restrain it from further expansion. In April 1940 the Pacific Fleet was ordered to remain at Pearl Harbor to serve as a deterrent to Japan. In the summer and autumn of 1940 America stopped the sale of aviation fuel and all scrap metal to Japan.

Further than this, however, America would not go, even in the face of the Tripartite (Axis) Pact, targeted against the US. Unlike Japan, America was a two-ocean power (Atlantic and Pacific) and Roosevelt and his military advisers were far more concerned with the threat posed to the western hemisphere by a Nazi victory in the Atlantic.

In the face of the American embargo and despite the talks held in Washington throughout 1941 between the new ambassador, Admiral Kichisaburo Nomura, and Cordell Hull, Japanese policy-makers gradually became

Topham Picture Library; left: US Library of Congress

▲ Unknown to them, their days are numbered. Led by a destroyer and with naval aircraft above, battleships of the US Pacific Fleet sail in line astern off Honolulu.

War Stories

Every young Japanese man underwent a standard two years of military service — the common man's greatest privilege. The dubiousness of the honour becomes apparent when one appreciates the nature of the training — 14 hours a day, six days a week, doing marathon marches and struggling (especially when weather conditions were extreme) to improve stamina. Working his men night and day on manoeuvres, an officer explained that his men already knew how to sleep — what he wanted them to do was learn how to stay awake!

convinced of the inevitability of war with the United States. The German attack on the Soviet Union in June 1941, with whom Japan had just signed a non-aggression pact, was the trigger. This removed any possibility of threat to Japan from the north, and the naval high command was able to convince the army and the politicians that now was the time to strike south.

FLASHPOINT APPROACHES

On 21 July 1941 the Japanese secured the agreement of the Vichy government to the virtual Japanese occupation of Indochina. Troops, air and naval units moved into bases in southern Indochina, placing them within striking range of the vulnerable colonies of South East Asia and the south-west Pacific. In response, American officials not only froze all Japanese assets in the United States but also placed a total embargo on all American exports to Japan, particularly those of oil. This was the flashpoint.

Both the army and navy were convinced that war was now inevitable, and although a diplomatic solution was sought, military preparations proceeded simultaneously. If the United States refused Japanese terms and no negotiated settlement was in sight by early October, then war would begin either in November or December 1941.

The question was: how would this war begin? An attack on Malaya or the Dutch East Indies, the so-called 'Southern Operation', would immediately bring the United States into the war. As the American Battle Fleet trekked across the Pacific to reinforce the Philippines, it would be whittled down by constant submarine attacks until the Japanese Fleet met in battle and crushed it.

However, Admiral Isoruku Yamamoto, Commander-in-Chief of the Combined Fleet, had authorised in December 1940 the preparation of a contingency plan for a pre-emptive strike against the American Fleet while it was anchored at Pearl Harbor. In order to conquer South East Asia, Yamamoto proposed first to cripple American naval strength in the Pacific on the first day of war and hopefully cause America to sue for peace.

Although Japan had the necessary numbers of carriers and aircraft to undertake such an attack, special training was necessary to overcome the problems posed by conditions at Pearl Harbor. The Japanese First Air Fleet, consisting of seven aircraft carriers, was the most modern, powerful and efficient carrier force in the world. Its 355

▼ Yosuka Matsuoka (left), Japan's Foreign Minister and always a strong supporter of the Axis Pact, with Adolf Hitler in Berlin, April 1941.

Topham Picture Library

▼ Flanked by his generals, Emperor Hirohito of Japan stands on a dais to inspect his troops in 1940. Although a figurehead of sacred standing, the Emperor enjoyed only limited political power.

Topham Picture Library; Inset: US National Archives

BATTLE DIARY
PEARL HARBOR

SEPTEMBER 1940
22 Japanese occupy northern Indochina
26 America imposes trade embargoes on Japan
27 Germany, Italy and Japan sign Tripartite
    pact

APRIL 1941
13 Japan and USSR sign non-aggression pact

JULY
26 America freezes Japanese assets in USA.

SEPTEMBER
3-6 Japanese decide on war with America if no
    diplomatic solution found

NOVEMBER
 5 Japanese war plans agreed at Imperial Conference with a deadline of December 1941
15 Japanese special negotiator arrives in
   Washington
26 US Secretary of State Hull puts his final pro-
   posals to the Japanese.
   Japanese First Air Fleet sails

DECEMBER
 7 Pearl Harbor attacked
 8 USA and Great Britain declare war on Japan

◄ **Militarism spread quickly in Japanese society. Young boys receive rudimentary training for war under the Rising Sun flag.**

aircraft, all modern monoplanes, Mitsubishi A6M Zero fighters, Aichi D3A Val dive-bombers and Nakajima B5N Kate torpedo-bombers, tried and tested in battle, had no equal. The crews were for the most part battle-hardened veterans, many with over 1,000 hours logged.

Despite this superiority, in the summer of 1941 Commander Minoru Genda, and the subordinate air commanders, Lieutenants Fuchida and Egusa, drove their men hard. Training at sea was supplemented by training on shore, mainly round the town of Kagoshima on Honshu, the geography of which bore a passing resemblance to that of Pearl Harbor. The town echoed to the buzz of low-flying aircraft as torpedo-bombers and dive-bombers exercised relentlessly.

Equally important was the development of special weapons. Existing bombs for the horizontal bombers

▼ **Yosuka Matsuoka (in glasses), the Japanese Foreign Minister, greets Dr Walther Funk, Nazi Minister of Trade, in Berlin, April 1941.**

◄ **Japan's people were united in the war effort. This group of girls marches with the flags of the Axis powers — Germany, Italy and Japan.**

▶ Pearl Harbor from the air, before the raid. In the centre is Ford Island, around which the US Pacific Fleet lies at anchor.

US National Archives. Inset: Popperfoto

▲ Pearl Harbor dry dock, only completed in 1941, was in use for the battleship USS *Pennsylvania* when the Japanese struck.

were inadequate for attacking the American Fleet battleships. A solution was found in the adaptation of 6 inch naval gun shells for dropping from aircraft. The addition of stabilising fins and a minor modification to the aerodynamic shape gave the Kates an effective weapon to smash through the armour of the American battlewagons.

Although the Japanese aerial torpedo, a variant of the 21 inch 'Long Lance' naval weapons, oxygen-propelled

and carrying 1,000 lbs of explosive, was the most effective weapon of its type in the world, the problem lay in its delivery in the shallow waters of the anchorage of Pearl Harbor. A solution had to be found to the problem of torpedoes running deep when dropped and burying themselves ignominiously in the mud. The addition of stabilising fins to the Mark II torpedoes in October 1941 solved this problem, allowing them to run successfully in only 39ft (12 m) of water.

Keystone Collection

◀ The Royal Hawaiian Hotel, Waikiki Beach, Honolulu, 1942—an odd mix of holiday sand and barbed wire.

BEFORE THE ATTACK

Pearl Harbor, on the island of Oahu in the Hawaiian Islands, just west of the capital city Honolulu, consists of 10 sq miles (26 sq km) of navigable waters, hundreds of anchorages, and covers a land area of 10,000 acres (4,000 ha). In December 1941 it had been the base of the Pacific Fleet for only 18 months but had adjusted to provide the extensive facilities required by the US Fleet. The evening before the attack had been a usual Saturday night with sailors at liberty in the bars, brothels, dance halls and clubs of Pearl City.

Life at Pearl was a leisurely peacetime existence with an unvarying routine: the week was spent in exercises by the Fleet and the weekend was spent anchored in Pearl. This rigidity rendered the task of Japanese intelligence agents working from the Japanese consulate all too easy, enabling them to forecast with remarkable accuracy not only what ships would be in harbour but also where they would be tied up. Such a lax peacetime attitude, encapsulated by one officer's comment that 'not much work was done in the afternoon', was to cost the Americans dear. However, Japanese intelligence could not predict that on the day of the attack, the US aircraft carriers *Lexington* and *Enterprise*, with their escorting cruisers and destroyers, would be at sea.

Not all agreed with the audacious plan to attack Pearl Harbor. Not only did the commander of the First Air Fleet, Admiral Nagumo, have doubts about its success, but the Naval General Staff felt that it might well end in disaster. Nonetheless Yamamoto insisted — to the point of threatening resignation — that only 'Operation Z' would give Japan a chance of success in a war with the United States.

As a concession, Yamamoto agreed to the participation of both conventional and midget submarines in the attack. The former were to lie in ambush off Oahu in anticipation of the American Fleet fleeing the air attack in confusion; the midget subs were to penetrate the harbour and torpedo whatever ships they could find.

The major ingredient in this daring scheme was surprise. To guarantee success the American Pacific Fleet had to be anchored unsuspectingly in Pearl Harbor. It was therefore decided that the attack fleet should approach from the north, maintaining radio silence and refuelling *en route* from accompanying tankers, and launch the strike 200 miles (320 km) from Hawaii. It was also decided that the strike should take place immediately upon the outbreak of war, a decision that was to have fateful consequences.

Popperfoto

With no satisfactory result from negotiations with the USA (despite the decision by the new Prime Minister Tojo to postpone the deadline until 1 December regardless of deteriorating weather that might hamper the attack fleet), in mid November the Pearl Harbor strike force was placed on alert for an attack day of 7 December and sailed for its concentration point off the deserted Tankan Bay in the Kurile Islands. To cover their movements the carriers sailed individually and maintained radio silence, while other ships assumed their call signs and broadcast bogus radio traffic.

After further training and briefing, the attack fleet sailed at dawn on 26 November 1941. Only a diplomatic breakthrough or being discovered by the Americans could halt Nagumo now. On 1 December 1941, as the fleet ploughed onwards, Tokyo took the fateful decision for war. A formal rejection of American conditions and a declaration of war was to be issued only half an hour before the aircraft were due over Pearl Harbor.

At 3.30 am on 7 December the aircrew were called from their sleep and briefed by their commanders. At 6 am the six carriers of the First Air Fleet swung as one into the wind and began to launch the first strike wave, ranged ready on deck, against Pearl Harbor. As the aircraft concentrated and swung on course, losing only one of their number, the deck crews immediately began to range the second wave ready for launch. The Pacific War had begun, though America had yet to realise it.

▲ Better safe than sorry — local US businessmen undergo basic training on Waikiki Beach. The drill is in case of a Japanese amphibious attack.

▼ Japanese pilots line up for an inspection. In spite of the rumours which American propaganda would have people believe, the Japanese pilots were very skilled.

Topham Picture Library

TORA! TORA! TORA!

As the Japanese formations peel off to hit their sitting targets, the battle-hungry crews have a single mission: to wipe the US fleet off the face of the Pacific.

The American forces in Pearl Harbor greeted Sunday 7 December as another peace-time rest day. Although they had received a 'war warning' from Washington on 27 November 1941, Admiral Husband E. Kimmel and Lt.-Gen. Walter C. Short had done nothing to make the fleet or its defences ready for a Japanese attack. Kimmel believed that in the unlikely event of war the Japanese would attack the Philippines rather than Pearl Harbor. Short interpreted his message from the War Department as a warning against sabotage.

WHAT ATTACK?

Although the defences were put on a limited alert, no long-distance reconnaissance was carried out, nor were the inadequate anti-aircraft defences bolstered. On board ship only half of the anti-aircraft positions were stood to and their ready ammunition was locked away.

Quite simply neither Kimmel, Short nor their subordinates expected an attack. This explains why two incidents immediately preceding the Japanese aerial assault were not treated seriously. At 03.50 a periscope was sighted at the entrance to the harbour and at 06.37 the destroyer *Ward* depth-charged and sank an unidentified submarine just outside the boom. The *Ward*'s contact report was not followed up with any degree of urgency. At 07.02 an army radar unit at Opana detected a large flight of aircraft some 40 miles (64 km) to the north. The duty pilot's reaction was to write it off as an expected flight of B-17s due in from the west coast of America.

At 07.56 am the Japanese formations broke up to attack their designated targets. To his disappoint-

◄Nightmare turns to reality on 7 December 1941 as the battleships of the US Pacific Fleet burn.

▶ Peace reigns over the entrance to the US airbase at Hickam Field before the Japanese attack. Inset: Japanese naval officers plan the Pearl Harbor attack which would take the Americans completely by surprise.

▼ Japanese Mitsubishi A6M2 Zero fighters run up their engines on board the carrier *Hiryu* prior to the Pearl Harbor attack, 7 December 1941.

Topham Picture Library; Inset: Süddeutscher Verlag
US National Archives
Topham Picture Library

ment, Fuchida could see no sign of the two American aircraft carriers, *Lexington* and *Enterprise,* both of which were at sea delivering aircraft to the garrisons at Midway and Wake Island. While the Vals and Zeros peeled off out of the blue skies, the Kates began their deadly runs against the American Battle Fleet, tied up two-by-two against Ford Island.

On the American airfields, as a precaution against the supposed danger of sabotage, aircraft were lined up wingtip to wingtip so that they could be more easily guarded. They were sitting ducks for Fuchida's airmen. At Hickam Field, dive-bombers and strafing fighters turned the neat ranks and hangars into a blazing shambles with the first shots of the harbour attacks at 07.56. The scene was repeated at Ewa, Wheeler Field and Kaneohe.

TORPEDOES LAUNCHED

As they had practised for so long the torpedo-bombers came in from east and west in four groups snarling low over the naval base before lining up on their targets. Twenty-four aircraft attacked 'Battleship Row' while another 15 attacked the cruisers and auxiliaries to the west of Ford Island. Unimpeded by anti-aircraft fire most of the Kates made perfect runs in formations of two or three, launching their torpedoes from around 70 ft (21 m) and 100 knots at their helpless targets.

▲ A map of Pearl Harbor, showing the positions of the US warships, carried by one of the Japanese pilots on the raid. The information was gathered by Japanese spies on Hawaii.

▼ A Japanese midget submarine, forced to beach on the island of Oahu.

◄ A comparison of US and Japanese naval power at Pearl Harbor.

BATTLE LINE-UP

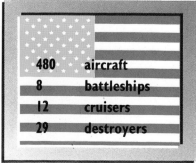

	US	
480	aircraft	
8	battleships	
12	cruisers	
29	destroyers	

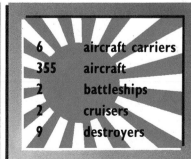

	Japan	
6	aircraft carriers	
355	aircraft	
2	battleships	
2	cruisers	
9	destroyers	

US National Archives

▶A Japanese aircraft flies over 'Battleship Row' in an aerial photograph by a Japanese pilot during the raid.

▼'Battleship Row' from the air. The ships *Maryland, Oklahoma, Tennessee, Arizona, West Virginia* and *Nevada* were packed tightly together — an easy target.

▼American sailors rush for cover from the hail of Japanese bombs on 'Battleship Row'.

While the Kates raced away over their targets, the crews anxiously waited to see how their weapons performed. To cries of 'Banzai!' (long live the Emperor!'), enormous spouts of water soared skyward, higher than the funnels of the battleships, as first one torpedo and then another ripped home. Six smashed into *West Virginia*, putting her on the bottom. Four others hammered into *Oklahoma*, capsizing her. One tore into *Arizona*, and two into *California*, the latter settling into the mud by Ford Island.

On the west side of Ford Island one torpedo slammed into the cruiser *Raleigh* and two into the old battleship *Utah*, now used as a target ship, while one weapon dropped by Lt Nagai of the *Soryu* burst against the cruiser *St Helena* and in doing so damaged the old minelayer *Ogala*.

Next into this cauldron of fire came the horizontal bombers. After making one abortive run due to turbulence, Fuchida led his formation back over Battleship Row. Flying at 9,000 ft (2,750 m), the highly trained bombardiers bent over their sights and aimed their 1,600 lb weapons at the inboard battleships,

which until that moment had escaped damage.

Almost immediately they achieved a spectacular success. One bomb, probably dropped by the star bombardier Kanai, knifed through B turret of the *Arizona* and exploded deep within the forward magazines of the striken battleship. A column of smoke and flame rose over 1,000 feet as it was engulfed in an explosion killing over 1,200 of its crew. One survivor remembered the *Arizona* 'sinking like an earthquake had struck it'.

Seven further bombs slammed into

WarStories

The events of 7 December 1941 produced a mixed reaction throughout the British and Commonwealth troops. One former soldier who served in Africa remembers, 'We were having a few beers when we heard about Pearl Harbor. Somebody said "Well, the Yanks will have to come in now on our side", so we thought we'd celebrate and sing the American National Anthem. Then an argument broke out as to whether it was *Yankee Doodle* or *Glory, Glory, Hallelujah*, so we compromised and sang *Roll out the Barrel* instead'.

Topham Picture Library

Roger-Viollet, Paris

◄ The full fury of the Japanese attack among the US ships. Inset: caught on the ground, an American bomber in flames. In the foreground, a Boeing B-17.

▲ The battleships USS *Tennessee* and *West Virginia* go up in flames. In spite of heavy damage, both ships were salvaged and recommissioned after the war.

the unfortunate ship as she sank. Other bombs hit the *West Virginia, Nevada* and *Maryland,* damaging them severely. Worse still, escaping oil fuel from the *Arizona* ignited and began to spread down Battleship Row, setting fire to the *Tennessee* and the *West Virginia.*

Into the midst of this mayhem flew two flights of American aircraft. The B-17s that had unexpectedly provided cover for Fuchida's formation arrived and were jumped by covering Zeros. Cannon fire raked the unarmed aircraft as they tried to put down wherever they could. A similar fate overtook a squadron of Marine Dauntless dive-bombers from the *Enterprise,* the surprised pilots standing no chance as the agile Zeros swarmed all over them.

The arrival of the second wave of Japanese at 08.40 am overlapped with the end of the first wave. This group of horizontal and dive-bombers, led by Lieutenant Shimakazi, added to the destruction as they peeled off in search of targets, raining down more bombs on the helpless Americans. Fighters and high-level bombers again concentrated on the airfields, working over the shattered remains of American airpower on Hawaii.

Eighty-one Val dive-bombers

Topham Picture Library

YAMAMOTO

Japan's foremost naval strategist, the short and stocky Isoruku Yamamoto inspired loyalty and dislike in equal quantities. In the inter-war period he served as naval attaché in Washington. This experience convinced him that Japan could not win a prolonged war against the United States, but such a view did not make him popular with the Japanese ultra-nationalists or the Navy General Staff. It is therefore ironic that as Commander-in-Chief of the Combined Fleet, he was the brains behind the strike at Pearl Harbor — the aim of which was to knock out the American Fleet and force

◄ Admiral Yamamoto, Commander-in-Chief of the Japanese Combined Fleet and architect of the Pearl Harbor attack.

Roosevelt to the negotiating table. Despite the stunning success at Pearl Harbor, the American Fleet recovered and Yamamoto tried to destroy it once again at Midway. But the Americans had anticipated his strategy and he was heavily defeated. After this setback he continued to direct operations in the Solomon Islands, forming his desperate plan of 'I-Go' — a huge naval air attack on the advancing Allies that was never carried out. He was killed on 18 April 1943 when, on an inspection tour of the Solomon Islands, his aircraft was intercepted and shot down by a squadron of long-range P-38 Lightning fighters. Yamamoto's most enduring legacy to future naval strategists was the use he made of carrier-borne aircraft.

Hulton Picture Library

JAPAN WARS ON U.S. AND BRITAIN; MAKES SUDDEN ATTACK ON HAWAII; HEAVY FIGHTING AT SEA REPORTED

▲ **From the left:** *Oklahoma, Maryland, Tennessee, West Virginia, Arizona* **and** *Vestal* **under attack. Inset: The** *New York Times* **breaks the news.**

US National Archives

under Lieutentant Egusa had orders to finish off as many of the American ships as possible. Jockeying for position for their dives they were hampered by increasing anti-aircraft fire and by poor visibility caused by smoke from the burning ships. Many concentrated on the *Nevada*, which was now under way, hoping to sink her in the channel. Five bomb hits sent her staggering aground.

Others put two bombs into the dry-docked *Pennsylvania* and more into the adjacent destroyers *Cassin* and *Downes*. In this phase of the attack the destroyer *Shaw* had her bows blown off, while the cruisers *Raleigh* and *Honolulu* were badly damaged by numerous bomb hits.

The overwhelming emotion felt by

▲ **A scene of chaos at Pearl Harbor dry dock. Destroyers USS** *Cassin* **and** *Downes* **are in the foreground, with the battleship** *Pennsylvania* **behind.**

▼ **A Consolidated PBY Catalina flying-boat amongst the wreckage of the naval airbase after the attack.**

Keystone Collection

GLOBAL WAR

The Japanese attack on Pearl Harbor transformed what had been an essentially European war into a worldwide conflict. Not only were the two most powerful countries in the Pacific now locked in a battle to the death, but the attack presaged a series of Japanese assaults that were to extend over an enormous area, from the Aleutians in the north to Australia in the south, from Burma in the west to Midway in the east. From a Japanese point of view, these assaults were part of a strategy of survival; to the Allies, they represented a widening of the war that was particularly burdensome. A new war in a new area of the world meant that new armies, airforces and navies had to be created.

▶ **The twisted wreckage of the USS** *Arizona* **on which hundreds died.**

TURNING POINT

Topham Picture Library

◄ **A civilian car, caught in the attack, stands abandoned and bullet-ridden. Three people apparently died in the car.**

Seventy-seventh Congress of the United States of America;
At the First Session
Begun and held at the City of Washington on Friday, the third day of January, one thousand nine hundred and forty-one

JOINT RESOLUTION

Declaring that a state of war exists between the Government of Germany and the Government and the people of the United States and making provision to prosecute the same.

Whereas the Government of Germany has formally declared war against the Government and the people of the United States of America: Therefore be it
Resolved by the Senate and House of Representatives of the United States of America in Congress assembled, That the state of war which is thrust upon the United States is hereby formally declared; and the President is hereby authorized and directed to employ the entire naval and military forces of the United States and the resources of the Government to carry on war against the Government of Germany; and, to bring the conflict to a successful termination, all of the resources of the country are hereby pledged by the Congress of the United States.

Sam Rayburn
Speaker of the House of Representatives.

H A Wallace
Vice President of the United States and President of the Senate.

Approved December 11 = 1941   305 p.

Franklin D Roosevelt

▲ **A grim-faced President Franklin D Roosevelt signs America's declaration of war on Japan – a turning point in the war.**

the American people when they heard of the devastation at Pearl Harbor was shock and outrage — tempered by anger. President Franklin D. Roosevelt and Secretary for the Navy Franklin Knox found it hard to accept the news when it arrived, feeling that there had to be some ghastly mistake. Nonetheless men at Pearl reacted well to the sudden shock of war, and courage and heroism was the order of the day.

SUPREME COURAGE

Men blown overboard clambered back to serve the guns; others manned fire parties. Dock workers made up rescue and repair parties, one group working on the bottom of *Utah* and *Oklahoma* to free trapped men by cutting through the bottom plates while the raid was still in progress. A small auxiliary, the YG-17, stood alongside the burning *West Virginia* to fight the fires.

Although the destruction wrought at Pearl Harbor was more than Yamamoto had hoped for it was by no means total. Fuchida was expecting to undertake a second attack to destroy the remaining ships and the oil tanks and the repair and maintenance installations that had been scarcely touched by the morning blitz.

Commander Minoru Genda wanted to seek out the American carriers and sink them. He and Fuchida were to be bitterly disappointed, Nagumo and his chief of staff, Ryunosuke Kusaka, deciding to run no further risks. They had crippled the American Fleet for the cost of only 29 aircraft lost and 74 damaged. The Japanese First Air Fleet therefore turned for home, satisfied with a job well done.

For the Americans, Pearl Harbor was a sorry sight. Eighteen ships, including all eight battleships, were

either sunk or heavily damaged, and no less than 164 aircraft were destroyed and another 124 damaged. A total of 2,403 service personnel had lost their lives and another 1,178 were wounded. However, the aircraft carriers still survived and sufficient cruisers and destroyers were operational to screen them from attack by Japanese ships.

Although the air bases had been badly damaged, Pearl Harbor itself could still function as a base and the oil tanks and the repair and maintenance installations still survived.

USA DECLARES WAR

Most importantly, by dint of efficient salvage work and repair, the American losses were not as catastrophic as first seemed. Fully 80 per cent of the damaged aircraft were repaired and all the sunken ships bar the *Arizona* were refloated and returned to service over the next two years.

No American could forgive or forget what Roosevelt called 'a day of infamy', and the next day the United States declared war on the Japanese nation.

▲ **The declaration of war on Germany signed by President Roosevelt on 11 December 1941.**

◄ **The aftermath of Pearl Harbor affected everyone—over 2,400 servicemen died and mass funerals were held to deal with the huge number of dead.**

▼ **Mute testimony to the effectiveness of the Japanese planning — a Boeing B-17 Flying Fortress stands, its back broken, on the airstrip.**

MOSCOW

BATTLE DIARY

OCTOBER 1941

2	Beginning of Operation *Taifun* (Typhoon)
6	Kleist reaches Sea of Azov
13	Vyasma pocket eliminated
14	German advance reaches Kalinin
15–16	Odessa evacuated by sea
19	Moscow evacuated but Stalin stays put

NOVEMBER

9	Germans capture Yalta
15	Assault on Moscow renewed
21	Fall of Rostov
23	Capture of Klin
24	Rostov evacuation in face of counter-attack
29	Moskva-Volga Canal crossed
30	Stalin approves counter-offensive plans

DECEMBER

5	Hitler halts drive on Moscow
6	Beginning of Russian counter-offensive
15	Soviets reoccupy Klin and Kalinin
17	German assault on Sevastopol begins
26	Russians begin counter-attack into Crimea
30	Russians recapture Tula

JANUARY 1942

7–8	New Russian offensive on northern sector
24	Russians recross River Donets
31	Soviet counter-offensive halted, except locally

FEBRUARY

24	Demyansk pocket completely sealed

MARCH

1	New Russian offensive in Crimea

APRIL

22	Relief of Demyansk pocket

ASSAULT ON MOSCOW

As the German army prepared to advance on Moscow,

its position seemed supreme – a situation the Russian

winter was to reverse dramatically

Topham Picture Library

▲ **Smolensk, October 1941. A German car equipped with loud speakers drives through the burning ruins, ordering the Russian troops to give up their weapons and surrender.**

◄ **Previous page: The violence of the German onslaught invades a Russian home. Shattered glass betrays a Nazi gunner's shelter.**

By October 1941 the great advances of Operation Barbarossa—Hitler's mighty attempt to subjugate the Soviet Union—had produced enormous booty for the German Army. Field Marshal Gerd von Rundstedt's Army Group South was now poised on a springboard pointing towards the River Don. On the Soviet side, the unfortunate Marshal Semën Budenny was removed from command and given a reserve posting, his place being taken by Marshal Semën Timoshenko.

But the Germans had lost time; moreover, according to General Günther Blumentritt, 'the results were not quite as satisfactory as they might appear at first glance. For one thing these great encirclements made very heavy demands on our panzer forces. For another, they were seldom entirely successful and large groups of the encircled enemy frequently slipped out of the pockets eastwards.'

GERMANY LOSES TIME

Army Group North had also made progress, despite the onset of the first autumn rains, and had reached the vicinity of Demyansk. By 16 September 1941—the day that Guderian and Kleist had completed the encirclement of the Ukrainian capital of Kiev—Manstein was able to announce that 'Nine enemy divisions were considered to have been destroyed and nine more badly battered'.

More significantly, he added, 'We still failed to find any real satisfaction in these achievements, for no-one was clear any longer what the actual aim of our strategy was or what higher purpose all these battles were supposed to serve.'

Manstein himself was now given a new appointment with Army Group South in the Crimea and command of his LVI Panzer Corps passed to General Ferdinand Schaal. Hitler then issued orders for a general reorganisation on the Eastern Front. Guderian's 2nd Panzer Group returned from Kiev to rejoin Army Group Centre, while Hoth's 3rd Panzer Group returned from the north.

The Führer had decided to leave the siege of Leningrad in the hands of the infantry, artillery and Luftwaffe, so Höpner's 4th Panzer Group (Reinhardt's XLI and Schaal's LVI Corps) was also detached to reinforce Army Group Centre, leaving behind the 3rd SS Division 'Totenkopf'.

Operation *Taifun* (Typhoon), the delayed advance on Moscow, officially began on 2 October but Guderian had already begun moving his troops northwards towards Orel a couple of days earlier because he was worried about the state of the roads. All the Panzer regiments were understrength after the summer losses, and although they were reinforced for Operation *Taifun*, many of the vehicles were battered and worn after the hundreds of miles they had driven.

Moreover, they were now facing a more potent adversary than they had previously encountered—the tough and canny Marshal Georgi Zhukov, the defender of Leningrad. Zhukov's Chief of Staff was the brilliant Vasily Sokolovsky and he had under his command two generals who were to emerge as among the best the Russians had, Ivan Koniev and Andrei Yeremenko.

Nevertheless, the initial stages of the new German offensive went off far better than anyone would have

WarStories

Volumes have been written about the Soviet Russians' austerity, lack of humour and grim outlook on life. A refreshing exception to this rule was the poker-faced Marshal Semën Mikhailovich Budenny. His appearance belied his fun-loving nature, and reports spread of a stag night he attended, which was held in a distillery. Throwing caution, his medals, uniform and firearms to the winds, he 'entered into the spirit' of the occasion by plunging enthusiastically into a brimming vat of wine with a bundle of similarly unclad ladies!

dared to predict. The first blow, spearheaded by Guderian's 2nd Panzer Group, fell on the Bryansk front, Yeremenko's command. Orel fell on 2 October and Guderian raced northwards, the Russians falling back in disarray before him. Another textbook encirclement took place at Bryansk when Guderian linked up with General Maximilian von Weich's Second Army.

Similarly, on what the Russians called the West Front, which was commanded by Koniev, the remainder of Höpner's forces swung north to link up with Hoth's 3rd Panzer Group, completing a second massive encirclement around Vyasma. Zhukov was recalled from Leningrad and was ordered by Stalin to find out what was going on

▲ General Oberst Erich Höpner, leader of the 4th Armoured Group, discusses the German advance with one of his men, Russia, October 1941.

◄ Summoned to the service of their country, a motley but dedicated crew of Russian partisans assembles to receive weapons. On the left the partisan receives a 7.62 mm Mosin-Nagant model 1930G rifle; the man, right, carries a PPSh/1941G 7.62 sub-machine-gun.

▲ A blaze of destruction from one of the Luftwaffe's aerial attacks glowing behind them, German infantrymen advance through the smoke on the trail of Moscow.

because what reports were reaching Moscow were fragmented and contradictory.

Reaching Koniev's headquarters on 7 October, Zhukov was told 'we don't know ourselves what is happening to the troops that have been encircled west of Vyasma'. Zhukov was forced to report to Stalin that 'there was no longer a continuous front in the west, and the large gaps could not be closed because the command had run out of reserves'.

Zhukov then set off to try to find Marshal Budenny, who had been entrusted with command of the Reserve

Bundesarchiv-Koblenz

Front after his failure to defend Kiev, but no-one at his headquarters knew where he was! He was eventually tracked down in Maloyaroslavets and asked what the defences consisted of on the road to Moscow. 'When I came through there', Budenny replied, 'I saw only three policemen.'

YET MORE PRISONERS

With typical energy, Zhukov began reorganising the reserves and pushing them into blocking positions around Mozhaisk, but he was unable to help the troops surrounded in the Bryansk and Vyasma pockets, some 660,000 more Russian prisoners being taken between 13 and 20 October when the two pockets surrendered.

At this point the German High Command was

▲ It is not only the men who are affected by the icy winter — horses weaken, vehicles sieze and oil thickens, impeding the Nazi advance.
◄ A Nazi soldier carrying a Mauser 7.91 mm 98K, throws a Steilhandgranate 39 (stick grenade) during an assault.

convinced the Red Army was finished. 'Prisoners', recalled General Blumentritt, 'told us that this new attack, launched so late in the year, had been completely unexpected. Moscow seemed about to fall into our hands.' Unfortunately for the Germans, the Red Army seemed unaware that it was defeated.

The new T-34 tanks were now coming off the production lines in ever greater numbers and, on top of this, several crack divisions of Siberian troops, vastly experienced in winter warfare, were being rushed westwards. Moreover, the weather was rapidly worsening. Showers turned into downpours which left the roads, such as they were, gluey quagmires in which wheeled vehicles had to be towed free by tanks.

EXHAUSTION

Moreover, the men were exhausted, having been marching and fighting continuously since June (and those who had taken part in the Balkan campaign for even

Tass News Agency; Below: Novosti Press Agency

BATTLE DIARY

BATTLE FOR MOSCOW

OCTOBER 1941
2 Beginning of Operation Taifun (Typhoon)
6 Kleist reaches Sea of Azov
13 Vyasma pocket eliminated
14 German advance reaches Kalinin
15/16 Odessa evacuated by sea
19 Moscow evacuated but Stalin stays put

NOVEMBER
9 Germans capture Yalta
15 Assault on Moscow renewed
21 Fall of Rostov
23 Capture of Klin
24 Rostov evacuated in face of counter-attack
29 Moskva-Volga Canal crossed
30 Stalin approves counter-offensive plans

DECEMBER
3 Hitler halts drive on Moscow
6 Beginning of the Russian counter-offensive
15 Soviets reoccupy Klin and Kalinin
17 German assault on Sevastopol begins
26 Russians begin counter-attack into Crimea
30 Russians recapture Tula

JANUARY 1942
7/8 New Russian offensive on northern sector
24 Russians recross River Donets
31 Soviet counter-offensive halted, except locally

FEBRUARY
24 Demyansk pocket completely sealed

MARCH
1 New Russian offensive in Crimea

APRIL
22 Relief of Demyansk pocket

longer). By 14 November, Guderian was forced to report that of 600 tanks with which his Panzer Group had commenced the invasion, only 50 remained serviceable.

Russian partisan groups were also becoming more active, exacting a heavy toll on supply convoys moving up towards the front line. The picture the Germans had painted early in October was rapidly fading. Nevertheless, it was decided to make one last try before the German Army had to go on to the defensive for the winter.

HARSH RUSSIAN WINTER

In the north the 3rd Panzer Group and Höpner's 4th, made good progress for a few days but then, says General Blumentritt, 'about the 20th of November the weather suddenly broke and almost overnight the full fury of the Russian winter was upon us . . .' With steadily decreasing momentum and increasing difficulty the two Panzer Groups continued to battle their way towards Moscow.

They managed to push through Kalinin and reach the Moskva-Volga Canal, then Höpner drove on to the Russian defences on the River Nara. A detachment of the 258th Infantry Division actually found a gap in the lines and drove through the night, reaching the western suburbs of Moscow on 2 December 1941, but they were thrown out again the following day by a determined tank attack. The drive to capture Moscow had failed. The battle for Moscow was about to begin.

▼ Soviet anti-aircraft gun crewmen, camouflaged and well-insulated, cover the advance of their troops against Luftwaffe attack.

NO RETREAT!

As badly equipped German troops struggle in appalling conditions, Marshal Zhukov seizes the initiative and launches a deadly Soviet counter attack.

The Russian winter of 1941 was one of the earliest and most severe on record, so severe that lubricating oil froze solid in vehicles' engines unless they were kept warmed, that ungloved fingers were welded by cold to any metal surface, that frostbite caused more casualties than enemy bullets and that sentries who fell asleep on duty were usually found dead—frozen solid at their posts.

HARSH REALITIES

This is the reality underlying the battle of Moscow, which lasted from 6 December 1941, when Zhukov launched his first offensive from north and south of Moscow, until the middle of April 1942 when it finally petered out and the Germans were themselves able to start planning a renewed offensive.

Supplies were short. German railway trains could not pull full loads because of ice on the tracks, and when they did get through they did not always bring what was really needed. On one occasion a trainload of cases of red wine arrived instead of the artillery ammunition expected. The bottles had all burst in the intense cold. Nor did all the Luftwaffe's efforts contribute a great deal, air-dropped supplies frequently falling far from the intended recipients, behind the Russian lines.

Süddeutscher Verlag; Inset: Bundesarchiv-Koblenz

◄ Field Marshal von Leeb (second from left), Commander of Army Group North, plots the campaign with General Höpner (second from right), Commander of the Fourth Panzer Army, Russia 1941.

ments in the form of two new 'Shock Armies' for his counter-attack—the First north-west of Moscow which was to strike across the Moskva-Volga Canal in the direction of Klin, and the Tenth south-west around Ryazan. Their aim was to split Field Marshal Günther von Kluge's Fourth Army away from its armoured support by driving wedges between it and the 3rd and 4th Panzer Groups on its northern flank and the 2nd on its southern.

Hitler had ordered 'no retreat', a command which many of his generals and field marshals regarded as insane. However, many of them were later to admit that it was the correct decision, because under the appalling weather conditions a withdrawal of

perhaps only three miles could have been achieved during each of the long nights. Instead of withdrawing, therefore, the Germans established defensive 'hedgehogs' with well-dug-in positions and entrenched artillery. Troops in the front 'line', where a line existed at all, could retire into these to allow the Soviet armour to expend itself fruitlessly in the bleak countryside, like cavalry in earlier days sweeping around the out-thrust bayonets of infantry squares. The Russians made determined efforts to deny the Germans any trace of shelter, whole villages being bombed and shelled indiscriminately so the infantry had no recourse but to dig themselves pathetic holes in the snow in which to shelter.

At home in Germany, Propaganda Minister Josef Göbbels launched a 'clothes for the troops' campaign but, although fur coats in their thousands were handed in, this first terrible winter would be almost over before they reached the combatants. For snow camouflage, German soldiers even wrapped bedsheets over the tops of their greatcoats. The Russians were generally much better off, being not only more suitably dressed but also more acclimatised to the extremes of temperature—especially the fierce Siberians. However, Zhukov was not given all the tanks he demanded, and those which did arrive were often crewed by men who had only had a few hours' training.

Zhukov had assembled reinforce-

▲ The war on the Eastern Front has taken a turn for which the Germans were entirely unprepared. Here German horse-drawn transport makes slow, painful progress through the appalling winter conditions.

▶ The relative strengths of the German invaders and Red Army defenders, October 1941.

| 950 | 1,400 |
| 770 | 1,700 |

BATTLE LINE-UP

| 800,000 | 1m |
| 9,150 | 19,000 |

► Kalinin, north west of Moscow, December 1941. Russian troops in winter uniform march past the bodies of their German enemies— a sad aftermath of the battle.

Novosti Press Agency. Inset: Imperial War Museum

БЕСПОЩАДНО РАЗГРОМИМ И УНИЧТОЖИМ ВРАГА!

ДОГОВОР о ненападении между СССР и Германией

КУКРЫНИКСЫ-41.

◄ Patriotic Russian propaganda—the intrusive rat, Hitler, can expect no quar- ter from the Soviets for his atrocities in their homeland. Bayonetting would be too good for him.

SUICIDE TACTICS

Adding to the problem of partisans in the German rear areas, Zhukov also deployed ski troops, Cossacks and parachutists far behind the lines. But Russian front-line tactics themselves were suicidal. The infantry came running out of the mists in great waves, stumbling in the snow, to be mown down in their hundreds and thousands by machine-gun, mortar and artillery fire. Time after time they attacked in this fashion and casualties caused Zhukov such

concern that a week into the campaign he had to issue a directive forbidding such head-on assaults.

Despite their losses, the Russians continued advancing and Guderian's 2nd Panzer Group, now renamed the Second Panzer Army, soon found itself in deep trouble.

ZHUKOV STRIKES

Zhukov's Fiftieth Army struck from Tula. 'Guderian's army,' the Marshal wrote, 'threatened by deep inroads on its flanks and lacking the forces to parry the attacks . . . began

MARSHAL GEORGI ZHUKOV

The greatest Soviet military leader of World War II was born in a village outside Moscow in 1896 and joined a crack dragoon regiment in 1914, winning two decorations from the Tsar.

He enlisted in the fledgling Red Army in October 1918 and joined the Bolshevik Party a year later, fighting and being wounded with the 1st Cavalry Army.

During the 1930s he became a forthright supporter of tanks and armoured warfare, and in 1939 conducted a successful campaign against the Japanese in Manchuria, having survived the 'Tukachevsky Purge' due to his civil war friendship with Stalin.

He was Chief of Staff during the Winter War with Finland but did

not have a field post, so avoided the disgrace of so many other Red Army officers, and was entrusted with the defence of Leningrad after the German invasion, before being removed to the Moscow front.

In 1942 he was in overall command of Soviet forces at Stalingrad and later played a major role in the Battle of Kursk in 1943, and the drive on Berlin in 1945.

After the war he was hailed as the 'saviour of Moscow', but Stalin decided to put him out to grass because he had become too friendly with Dwight D Eisenhower. After being Minister of Defence under Khrushchev, he died in 1974.

► Mastermind of the Russian winter victory—Marshal Zhukov.

Popperfoto

▶The push towards Moscow must go on. German troops mount an assault on a Russian village, dropping into action under the cover of their Panzer Mk III. Inset: another Soviet village comes under German attack.

to pull back rapidly through Uzlovaya and Bogoroditsk towards Sukhinichi, leaving behind heavy weapons, trucks, tractors and even tanks.' The Second Panzer Army was forced to retreat because the second Army, on Guderian's right flank, was already falling back and this would have left Guderian vulnerable to encirclement. A fortnight later Hitler sacked him—just one of several major changes to take place in the German officer corps.

SURROUND AND DESTROY

Kluge's Fourth Army was soon in a bad way as well. According to General Blumentritt, Zhukov, having obtained his first objective in forcing Guderian to retreat, then split his forces, some heading towards Kaluga, others advancing in the Oka sector and still more in the direction of Maloyaroslavets. 'Russian intentions were obvious. They were planning a wide double encirclement with the ultimate aim of surrounding and destroying (the Fourth Army) in its present positions west of Moscow.' The Germans had no reserves and only one road still lay open towards the west and their supply line.

DISMISSED

Kluge decided to withdraw, but a direct order from Hitler forbade this. At this point, on 18 December, Field Marshal von Bock—commander of Army Group Centre—was forced to give up his post because of ill health, and Kluge assumed overall control. His Chief of Staff, Blumentritt, took

▲ The brilliant Panzer commander, General Erich von Manstein, pictured in the Crimea, 1942. Inset: Christmas far away—a German morale-boost for home

over the Fourth Army itself, pending the arrival of General Kubler on the 26th. Meanwhile, back in Berlin, the Army's C-in-C, Field Marshal Walter von Brauchitsch, himself took retirement because he could no longer agree with Hitler's decisions. Other capable officers who were dismissed or forced to resign because of the Führer's tantrums included von Rundstedt, whose Army Group South had been thrown out of Rostov-on-Don back to Kharkov, Höpner and von Leeb.

On Christmas Eve 1941, the Fourth Army's situation was extremely precarious. It still retained its headquarters at Maloyaroslavets but all that lay between it and the Russians were the 50 surviving tanks of the 19th Panzer Division. Other formations were in an even worse state: Höpner's four Panzer divisions

◄ A German address to the Russian people—the arrival of the Wehrmacht will liberate them from the oppressive regime—they should welcome Nazi rule.

Top, Top Left, Left: Bundesarchiv-Koblenz

WarStories

Supplies—or rather a woeful lack of them—became the greatest cause of dissatisfaction amongst the German forces, battling through the savage Russian winter towards their goal, Moscow. The drop of a consignment of food or warm clothing was, therefore, an occasion to celebrate. Imagine, then, the sense of irony and anti-climax amongst the men when the eagerly-awaited bundles were ripped open, only to reveal one of the very few things for which they had absolutely no use at all—two tons of condoms!

had less than 15 tanks apiece. At the last minute, on Christmas Day, Blumentritt transferred Fourth Army's HQ westwards to Yukhnov, where Kubler assumed command. Then, miraculously, the Russian attacks against Army Group Centre faltered to a standstill, the troops too exhausted to advance any further and their ranks decimated. Kluge's forces at this point occupied a line roughly running from Rzhev in the north through Vyasma to Bryansk in the south. Zhukov had not completely shot his bolt, however, and on the night of 7/8 January 1942 he launched a new offensive north of Moscow with the intention of cutting off the German troops besieging Leningrad.

HOLD THE LINE

In the middle of a blizzard, the First and Third Shock Armies and the Eleventh and Thirty-Fourth Armies threw their might against General Ernst Busch's Sixteenth Army in the gap between Lakes Llmen and Seliger. The 290th Infantry Division was virtually annihilated and the 30th Division thrown back in disorder with heavy casualties. This left the line held almost solely by SS General Theodor Eicke's 3rd 'Totenkopf' Division, whose defence over the next

Topham Picture Library; Below: Novosti Press Agency

◄ **A brief glimmer of warmth in the push towards Moscow—a group of German soldiers huddle around a campfire—a small defence against the temperatures of −35°C and under.**

Bundesarchiv Koblenz

▲ **Comradeship in war between two German soldiers, enjoying a well-earned smoke.**

three months was an epic of courage and determination.

The division had already suffered heavily in the summer and autumn fighting, losing nearly 9,000 casualties—roughly 50 per cent of its strength—and replacements only totalled about half this number.

However, the division did have two advantages. The SS commissariat had been more farsighted than its army counterpart, and large stocks of warm winter parkas, boots and hats had been issued to its men. Moreover, during December 1941, the Russians had made only limited moves on the division's front, and it had been able to construct bunkers and trenches in the Valdai hills, a natural defensive position.

WINTER CLOTHING

At the outset of the Russian campaign the only winter clothing available to German troops was the standard double-breasted, calf-length field grey great-coat, together with leather marching boots and a pair of woollen gloves. Woefully inadequate in the face of the appalling Russian winter (a time by which, at least in the Führer's eyes, Germany would be victorious), it was a situation that could not continue. As a consequence during the winter of 1941–42 a wide variety of civilian Russian clothing was pressed into service, including quilted jackets, fur waistcoats and fur hats. Later a

The icy, demoralising trudge goes on for German soldiers, Moscow sector, December.

proper two-piece reversible blanket-lined suit was issued, one side being grey and the other white, together with a fur-lined cap with ear flaps. The Waffen SS had their own pattern pile-lined hooded parka but this was so thick it restricted mobility and later alpine-type anoraks with deep chest pockets and drawstring fastening became popular. Soviet troops were also issued with a double-breasted greatcoat called a kaftan in dark grey or khaki. To complement these they also wore quilted collarless jackets and trousers, thick felt boots, wadded with straw, and the *schlem*, a peaked, pointed cloth helmet with ear flaps. Both sides wore loose white cotton smocks over everything else for snow camouflage.

Imperial War Museum

THE RED TIDE

Five of the division's battalions had to be rushed to the important rail and road junction of Staraya Russa and two more to Demyansk in order to stem the 'Red tide', and von Leeb resigned when Hitler refused his troops permission to retire. By 20 January the 'Totenkopf' and other isolated units were completely cut off except at Staraya Russa, where they established a 'breakwater'. Three weeks later the Russians had surrounded all of six divisions, including the 'Totenkopf', in the area around Demyansk.

The situation was so critical that Eicke had to order all his walking wounded back into the line from the field hospitals. Mere companies, sometimes of only 40 or 50 men, had to repulse assaults on a divisional scale—and succeeded. The only villages the Russians recaptured were those in which every 'Totenkopf' soldier had died. Awards of Knights' Crosses became almost commonplace.

TO THE LAST MAN

By the end of February only isolated groups of soldiers still fought on, separated by the wilderness and the

◀ A poster in praise of the partisans— the German advance is met by continued opposition, the rear area troops under constant threat from snipers.

enemy from their comrades. Despite Zhukov's earlier directive, though, the Soviet infantry still swept forward in suicidal waves, their attacks only being halted when the last man had been killed. The Germans could no longer evacuate their wounded to hospital, and only the Luftwaffe kept them supplied, ammunition being the top priority. A mere 400 reinforcements were flown in early in March. Still the invasion force managed to hold out, although their lines penetrated everywhere.

WEATHER IMPROVES

Then, in the second week of March, the weather began improving and with it the supply situation. An attempt to relieve the survivors in the Demyansk pocket could now be planned, and General Walter von Seydlitz-Kurzbach's 10th was assembled to strike towards them from the direction of Staraya Russa, over the River Lovat. Supported by the greatest concentration of aircraft seen over the northern front all winter, Seydlitz's attack began on 22 March but was brought to a halt six days later.

Clearing a path through the Russian defences took another fortnight and it was not until 14 April, with spring in the air, that Eicke's emaciated command in the pocket was able to strike westwards to effect a linkup. On 22 April 1942,

REPRIEVE

On 4 August 1941, Hitler met his Generals at Novy Birissov, the Headquarters of Army Group Centre on the Eastern Front. He confirmed that the Panzers were to divert from a direct attack on Moscow and go north and south to assist at Leningrad and Kiev respectively, saying that Moscow was little more than a 'geographical expression'. What was important was the destruction of the Russian army and the seizure of resources in the Ukraine. General Heinz Guderian, Commander of Panzer Group 2, pointed out that Moscow lay wide open to attack, but the Führer was adamant. The diversions achieved a great deal, but the defenders of Moscow gained the respite they needed to hold the capital.

▶Germans with an MG34 machine-gun lie in wait in a frozen foxhole.

TURNING POINT

Bundesarchiv-Koblenz

after 73 days of isolation, the 'Totenkopf' Division re-established contact after forcing a passage of the River Lovat, swollen by the thaw.

MOSCOW STANDOFF

The German Army may have failed to take Moscow, but Zhukov had also failed in his attempt to throw it right back. After a pause in which a number of divisions had to be sent back to the west to be brought up to strength and re-equipped, the German offensive would be resumed. The battle of Moscow was at an end. The next goal for the German troops was to be Stalingrad, the gateway to the Caucasus.

▶ In a rain of German shells, a Russian medic helps a wounded soldier.

▼ Red Square, Moscow, 7 November 1941. Russian troops on parade mark the anniversary of the 1917 revolution – then march on to the front nearby.

MIDWAY

BATTLE DIARY

MAY 1942

28–30   Japanese forces sail to implement Operation M1
American carrier forces leave Pearl Harbor to rendezvous off Midway

JUNE

3   Operation M1 begins with assault on Aleutians

4   Start of the Battle of Midway

04.30   Nagumo begins to launch strike against Midway

05.30   Catalina sights Nagumo's forces. Midway begins to launch strike aircraft and prepare for attack

06.30   Japanese attack on Midway begins

07.00   American carriers begin to launch strike

07.30   Japanese floatplane from *Tone* sights *Yorktown*

09.20   Nagumo swings north to close range

09.20–10.15   American torpedo-bombers attack

10.23–10.30   American dive-bombers attack, crippling *Akagi*, *Kaga* and *Soryu*

11.00   *Hiryu* begins to launch strike against American carriers

12.00   Japanese strike attacks and damages *Yorktown*

13.30   *Hiryu* launches further strike

14.30   Japanese strike cripples *Yorktown*

15.30   Crew of *Yorktown* abandon ship
Hornet and *Enterprise* launch strike

17.00   American strike attacks and cripples *Hiryu*

JAPAN PUSHES ON

Japan's list of victories continues to grow and grow, with the Allies impotent to resist. Japanese morale is high. Even the great land mass of Australia is viewed as a possible conquest.

▲ **Gun-crew on board a Japanese destroyer in the Pacific prepare for action. This is probably a training exercise; respirators were both uncomfortable and unwieldly, so were rarely worn in battle—in spite of the fact that they were designed to filter out the smoke from a hit.**

Hulton Deutsch Collection

The early months of the war had brought Japan astonishing successes. By June 1942 she had the conquests of the Philippines, Burma, Malaya, and the Dutch East Indies under her belt. What's more, all this had been achieved for far less than the anticipated naval losses of over 20%. Nonetheless, the situation brought with it its own set of problems.

WHERE NOW?

The question was, where to now? Admiral Nagano's Naval General Staff were in favour of either a push westwards against the British possessions in India and Ceylon, or a southward advance to the Australian land mass. But this kind of prolonged struggle was seen as fatal

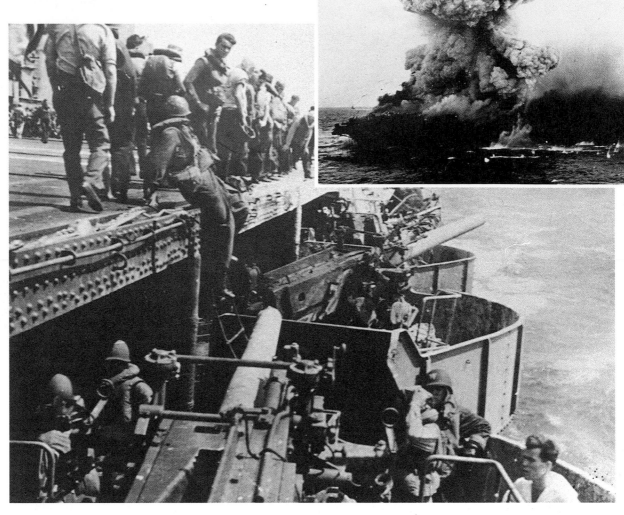

▶Scene aboard the US aircraft carrier *Lexington* in the aftermath of the Japanese air attack, Coral Sea, 8 May 1942. The damage seems survivable at this stage; but the inset shows fires from the violent explosion that rocked the *Lexington* at 12.47 the same day, which soon raged out of control. A destroyer was able to pick up many survivors. The Coral Sea battle proved a costly stalemate for the US.

US National Archives

▼An American postcard of 1942 promises the destruction of Japanese airpower in the Pacific—a promise soon to be fulfilled.

I & V Holt Collection

BLACKOUT of the RISING SUN

to Japanese interests by Admiral Yamamoto and the staff of his Combined Fleet. They argued that the first priority for Japan was the destruction of the United States' Pacific Fleet, particularly the aircraft carriers. These had been at sea when the surprise attack on Pearl Harbor was sprung, and posed a threat long foreseen by Yamamoto.

He proposed an attack on the Northern Pacific island of Midway, in preparation for an advance on the Hawaiian islands. Such an action, it was argued, would draw the US Pacific Fleet out for a decisive battle for control of the Pacific, long before the Allies gained material superiority.

OUT OF FAVOUR

This plan found little favour with the Imperial Japanese Army, wary of committing such large numbers of troops for naval operations, their eyes firmly fixed on Russia and the mainland of Asia. Instead the Army forced the Naval General Staff to adopt a much less ambitious plan to isolate the Australian mainland.

As the debate carried on the modified plan was put into action when Lae and Salamaua in New Guinea were occupied in early March. But as preparations for the conquest of Port Moresby, the gateway to Papua, got under way, Japan was shaken by the Doolittle raid on Tokyo, an event which brought the war a little too close to home and undoubtedly strengthened Yamamoto's hand. On 5 May, the Naval General Staff acquiesced, Admiral Nagano ordering Yamamoto to 'carry out the occupation of Midway Island.'

Japan was now in very real danger of over-extending her resources. The attack on Port Moresby had originally been scheduled for early March but the presence of US aircraft carriers in the region had resulted in its

cancellation until the V Carrier Division could return from the Indian Ocean, under the command of Rear Admiral Chuichi Hara, with the powerful carriers *Shokaku* and *Zuikaku* in its ranks. The rest of the ships came from the Fourth Fleet under the command of Vice-Admiral Shigeyoshi Inouye, the operation's overall commander.

The invasion of Port Moresby, Operation MO, was a relatively simple one, intended to bring the north coast of Australia within the range of Japanese bombers and protect Japanese advances into the south-west Pacific. Inouye expected opposition to the advance but did not believe that it would involve more than one aircraft carrier. He believed that once an airfield could be established at Tulagi in the Solomon Islands and air superiority was therefore established, the Allies would find the Japanese movements difficult to follow and thus would enable the Invasion Group to land. As the Allied task force entered the Coral Sea, between New Guinea and the Queensland coast, it would be destroyed in a pincer movement. Or so ran the theory.

AIR STRIKE

When Tulagi was invaded on 3 May, the Americans had gathered two task forces in the area under the command of Rear Admiral Frank Fletcher. One, Task Force 17, was built around the carrier USS *Yorktown*, while the carrier USS *Lexington* spearheaded Task Force 11. On the morning of 4 May *Yorktown* launched three air strikes against Japanese landing forces although, despite the returning pilots' optimistic claims, the results were somewhat disappointing. Nevertheless, the Japanese did abandon the build-up of their garrison on Tulagi.

Peter Newark's Western Americana

US National Archives

Yorktown withdrew to rendezvous with *Lexington* and refuel from the ill-fated *Neosho* before heading northwest on 6 May to search for the Port Moresby Invasion Force which had been sighted by American land-based aircraft at midday off the eastern tip of New Guinea. Planning to send in his cruisers to attack the Invasion Force, Fletcher kept back his aircraft for use against any Japanese carriers.

Unknown to Fletcher, Vice Admiral Takagi's fleet carriers were behind him, having come round the Solomon Islands. Takagi assumed that the US carriers were to his north-east, but elected to search to the southeast to ensure that no one was behind him. At dawn on 7 May, a Japanese float-plane flashed the news that it had sighted an aircraft carrier and a cruiser. In fact, what was assumed to be one of the US carrier task forces consisted

▲ Following hits from aerial torpedoes, the *Lexington* starts to list heavily. Men can be seen swarming down ropes; many had queued patiently, waiting for the order to abandon ship. Hours later, the 'Lex' was scuttled by an American destroyer.

◄ Survivors from the crippled *Lexington* scramble aboard a US destroyer, Coral Sea, 8 May 1942.

BOMBING OF DARWIN

Darwin, the main port of Northern Australia and therefore the main supply base for ABDACOM (American, British, Dutch, Australian Command), was attacked on 19 February 1942. In an attempt to cripple Allied supply lines, 135 aircraft, Pearl Harbor veterans from Nagumo's First Air Fleet, were launched from four fleet carriers. With negligible opposition it was almost target practice as the Japanese aircrews sank five ships and damaged three others severely enough to cause them to be beached. The port itself was heavily damaged with 240 people killed and 150 wounded. This savage bolt from the blue caused considerable alarm and panic in an Australia that had been hitherto insulated from the events of the war.

▶ Australian gunners man a 4.7 inch heavy anti-aircraft gun outside Darwin, some time after the Japanese attack.

Topham Picture Library

海の強者になるためだ
鍛へよ強く
逞しく

海軍志願兵徴募中
詳細は至急最寄の市區町村役場へ問合せの事

Marshall Cavendish Library

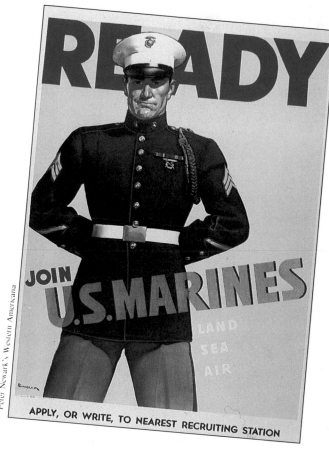

READY

JOIN
U.S. MARINES
LAND
SEA
AIR

APPLY, OR WRITE, TO NEAREST RECRUITING STATION

Peter Newark's Western Americana

▲ Japanese propa-
ganda poster of 1942
salutes the recent
victories of the Navy,
while the US Marine
Corps appeals for
volunteers.

of the oiler *Neosho* and the destroyer *Sims*, both of which
were overwhelmed by the Japanese airmen, furious at
their mistake.

Fletcher was to do little better. On the same morning a
scout from *Yorktown* reported two carriers 200 miles to
the north-west. Only after launching a strike was it
discovered that the target was actually two cruisers.
Nevertheless, Fletcher allowed the strike to proceed.

Meanwhile, the Lexington sighted a small carrier, the
Shoho, and the Covering Force for the invasion. US
airmen swooped down on the converted freighter and
scored 13 bomb hits and seven torpedo hits that left her a

burning wreck. The US carriers spent the rest of the day
trying to locate one another in the poor weather that
closed in on the Coral Sea. Takagi, who had some idea of
where Fletcher's carriers were, launched a tentative strike
in the late afternoon which got hopelessly lost after being
intercepted by Wildcats from Task Force 17.

FIRE AND FURY

Early next morning, both sides located each other and
launched large-scale strikes. That launched from the
Yorktown and *Lexington* was largely uncoordinated with
both groups attacking separately, concentrating on the

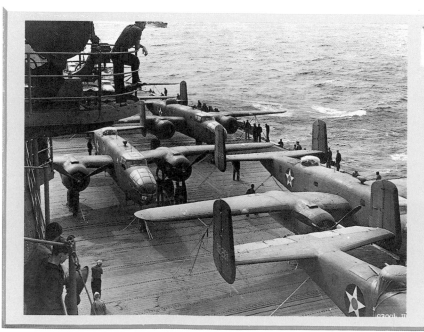

Lopham Picture Library

DOOLITTLE RAID

On 18 April 1942, the war was brought home to Japan
when 16 Army B-25 Mitchell land-based aircraft flew
off the flight deck of the carrier USS *Hornet* and
bombed Tokyo before landing secretly in Nationalist
China. Intended to raise Allied morale rather than
cause much damage to the Japanese capital, the daring
raid led by Lieut. Colonel James H. Doolittle was not
without its success. Mortified by the excursion into
Japanese airspace, the Navy accepted Yamamoto's
plan to extend Japan's air defence perimeter.
Operation MI, the invasion of Midway Island, was
therefore rescheduled for the first week of June and
allocated resources originally meant for Operation
MO, the attack on Port Moresby.

◄ Converted B-25 bombers pack the deck of the carrier
USS *Hornet* as airmen prepare to bomb Tokyo, April 1942.

WarStories

One US sailor aboard the USS *Lexington* in the Coral Sea had just cause to thank his girlfriend. Though she was 12,000 miles away in Maryland, Anna Lee Etchison probably saved electrician Richard Bachman's life.

As Japanese planes attacked the *Lexington*, a flying chunk of metal hit a metal cigarette case, a gift from Anna, that he carried in his pocket. If it had not been for the case deflecting the chunk, his leg would have been torn off, which would have prevented his escape from the doomed carrier. The couple were reunited two weeks later.

Shokaku. Running into heavy fighter opposition and a furious gun barrage, the inexperienced American pilots could not repeat the damage done to the *Shoho*, scoring only three bomb hits for the loss of 43 aircraft. Although they reported two carriers as 'burning fiercely' and 'settling fast', the *Shokaku*, badly damaged, was able to transfer its remaining aircraft to *Zuikaku* and return to Truk en route to Japan.

TORPEDO ATTACK

At the same time, a similar scene was being played out as the Japanese strike showed the difference in quality between themselves and the novice Americans. The strike bored through an inadequate Combat Air Patrol and in an attack lasting some 40 minutes put one bomb onto the *Yorktown* and two into the *Lexington*, while the latter was caught by a torpedo attack, with Kates attacking from both sides, resulting in a temporary list to port. Despite the damage, both carriers were soon operational again, landing aircraft and preparing another attack. But disaster was soon to strike.

Sparks from one of the *Lexington*'s generators ignited vapour escaping from the damaged fuel pipes and set off a lethal chain reaction of fire and explosions. Despite brave damage control work, she had to be abandoned, most of her crew being saved, before she was sent to the bottom by one of her escorts at 8 pm.

The loss of the *Lexington* changed the face of the battle. From a point at which the Americans had two operational carriers to the Japanese one, with more aircraft, Fletcher and his Commander-in-Chief back in Pearl Harbor, Chester Nimitz, now had to weigh the possibility of reinforcements joining the surviving Japanese carrier. Ordered by Nimitz to conserve his carrier strength, Fletcher withdrew from the arena and set course for Noumea in New Caledonia, leaving the Japanese in control of the Coral Sea.

THE PURSUIT ENDS

This supremacy was to be short-lived. The invasion of Port Moresby had already been postponed until air superiority could be won. Takagi initially began to withdraw from the scene when he received orders from an irate Yamamoto to finish off the American carrier force. Half-heartedly cruising the area for another two days he called off the pursuit and returned to Truk, fearful of American land-based power.

In terms of numbers, the Coral Sea was a victory for the Japanese, sinking one fleet carrier, one oiler and a destroyer in exchange for one light carrier sunk and a fleet carrier damaged. However, strategically it was a clear American victory, as the Japanese drive south was checked with the postponement and then the cancellation of Operation MO.

Almost as important, the damage to the *Shokaku*, the sinking of the *Shoho* and the decimation of both air groups deprived Yamamoto of two of his newest and most powerful carriers at a time when they were most needed, for Operation MI, the planned invasion of Midway Island.

▼Having sustained bomb damage in the Coral Sea, the US carrier *Yorktown* undergoes emergency repairs in dry dock at Pearl Harbor, May 1942. Dockers worked night and day on her and, to the astonishment of the Japanese, she appeared at the Battle of Midway.

▼An American poster calls on US citizens to buy War Bonds—government stock, sold at a fixed rate of interest. The money would fuel the war effort.

Peter Newark's Western Americana

To Have and to Hold!!

WAR BONDS

◄The sequence of events in the early Pacific War.

▼Specially made flag to denote the Allies—United Kingdom, United States of America, China, Russia and Free France.

US National Archives Inc — Marshall Cavendish

BATTLE DIARY

MIDWAY AND CORAL SEA

MARCH 1942
8   Japan invades New Britain
9   Dutch East Indies capitulate
    Further debate in Tokyo on
    Japanese strategic intentions

APRIL
18   Doolittle raid

MAY
3   Japanese invade Tulagi. Port
    Moresby invasion force sets sail
7-8   **Battle of the Coral Sea**
28-30   Japanese forces sail to implement
    Operation MI. US carrier forces
    leave Pearl Harbor to rendez-
    vous off Midway

JUNE
3   Operation MI begins with assault
    on Aleutians
4-6   **Battle of Midway**

FORTUNES REVERSED

With stalemate the order of the day in the Southern Pacific, Japan's eyes turn to Midway Island and the elimination of America's outnumbered Pacific fleet. The result is a complete reversal in fortune.

▲The cap badge worn by an officer of the Imperial Japanese Navy.

▲ Japanese troops occupy the island of Attu in the Aleutians, June 1942. The island was of little strategic value. Dutch Harbor (left) in the aftermath of a Japanese air attack, 3 June 1942.

On 5 May, Japanese Imperial Headquarters issued the operational orders for the next stage of Japanese expansion, Operation MI. Its aim: to capture Midway Island, some 1,100 miles (1,770 km) from Hawaii, in order to weaken America's perimeter defences and at the same time bring America's weakened carrier forces to battle. At the same time Attu and Kiska Islands in the Aleutians, a chain of islands off the Alaskan coast, would be invaded as a diversion which would also eliminate them as possible bases for air attack against the Japanese mainland.

THE FLEET SETS SAIL

On 28 May, the four carriers of Vice Admiral Nagumo sailed with their powerful escort from Japan. On 30 May the Main Body under Admiral Yamamoto and the Covering Group under Vice Admiral Kondo sailed from Ashijarima. These powerful forces began to converge on Midway under cover of bad weather. Another smaller force made its way to the Aleutians.

Unknown to the Japanese, the Americans were ready and waiting at

Midway. Confident that their codes could not be broken, Japanese Combined Fleet Headquarters had despatched the orders for the attack on Midway by lengthy radio messages. But by the middle of May the highly efficient American code-breaking and traffic analysis organisation in the Pacific was providing Admiral Nimitz with full details of the forthcoming Japanese attack. Accordingly, Midway Island was reinforced with more aircraft to supplement the carrier task forces which were rushed back from the South Pacific. Task Force (TF) 16, consisting of USS *Hornet* and USS *Enterprise*, could simply put into Pearl Harbor to refuel and rearm; for TF17, USS *Yorktown*, it was more difficult. Damaged by bombs and torpedoes at Coral Sea, *Yorktown* had to be drydocked at Pearl Harbor as soon as she arrived on 22 May 1942. It was estimated that it would take at least three months to repair. But Nimitz, conscious of the significance of the impending battle, insisted on repairs being carried out

▶ In early June 1942, a Mitsubishi A6M Zero fighter was recovered by the Americans from Akutan island in the Aleutians (upper). Repaired, it is test flown in San Diego, California (lower), revealing its vulnerable areas. This captured Zero gave rise to the development of the F6F Hellcat.

in only three days.

Command of the US forces rested with Rear Admiral Fletcher, commander of TF17, with Nimitz at Pearl Harbor keeping a close watch on the battle. But the commander of TF16, Rear Admiral Halsey, the most experienced carrier commander in the US Navy, had been hospitalised at Pearl with a skin complaint brought on by strain. In his place he recommended the inexperienced cruiser

◀ Douglas SBD Dauntless carrier-based dive-bombers fly over Midway Island, June 1942. Their role in the Battle of Midway was crucial. The Japanese aircraft carrier *Akagi* (inset) tries to avoid American air attack, Midway, 4 June 1942.

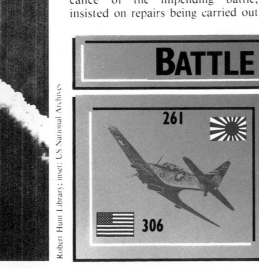

BATTLE LINE-UP

Japan	Aircraft Carriers	US
261 🇯🇵		306 🇺🇸

US 🇺🇸		Japan 🇯🇵
3	AIRCRAFT CARRIERS	4
0	BATTLESHIPS	2
8	CRUISERS	3
15	DESTROYERS	11

◀ The opposing US and Japanese forces as they lined up at the Battle of Midway June 1942.

War Stories

Although staunchly together and fighting on the same side, there was always good-natured rivalry among the Allied Forces, particularly between Britain and the USA. Once, as a powerful US warship passed a Royal Navy ship at sea, a message was sent to the Brits: 'Greetings to the second biggest navy in the world'. Quiet reigned in the signals cabin as the Royal Navy captain, unmoved, sent back his reply. His message read, 'Greetings to the second best navy in the world'. Full marks to the RN!

▼ **Grumman TBF Avenger torpedo-bombers show their lines, Midway, 1942.**

US National Archives

commander, Rear Admiral Raymond Spruance, which turned out to be an inspired choice.

The intention was for the out-numbered American forces to ambush the Japanese carriers before they knew where the American carriers were. To this end the Americans had sailed from Pearl Harbor before the Japanese submarine scouting picket line was in place and maintaining radio silence, had rendezvoused at Point Luck, some 200 miles (320km) north-east of Midway.

MASTER PLAN

Admiral Yamamoto's master plan began to unravel on the morning of 3 June 1942 when at 9.00 am a Navy Catalina flying boat sighted the transports of the occupation force some 700 miles (1125 km) west of Midway. High level bombing attacks by Army B-17s and low level night torpedo attacks by 'Black Cat' Catalinas caused little damage.

In accordance with the plan, Nagumo began his strike against Midway at 4.30 am on 4 June. Unaware of the trap awaiting him, but cautious nonetheless, he launched only half of his strike force.

One hour later, as Nagumo's forces were sighted, Midway launched all available attack aircraft against the Japanese carriers. Spruance raced south-west with TF16, with Fletcher following after he had recovered his search planes, in a position to launch against the Japanese carriers as soon as they were within range. Spruance, with the advice of his chief of staff, Captain Browning, decided to launch his strike at 150 miles (240 km), the limit of his aircraft's range, in order to get his blow in first. At 7.00 am he launched a full-strength attack from the *Hornet* and *Enterprise*.

Meanwhile, as the Japanese strike closed on Midway it was bounced by the Midway Marine fighter squadron but the obsolete Buffaloes and

▲ **Like all major US ships, the *Yorktown* had its own badge—an eagle perched on a cannon.**

CHESTER W. NIMITZ

As the pre-war Chief of the Bureau of Navigation, Admiral Chester Nimitz had developed a strong reputation for getting the job done with a minimum of fuss. Appointed to the Command of the US Pacific Fleet in January 1942 in succession to the unfortunate Admiral Kimmel, the man held to be responsible for the debacle at Pearl Harbor, he became Commander in Chief Pacific Ocean Area two months later. With his headquarters at Pearl Harbor, he became a key figure in the Pacific War despite not being as flamboyant as some of his better known subordinates such as William 'Bull' Halsey.

A quiet and thoughtful individual, he nonetheless enjoyed a good working relationship with both his acerbic superior, Admiral Ernest King, and his key subordinates commanding the Third and Fifth Fleets, Rear Admiral Raymond Spruance and Vice-Admiral Halsey. More than any other man, Nimitz was responsible for the United States Pacific Fleet's move from the defensive to the offensive within a year of the outbreak of war in the Far East. Fittingly, it was Nimitz, the coordinator of American strategy in the Central Pacific, who signed the Japanese surrender on behalf of the United States of America on board the USS *Missouri* in Tokyo Bay on 2 September 1945.

▶ **Admiral Chester Nimitz, Commander of the US Pacific Fleet.**

Main picture: the US carrier *Yorktown*, badly mauled at Coral Sea, comes under heavy air attack.

Wildcats were cut out of the sky by the agile Zeros.

At this moment the first attacks by aircraft from Midway against the Japanese carriers began. Six of the new Grumman Avenger Navy torpedo bombers under Lt. L K Fieberling were the first to go in. Three were shot down by the waiting Zeros of the CAP (Combat Air Patrol). The remainder dropped their obsolete torpedoes, which the *Akagi* easily dodged, but only one survived to return to Midway. Close on the heels of the Avengers, four Army B-26 Marauder twin-engined bombers bored in. Their crews had never trained with torpedoes: two survived to drop their torpedoes but, not surprisingly, no hits were scored.

GAME OF RISK

At 7.30 a single floatplane from the *Tone* signalled that it had sighted American ships less than 200 miles (320 km) from Nagumo's fleet. Nagumo was in a dilemma: his first strike wave was returning from Midway, low on fuel and anxious to land as quickly as possible, while the second wave, only partly rearmed, cluttered up the hangars and flight-decks of his carriers. Pressured by his bold subordinate Yamaguchi, Nagumo decided to take the risk of landing the Midway force before launching a strike against the American ships.

It was not to be. The Japanese CAP and lookouts shouted warnings of incoming torpedo bombers. First in, between 9.20 am and 9.35 am, were the 15 obsolete Devastators of *Hornet*'s Torpedo 8 commanded by Lt. John Waldron. Determined to get a hit, Waldron led his squadron

◀ **This remarkable photograph shows a Japanese Nakajima B5N 'Kate' torpedo-bomber flying through anti-aircraft fire at zero feet towards a beleaguered US warship, Midway, 4 June 1942.**

The Japanese carrier *Hiryu* burns after having been hit by aircraft from USS *Enterprise* late on 4 June 1942. *Hiryu* was scuttled the next day.

▼ A Japanese *Mikuma*-class cruiser under heavy air attack, 5 June 1942—one of the final acts of the Battle of Midway.

Japanese destroyer. Hot on his heels came 18 Dauntlesses from *Yorktown* led by Lt-Commander Lesley. The Japanese force had lost its cohesion through manoeuvring to avoid the torpedo bombers with *Hiryu* out of the box formation 10 miles (16 km) to the north. Moreover, all the Zeros had been pulled down to sea level by the Devastators and were short of fuel and ammunition. The flight decks of all four Japanese carriers, which were just about to launch their strike, were covered with aircraft, while the decks were littered with discarded ordnance.

OVERWHELMED

Enterprise's Dauntlesses peeled off into their steep attack dives at 10.23 am, looking like a 'beautiful silver waterfall' as they screamed down on to the *Akagi* and *Kaga*, bringing up the rear of the Japanese formation. Two bombs on Nagumo's flagship bored through the flightdeck and turned the hangar into a blazing inferno as the abandoned munitions exploded. *Kaga* staggered to a halt, her fire-fighting teams overwhelmed. The Dauntlesses of *Yorktown* led by Lesley had equal success against *Soryu*, which was hammered by three hits in quick succession.

Over the next three hours the crews struggled to save their ships from the fires and explosions that were ravaging them but had to give up the

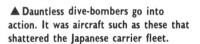

▲ Dauntless dive-bombers go into action. It was aircraft such as these that shattered the Japanese carrier fleet.

straight in, even though he had lost touch with his fighter escort. Bounced by 40 Zeros before they reached dropping range, all the Devastators were shot down and no hits were scored. Only one man out of 45 survived. A similar slaughter overtook Commander Lindsey's Torpedo 6 from *Enterprise* and Commander Massey's Torpedo 3 from *Yorktown* in their attacks. Again, no hits on Japanese ships.

TIDE TURNS

However, the payoff for the sacrifice of the torpedo-bombers was about to come. Lt. McClusky, commanding the 25 Dauntlesses from the *Enterprise*, had had more luck, following the course of a returning

unequal fight and abandon ship. *Soryu* lingered on with a volunteer damage control crew until 1400 when the submarine *Nautilus* administered the *coup de grace*. At the same time, *Kaga* succumbed when her hull blew apart as her fuel tanks erupted. *Akagi* remained afloat until early the next day when one of her escorts put four torpedoes into the stricken hulk.

Nagumo, forced to transfer his flag to the cruiser *Nagara*, temporarily passed command to Rear Admiral Abe. In command of a powerful force, Abe felt that there was still a chance of victory and ordered *Hiryu* to launch a strike against the American carriers. At 10.58 am, Captain Yamaguchi ordered 18 Vals plus six escorting Zeroes into the air against TF17, holding back his torpedo bombers.

JUBILATION

As they recovered their aircraft there were scenes of jubilation on the American carriers—tempered by the realisation of the horrendous cost in aircrew. The last of the aircraft were being landed when *Yorktown*'s radar detected bandits 32 miles (51 km) out at 11.52 am. Eight Vals broke through the cordon of fighters and anti-aircraft fire and put three bombs into the veteran carrier, starting a fire in the hangar and damaging *Yorktown*'s engines, reducing her speed to 6 knots.

Fletcher took the agonising decision to transfer his flag and ordered Lesley's remaining Dauntlesses to be transferred to *Enterprise*. However, by 1.40 pm *Yorktown*'s experienced damage control crews had the fires out and the *Yorktown*

under way at 20 knots with a CAP of eight Wildcats circling protectively.

The surviving Japanese pilots had returned to *Hiryu* believing they had knocked out one of the American carriers. With TF16 located by a scout, Nagumo ordered the last of his aircraft, 10 Kates and six Zeros, against *Hornet* and *Enterprise*. Due to inaccurate information these last remnants of the once proud Japanese air groups attacked *Yorktown*, believing the two undamaged American carriers had split, rather than *Hornet* and *Enterprise*. Although the CAP and anti-aircraft fire prevented a co-ordinated attack, four Kates launched torpedoes at the port side of *Yorktown*. Unable to manoeuvre fully due to lack of speed, Captain Buckmaster could only watch helplessly as two hit forward and amidships. Her generators knocked out, leaving her without light or power, the *Yorktown* went dead in the water and began to list 26° to port.

At 2.45 pm American search

◄ Midway consists of two islets, seen here in November 1941. The airfield is on Eastern Island.

▼ The air raid on Midway caused damage but it remained operational.

▼ The Japanese heavy cruiser *Mogami*, **battered and burning after a collision and subsequent US air attack at the Battle of Midway. Recovered and repaired, *Mogami* was eventually sunk at the Battle of Leyte Gulf in October 1944.**

planes had finally located the *Hiryu*, and Spruance ordered a strike to finish off the last surviving carrier of the Japanese force. Despite the decimation of the air group of the *Enterprise*, he was able to launch 24 Dauntlesses at 3.30 pm.

OPEN TARGET

These located the *Hiryu* at 5.00 pm and tipped into their dives, scoring four hits in rapid succession that blasted open the flight deck and set her afire. The *Hiryu*, trailing flame and smoke, remained afloat, a target for the ineffective B-17s from Midway, until the next day when she was finally abandoned.

Although stricken by the news that morning of the loss of three carriers, Yamamoto had immediately ordered the two carriers with the Aleutian task force to steam south and ren-

▼ The insignia of aircraft-carrier squadron VF-3: Felix the cat.

MIDWAY TO VICTORY

TURNING POINT

Before the Battle of Midway, the Japanese had encountered little resistance to their rampage through the Pacific and Far East; Midway stopped them in their tracks. The Americans destroyed more Japanese ships and aircraft than they lost, doing so in a way that was both novel and dramatic. Their realisation that the aircraft carrier rather than the battleship now held the key to naval victory allowed them to concentrate naval and air resources against a Japanese fleet badly split into small groups; their reading of Japanese codes enabled them to deploy their forces at the right time in the right place; their bravery and tactical skill did the rest. At Midway the tide was halted; it was the beginning of the road to victory.

▼ Anti-Japanese propaganda in the form of a book of matches for the men of the US Pacific Fleet.

Strike 'em Dead
REMEMBER PEARL HARBOR
CLOSE COVER BEFORE STRIKING

▶ Vulnerable Douglas TBD Devastator torpedo-bombers on the USS *Enterprise*.

Peter Newark's Western Americana

▼ Crew members prepare to abandon *Yorktown* as she lists dangerously to port. Hit by bombs and torpedoes, she wallows helplessly (inset) guarded by a destroyer.

dezvous with him and Admiral Kondo as quickly as possible. Spruance, however, refused to fall in with Yamamoto's plans. After recovering his last strike he withdrew eastwards with his two intact carriers and their battered air groups. He calculated that he had won the battle and that it was now his job to protect Midway rather than risk his carriers.

By midnight, with the failure of his plan to bring the American forces to battle, Yamamoto was faced with a dilemma. He could go ahead with the Midway invasion, and risk his vulnerable surface ships being caught by American air attacks, or could abandon Operation MI and save his forces to fight another day. With a heavy heart Yamamoto followed the advice of his chief of staff, Admiral Ugaki, and took sole responsibility for cancelling his plan: 'I am the only one who must apologise to His Majesty.'

Yamamoto's ordeal was not over. As the four heavy cruisers of the

US National Archives

Peter Newark's Western Americana

▲ Fires smoulder inside the skeleton of an aircraft hangar at Midway, 24 hours after the Japanese air attack.

bombardment force turned for home, a submarine alert caused the *Mogami* to ram the *Mikuma*, leaving them both crippled. Three strikes were launched from the returning American carriers on the morning of 5 June against the two helpless cruisers, sinking the *Mikuma*.

Some measure of revenge was gained when a Japanese floatplane stumbled across the *Yorktown*. After drifting all night, a tow had been passed to the crippled carrier on the morning of 5 June and a salvage crew made up of volunteers from her crew put on board in the afternoon. In the early afternoon of the next day four torpedoes fired by the submarine *I-168* found their mark. One blasted the escorting destroyer *Hammond* clean in two while two others ripped open the starboard side of the *Yorktown*. Buckmaster and his crew again had to abandon ship, but

now for the last time. The *Yorktown* finally capsized at 5.00 am on 7 June.

STUNNING VICTORY

A simple reckoning of the figures of the Battle of Midway reveals that the Americans had won a stunning tactical victory against all the odds. The Japanese lost four aircraft carriers to the Americans' one, 261 aircraft to the Americans' 137 and 3,500 dead to the Americans' 307. This was partly due to the excellent intelligence which enabled Nimitz to deploy his outnumbered forces to the best advantage. The skill of the American Dauntless pilots combined with the luck and the indecision of Nagumo to win the battle by crippling three Japanese carriers in barely 15 minutes of frantic action. From that point on, Nagumo and Yamamoto were chasing a lost cause.

▼ A Grumman F4F Wildcat fighter, minus its wings and with a collapsed undercarriage, shortly after the air raid on Midway.

▲ The sad aftermath of battle: American servicemen killed at Midway are honoured.

◀ With damaged aircraft in the foreground and a heavy cruiser behind, the Americans take stock: Midway has been an undisputed victory.

EL ALAMEIN

BATTLE DIARY

JUNE 1942

24	Rommel begins pursuit of Eighth Army from Tobruk to Mersa Matruh
26–28	Battle of Mersa Matruh; Eighth Army pulls back to El Alamein Line
30	Beginning of First Battle of El Alamein; Rommel attacks in centre

JULY

7–8	Australian raid against Ruweisat Ridge
10–11	Successful Allied counter-attack in north
13–16	German attacks repulsed with heavy losses
17	Rommel ceases attack and takes up defensive positions
21–22	Auchinleck launches unsuccessful counter-attack
26	Further Allied attack beaten back with heavy losses

AUGUST

7	Montgomery appointed commander of Eighth Army
12	Montgomery arrives in Cairo. Both sides rebuild their strength and lay minefields
31	Renewed German attack towards Alam El Halfa

SEPTEMBER

2	German attack called off
23	Rommel flies home on sick leave; Stumme takes over command

OCTOBER

6	Montgomery finalises outline for Second Battle of El Alamein
23	Second Battle of El Alamein begins in north
24	Stumme dies
25	Rommel returns, XXX Corps makes good progress against 164th Infantry Division, but elsewhere Allied attacks contained
26–29	Inconclusive fighting all along front

NOVEMBER

2	Beginning of Operation Supercharge
3–4	Rommel begins withdrawing
5	Afrika Korps pushed back from Fuka
8	Torch landings in Morocco and Algeria

MOVE INTO EGYPT

As Rommel's troops struggle eastward toward their next goal – the Nile Delta – the Allies gather all their strength at El Alamein.

While his victorious troops celebrated in the smouldering ruins of Tobruk, helping themselves freely to the vast stocks of food, drink and cigarettes, and messages of congratulation poured in from every quarter, *Afrika Korps* commander Erwin Rommel was in a towering rage.

He had not been interested in securing luxuries but rather, with his eyes now fixed firmly eastwards towards Cairo and the Pyramids, had pinned his hopes on petrol, water and motorised transport so that the Italian infantry under his command could keep up with his own armoured divisions. To his fury, the port's defenders had succeeded in burning much of the petrol, wrecking many of the trucks and destroying the water distillation plant. To a professional soldier like Rommel, even the award of the coveted Field Marshal's baton was poor recompense.

Rommel was somewhat mollified on 23 June by the news that his 90th Light Division had captured almost intact a huge supply dump at Fort Capuzzo on the Egyptian frontier which had been abandoned by the Allies in their disorganised retreat. On the following day, therefore, he launched the *Afrika Korps* in a wide southerly hook around the frontier defences, which had, in fact, already been abandoned following the fall of Tobruk, and raced towards Mersa Matruh where Major-General Neil Ritchie had halted Eighth Army's headlong flight and was preparing to make a stand. At this point General Sir Claude Auchinleck, the British C-in-C Middle East, sent the unfortunate Ritchie on leave and assumed personal command in the field.

DRAWN TO THE LINE

The Eighth Army was in a sorry state after its mauling at Gazala, despite the arrival of Lieutenant-General W G Holmes' X Corps from Syria. To Holmes' south, Lieutenant-General 'Strafer' Gott's XIII Corps merely comprised one brigade of 5th Indian Division, the 29th, plus the 4th and 22nd Armoured Brigades of 1st Armoured Division with 169 assorted Crusader, Grant, Stuart and Valentine tanks. Gott was reinforced on the 26th, though, by the arrival of Major-General Bernard Freyberg's weary New Zealand Division. Lieutenant-General C W Norrie's XXX Corps, meanwhile, was further east, already working frantically to prepare the Alamein position.

▲ A German 88 mm Flak gun, used in the anti-tank role, engages British armour during the early stages of the Battle of El Alamein.

Imperial War Museum

▲ German troops dig in close to the Alamein Line, August 1942. Although they do not yet realise it, their days of success in North Africa are over.

▼ Under the merciless glare of a desert sun, German soldiers keep watch for British movements on the Alamein Line. At the end of an overstretched line of supply and facing a desperate enemy, these men are soon to find the tide of war turning against them.

The El Alamein 'Line' was the last possible defensive position west of the Suez Canal, and was only 55 miles (88 km) from Alexandria — less than a day's march if the German armour achieved a breakthrough. Taking its name from a lonely railway station a mile or so from the coast, it was a line some 40 miles (64 km) long stretching from the sea to the Qattara Depression. The latter, bounded by a 700 foot (215 m) high escarpment, was a vast bowl of treacherous sand virtually impassable to motor vehicles, which at last gave Eighth Army a secure southerly flank which could not be bypassed. Any attack on the Alamein position would therefore have to be frontal, denying the German panzers the advantage of mobility which they had exploited so skilfully hitherto.

Major-General Fritz Bayerlein, a senior German staff officer, described the position as 'a stony, waterless desert where bleak outcrops of dry rock alternated with stretches of sand sparsely clotted with camel scrub beneath the pitiless African sun'. In the centre of the position were two prominent east-west ridges, Miteiriya and Ruweisat, with Alam el Halfa to their east and the less prominent Bab el Qattara to their south. It was around these that Auchinleck would prepare for the Eighth Army's last stand.

On 26 June Auchinleck decided not to try to contest the Mersa Matruh position, but to withdraw X and XIII Corps again towards Alamein as soon as Rommel moved. Rommel himself, in truth, was not well equipped to sustain his pursuit of Eighth Army. The 15th and 21st Panzer Divisions were reduced to a mere 60 tanks, the Italian 'Ariete' and 'Trieste' to just 44, while his total infantry strength was barely 9,000, of whom 2,500 were German and the remainder Italian. Nevertheless, on the evening of 26 June, he launched an attack on Mersa Matruh.

HOT PURSUIT

In the south, the weakened 15th Panzer Division was checked by 1st Armoured Division's two brigades, but the 90th Light Division penetrated the centre of the position on the 27th. Then 21st Panzer Division, on 90th Light's southern flank, wheeled south to come in on Freyberg's New Zealanders at Minqar Qaim from the north-east. During the ensuing battle, Freyberg himself was badly wounded and the lack of his firm hand added to the general confusion. 21st Panzer Division was finally checked by the timely arrival of some 1st Armoured Division tanks which saved the situation turning into a disaster.

That evening, Gott issued XIII Corps with the order to retreat but failed to notify the New Zealanders, whom he believed no longer existed as a viable fighting formation.

MONTY'S HOUR

Bernard Law Montgomery was born a bishop's son in 1887 and spent his formative years in Tasmania before his family moved to England. Not among the most popular aspirants at Sandhurst, he nevertheless made his mark by sheer hard work, later gaining the Distinguished Service Order as a lieutenant on the Western Front during World War I.

With the reputation of being something of an eccentric, Montgomery was a perfectionist in his military duties and, like Rommel, had written a book on infantry tactics. After slow promotion in the peacetime army, his tenacity and attention to detail were rewarded when he was appointed commander of Auchinleck's battered Eighth Army in August 1942 – a decision which was to turn the tide in the Desert War. His victory over the Axis forces made him a hero in his country, which conferred upon him the title of Viscount Montgomery of Alamein after the war.

BATTLE DIARY
LINING-UP FOR EL ALAMEIN

JUNE 1942
24 Rommel begins pursuit of Eighth Army from Tobruk to Mersa Matruh.
30 Beginning of First Battle of El Alamein. Rommel attacks in centre.

JULY
13—16 German attacks repulsed with heavy losses.
21—22 Auchinleck launches unsuccessful counter-offensive.
26 Further Allied attack beaten back with heavy losses.

AUGUST
5 Winston Churchill visits El Alamein.
7 Montgomery appointed commander of Eighth Army.
31 Renewed German attack towards Alam el Halfa.

SEPTEMBER
2 German attack called off.
23 Rommel flies home on sick leave; Stumme takes over command.

OCTOBER
23 Second Battle of Alamein begins in the north.
25 Rommel returns; XXX Corps makes good progress against 164th Infantry Division, but elsewhere attacks contained.
26—29 Inconclusive fighting all along front.

NOVEMBER
2 Beginning of Operation 'Supercharge'.
3—4 Rommel begins withdrawing.
5 Afrika Korps pushed back from Fuka.
8 'Torch' landings in Morocco and Algeria.

However, Auchinleck had earlier given Freyberg contingency orders to withdraw to Bab el Qattara, and the New Zealanders broke out eastwards during the night, straight through 21st Panzer Division's positions. There was fierce hand-to-hand fighting, but the majority of Freyberg's men escaped to fight another day.

Gott's withdrawal left Holmes' X Corps isolated in Mersa Matruh without armoured support and surrounded by superior forces, and by the time they broke out during the evening of the 28th, the village of Fuka to their east had already fallen into German hands. Lacking transport, for most of their vehicles had been earlier handed over to the New Zealand Division, they split into separate columns and headed towards El Alamein, but some 7,000 men were captured, roughly two-fifths of the corps' strength.

Auchinleck's first experience of direct command in the field had not been a happy one. Could he hold at Alamein? All rested on Norrie's comparatively fresh XXX Corps, for although the 9th Australian Division was in transit from Syria, it could not hope to reach the line until 1 July, and the rest of his troop dispositions left wide gaps through which Auchinleck prayed his armour could contain any assault.

The First Battle of Alamein lasted from 30 June to 17 July, beginning with brief clashes on the first day followed by the main German assault on 1 July. Movement and navigation were hampered by a sandstorm, so instead of penetrating

▲ Lieutenant-General Bernard Montgomery poses in front of his Lee-Grant command tank, October 1942. He wears his distinctive 'two-badge' beret.

▼ As infantry soldiers wait to follow through, a British Crusader tank, its commander dangerously exposed, moves to protect the approaches to Mersa Matruh, June 1942. The town was soon to fall to Axis forces.

◄ The crew of a British 6-pounder anti-tank gun come under enemy fire, Alamein, July 1942. The 6-pounder – a long-overdue replacement for the puny 2-pounder anti-tank gun – offered, for the first time, a degree of protection against German panzers.

Auchinleck had hoped, he launched the 9th Australian and 1st South African Divisions down the coast against the hapless Italian 'Sabratha' Division on the 10th, nearly annihilating it and penetrating west to Tel el Eisa, on the *Afrika Korps'* northern flank, on the 11th.

HEAVY LOSSES

Realising the danger he was in, Rommel threw what was left of 15th Panzer Division into a counter-attack, which was halted by a deadly artillery barrage. Similar attacks by 21st Panzer Division on the 13th and 14th were equally unsuccessful. Now it was the New Zealanders' turn again. Attacking from the south-east, they overran the Italians at Deir el Shein but were in turn counter-attacked by 15th Panzer and the 'Brescia' Divisions and forced back with the loss of 1,500 prisoners because the 22nd Armoured Brigade, which was supposed to have supported them, was late in arriving on the scene. However, the operation left Eighth

◀ **Soldiers of the Scots Guards occupy trenches in the Alamein Line. Inset: A British infantryman hugs the ground as a 2,000 lb (1,000 kg) bomb, dropped by the RAF, explodes on enemy positions.**

▼ **Prime Minister Winston Churchill (right) inspects a British medium gun, August 1942.**

between Miteiriya Ridge and the main El Alamein perimeter, 90th Light Division bumped headlong into 3rd South African Brigade and had to retire. Further south, 15th and 21st Panzer Divisions overran the 18th Indian Brigade at Deir el Shein in a costly battle which lost them 18 tanks. There were further inconclusive armoured clashes around Ruweisat on 2 July, and on the 3rd a spirited counter-attack by the New Zealanders, charging with fixed bayonets, reduced the 'Ariete' Division to only five tanks and took some 350 prisoners.

ROMMEL TAKES STOCK

Rommel was forced to retire to a shortened line between Ruweisat and the coast some four miles (6 km) west of the main Allied lines to reconsider the position. He had only 36 tanks left and his ammunition was running low. There was a lull for the next few days, although a raid by the Australians along Ruweisat Ridge during the night of 7/8 July caused panic in 15th Panzer Division.

With the *Afrika Korps* dangerously extended, as

RULERS OF THE SKY

At the time of Second Alamein, Air Chief Marshal Sir Arthur Tedder's Desert Air Force was stronger than it had ever been, the RAF squadrons augmented by new Australian and South African formations.

Axis supply ships and harbours were primary targets, and night after night formations of Wellingtons, Bostons and Albacores flew hundreds of sorties against Tobruk, Sollum and Mersa Matruh. Then, when daylight came, it was the turn of the Hurricane, Spitfire and Kittyhawk fighters. Sometimes flying as many as eight sorties per day, they prowled over the Axis lines, wearing down Germany's most veteran pilots. Trucks, convoys, supply dumps and airfields were bombed time and again. Although the troops of Eighth Army gave Montgomery his victory, it was equally down to the efforts of the DAF.

An RAF Hawker Hurricane at its base in the Western Desert.

Army once more in firm possession of Ruweisat Ridge and on the 16th Rommel had to commit his last reserves, including elements of the new 164th Infantry Division, which was still in the process of being formed.

By the 17th Rommel had shot his bolt and was dispirited when Field Marshal Albert Kesselring, C-in-C for the Mediterranean theatre, visited his headquarters. The *Afrika Korps* would have to go on the defensive until it could be reinforced for another effort some time in August. But Auchinleck struck first. After a week of comparative inactivity, reinforced by one fresh armoured and two infantry brigades, he struck on the night of 21/22 July. However, Rommel had also been reinforced and now included the German Ramcke 1st Parachute Brigade and Italian 'Folgore' Parachute Division under his command, while he had sown numerous minefields of his own. During this attack, the newly arrived British 23rd Armoured Brigade lost no fewer than 93 of its 104 tanks to German anti-tank guns largely because it refused to co-operate closely with accompanying infantry.

FAMOUS VISITOR

Towards the end of July, further attempts by the Allies to break through the enemy lines were thrown back with heavy losses. Auchinleck was forced to report to Whitehall that he had to resume the defensive. Prime Minister Winston Churchill himself flew out to Egypt to inspect the position on

▲ A German SdKfz 251, armed with machine guns, negotiates stony terrain.

▼ Germany motor-cycle troops, muffled up against the sand, await orders.

5 August. He decided to replace Auchinleck by General Sir Harold Alexander and offered 'the Auk' the new command of Persia and Iraq, entrusting leadership of Eighth Army in the field to General Gott. As it happened, Auchinleck declined the new post and returned to India. Before he could assume his post, Gott was killed on the 7th when his aircraft was shot down and Churchill made what was to prove a momentous decision — he replaced him with Lieutenant-General Bernard Law Montgomery.

MONTY GOES TO WAR

After his failure to break through British positions in Egypt in July, Rommel tried again during the night of 31 August/1 September with a strong attack against the southern sector of the Alamein Line. His intention was a virtual replay of the assault against the Gazala Line in May that same year, which had resulted in the fall of Tobruk: a quick penetration by his tanks followed by a sweeping thrust northwards, east of Alam el Halfa Ridge to the coast, cutting off Eighth Army's line of retreat.

Unfortunately for him, the plan failed because the Eighth Army's commander, Montgomery, was forewarned by the 'Ultra' cryptologists, who by this time were well versed in deciphering the German 'Enigma' codes, with the result that Rommel's divisions ran headlong into concentrated fire from hull-down tanks and well dug-in anti-tank guns on Alam el Halfa Ridge. On 2 September he was forced to call the operation off. Montgomery now had the time he needed to carry out a well planned offensive, designed to rid North Africa of the 'Desert Fox' once and for all.

WarStories

For reasons of safety, British families were evacuated from Cairo. Just before the family of one British official left, their small son asked if he could go to see 'Gordon' again – the life-size statue of General Gordon, mounted on a camel. The boy's father was touched as he saw him look wistfully at the statue, then say sadly, 'Goodbye Gordon'. The father was proud of his son's patriotism – until, as they walked away, the boy asked thoughtfully, 'Dad, who is that man sitting on top of Gordon?'

MONTY'S TRIUMPH

After taking severe punishment from Montgomery's reinforced Eighth Army, a battered Afrika Korps gets ready for the final blow.

▲ A black desert rat – symbol of the British 4th Armoured Brigade.

◀◀ The Germans reach El Alamein – but only as prisoners of war, taken during the early stages of the battle in late October 1942.

▶▼ Field Marshal Rommel confers with his aides in the desert. Below: As a guncrew keep watch, German troops move up to the front line.

Following a worldwide series of military disasters earlier in the year, Prime Minister Winston Churchill was desperate for a victory before the end of 1942 to restore flagging morale at home. In selecting Lieutenant-General Montgomery to command the Eighth Army in the Western Desert, he proved to have made a wise choice.

Montgomery was not one for the inspired guess or the intuitive masterstroke, but his planning was meticulous. And at last he had the tools to do the job he had been entrusted with.

Eighth Army began to receive reinforcements almost immediately after Monty reached Cairo on 12 August. XXX Corps, taking the northern sector of the line, was now commanded by Lieutenant-General Oliver Leese. It comprised the 51st Highland, 4th Indian, 9th Australian, 1st South African and 2nd New Zealand Divisions, plus the 23rd Armoured Brigade Group. XIII Corps, holding the southern sector and also under a new commander, Lieutenant-General Brian Horrocks, consisted of the 44th and 50th Divisions, 7th Armoured Division, the 1st and 2nd Free French Brigade Groups and the 1st Greek Infantry Brigade Group.

The mobile reserve comprised the 1st and 10th Armoured Divisions in X Corps under Lieutenant-General Herbert Lumsden. They included 252

of the brand-new American-built M4 Sherman tanks in their strength.

BATTLE PLAN

The main attack on Rommel was to be spearheaded by XXX Corps, which would clear passages through the extensive Axis minefields for X Corps to exploit with its tanks. However, having initially planned a real 'Blitzkrieg' by X Corps, Montgomery changed his mind — much to Lumsden's disgust — and ordered him to advance no further than a line just forward of Kidney and Miteiriya Ridges and then to deploy defensively so as to bring the German tanks against his at a disadvantage.

Montgomery had, in his own words, decided to 'crumble' the enemy infantry while letting their panzers

◀ The comparative strengths of Allied and Axis forces at Second Alamein, 1942.

▼ A German engineer lifts anti-tank mines at Mersa Matruh.

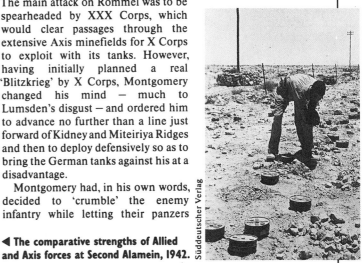

Roger-Viollet, Paris; top: Imperial War Museum

Süddeutscher Verlag

BATTLE LINE-UP

🇬🇧 530	🇩🇪 350	🇬🇧 1,029	🇩🇪 489
🇬🇧 195,000	🇩🇪 104,000	🇬🇧 2,311	🇩🇪 1,219

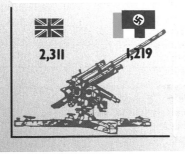

▼ German mechanised units move forward across the featureless desert west of Alamein, October 1942. The lack of cover leaves them dangerously vulnerable to Allied air attack.

▼▼ With bayonets fixed, British infantry move forward through the dust and smoke of an artillery barrage towards Axis positions.

wear themselves out fruitlessly. Meanwhile Horrocks would launch diversionary attacks to pin the enemy forces facing XIII Corps and prevent them moving north to interfere in the principal sector. It was a risky plan because the enemy also had his flanks secured by the same natural obstacles, and if the infantry failed to achieve a breakthrough, the British armour would be decimated by the skilled German anti-tank gun crews.

While morale was high in Eighth Army due to Montgomery's energetic public relations, it had sagged in *Panzerarmee Afrika* (as the combined German and Italian forces were now known), because Rommel himself was no longer with them. He had suffered increasingly throughout the summer from blood and stomach complaints as well as psychological depression after two failures to break the Alamein Line, and had been sent home on sick leave on 23 September. His replacement was General Georg Stumme, a veteran

Panzer commander from the French and Russian campaigns but virtually unknown to the troops in Africa.

Stumme's dispositions were as recommended by Rommel before his departure, with German units interspersed at regular intervals in the Italian infantry lines and three groups of mobile divisions behind them—15th Panzer and 'Littorio' in the north and centre, backed by 90th Light and 'Trieste' in immediate reserve, and 21st Panzer and 'Ariete' in the south.

ZERO HOUR

'About 9 pm we moved forward and took up our positions on the start line. It was deathly still and a full moon lighted the bleak sand as if it were day. Suddenly the silence was broken by the crash of a single gun, and the next moment a mighty roar rent the air and the ground shook under us as salvo after salvo crashed out from hundreds of guns. Shells whined over our heads in a continuous stream, and soon we

saw the enemy line lit up by bright flashes.'

With these words Major H P Samwell, an officer in the Argyll and Sutherland Highlanders, recorded his impression of the start of what has entered history as the Second Battle of El Alamein. As a conflict, it may have been a mere skirmish compared with what was happening in Russia, but it was to herald the beginning of the final Axis defeat in North Africa.

The British attack was preceded by an 882-gun artillery barrage, the greatest the desert had ever witnessed. It began at exactly 9.40 pm on the moonlit night of 23 October. In the Allied lines there was tense silence while the seconds ticked away. 'As the second hand of my watch reached zero hour,' recalled one Scottish gunnery officer, 'I gave the order to fire ... For a split second I thought I must have made a mistake, but almost instantaneously the ground shook and the air vibrated as the artillery of the

Süddeutscher Verlag

Imperial War Museum

War Stories

The Italian fighting men may or may not have been aware of the general contempt in which they were held by the Allies, but whether they knew it or not, they did little to dispel their reputation as a nation of military buffoons. Two high-ranking Italian officers were taken prisoner in the Egyptian desert and, fuming and fretting, they complained to their British captors that they were at the front as observers of British methods, not as combatants. One of them was heard to say, 'This is an absolute outrage. We were just looking.'

whole Eighth Army opened up. That was the last shouted order I was to give that night.'

BAYONETS FIXED

As the barrage rolled forward over the stunned Axis positions, thousands of men from the four divisions entrusted with the initial assault rose to their feet and began to advance, bayonets glinting evilly. They comprised Major-General Leslie Morshead's Australians, Freyberg's New Zealanders and Major-General Dan Pienaar's South Africans, accompanied by the skirling bagpipes of Major-General Douglas Wimberley's Highlanders. Bofors anti-aircraft guns fired tracer over their heads to mark the lines of advance through the minefields. Feint 'raids' on either flank of the main line of advance helped confuse the enemy, while in the south Horrocks also advanced to pin the 21st Panzer and 'Ariete' Divisions.

Major Samwell recalls that as the

▶ British 25-pounders are fired during a night attack, their gun flashes illuminating the scene in an unearthly way.

Popperfoto

SHERMAN TANK

The arrival of the American M4 Sherman tank in the Western Desert, 252 of which had reached the Eighth Army by the beginning of Second Alamein, came as a nasty shock to the German panzer crews. Developed from the M3 Lee-Grant, with similar low hull shape and suspension and the same Wright air-cooled radial engine, it was a fast-moving and effective weapon upon which Allied tank commanders now pinned all their hopes.

The M4 was the first US-built tank with a 75mm gun in a fully-traversing turret, giving close parity with later marks of the German Panzer IV.

By 1944, however, the M4 had been outclassed by the German Tigers and Panthers and became a virtual deathtrap for its crews. Known to the Germans as the 'Tommycooker', the Americans ironically called it the 'Ronson' – it lit first time!

Marshall Cavendish Library

▼ Dug-in to a prepared position, yet still exposed because of its high profile, a German 88 mm Flak gun prepares to engage British armour at El Alamein. The white rings on the barrel denote previous tank 'kills'.

Süddeutscher Verlag

German and Italian machine-gun fire intensified, the Argyll and Sutherland Highlanders' line broke up 'into blobs of men all struggling together... To my left and behind me some of the NCOs were rounding up prisoners... In front of me a terrified Italian was running round and round with his hands above his head screaming at the top of his voice.'

But signs of initial success were shortlived. In most places the Axis line held and their artillery and mortars pounded at the narrow lanes through the minefields. Thus, while 1st and 10th Armoured Divisions started rolling forward at 2.00 am on the 24th, they were only able to make slow progress and were rapidly challenged by the 15th Panzer Division. The historian Sir Michael Carver later described the scene as looking like 'a badly organised car park at an immense race meeting held in a dust bowl'!

By the evening of that day, though, the Allied infantry were in a fairly strong position despite fiercer opposition than expected. But 1st Armoured Division had only succeeded in getting a few of its tanks through the minefields and 10th Armoured was seriously lagging behind. The latter's commander, Major-General Alec Gatehouse, was roundly castigated over the telephone by Montgomery in the middle of the night and told in no uncertain terms to move his headquarters up from its position 10 miles (16 km) behind the front and get his tanks into action.

DEVIL'S GARDEN

In fairness, it was not really the fault of the armoured division commanders. The sappers who had preceded the tanks with white tapes and shielded lanterns to clear paths through the extensive minefields — which became known as the 'Devil Garden' — had an extraordinarily difficult task. Inching forward in the bright moonlight, even those parties with mine detectors could only advance perhaps 100 yards (91 m) in an hour, while those who had to use their bayonets to probe the treacherous sands could only manage half that. And even when the mines had been identified and marked, they still had to be defused and moved to safety. Many mines were also connected together with trip wires to add to the hazards.

The unfortunate German commander, Stumme, died of a heart attack when his car came under fire from some Australian infantry during the day. He was temporarily replaced by Lieutenant-General Ritter von Thoma, but an urgent telephone call from Hitler himself brought Rommel flying to the rescue on the 26th. His firm hand back at the helm was quickly detected by the Allies, but Rommel still had problems, one of the most acute being the usual lack of adequate petrol to keep his panzers moving. And this time not even his tactical flair could save the *Panzerarmee Afrika*.

However, the first phase of the battle had gone rather awry for the British so Montgomery decided to leave things as they were around Miteiriya Ridge and concentrate on the north, using the 9th Australian Division supported by 1st Armoured Division against the 164th Infantry Division. Montgomery's casualties were heavy — about 6,000 men and 300 tanks by this time — and Axis morale revived with the return of their hero. Rommel himself was less confident after receiving the news that two tankers bringing desperately needed petrol across the Mediterranean had been sunk.

SHOOTING GALLERY

The following days were characterised by a dogged Australian advance, well supported by 1st South African and 4th

Imperial War Museum

◄▲ In an effort to fool the enemy about British strength, tanks are camouflaged to look like lorries.

DECEPTION IN THE DESERT

With Eighth Army and *Panzerarmee Afrika* facing each other from positions only an average of 4 miles (6.5 km) apart, Montgomery realised that he would have to take extraordinary precautions to disguise his real intentions in battle. An elaborate deception operation, codenamed 'Bertram', was therefore put in hand. At the southern end of the Alamein Line, dummy HQ buildings, barrack tents and supply dumps with empty petrol cans were set up, and fires lit at night to suggest a major troop concentration. Trenches and gun emplacements were dug and imitation minefields laid, while the Air Force deliberately allowed Axis reconnaissance aircraft to photograph the activity. Trucks had their silhouettes altered with canvas awnings to resemble tanks from a distance, and sappers even constructed a dummy water pipeline using empty oil drums, while signallers kept up a steady flow of coded radio traffic between bogus divisions.

In the north, similar dummy positions were laid out while the fighting divisions were all kept well to the rear so the newly-arrived troops could train for the coming assault. As the deadline for the attack approached, real divisions were filtered into their positions at night and dummy vehicles and supply dumps replaced with genuine ones so the enemy was not aware of the change in status.

Much of the Eighth Army's success on this front was due to these effective measures.

DESERT VICTORY

The Second Battle of Alamein, fought in late October/early November 1942, was recognised at the time as a turning point in Britain's war against the Axis. After nearly a year of defeat on all fronts, Montgomery's victory, however hard-won, was a unique event, forcing Axis units to withdraw and proving that Rommel, despite his reputation, could be outfought. Admittedly, the victory was not Montgomery's alone – the First Battle of Alamein, conducted by General Auchinleck, had blunted Rommel's advance and forced the Axis on to the defensive—but there could be no doubt that the British had found a man to match the needs of the time. Montgomery represented a new generation of commanders, intent on victory. Second Alamein was the first step.

Imperial War Museum

Indian Divisions after the sorely tested New Zealanders were pulled back to rest, and indecisive tank encounters in which the German panzers lost heavily. On the 29th Montgomery planned to throw everything into his breakout attempt, which was codenamed Operation 'Supercharge'.

The operation commenced with another massive artillery barrage at 1.00 am on 2 November, the revitalised New Zealanders clearing a 400-yard gap in the Axis lines. Then the tanks of 9th Armoured Brigade rolled forward. The result was the disaster which Lumsden had hoped at all costs to avoid. Silhouetted against the rising sun, the British tanks were like ducks in a shooting gallery to the German 88s, and 70 were destroyed in an hour. The 1st Armoured Division was then committed and the rest of the day saw a fierce but inconclusive struggle in which both sides lost heavily.

ROMMEL BACKS OUT

Low on petrol and ammunition, by 8.15 on the evening of 3 November Rommel had decided he had no option but to retreat. Hitler ordered him to hold fast but the Allied troops broke through his lines in several places during the night and retreat became inevitable.

The withdrawal was orderly, and mobile German tank and anti-tank units prevented Montgomery from fully exploiting the situation, using their ingrained battlefield know-how to

thwart all the efforts of troops and commanders who were in many cases still very fresh to desert warfare. Rommel, obeying another direct order from Hitler, attempted to halt the pursuit at Fuka on 5 November but was pushed back again, heavy rain over the next 24 hours slowing operations down seriously on both sides.

Then, on 8 November, came the news that British and American troops had been landed by sea near Casablanca, Oran and Algiers. Operation 'Torch' was under way and the *Afrika Korps* was trapped between forces which far outnumbered any reinforcements they could hope to expect.

▲ The Second Battle of Alamein cost Montgomery 13,500 casualties: here the crew of a British tank, knocked out in the battle, lie in a makeshift grave, marked by helmets and a cross.

▼ As Rommel retreats in the aftermath of Alamein, British forces capture stockpiles of abandoned equipment – in this case the remains of German Bf-109 fighter aircraft at El Daba, on the Egyptian coast.

Süddeutscher Verlag

▲ Australian troops bring in a wounded German prisoner. In all, the Axis lost 24,000 men as prisoners.

STALINGRAD

BATTLE DIARY

JANUARY 1942

18–31   Timoshenko's abortive winter offensive

MAY

12   Timoshenko renews offensive

15   Manstein clears Kerch peninsula

23   German pincers seal off Timoshenko's forces around Kharkov

JUNE

2   Assault on Sevastopol begins

28   Opening of Army Group South's summer offensive

JULY

3   Fall of Sevastopol

9   Fall of Voronezh

AUGUST

9   Army Group A reaches Maikop oilfields

11   6th Army reaches Don

23   14th Panzer Corps reaches Stalingrad

SEPTEMBER

2   Beginning of battle for Stalingrad

10   48th Panzer Corps joins battle

13   Soviet 62nd and 64th Armies divided

OCTOBER

4   Renewed assault begins

15–23   Tractor Factory captured. Barricade Factory falls

NOVEMBER

10   Last German attempt to clear Stalingrad

19   Beginning of Soviet counter-offensive

23   6th Army surrounded in Stalingrad

DECEMBER

12–24   Manstein's abortive relief attempt

JANUARY 1943

8   Paulus refuses to surrender

31   Paulus surrenders

FEBRUARY

23   Last German forces in Stalingrad surrender

Associated Press

TARGET STALINGRAD

Spread out over hundreds of miles of Russian steppe, the German panzers seem unstoppable – until they reach the borders of Stalingrad.

After the German Army's failure to take Moscow in 1941, and its desperate struggle to hold a line during the bitter winter fighting that followed, Hitler rearranged his objectives. The attack on Moscow would not be resumed; instead, the weight of the German spring and summer offensive in 1942 would fall in the south. The initial aim was to complete the capture of the Crimea, followed by a two-pronged drive towards Stalingrad (today renamed Volgograd), 300 miles east, and the Caucasus Mountains, even further away. These were not just propaganda targets, for Stalingrad's factories were churning out roughly a quarter of all Russia's new tanks and other armoured fighting vehicles, while Hitler had decided that the best way to defeat the Soviet war machine was by denying it its lifeblood – the black gold from the oilfields around Maikop, Grozny and Baku in the Caucasus.

▲ A bottleneck forms as German troops approach a defended village in southern Russia, summer 1942. The head of the column is under enemy fire, and Blitzkrieg is slowing down.

Even before German plans were finalised in April, the Red Army had struck first, in an ill-conceived attack either side of Izyum designed to recapture Kharkov. This did succeed in driving a salient deep into the German lines from 18-31 January 1942, but made no headway towards Kharkov. By the

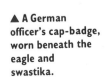

▲ A German officer's cap-badge, worn beneath the eagle and swastika.

▶▶ World War II propaganda poster depicting Hitler as a bloodthirsty monster greedily devouring the peoples of Europe.

▶ A German officer pauses to discuss the advance with the crew of a Panzer Mk IV, while Russian civilians look on.

▼ German engineers construct a fairly sophisticated bridge over the bed of a stream, left dry by the summer weather. In autumn, the rain will turn this into a significant obstacle.

MANEATER

France Rumania Poland
Greece Belgium
Jugoslavia

Reproduced from the original design presented to Lord Beaverbrook on the instruction of M. Stalin.

Imperiaal War Museum

▼ German motor-cycle reconnaissance troops on the Eastern Front, on the road to the Caucasus, summer 1942. The motor-cycle combination is armed with an MG 34 machine gun.

end of the month Field Marshal Fedor von Bock's German Army Group South had managed to stabilise the situation.

Although fighting continued at a fierce level, no further progress was made by either side until 12 May, when Defence Commissar Marshal Semyon Timoshenko launched a renewed assault north and south of Kharkov – six days before von Bock had planned to begin his own new offensive to cut off the Soviet salient. Timoshenko made the mistake of withholding too many reserves until too late. When von Bock counter-attacked in the south on the 17th with First Panzer and Seventeenth Armies, rapidly reinforced by Sixth Army

War Stories

On the Russian Front, the German Army was often harassed by fast-moving partisans who were totally familiar with the countryside. When the Germans sent out patrols against the partisans, they deliberately put non-smokers at the front. This was due to their sense of smell being more acute than that of the smokers, and they could pin-point the whereabouts of partisan groups by the pungent smell of strong Russian tobacco which lingered in the air after the partisans had passed.

from the north, the Soviet Marshal was encircled near Izyum with severe losses comparable to those of the previous summer's battles.

This Soviet defeat, coupled with the success of General Erich von Manstein's Eleventh Army in driving the Russians out of the Crimean Kerch peninsula (and finally capturing the fortress port of Sevastopol on 3 July, for which he was promoted to Field Marshal), gave Hitler enormous encouragement. On 28 June *Fall Blau* ('Case Blue', the operational codeword for the drive on Stalingrad and the Caucasus) was launched. Army Group South would be divided into two for this, with Army Group A under Field Marshal Siegmund Wilhelm List and Army Group B under von Bock. List commanded General von Kleist's First Panzer Army and General Richard Ruoff's Seventeenth Army, while von Bock had General Hermann Hoth's Fourth Panzer Army and the Second and Sixth Armies under Generals Maximilian von Weichs and Friedrich Paulus respectively.

HEADING FOR DEFEAT

The basic plan was for Army Group B on the northern flank to strike towards the Volga river and Stalingrad after first clearing the western bank of the River Don. Meanwhile, Army Group A would move in a more south-easterly direction to seize the Caucasian oilfields. The inherent danger in the plan, well appreciated by Army Chief of Staff General Franz Halder, was that the long left flank of Army Group B, separated by hundreds of miles from Army Group Centre, was only weakly protected by Hungarian, Italian and Rumanian divisions of low morale and dubious fighting ability.

The groundwork was laid for the greatest defeat the army of the Third Reich had yet to sustain and which, coupled with the American triumph at Midway (June 1942), Montgomery's victory at El Alamein and the Allied landings in French North-West Africa (November 1942), would mark the turning point of the war.

To begin with, it seemed as though *Blitzkrieg* was working again as the panzers steamrollered forward, although it was noticeable that the Soviet Army had learned from its previous defeats and was able to retreat in a more orderly fashion, avoiding the massive encirclements of the earlier part of the campaign.

The offensive opened on 28 June 1942 with the usual barrage and Stuka bombardment, Army Group B moving off first because the intention was to stagger the punches to keep the Russians off balance. Hoth's Fourth Panzer Army broke through the Soviet defences to the east of Kursk, and within a week German troops had reached the River Don either side of Voronezh. Field Marshal von Bock was particularly concerned about the threat posed to his flank by the strong Soviet forces around Voronezh, commanded by General Nikolai Vatutin. As a result he committed General von Weichs' Second Army to taking Voronezh, a task which was not completed until 8 July because of fanatical Russian resistance.

Hitler, infuriated at the delay to his plans, dismissed von Bock and put von Weichs in command of Army Group B. He also took Fourth Panzer Army away from Army Group B, sending it south-east to join Army Group A's drive towards Rostov and the Caucasus – a move which created a monumental traffic jam on the steppes as it cut across the path

▼ Despite the image of panzer formations racing ahead, most German transport and artillery was horse-drawn during the Russian campaign.
▼▼ General Hoth (foreground) watches as elements of his Fourth Panzer Army set off for the Don river, 28 June 1942.

Main Picture and insets: Bundesarchiv-Koblenz

of Sixth Army. Hitler also denuded von Weichs of about half his motorised transport, in doing so bringing his advance to a virtual standstill.

RUSH FOR THE OIL FIELDS

The arrival of Hoth's Fourth Panzer Army to reinforce von Kleist's First Panzer Army caused further congestion in the Donets basin and proved to be totally unnecessary in any case. One NCO from the 14th Panzer Division recalled that 'Russian resistance was so slight that many of the soldiers were able to take off their clothes and bathe', because most Soviet divisions east of the Don had been withdrawn to the north and east. Once engineers had repaired or replaced the bridges over the Don, von Kleist roared forward at a cracking pace, reaching Proletarskaya on 29 July, Stavropol on 5 August and Malikop on the 9th, while other units headed towards Grozny. On the 22nd, German alpine troops scaled Mount Elbrus, at 18,481 feet the highest peak in the Caucasus, to plant the swastika flag on its summit.

Seeing that von Kleist did not need Hoth's assistance, Hitler split Fourth Panzer Army up, leaving Hoth with just the XLVIII Panzer Corps and four infantry divisions, two of them Rumanian, and sending the XIV Panzer Corps back northwards to join Sixth Army. By this time it was mid August and Stalingrad, which would almost certainly have fallen in July had von Weichs been able to move more quickly, had now been greatly reinforced. As it was, Paulus had not succeeded in forcing his way across the River Chir to the Don until 11 August, after a four-day battle which virtually destroyed two Soviet armies, one of them armoured. This still left strong Russian forces to the north of Kletskaya on the Don which were to play an important part in the events to follow.

A week later Paulus' exhausted troops were across the Don but the infantry lacked the strength or tne fuel to push the remaining 35 miles, so XIV Panzer Corps was sent ahead, reaching the outskirts of Stalingrad on the 23rd at the end of a dangerously narrow supply corridor. On that day and throughout the whole night, the Luftwaffe laid on its largest

Roger-Viollet, Paris

Marshall Cavendish Library

THE 8-MONTH SIEGE

Before the German Army could resume its eastward drive in 1942, the major fortified naval base of Sevastopol had to be secured. It would otherwise have acted as a sally port from which Russian troops could strike the extended German flank.

Sevastopol was first attacked in November 1941 but did not succumb to German pressure until the siege had lasted for 247 days. The German Army brought up over 50 large-calibre rail guns and self-propelled 'Karl' mortars to pummel the garrison into submission, as well as blockading access via the Black Sea.

General von Manstein's final assault began on 7 June 1942 with the artillery supported by hundreds of Luftwaffe bomber sorties every day. The grim determination of the Soviet defenders to deny every building or strongpoint to the attackers should have acted as warning for what was later to transpire in Stalingrad, but the message did not sink in at the time and was erased in the euphoria of the Russian surrender.

However, many Red Army soldiers managed to escape to join the partisans behind German lines, so victory was not all complete.

Bundesarchiv-Koblenz

air raid ever against a single target, and by dawn on the 24th the city was a raging inferno, its many wooden buildings being particularly vulnerable.

STALINGRAD IN FLAMES

The glow of the flames from the burning city could be seen by Paulus' troops even over all those miles. One German soldier wrote to his wife, 'All of us feel that the end, victory, is near'. What the troops in the front line did not realise, though, was the weakness of Army Group B's flanks, guarded on the left by the German Second Army together with the unreliable Second Hungarian, Eighth Italian and Third Rumanian Armies, and on the right by the Fourth Rumanian Army. These allied troops were to prove hollow reeds indeed. Moreover, Stalin was shortly to remove Timoshenko from command and appoint the 'saviour of Moscow', Marshal Georgi Zhukov, in his place.

Stretched out for 30 miles along the western bank of the Volga, Stalingrad's northern industrial sector and the southern power station provided the main targets for German attacks. While women and children waited in dug-outs to be evacuated from the devastated city by night, any remaining civilians were mobilised to hold an inner defence line, making it an 'impregnable fortress' in Stalin's own words.

The battle for Stalingrad was one in which individual tanks and tiny groups of men fought with guns, bayonets and fingernails, clawing through half-burnt timbers and bricks to get at each other. Major advances were measured in feet and inches rather than in miles and were conducted by platoons and companies rather than divisions and armies. Miniature replicas of World War I trench warfare recurred, the 'no-man's-land' between opposing forces being no wider than a

▲ **A Soviet T-34 tank burns after having been hit by German anti-tank fire, southern Russia, 1942.**

◄ **SdKfz 251 half-tracks of the German Sixth Army wait to cross the River Don. These men will not be coming back.**

▼ **The Germans approach Stalingrad, summer 1942. At this stage, victory seemed in sight, but the tide was soon to turn.**

narrow street.

'Security' became a bunker dug beneath the comforting steel thickness of an abandoned tank, its walls shored up with logs and planks. German tactical mobility and superiority were sacrificed on the altar of a smouldering funeral pyre because, one for one, the average Russian soldier was every bit a match for the average German in terms of tenacity and conviction, even if not in terms of education and discipline. The really elite German troops who might, possibly, have made the difference – the men of the Army's Grossdeutschland and the Waffen-SS's Leibstandarte Adolf Hitler, Das Reich and Totenkopf Divisions – had been withdrawn to France for rest and refit. They would return later to an apocalypse of their own.

As Sixth Army finally approached Stalingrad on 2 September to relieve the isolated XIV Panzer Corps, the Soviet Sixty-Second and Sixty-Fourth Armies were withdrawn within the city boundaries. This marks the 'official' beginning of the battle of Stalingrad, even though perimeter fighting had already been going on for ten days. The Germans came to call it the *Rattenkrieg*, or 'war of the rats': it was a nightmare of slow-moving urban fighting.

Bundesarchiv-Koblenz

Nach Stalingrad! 13 Km.

CAMPAIGN

NIGHTMARE OF THE STREETS

In the bombed-out city, every building and street corner are fought over with desperate ferocity.

As soon as the fighting during September began to bog down in a war of attrition – which the Germans could not hope to win because there were no adequate reserves – wiser heads than Hitler advised a withdrawal to a defensible winter line behind the River Don. But the Führer persisted – there would be no retreat from the Volga. The commander of Army Group B, General von Weichs, and General Hoth, whose XLVIII Panzer Corps had joined the fighting on 10 September, were particularly anxious about their flanks and concerned that their principal panzer

Fortunately, Chief of Staff General Kurt Zeitzler persuaded Hitler in the nick of time to permit these forces to fall back, and radioed the order to them before the dictator could change his mind – as he did half an hour later!

Nevertheless, the arrival of XLVIII Panzer Corps, led by Lieutenant-General Werner Kempf, had an immediate effect on the battle. Fighting through the deep ravines and gullies south of the city, they severed the Soviet Sixty-Fourth Army from the Sixty-Second and reached the bank of the Volga, while Lieutenant-General Walter von Seydlitz-Kurzbach's LI Corps se-

cured Gumrak airfield to the west and pushed forward to the prominent Mamayev Hill which dominated the city.

Things seemed to be going well and on 26 September the swastika flew from the top of the government buildings in Red Square. But this victory was an illusion. The Russian troops were kept adequately supplied by the constant stream of ferries from the eastern shore of the Volga, while Marshal Georgi Zhukov, overall Soviet commander in the Stalingrad sector, was able to keep his Sixty-Second and Sixty-Fourth Army commanders, Generals Chuikov and Shumilov, fully up to strength by sending in fresh troops to replace casualties. During September alone, he funnelled nine infantry divisions, two tank brigades and a rifle brigade into the city.

By 6 October General Friedrich Paulus, commander of the German Sixth Army in Stalingrad, had lost 40,000 men. Soviet casualties were immensely higher (although they have never admitted a figure), but they could afford them.

▼ **Arm badge worn by a Marshal of the Soviet Union.**

◄ **Wreathed in the smoke and dust of bombardment, the industrial suburbs of Stalingrad sprawl in front of the German attackers. The grain elevators visible against the skyline are to become hotly contested killing grounds.**

strength was being frittered away in house-to-house fighting for which it was totally unsuited.

The task of clearing Stalingrad should have been left to the infantry and the tanks held as a mobile reserve against the Soviet counter-attack which was bound to fall sooner or later. General von Kleist, who had replaced Field Marshal List as commander of Army Group A after the latter was sacked by Hitler on 9 September, also worried that a strong Russian attack south of the city could cut off his command.

◄ **German infantry, armed with an MG 34 machine gun and Mauser M98K rifle, lay down support fire as troops move into the suburbs of Stalingrad, September 1942.**

Hulton Deutsch Collection

BATTLE LINE-UP

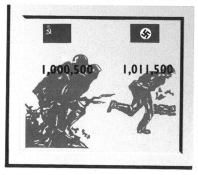

1,000,500   1,011,500

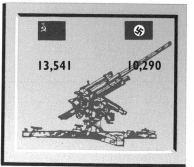

13,541   10,290

◄ German soldiers deploy a 7.5 cm light infantry-support gun during street fighting.

Bundesarchiv-Koblenz

RENEWED ATTACKS

During the second week in October Paulus received meagre reinforcements in the form of five assault pioneer (engineer) battalions and a single understrength panzer division detached from Army Group A. The engineers were tough troops, well trained for this sort of fighting, and on 15 October finally captured the tractor factory in the north of the city which had been a real thorn in Sixth Army's side. The *Barrikady* (Barricade) Factory fell on the 23rd, and half the *Krasny Oktyabr* (Red October) Factory.

Heavy fighting went on around the city's massive grain elevators, as Andrei Khozyanyov, a Soviet naval-infantry officer, bears witness: 'At noon 12 enemy tanks came up from

▼ German infantry advance against a backdrop of the burning city.

► A machine-gun team moves forward to take up a good firing position.

War Stories

Hearing that nine attempts had failed to blow the bridge over which German tanks were to arrive, a Russian woman partisan took her 1-year old daughter, wrapped in a bundle with a powerful time-bomb, and a basket of apples, to cross the bridge to go to market. The guard took some of her apples but let her pass. Half way over, she stopped to change her wailing toddler's nappy and deftly attached the device to a girder. Three hours later the bridge blew up – and took a month to repair!

BATTLE DIARY
STALINGRAD

JANUARY 1942
18- Timoshenko's winter
31 offensive
JUNE
28 Opening of Army Group South's summer offensive
JULY
3 Fall of Sevastopol
AUGUST
11 Sixth Army reaches the Don
23 XIV Panzer Corps reaches Stalingrad
SEPTEMBER
2 Beginning of battle for Stalingrad
OCTOBER
15 Tractor Factory captured by Germans

23 Barricade Factory falls to Germans
NOVEMBER
19 Beginning of Soviet counter-offensive
23 Sixth Army surrounded in Stalingrad
DECEMBER
12- Manstein's relief
24 attempt fails
JANUARY 1943
10 Beginning of final Soviet offensive to take Stalingrad
31 Paulus surrenders
FEBRUARY
2 Last German forces in Stalingrad surrender

Bundesarchiv-Koblenz

Topham Picture Library

continued to fire at the enemy's infantry, preventing them from entering the elevator. Then a Maxim, together with a gunner, was blown up by a shell, and the casing of the second Maxim was hit by shrapnel, bending the barrel. We were left with one light machine gun. Fighting flared up inside the building. We sensed and heard the enemy soldiers' breath and footsteps, but we could not see them in the smoke.'

By the end of October, Sixth Army effectively controlled the city, only isolated Russian pockets of resistance still clinging tenaciously to the western bank of the Volga. But Paulus was stretched as far as he could go. A final attempt to clear the city on 10 November, spearheaded by four more newly arrived pioneer battalions, made little headway. German casualties were horrific.

LAST OF THE ALLIES

At 7.20 on the freezing cold morning of 19 November the long expected Soviet counter-offensive fell on the hapless Rumanian Third Army to the north-west of Stalingrad, heralded by a barrage of 3,500 guns. The Soviet forces comprised General Nikolai Vatutin's South-West Front, which included three tank corps, and General Rokossovsky's Don Front.

the south and west. We had already run out of ammunition for our anti-tank rifles, and we had no grenades left. The tanks approached the elevator from two sides and began to fire at our garrison at point-blank range. But no-one flinched. Our machine guns and tommy guns

Süddeutscher Verlag

The Luftwaffe's most highly decorated pilot, Hans Rudel, was flying his Stuka over the lines that morning. 'What troops are those coming towards us? Masses in brown uniform – are they Russians? No. Rumanians. Some of them are even throwing away their rifles in order to be able to run faster.'

Zhukov had assembled three armoured and four cavalry corps plus 19 infantry divisions along the Don around Kletskaya, the salient which von Weichs had earlier bypassed, and their full weight was now funnelled into the corridor between the Don and the Chir, aimed at Kalach, the town lying astride Sixth Army's supply lines.

The two sides in the coming struggle were, on paper, fairly evenly matched. However, what the figures do not show is the lack of fighting spirit among the Germans' allies, or the poor quality of their equipment, especially tanks. And, of course, Zhukov had the major advantage of the initiative – he was able to concentrate his forces to give much greater local superiority.

CLOSING THE TRAP

Over 500 tanks were committed to the Russian assault, which swept the unfortunate Rumanians aside like chaff. Hoth's reunited Fourth Panzer Army – an army in name only, for its

divisions were barely of regimental strength – was helpless to stem the tide. The XLVIII Panzer Corps was all but annihilated within 24 hours and its commander, Lieutenant-General Ferdinand Heim (who had taken over from Kempf), was recalled and jailed, later to be released with the rank of private. The remnants of von Weichs' forces withdrew in confusion behind the Chir.

On 21 November Soviet troops were menacing Paulus' rear and he

had to withdraw his headquarters hastily to Gumrak airfield. Meanwhile, south of Stalingrad, two tank corps under the command of General Andrei Yeremenko attacked the Fourth Rumanian Army with similar results, and on the 23rd the two pincers met near Kalach, sealing Sixth Army within the Stalingrad perimeter.

Hitler now recalled Field Marshal Erich von Manstein from the Leningrad front and appointed him

▲ General Vassili Chuikov (second from left), commander of the Soviet Sixty-Second Army, in his command post at Stalingrad. General Chuikov was responsible for defending the city throughout the battle.

Hulton Deutsch Collection

Novosti Press Agency

◄ **German troops enter the shattered remains of the Barrikady Factory, scene of bitter fighting during October 1942.**

▼ **As the winter weather closes in, the Soviet troops can now begin to root out the Germans, January 1943.**

▲ **Soviet gunners fire into fast-deteriorating German positions during the Red Army counterattack in the Caucasus.**

commander of a rechristened Army Group Don. This was as much a misnomer as 'fortress' Stalingrad. Apart from Sixth Army trapped in the city, he had the remnants of one SS and five army panzer divisions, two motorised divisions, six infantry divisions, three poor quality Luftwaffe field divisions and the survivors from 14 Rumanian and Italian divisions. And this was after reinforcements arrived during December.

It was not a force to inspire confidence, but the ever-energetic von Manstein set to with a will despite contradictory demands from Berlin. He was not just to stabilise the line, but to recapture the lost ground and re-open a channel into Stalingrad – not so that Sixth Army could break out, but to strengthen its hold on the city.

In his first task von Manstein succeeded where few others could and, although forced to give ground here and there, established a reasonably secure line behind the Chir and prevented a Soviet attempt to recapture Rostov, which would have trapped Army Group A to the south. His forces even managed to get to within 30 miles of Stalingrad, but Paulus' fuel situation would only have allowed the trapped Sixth Army to traverse about half that distance even if Hitler had allowed him to

Popperfoto

Novosti Press Agency

▲ **The heavy and continued German bombing during the battle for Stalingrad reduced the prosperous city on the Volga to a pile of rubble.**

Bundesarchiv-Koblenz

attempt a break-out – which he still refused.

MELTED GUNS

In the city, conditions were almost indescribable. As the German Chief of Staff, General Zeitzler later wrote: 'Supplies to the troops had ceased almost completely. The troops lacked food, ammunition, fuel, equipment of every sort. If something were lost, it was gone forever and could never be replaced. Many artillery units fired off their last shells and then destroyed their guns. Truck drivers, when their petrol tanks were empty, set fire to their vehicles. Whole formations melted away. The Sixth Army was consumed as by a fire until all that was left was a slag.'

All the horses had already been eaten and the men foraged for stray cats and even rats to take the edge off their hunger. The wounded were in an even worse state, lying unattended in the streets in their thousands, for Paulus had had to take the agonising decision that only those troops still capable of fighting should be fed from the meagre supplies remaining. Reichsmarschall Göring's vain boast that the Luftwaffe could keep the invaders of Stalingrad supplied had failed miserably. Where 500 tons of food and ammunition were needed each day to feed a starving army, only about one tenth of that amount managed to be flown in.

▲ Soviet troops, clad in winter clothing, take up positions amid the ruins of Stalingrad.

▶ A Soviet soldier rests his gun on a comrade's shoulder so that he can use it in an anti-aircraft role.

GERMAN FORCES CRUMBLE

By now, everything which could be burned had already been burned so there was no way fires could be lit for heating or cooking, even had there been anything left to cook. Practically every man was suffering from various degrees of frostbite. There was hardly any ammunition left, and what there was was reserved for the men beating off Russian attacks, so Soviet soldiers learned that they could move around quite freely, knowing that if they did nothing aggressive they would not be shot at.

When the snowbound Gumrak airfield fell to the steadily closing Soviet troops on 22 January 1943, the climax was close. The Sixth Army

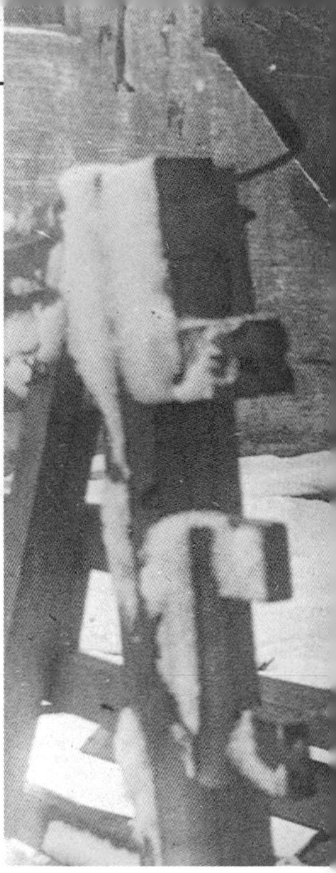

◀▲ The hammer and sickle symbol used on cap bands for artillery officers of the Soviet Army.

Popperfoto

◄ **January 1943: Soviet infantry advance in search of signs of German resistance which, by this time, is almost dying out.**

▼ **Soviet snipers use the ruins of buildings in Stalingrad as cover.**

news of his promotion to Field Marshal. By first light Russian troops were outside his headquarters bunker and he ordered his radio and coding equipment destroyed. A few minutes later he surrendered. The last remaining German resistance in the city was squashed on 2 February. Of the once proud Sixth Army, some 91,000 officers and men began the march to Siberia. Only 7,000 survived to return home a decade later.

was reduced to two and then to three isolated pockets of resistance which succumbed one by one.

On 30 January Paulus radioed a greetings message to Hitler on the anniversary of the dictator's assumption of power, saying 'the swastika still flutters over Stalingrad. May our struggle stand as an example to generations yet unborn never to surrender, no matter how desperate the odds.'

That night Paulus received the

TURNING POINT

POOR STRATEGY

The German summer offensive of 1942 showed the weakness of Adolf Hitler as a strategist. His decision to attack into the Caucasus, aiming for the Soviet oilfields and, eventually, for a link-up with Rommel in the Middle East, was over-ambitious and ran the risk of a Soviet counter-attack. When this was recognised, it was already too late to reverse the commitment of Army Group A, yet Hitler insisted on recalling the XIV Panzer Corps to attack Stalingrad itself. This was a major mistake, weakening Army Group A while doing little to ensure the capture of an urban area in which tanks only played a limited role. In the end, his bold aims were more than the German forces could manage.

► **The Soviet flag is hoisted in central square in Stalingrad, 31 January 1943.**

SICILY

BATTLE DIARY

JANUARY 1943

14   Opening of the Casablanca conference during which Operation 'Husky' is given go-ahead

MAY

9   Operation 'Mincemeat': The Man Who Never Was

JUNE

11   Pantelleria captured

JULY

9 (19.40)   German and Italian Field Divisions placed on alert

10 (02.45)   H-Hour for Allied invasion of Italy

10–11   Germans attack American beachhead at Gela. American airborne reinforcements fired on by own troops over beachhead

13   German paratroopers flown as reinforcements

13–17   Battle of Primosole Bridge

18–22   Patton's drive for Palermo

20   45th US Infantry capture Enna

25   Mussolini is arrested

27   German Army starts evacuation of Sicily

AUGUST

5   Catania falls

17   Patton enters Messina

BEACHHEAD SICILY

US Library of Congress

Spurred by their latest successes, the Allies prepare for their next task – freeing Nazi-occupied Europe.

▲▲ Montgomery's cap badges (Field Marshal's on right); Patton's three stars, worn on his helmet.

▲ War correspondents gather to hear from President Roosevelt and Prime Minister Churchill about the details of the Casablanca Conference, January 1943.

In January 1943 Prime Minister Churchill and President Roosevelt met in the Moroccan city of Casablanca to discuss Allied strategy now that the war in North Africa was drawing to a close. There was bitter disagreement which revealed very wide differences in the ways and means of defeating the Axis powers in Europe.

The Americans maintained that Germany could only be defeated after her army had been beaten in the field. This could only be achieved by threatening to invade Germany and the shortest route to Germany lay through northern France. The Americans had the confidence, manpower and resources to match, so they were not in

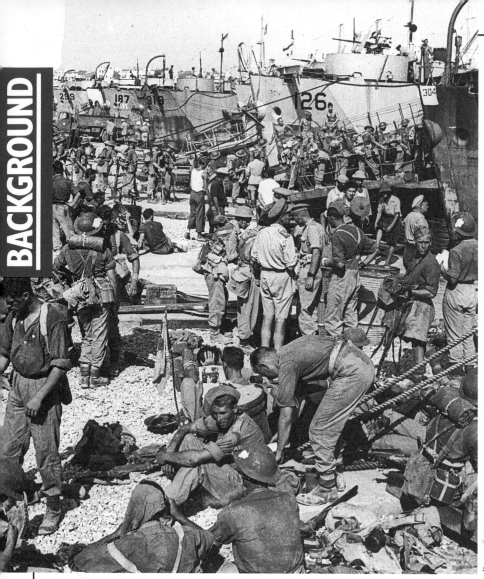

Popperfoto

the least discouraged at the prospect of bitter, relentless battles that might lie ahead if their strategy was adopted.

The British had fought such battles during World War I and were determined to follow a more flexible and indirect strategy which capitalised on the Allies' strengths as maritime powers. Their answer was to wear the Germans down until final victory was assured. In this context the Balkans and eastern Mediterranean had an obvious appeal. The partisans were giving the Axis a hard time in Yugoslavia; the Greeks, it was reckoned, were ripe for an uprising and there was always the prospect of luring neutral Turkey into declaring war on Germany.

DIVERSE VIEWS

Roosevelt and his staff would have none of these 'hare-brained' schemes, which they felt would only detract from the main purpose. It was on this issue that the Americans and British differed. Whereas the former saw the invasion of France as a first step leading to a decisive set-piece battle, in the British scenario it was much later in the scheme of things.

Stalin did not attend the conference, but the Soviet leader was suspicious of his allies, believing they were quite prepared to allow the Red Army to shoulder most of the burden of defeating the Germans. Stalin demanded an Anglo-American army fighting on mainland Europe as soon as possible, to draw some of the enemy forces away from the Eastern Front.

After considerable debate at Casablanca, the Americans reluctantly accepted the British view that a large-scale invasion of France was out of the question for that year. There was neither the trained manpower nor the resources to launch such a risky enterprise.

TARGET SICILY

Thus an operation against Sicily made some sense to all parties. The island's conquest opened up the Mediterranean and freed the Suez Canal route for

▲ Men of Montgomery's Eighth Army board the landing ships that will take them to Sicily, July 1943. Despite apparent chaos, such loading had to be done systematically.

▲ Gilt metal collar insignia for US infantry officers.

▶ Landing craft and launches of the invasion fleet plough across the Mediterranean, heading for Sicily.

Robert Hunt Library

BATTLE DIARY

SICILIAN OVERTURE

JANUARY 1943
14 Opening of Casablanca conference.

MAY 1943
9 Operation Mincemeat—body of British officer found on seashore in Spain.

JUNE 1943
11 Pantelleria captured.

JULY 1943
9 German and Italian Field Divisions placed on alert.
10 2.45 am: H-Hour for the invasion of Sicily.
10 Eighth Army captures Syracuse.
10/11 Germans counterattack US beachhead at Gela.
13/17 Battle of Primosole Bridge.
16 1st Canadian Infantry capture Caltagirone
18/22 Patton's drive for Palermo.
20 45th US Infantry Division capture Enna.
25 Mussolini ousted and is subsequently arrested.
27 German Army starts evacuation.

AUGUST 1943
5 Catania falls.
17 Patton enters Messina.

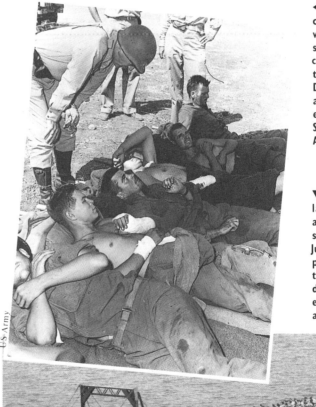

▲ Lieutenant-General Patton adopts a thinking pose, pearl-handled revolver at the ready. He often 'shot from the hip' in dealing with others.

Popperfoto

STAR-STUDDED HERO

When the US Seventh Army landed on the beaches at Gela, their commander was a 58-year old general who was at least ten years older than other field commanders. Yet George S Patton had all the fire and zip of a man half his age. He saw himself as the Allied 'Rommel', bold, aggressive and a daring leader of armoured forces. How others saw him has divided the military fraternity to this day.

There were those who, motivated by his aggressive style of leadership, found that elan and morale could make all the difference between success or failure on the battlefield. To others he remained a braggart, a man of profanity and bravado, a prima donna with indifferent military skills whose successes were really due to enemy weaknesses.

Sicily established Patton as the great popular hero, at least for a while. The race to Messina captured the public imagination, but his fall from grace was equally dramatic. The press exposed a couple of incidents when Patton assaulted soldiers who were suffering from shell shock. The public scandal nearly finished his career and it was almost a year before he was given a field command again.

He led the Third Army across Europe from France to Czechoslovakia. In December 1945, Patton was fatally injured in a car accident in Mannheim, Germany, and is buried in Luxembourg.

---

convoys to Iran, where supplies were sent overland to Russia. Sicily had many airfields from which bombing raids could be launched against southern Europe. A continued Allied threat would force the Germans to strengthen their defences, drawing troops away from both the Eastern Front and northern France, still the ultimate Allied objective.

The British also believed a conquest of Sicily might be sufficient to knock Italy out of the war, though no one saw the Italian peninsula as the main route to Germany. Previous staff studies had already concluded that it was too long and too easily defended.

Sicily, then, was to be the next target after North Africa had been secured. For the Americans the island's conquest was seen as a fitting end to the Mediterranean campaign, whereas for Churchill it marked the beginning of all sorts of opportunities in the eastern Mediterranean. The British Prime Minister was reasonably confident he could persuade the President to continue into Italy or even the Balkans when the time came.

Lieutenant-General Dwight D Eisenhower was appointed Supreme Commander, with Air Chief Marshal Sir Arthur Tedder as his deputy. There were to be two armies for the enterprise: the American Seventh Army under Lieutenant-General George S Patton and the Eighth Army under the vastly experienced and very successful Lieutenant-General Bernard Montgomery. Together they formed the Fifteenth Army Group under General Sir Harold Alexander, who thus had operational responsibility in the field.

In the event Operation Husky, the code-name for the invasion of Sicily, was hugely successful, but from the outset there were considerable difficulties involved in both its planning and preparation. Husky was the biggest amphibious operation of the war to date and the first against a defended beachhead since Gallipoli in 1915; the planners were very much mindful of what a disaster that had proved to be. They knew too that any mistake on their part would put at risk the only trained forces available; their destruction could cause fatal damage to the Allied prospect for victory.

US Army

Robert Hunt Library

◄ **Lt.-Gen. Patton chats with wounded US soldiers—in this case members of the 3rd Infantry Division—as they await air evacuation from Sicily to North Africa, July 1943.**

▼ **An improvised landing barge approaches the shore at Sicily, 10 July 1943. It is packed with troops, dangerously exposed to air attack.**

US Library of Congress

▲ A spectacular explosion marks the demise of an American cargo ship, hit by a German bomber off the Sicilian coast, July 1943. Inset: The Allied fleet gathers in a North African harbour for Operation Husky. As with all amphibious landings, fire support from warships offshore was crucial.

FAVOURABLE MOON

At Casablanca it had been decided that Sicily would be invaded one night in the second week of July. Then the moon would light the way for the airborne attack but set in time to conceal the approach of the assault from the sea. It was the first and only time during the war that an amphibious invasion was attempted at night.

But until the war was over in North Africa nobody could plan on the amount of time that was needed for training in amphibious warfare. First the assault divisions would need time to rest, re-equip and make good their battle losses.

Montgomery attended a presentation on the plan in April 1943 and didn't like it at all. The invading forces were to hit widely scattered beaches along the whole of the southern coast, with the Americans targeting Palermo, the island's capital, and the British Syracuse on the east coast. To Montgomery this meant they were beyond mutual support should the need arise, and this invited defeat in detail. That risk was unacceptable and he insisted the plans be changed. Montgomery's was a lone voice, for the other senior commanders disagreed, but he had the reputation and experience. The planners went back to the drawing board and started again.

CONTINGENCY PLANNING

The enemy had their problems, too. Defeat at Stalingrad in February 1943 and in North Africa in May exacted a heavy toll on German manpower. They knew the Allies must strike next in the Mediterranean, but there were simply not the resources adequately to cover every eventuality. Neither could more of the burden be shouldered by the Italians. Hitler and his generals were under no illusions about their Axis partner. Defeat in North Africa had marked the end of Italy's Empire and induced a great war weariness among the people. Morale in the armed forces was at rock bottom. Poorly armed, with obsolete equipment, few of their units, army or air force, could play a meaningful role in battle. But the Italians did make a major contribution as occupation and garrison troops throughout much of southern Europe. Their sudden collapse or disaffection would simply place further strains on the already over-stretched resources of the Third Reich. Berlin ordered the preparation of a contingency operation, *Plan Achse*, just in case the Italians collapsed and the Germans were forced to assume their responsibilities.

An invasion of Sicily was envisaged in the contingency plans by the German High Command. Sardinia and Greece were also listed. There were precious few troops that could be spared to meet these threats. Field Marshal Albert Kesselring, C-in-C South, was given the *Hermann Göring* Panzer Division, an armoured unit officially part of the Luftwaffe, and the 15th Panzer Grenadiers for Sicily. The main line of defence was the Italian Sixth Army, some 200,000 men, commanded by the 66-year-old General Alfredo Guzzoni, recently brought back from retirement and serving in Sicily for the first time. He had eight coastal divisions, locally recruited, inadequately trained and regarded by Lieutenant-General Fridolin von Senger und Etterlin, Kesselring's liaison officer with Sixth Army, as worthless. There were four field divisions, of which only one, the *Livorno*, had anything like the trained men and weapons to make a useful contribution. The Germans were under no illusions: if the Allies invaded Sicily, theirs would be a delaying action, buying time and hoping they could make good their escape across the Strait of Messina to the Italian mainland.

Montgomery approved the revised plans for the invasion in June. The chosen landing beaches stretched for some 85 miles either side of Cape Pessaro and divided into three sectors—American, Canadian and British. The latter were accorded the primary role. Montgomery's Eighth Army was to strike hard up the coast road for Syracuse and then on to Catania and Messina.

The Americans, still seen as new to war by the condescending British, were required to protect Montgomery's flank and rear. This was very much a secondary role and one deeply resented by Patton and his subordinate commanders, though they knew Eisenhower dare not intervene on their behalf.

BOMBED FORTRESS

The Allies had to maintain utmost secrecy in their planning. They produced a cover story to induce the enemy into believing that perhaps Sardinia was the target, code-named Operation Mincemeat. Another island also had to be neutralised before the invasion. Pantelleria, situated between Sicily and Tunisia, had a tremendous reputation created by enemy propaganda and, because it was fortified, there was no way of verifying the truth. So it had to be assumed that there were nests of small gunboats (E-boats) and swarms of dive-bombers lurking in bomb-proof shelters and waiting to fall on any invading force which dared to stray into Italian waters.

The entire British 1st Infantry Division were loaded into landing craft and, on 11 June 1943, after a massive air and naval bombardment, a small contingent landed on the island. There was no enemy resistance, but was this a foretaste of things to come?

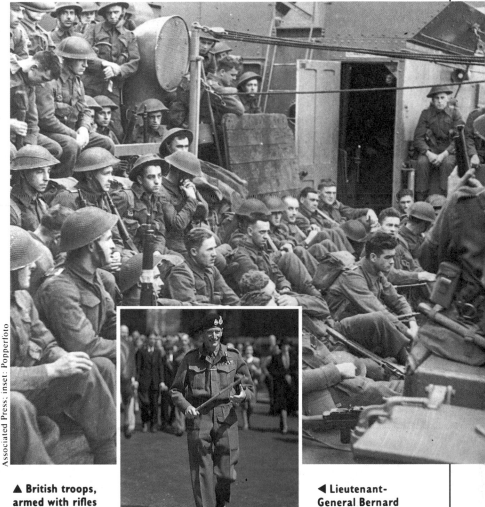

Associated Press; inset: Popperfoto

▲ **British troops, armed with rifles and Bren guns, prepare for the landings on Sicily.**

◄ **Lieutenant-General Bernard Montgomery, commander of British troops.**

Kobal Collection; inset: Marshall Cavendish

▲ **'The Man Who Never Was' in the movie and in reality (inset).**

OPERATION MINCEMEAT

On 9 May 1943 the body of Major William Martin, a British officer in the Royal Marines, was washed up on the shores of southern Spain. Attached to his wrist was a briefcase containing the Allied order of battle for the invasion of Italy. But this wasn't a terrible accident—in fact, the British were counting on Spain's fascist government to allow the *Abwehr*, German Intelligence, to have sight of the documents. They showed the Allied invasion would begin in Sardinia and thence on to northern Italy via Genoa with a feint attack on Sicily.

It was all a ruse to attract enemy forces away from the painfully obvious target of Sicily. The Royal Marine was a man found dead in London of natural causes. He had died of pneumonia, with symptoms similar to drowning. Scotland Yard and Special Branch made extensive enquiries and confirmed that he had no known relatives. Given a complete new identity, even down to letters and personal items, his body was dumped by a submarine to simulate an air crash en route to Gibraltar. The operation has been popularly dubbed 'The Man Who Never Was.'

Ultra intercepts soon confirmed that the Germans had fallen for the plan. They ignored Mussolini's appeals and strengthened the garrisons in Sardinia, northern Italy and southern France, while just two divisions were deployed to Sicily.

ASSAULT ON SICILY

the first blow in the liberation of Europe.

Lieutenant-General Bernard Montgomery and Lieutenant-General George Patton, commanders of the Anglo-Canadian and US assault forces respectively, had units of amphibious shock-troops at their disposal. Airborne forces, Commandos and Rangers were invaluable in isolating beachheads and securing the flanks of landing operations, when they were used properly.

PHASE ONE

In the first phase 100 American Dakotas and 30 British Albemarles left their Tunisian airfields at dusk as 'tugs', each pulling a Waco or Horsa glider. In the latter were 1,500 men of the 1st British Airborne Division in their first major operation of the war. Their task was to capture the Ponte Grande viaduct between the British beach and enemy reserves in Syracuse.

Two hours later a further 230 Dakotas of the 52nd Carrier Wing set out with 3,400 young American paratroopers from the 82nd Airborne, a division which had yet to celebrate its first birthday. Under their youthful leader, Colonel Jim Gavin, the 505th Regimental Combat Team was ordered to seize and hold Piano

Operation Husky did not begin well. On 9 July 1943, the day before the planned landings in Sicily, a sudden and violent storm swept over the Allied armada in the Mediterranean. Waves running before the gale-force winds broke over the crowded transports and flooded the troop decks.

There were 2,500 ships at sea in the biggest 'D-Day' of the war so far. As darkness fell and the winds persisted, conditions aboard the flat-bottomed, shallow hulled LCTs (landing craft, tank) and LSTs (landing ships, tank) were almost unbearable.

The gale did moderate after midnight, as the forecasters had predicted, but there was still a heavy sea running, which made it even more difficult for the encumbered troops as they clambered in the dark down scrambling nets to the landing craft, pitching in six-foot waves below.

The fleets anchored some eight miles (13 km) off their appointed beaches and, as the moon appeared, the skies above filled with the sound of labouring aircraft engines. The airborne divisions were about to deliver

◄ **A British-crewed M4 Medium tank (Sherman) noses out of its landing craft into shallow water, Sicily, 1943. It is armed with a 75 mm gun.**

▼ **As landing craft discharge their cargoes, British beach engineers start to sort out the inevitable chaos of an amphibious landing.**

▶ **The battle line-up reveals an Allied supremacy in almost everything but manpower— boosted on the Axis side by the Italians.**

◄ **British troops manhandle supplies and vehicles ashore on the Sicily coast. The soft nature of the sand is clear.**

BATTLE LINE-UP

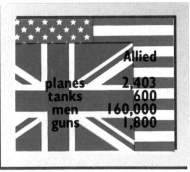

	Allied
planes	2,403
tanks	600
men	160,000
guns	1,800

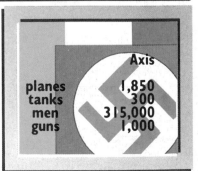

	Axis
planes	1,850
tanks	300
men	315,000
guns	1,000

Lupo, the high ground beyond Gela which overlooked the beaches where the 1st US Infantry Division were to land before daybreak.

The storm-force winds conspired with raw aircrews, who were inexperienced in night flying and made appalling errors in navigation, to produce a tragedy. Only 54 of the gliders landed in Sicily, let alone anywhere near their targets. The remainder, prematurely released, came down in the sea and their occupants drowned. Just 12 gliders with less than 100 men aboard landed near Ponte Grande, but they were enough to secure the viaduct. This tiny group held the bridge against overwhelming odds until the 5th Infantry Division reached them in mid-afternoon.

Enemy defences were formidable. They began at the water's edge with extensive use of barbed wire. Camouflaged concrete pillboxes with heavy machine guns and gun emplacements were dotted along the coast at regular intervals and these were usually flanked by earthworks.

Further inland there were

▼ American soldiers fire their 81 mm mortar in support of an infantry attack in rural Sicily.

▶ German troops man defensive positions on the Sicily coast. They were to be overwhelmed when the Allies attacked in July.

orchards, fields, vineyards and terraced olive groves, which all favoured the defence. Every coastal road junction was heavily defended with concrete pillboxes and trenches. Finally, along all the valleys and roads that led inland there was more barbed wire, as well as pillboxes and minefields.

Field Marshal Albert Kesselring, the Axis commander, was in a quandary over the deployment of his mobile forces. Like Field Marshal Erwin Rommel later in Normandy, he was torn between keeping them concentrated inland or split into smaller groups close to the beaches, ready to counter-attack immediately. Kesselring chose the latter and two German divisions—the *Hermann Göring* Panzers and the 15th Panzer Grenadiers—were divided into four battle groups across the island, covering the beaches from Palermo to Syracuse.

Even though the armada had been detected and Lieutenant-General Fridolin von Senger und Etterlin, Kesselring's liaison officer, had placed the Germans on alert, none of the defenders expected the Allies to be so foolish as to attempt a landing on such a wild and tempestuous night; the Italians in the coastal divisions retired to their beds.

Theirs was an especially rude awakening. H-Hour for the seaborne assault was 0245 hours on 10 July: a moment fixed in the minds of thousands of Allied troops. As the assault waves headed inshore, the protecting warships opened fire. A variety of specialised ships and landing craft made their debut at Sicily, none more fearsome than the LCT(R) (landing craft, tank (rocket)), a British invention. This was a landing craft which fired a thousand 5-inch rockets in rapid salvoes. Their contribution to the battle lasted four minutes but it was devastating; the effect was the equivalent of a barrage from 30 regiments of field artillery, or 30 cruisers each with a broadside of a dozen 6-inch guns.

SCATTERED LANDINGS

Total surprise, overwhelming fire and indifferent quality of the coastal divisions allowed the Allies to come ashore without much interference. This was just as well since the landings were marked by considerable chaos and confusion, especially on the American beaches.

Süddeutscher Verlag

Robert Hunt Library

War Stories

American troops landing in south eastern Sicily found an abandoned Italian command post and went in to look around. Among the first in was an American correspondent of International News Service, who spoke fluent Italian and, when the phone rang, he answered it. The caller was a high ranking Italian officer who wanted to know if the rumour was true, that Americans were landing in the area. The bilingual American replied that of course it was not true. 'Fine', the officer said, and hung up.

◄ British infantry advance to seize a railway station. The trucks provide useful cover—not least for the cameraman.

▼ As artillery shells explode in the background, an American infantryman acting as 'point' for his section—moves forward to probe enemy defences.

Poor navigation resulted in troops being dumped on the wrong beaches.

Heavy surf was unexpected and unplanned for. Some landing craft broached, struck the beach broadside and were stranded. Others discharged their men in neck-deep water as coxswains, in their eagerness to land their charges, dropped the ramp too soon. Add darkness to all this confusion and it was just as well the enemy failed to offer any serious resistance.

The British assault formations—the 5th Infantry and 51st Highland Divisions and the 231st Independent Brigade with Commandos on the open flank—landed astride Pachino peninsula. Despite some patchy enemy shelling, the troops quickly moved inland and by evening secured all their objectives. The advanced guard of the 5th Infantry moved into Syracuse at dusk, the first prize of the campaign.

The Americans' immediate ob-

SMILING ALBERT

Albert Kesselring was born in 1885 and had served with the German Imperial Army during World War I. He transferred to the Luftwaffe, and at the outbreak of World War II commanded airfleets in Poland, France and in the Battle of Britain.

Kesselring took his *Luftflotte II* to Italy in the winter of 1942. As the senior German officer in the theatre, 'Smiling Albert' had a happy disposition which allowed him to work well with other services and allies. He also had a much higher regard for the Italians than many other German officers, and was convinced of the importance of defending the country as far southwards as possible.

As Commander-in-Chief of all Axis forces in the Mediterranean, Kesselring directed the masterful German retreat through Italy. He died in 1960.

► Field Marshal Kesselring chats with Luftwaffe personnel.

jective after coming ashore was the clutch of airfields and landing grounds around Gela. A composite force of Rangers and engineers under Colonel William Darby seized Gela town and ousted the Italian garrison.

The enemy reacted more strongly to the American landings. Throughout D-Day the beach and ships offshore were bombed and shelled and this further delayed proceedings.

Battle groups from the *Livorno* Division attempted to recapture Gela but were stopped by Darby's Rangers, dug in around the town and using captured 77 mm shore battery artillery for support. The enemy were also disrupted by small groups of marauding American paratroopers, who caused further mayhem and confusion by attacking the Italians from the landward side.

There was little co-ordination among the defenders. Indeed, the Germans were under orders to attack without waiting for the Italians. General Conrath, commanding the *Hermann Göring* Panzer Division, planned to unleash his stormtroopers at the beachhead before nine in the morning. But he was an ex-policeman, appointed for his political zeal rather than his military expertise. His division's battle groups had to contend with poor roads and heavy Allied air attacks so that it was early afternoon before they could make their presence felt.

A tank column, which included some of the awesome PzKpfw VI Tigers and was led into battle personally by Conrath, headed for the thin American line on the Piano Lupo, all that stood between the panzers and the congested beaches. They overran a battalion of the 45th

Robert Hunt Library

▲ American infantry march through an approving crowd in the captured village of Corleone.

▼ Never willing accomplices of the Nazis, Sicilians gather round a British Bren-gun carrier.

Imperial War Museum

STEADFAST PARAS

The Primosole bridge spanned the Simeto river and was of vital importance as the only gateway into the Catania plain and its airfields.

On the night of 13/14 July, 1943, 1,900 men from the 1st British Airborne Division set out to capture the bridge by parachute and glider.

In the event, less than 200 men with three anti-tank guns reached the bridge. They did overpower the guard and remove demolition charges placed by Italian engineers. However, unbeknown to the Allies, the machine-gun battalion of a German Parachute Division had just been dropped on to that very area.

The two paratroop forces were immediately locked into a deadly battle, but the tiny British unit, though heavily outnumbered, clung grimly to the bridge until relieved two days later.

▶ **British airborne troops train for a night-drop.**

US Infantry Division and it looked as if the Americans could be in serious trouble. But the paratroopers and infantry on the heights held firm until reinforcements arrived. The German tank crews were inexperienced and their Tigers mechanically unreliable, while the terraced olive groves impeded their advance. Darby's Rangers had also become adept at handling their Italian field pieces and, when they joined in, the German attack stalled.

By the end of the first day the Americans were safely ashore and those on the flanks consolidated and extended their perimeter. The forward elements of the 45th Infantry Div. on the right flank had penetrated seven miles (11 km) inland, and Major-General Lucian Truscott's 3rd US Infantry Div. on

◀ **An American M7B1 'Howitzer Motor Carriage' (self-propelled gun) races forward to engage the enemy in the town it is entering.**

▼ **Italian troops waving white flags come forward to surrender to the Eighth Army, August 1943. The campaign is over– next stop, the Italian mainland.**

Imperial War Museum

the left were well established. The weakness lay with the 1st US Infantry Div. in the central sector, where the Piano Lupo was not properly reinforced and the beaches were under bombardment.

Patton played safe and called for additional forces. Colonel Reuben Tucker's 504th Parachute Regiment Combat Team left Tunisia at dusk in 147 Dakotas to reinforce the central sector and Piano Lupo.

FATAL ERROR

The Americans arrived over the beachhead in darkness and just 45 minutes after a very heavy enemy air raid on the anchored invasion fleet. Gun crews were still at battle stations. Even though orders had

▼ German paratroops are rushed forward as reinforcements to oppose the Allied landings, 15 July 1943. Their efforts prove to be in vain, for the Allied troops are soon to reach the road to Messina.

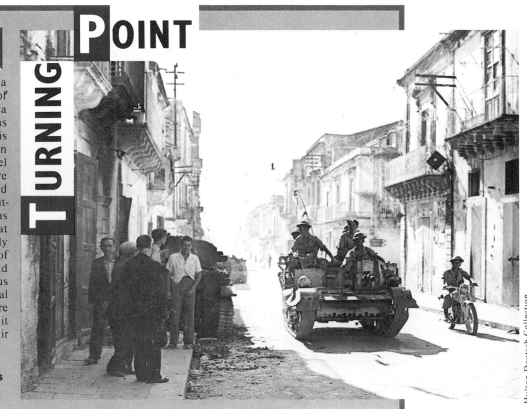

▶ Men of the 6th Battalion, Royal Inniskilling Fusiliers, clear buildings in a Sicilian village. Fighting in built-up areas was something new for the Eighth Army.

Süddeutscher Verlag

been given that the friendly aircraft were expected, a single gun on one ship opened fire. Within seconds every anti-aircraft gun in the fleet was firing on the close-packed ranks of Dakotas flying overhead. Some planes turned away and of those who pressed ahead ten were shot down before they could drop the paras. Another 17 were shot down empty on the return trip and a further 37

limped badly damaged back to North Africa, many with dead and wounded paratroopers still aboard. There were just 500 paratroopers assembled at the dropping zone; the remainder, some 1,200 men, were scattered the length and breadth of Sicily.

The most dangerous counterattack came early the next morning—11 July. Conrath's panzers were joined by the *Livorno* Division in a

TURNING POINT

DISAGREEMENT

Operation Husky was indicative of a potentially damaging difference of Allied opinion. Once North Africa had been cleared, the Americans were keen to defeat the Axis powers by a direct assault on Germany with a cross-Channel invasion. Churchill was well aware that an invasion of France required far more preparation and commitment of resources than was apparent in 1943. He realised that attacks against the 'soft underbelly of Europe' had the advantage of knocking Italy out of the war and securing the Mediterranean, thus also aiding Britain's colonial interests. The British view was more realistic, but the reasons behind it were not fully appreciated by their Allies. Friction ensued.

▶ A British Bren-gun carrier moves freely through a town in Sicily.

Hulton Deutsch Collection

Süddeutscher Verlag

coordinated attack on the beach at Gela. Together they were to envelope the beachhead in a pincer movement, the *Livorno* from the north and west, *Hermann Göring* in three columns from the east. Once they had broken through the Americans on the Piano Lupo, Conrath planned to concentrate his division on the Gela plain and then rampage with his Tigers across the beachhead.

ALLIED BREAKTHROUGH

The *Livorno* attacked bravely enough but ran into a determined Ranger defence which included among its repertory of firepower 6-inch salvoes from the USS *Savannah*, a cruiser offshore. Broken and routed, the *Livorno* was finished as a fighting unit. With the Germans it was another matter; their attacks got underway at 0600 hours and for a while the situation was quite tense. American outposts at Ponte Dirillo were overrun and the panzers were in danger of breaking through when Gavin and his paratroopers attacked from the rear. Their battle lasted until noon but was enough to divert one German battle group from the beachhead. Conrath personally led another column which assaulted the weakly held Piano Lupo. They came within 2,000 yards of the beach, which was fired upon by the panzers. The Germans were met by a storm of fire which left 16 panzers ablaze.

It took the Allies 30 days and cost them 23,000 casualties to reach Messina and even then Montgomery's troops weren't the first into the town, in what was dubbed the 'Race for Messina'. Syracuse had fallen easily enough and the Italian garrison at Augusta, further up the coast, was preparing to surrender formally when the Germans took a hand. In marked contrast to the Allies, two battalions from the 1st German Parachute Division in Avignon were dropped accurately into the battle and from then on it was a different story.

There was a fierce battle for the Primosole Bridge, the gateway to Catania, and the British attack on the city became bogged down before a skilled defence which made every use of the formidable terrain.

Montgomery's Eighth Army had attracted the bulk of the Germans to their front and this left the way open for Patton. On 19 July and against weak Italian defences, Patton created a Provisional Corps and drove his armour hard for Palermo. They captured the port on 22 July.

HEADING FOR MESSINA

The reality of the Race for Messina was a tough slogging battle along the coastal road and into the mountainous interior.

Catania eventually fell on 5 August and Patton won the Race to Messina. He entered the city on 17 August but the enemy had gone.

For the Allies, Sicily was a painful transition from a North African to a European war, while the Germans conducted a most successful rearguard crowned by a brilliant evacuation. Between 11 and 17 August they brought all their units and the bulk of their equipment out of Sicily. More ominous was the confidence Sicily had given the German High Command to make a fight for Italy rather than abandon the peninsula entirely. The war in the area had only just began.

◄ German officers, held in an Allied POW camp on Sicily, are issued with rations under the watchful gaze of their British counterparts.

▼ Cheerful-looking Italian troops march into a village near Messina, displaying all the signs of surrender. By August 1943, the Italian Army had virtually collapsed.

KURSK

BATTLE DIARY

DECEMBER 1942

16   Start of Russian winter counter-offensive

JANUARY 1943

12   Second phase of Russian counter-offensive begins

FEBRUARY

2   Last German units in Stalingrad surrender

8   Russians recapture Kursk

16   Russians recapture Kharkov

20   Guderian appointed Inspector General of Armoured Troops

22   Manstein launches spring offensive

MARCH

15   Germans recapture Kharkov

18   Germans recapture Belgorod

MAY

4   Kursk attack plan approved

13   Last German units in Tunisia surrender

JULY

4   Manstein begins attack in southern half of Kursk salient

5   Model begins attack in northern half of Kursk salient

7   Ninth Army's advance halted

10   Allies land on Sicily

12   Major tank battle around Prokhorovka – over 1,500 armoured
      vehicles involved

13   Hitler orders halt to attacks at Kursk

14   Red Army launches its counter-attack

23   All German gains around Kursk wiped out

LAST VICTORIES

Ringier Dokumentationszentrum

After their victory at Stalingrad, the Red Army hurled itself at the remaining German forces in southern Russia, in the process crossing swords with a master tactician.

▲ A German headquarters' column travels a lonely road across the wintry steppes. In the early months of 1943 the *Wehrmacht* achieved its last victories in Russia.

▲▲ Unit insignia of the 11th Panzer Division.

T he decisive battles on the Eastern Front all took place in southern Russia during 1942 and 1943. In this enormous region south-east of the Pripet marshes, the great rivers Dnieper, Donets, Don and Volga all run in a roughly north to south direction, forming the only effective defence positions in the predominantly flat landscape.

Furthermore, the industry of the Donets basin and the oilfields of the Caucasus between the Black Sea and the Caspian Sea were vital parts of the Russian war machine. As a result, the course of the war in the East was largely determined by the fighting for control of these water barriers, the bridges over them and the railway centres that served both armies and industry.

After the relative failure of the Russian winter offensives of early 1942, Hitler gave his generals conflicting goals for their efforts later in the year. They were instructed to take Leningrad at the northern end of their line while simultaneously advancing into the Caucasus region, more than 1,000 miles (1,600 km) to the south.

To make matters worse, the field commanders were supposed to undertake these Herculean tasks with many units down to 50 per cent or even 35 per cent of normal strength. Meanwhile, the Russian armies were building up and at least 360 divisions were eventually identified by the Germans. Though much of their equipment had been obsolete at the start of the war, by 1942 the Russian divisions were increasingly well supplied with modern T-34 tanks, artillery of all calibres and crude but reliable small arms.

SUB-ZERO CONDITIONS

Furthermore, while the German Army suffered badly from the cold between October and May each year, and many casualties were caused by simple frostbite, standard Russian equipment was designed for sub-zero conditions. Whether it was a uniform, a sub-machine gun or a tank, the equipment did not prevent men – and women – from fighting on whatever the temperature.

As the summer of 1942 wore on, following a Russian offensive in the direction of Kharkov, the main weight of the German offensive in the south was switched from the Caucasus to Stalingrad on the Volga. It was only after Rostov-on-the-Don was retaken by the Germans in mid July that the German Army Group A under Field Marshal Wilhelm List was ordered to turn south to occupy the Caucasus. The purpose behind this move was to seize the Transcaucasian oil fields on the far side of the Caucasus mountains.

This was an apparently attractive move because with one blow it could solve the main German supply problem and cut Russian oil output. But after a rapid initial advance,

▶ Soviet tank crews proudly stand in front of their new T-34s. The tanks were paid for by communities in central Siberia.

▼ A German StuG III assault gun is backed into a shelter. Such vehicles made up an increasing proportion of German armour production.

WarStories

Lice and parasites dogged the Russian partisans but one, a former zoologist, found that if he left his clothes over an ant-hill, the parasites were cleared in minutes! Another group of sappers were enjoying the luxury of a steam bath as their clothes were being disinfested in a specially rigged-up chamber next door. Suddenly they heard explosions and rushed out, stark naked, certain they were under attack. In fact, it was the grenades, cartridges and detonators they had left in their pockets, set off by the heat.

Süddeutscher Verlag

Ringier Dokumentationszentrum

▲ British swordsmith Tom Beasley forges the Stalingrad Sword in 1943. The sword was presented to Stalin by Churchill

Novosti Press Agency

▲ Civilians return to Kursk following the town's liberation from the Germans on 8 February 1943. They returned to find devastion left by the Germans, who destroyed anything of military use.

▶ Soviet troops on the offensive.

Popperfoto

at the Teheran conference in November 1943, in honour of the Red Army's victories in its 1942-3 winter offensive.

THE BIGGEST TANK BATTLE

DECEMBER 1942
16 Start of Soviet winter offensive

JANUARY 1943
12 Second phase of Soviet offensive begins and Germans retreat

FEBRUARY
2 Last German units in Stalingrad surrender
8 Russians liberate Kursk
16 Kharkov falls to the Russians
20 Manstein launches his counter-offensive

MARCH
15 Germans recapture Kharkov for the last time

MAY
4 Kursk plan of attack approved despite Hitler's fears

JULY
4/5 Beginning of German attacks on Kursk salient
7 Advance of German 9th Army halted
12 Major tank battle around Prokhorovka – the panzer's death ride
13 Hitler orders halt to attacks at Kursk
14 Red Army launches its counter-attack
23 All German gains around Kursk recovered

AUGUST
23 Kharkov liberated for last time

the move petered out for lack of fuel and Hitler sacked List out of hand for the failure. Not only did the Caucasus operation divide the German forces and weaken each part so much that both Stalingrad and the oil fields remained unattainable, it also left the whole of Army Group A liable to be cut off from the rest of the German forces, any time that the Russians recaptured Rostov.

This strategic uncertainty of purpose contributed to the loss of Stalingrad but an attempted rescue operation, codenamed Winter Storm, brought Field Marshal Erich von Manstein on to the scene. Despite Manstein's acknowledged ability, however, Winter Storm failed, Stalingrad fell and at the turn of the year, the Russians started to advance in the direction of Rostov and Kharkov and Dnepropetrovsk.

Simultaneously with the advance on Rostov, the Russians launched an offensive on the Transcaucasian front with the hope of trapping Army Group A south of the Don. One Panzer Army scrambled across the Don before Rostov was retaken by the Soviets but the rest of the German forces in the Caucasus had to escape by boat,

across an arm of the sea to the Crimean Peninsula. At this point, the Germans were more or less back where they had started in early 1942 – all their efforts and all the casualties they had suffered were in vain. In the circumstances it was remarkable that Manstein could even contemplate striking back.

Nevertheless this was what he was doing as four Russian Fronts (Army Groups) pushed him back to Kharkov and a partisan revolt broke out in the city. After some fighting, SS General Paul Hausser ordered evacuation of the city on 14 February 1943, despite a direct *Führer* order to the contrary. Manstein pulled his forces right back and lured the Russians on until they almost reached Dnepropetrovsk on the River Dnieper, something like 425 miles (700 km) west of Stalingrad as the crow flies. No army could advance so far and so fast without some degree of disorganisation and at Dnepropetrovsk, Manstein as the new commander-in-chief of Army Group South had gathered 12 infantry and 12 panzer divisions ready for a counter-attack.

CHANGE OF GAUGE

The severity of Russian supply and organisation problems can be judged from the way the Germans had methodically converted the wider gauge Russian railway lines to European gauge as they advanced. In consequence all the Red Army's supplies had to be trucked 65 miles (105 km) overland to the railway centre of Kharkov until the tracks had been ripped up and relaid to the Russian gauge again.

In addition, superior German tactics and the greater freedom of manoeuvre that German officers were trained and encouraged to employ paid off in dozens of local successes. These helped to stave off the inevitable consequences of Russian superiority in men and, as time went on, in equipment and supplies.

A typical example is the action fought on 25 January 1943 by Major-General Herman Balck's 11th Panzer Division, part of Army Detachment Hollidt.

Russian units had secured a bridgehead at the confluence of the Rivers Don and Manych, and the Germans set out to eliminate it. The Russian tanks were dug into hull-

◄ **A German stands sentry over an anti-tank gun emplacement in the spring rains of April 1943.**

down positions so that only the tops of the turrets appeared above ground level. This made them very difficult to hit, and so it would have been foolish to attack frontally. Balck therefore launched a feint attack with his armoured cars and half-tracks from the north to lure the tanks out of their prepared positions, while covering his real intentions with a smokescreen laid down by the divisional artillery. Then he sent his tanks, together with their supporting panzergrenadiers, in from the south. After a few minutes' pandemonium, the Russians fled in headlong retreat. The German casualties were one dead and 14 wounded – the Russians lost 20 tanks and about 500 men.

PINCER ATTACK

The loss of Kharkov incensed Hitler and he flew to Manstein's headquarters at Zaporozhye on 17 February 1943 to demand an explanation – probably the closest the *Führer* got to the battle front in the course of the war. Manstein duly gave him both barrels. Colonel – General Hermann Hoth's Fourth Panzer Army (XLVIII and II SS Panzer Corps) and Lieutenant-General Eberhard von Mackensen's First Panzer Army (XL and LVII Panzer Corps) were, he explained, now in position for a pincer attack against the South-West Front, with the aim of driving the Russians back across the River Donets. The combined panzer armies could then hit the Russian left flank and recapture Kharkov in the process.

Later, working in conjunction with Schmidt's Second Panzer Army diverted south from Army Group Centre, Manstein planned to encircle the remaining Russian forces in the vicinity of Kursk. This would leave the German army in a very strong position for a renewed major offensive later in the year. It was a bold plan, typical of Manstein in its essential simplicity, and on 19 February, Hitler left the Field Marshal with his blessings – after Russian tanks had been reported half a dozen miles away from Zaporozhye – and flew back to his own forward headquarters at Vinnitsa in Poland.

With his two panzer armies and the choice of ground for his attack, Manstein could assemble something like a seven to one local superiority in tanks while the Luftwaffe had a three to one superiority in the air. The first two

A MASTER OF TACTICS

Erich von Manstein was born in Berlin on 24 November 1887. He joined the Imperial Army in 1906, and fought with distinction during the First World War. His natural aptitude for soldiering earned him steady promotion, even in the tiny inter-war army. Manstein served as chief-of-staff to an army group during the Polish campaign. The plan for a thrust through the Ardennes adopted for the attack on France in 1940 was largely his idea. During Operation Barbarossa, he commanded a panzer corps, before being given charge of the Eleventh Army. After the battle of Kursk, his preference for a mobile defence and his open disagreements with Hitler led to his dismissal in March 1944. A British military court found Manstein guilty of war crimes in 1949. He died in 1973.

▶ **Manstein (in white) confers with subordinates before the battle of Kursk.**

The citizens of Kursk start clearing away the rubble left behind by the demolitions of the retreating Germans. They were not only faced with the task of rebuilding their shattered city; soon they would be digging trenches for the elaborate defences the Red Army constructed in the Kursk salient.

phases of the plan worked well. Fourth Panzer Army hit General Nicolai Vatutin's South-West Front on the 20th and sent his forces reeling. Many Russian units were isolated or immobilised for lack of fuel and defeated in detail. Vatutin tried to continue with the attack but the panzers would not be denied and by the end of the month the Russians were back behind the River Donets, having lost or abandoned 615 tanks.

The Germans next turned their attention to the Voronezh Front further north. With forces already weakened because the Third Tank Army had already been sent to aid the South-West Front and smashed by the Germans while it was off balance re-aligning its front, Colonel General Filipp Golikov tried to hold a defensive line south of Kharkov. It was no good and the city fell to the Germans once again on 15 March. Golikov lost 72,000 men killed and captured and lost another 600 tanks.

Only the weather intervened to prevent Manstein's grand plan from achieving total success. An unexpected warm front arrived, the snow thawed and the ground, as ever in the Russian spring, turned into a quagmire over which the tanks could not operate. The result was that while the Germans had stabilised the situation in the south and established a strong position, there still remained a great western bulge, or salient, in the line between Belgorod and Orel. With just 140 serviceable tanks spread around 16 panzer divisions, this pause could not have come at a better time for the Germans.

BATTLE-WORN

As usual, the thaw lasted six weeks, giving time for the German field workshops to catch up with their backlog of repairs, but the tanks were spread more thinly than at the start of any previous year. While the Battle of France was fought by panzer divisions made up of four tank battalions deploying perhaps 500 fully-serviceable tanks between them, most panzer divisions were now down to a couple of tank battalions with a total of no more than 160 or 200 battle-worn tanks. Most of these had only been patched up and were liable to break down under strain. Any factory-fresh tanks tended to be allocated to newly formed Divisions.

Rivalry between the Artillery and the armoured forces was also hampering the efforts of General Heinz Guderian, newly appointed Inspector-General of Armoured Troops,

to rebuild the depleted panzer divisions. The rivalry centred on the Jagdpanzers (self-propelled anti-tank guns) and the assault guns which were tank chassis fitted with large calibre guns but without a revolving turret. One battalion of Jagdpanzers was supposed to be allocated to each panzer division to deal with the T-34s that were causing havoc among the standard MK IV panzers.

So while Guderian sought to combine tanks, Jagdpanzers, assault guns and infantry into effective new panzer units, artillery generals intrigued amid the chaos of the German supply and procurement system to divert production into assault guns which they managed to keep out of Guderian's control. Thus only small quantities of Jagdpanzers reached the panzer divisions, and instead of entering the summer campaign of 1943 with their customary numerical and technical superiority, German armoured tactics in the summer campaign of 1943 hinged on protecting the vulnerable Mk IVs by mixing them with small quantities of the new Tiger tank in the broad axe-shaped *panzerkeile* formation, so far had the balance tilted against the Germans.

Dejected and disarmed, a group of Russian POWs is shepherded into captivity. But by late 1943, the Germans could no longer counteract Russian superiority by taking hundreds of thousands of prisoners at a time. It was only a matter of time before numbers told.

CLASH OF STEEL

Peter Newark's Military Pictures

The fate of German arms in the East was decided in a titanic struggle of men and tanks at Kursk in the summer of 1943, as both sides chose to gamble all on one battle.

The single greatest armoured battle the world had ever seen took place on 12 July 1943. It involved 1500 Russian and German tanks, and remained unrivalled in size until the Arab-Israeli wars of the 1960s and 1970s. It was the climax to the great German summer offensive, code-named *Zitadelle* (Citadel), which was designed to pinch off and destroy the two Soviet Army fronts in the Kursk salient and pave the way for further operations northwards to isolate Moscow from the east and retrieve the ground lost in the south since Stalingrad. If the attack had been launched earlier in the year, as Field Marshal Erich von Manstein had originally planned, it would have stood a good chance of success against the overstretched Soviet forces. After a three-month pause, it was doomed to failure.

Both sides could see the opportunities – and the dangers – presented by the Kursk salient. To Chief-of-Staff General Kurt Zeitzler, who persuaded Hitler to accept his plan despite misgivings from General Heinz Guderian and Manstein among others, it offered a chance to destroy substantial Soviet forces and regain the initiative. Originally scheduled for May, the operation was postponed several times, one of the reasons being a meeting between low-ranking German and Russian diplomats in June: Stalin, angry over the Western Allies' failure to open the Second Front, had offered an armistice if the German Army would withdraw behind 1941 frontiers, but Hitler wanted to establish an independent, neutral Ukraine, and this the Russian dictator obviously could not accept.

The final plan for the attack was agreed on 4 May, nine days before the German surrender in Tunisia, but there were still doubts about its feasibility, since it was obvious the Russians would easily be able to see the build-up and take appropriate precautions. The German staff would have been even more worried had they

Ringier Dokumentationszentrum

BATTLE LINE-UP

GERMAN		SOVIET	
MEN	900,000	MEN	1,300,000
TANKS	2,700	TANKS	3,600
GUNS	10,000	GUNS	20,000
AIRCRAFT	2,000	AIRCRAFT	2,400

▲ A Tiger tank rolls forward as the German build-up for Kursk begins. Its 88 mm gun outranged the T-34's 76.2 mm gun.

◄◄ A dead German crewman lies by the wreck of a Panzer Mark IV.

◄ The opposing forces at Kursk.

Ringier Dokumentationszentrum

south of Orel and launch a two-pronged attack either side of Ponyri. In terms of armoured formations, it was weaker than Manstein's southern attack force with only four panzer divisions (2nd, 9th, 18th and 20th) plus a single Tiger battalion (505th) and two *Elefant* battalions (653rd and 654th). In the south there were two panzer groups, Hermann Hoth's Fourth Panzer Army and Army Detachment Kempf (named after its commander). Between them these comprised the 3rd, 6th, 7th, 11th and 19th Panzer Divisions and *Grossdeutschland* which was a panzer division in all but name, plus the similarly equipped 1st, 2nd and 3rd SS Panzer Divisions: *Leibstandarte, Adolf Hitler, Das Reich,* and

known about the 'Lucy' spy ring. On 10 May Guderian faced the *Führer*. 'How many people', he asked, 'do you think even know where Kursk is? It's a matter of profound indifference to the world whether we hold Kursk or not.' Uncharacteristically, Hitler agreed with him. 'You're quite right. Whenever I think of this attack my stomach turns over.' The German dictator should have followed his own gut feeling, for the Russians also saw the salient as a springboard from which they could resume the offensive. However, the Soviet High Command wisely decided to play a waiting game. General Nicholas Vatutin's Voronezh Front and General Konstantin Rokossovsky's Central Front within the 'bulge' would be reinforced, but they would take up a defensive stance. They would blunt the panzer assault, inflict heavy casualties and regain the initiative which had been lost with the fall of Kharkov. General Ivan Koniev's Steppe Front would be held behind them as an instant reserve.

DEFENCE IN DEPTH

To speed his preparations, Marshal Georgi Zhukov, who was in overall command, conscripted over 300,000 local people from Kursk and other towns in the salient such as Ponyri,

Lgov and Oboyan to begin preparing an elaborate series of fortified lines in concentric fashion, like the skins of an onion, to give defence in depth. The salient had a 345 mile (550 km) perimeter and this meant digging over 6,000 miles (11,200 km) of trenches, with minefields and anti-tank 'hedgehogs' concealing dug-in tanks and guns in carefully camouflaged strongpoints. Great attention was also paid to anti-aircraft defence and eventually the Soviet forces around Kursk were stronger even than those in front of Moscow.

The German plan was predictable, with its attacks taking place astride the main north-south road through Kursk. In the north, General Walther Model's Ninth Army would assemble

▲ **Three Tigers advance across the Russian plain. Heavy tank battalions using the Tiger made up the tips of the German armoured thrusts at Kursk.**

◀▼ **General Model, Ninth Army Commander (centre), confers with subordinates.**

▼ **The gun crew of a German howitzer duck as a shell explodes.**

Ringier Dokumentationszentrum

THE PRODUCTION BATTLE

The German panzer divisions at Kursk were equipped with a new generation of tanks, designs that were the product of three years' experience of war. However, manufacture of the much needed replacements for the Panzer Mark IIIs and IVs was considerably slowed by the multiplicity of models being built, and the complex, high-tech designs of the new Tigers and Panthers. The net result of these factors was a limit to the numbers of tanks that Germany was able to produce compared to the Soviets, resulting in a substantial inferiority on the battlefield. This disparity in production was the reason why German armoured strength at Kursk, at 2,700 vehicles, was 61 per cent of the number serving on the Eastern Front, while the Soviet total of 3,600 amounted to less than 40 per cent of that of the Red Army.

► Turrets being installed on Tiger tanks. The Tiger's new design and heavy armour could not compensate for low numbers.

Ringier Dokumentationszentrum

Tass

◄ As the Germans near Prokhorovka, reinforcements are hurried forward. These T-34s carry infantry to the front line. Overhead, Pe-2 dive bombers race in for a strike.

► ► Marshal Georgii Zhukov took charge of the fighting around Prokhorovka at its critical phase.

▼ Tigers break through the Red Army's lines, passing a wrecked T-34 Model 1943.

reinforced from Steppe Front by the Fifth Guards Army and Fifth Guards Tank Army.

Model's attack was scheduled to start at 3 am on 5 July but the Russians, forewarned of the exact time by a Hungarian deserter, struck the first blow. At 2.20 am they commenced a massive artillery bombardment on Ninth Army's start lines. Casualties were heavy because the German troops were largely in the open and in the ensuing confusion they were unable to begin moving forward until 90 minutes after the planned deadline. It was a foretaste of worse to come.

Model's forces, the infantry preceding the tanks to clear a path, were unable to make much headway, hacking their way through the first line of defences under murderous crossfire and gaining only six miles

(10 km) on the first day with many units bogged down by minefields whose density in places was over 5,000 per mile. The Soviet artillery and *Katyusha* rocket fire was especially murderous. A further three or four miles were covered on the second day but on the 7th the attack was stopped in its tracks on the ridge in front of Olkhovatka, only 12 miles (19 km) from Ninth Army's starting point. The *Elefants* proved useless when separated from their supporting infantry and, as Guderian had feared,

Tass

Totenkopf. Each of the SS divisions and *Grossdeutschland* contained an integral Tiger company of between 13 and 15 tanks. In addition, Hoth had the 503rd Heavy Tank Battalion with a further 45 Tigers, making the greatest number so far assembled in one spot.

Model, whose main line of advance lay down the axis of the Orel-Kursk railway line, was faced by the Soviet Thirteenth Army. Manstein's line of attack was two-pronged, Fourth Panzer Army being intended to strike from Tomarovka through Prokhorovka and skirt Oboyan while Army Detachment Kempf would advance on its right from Belgorod to bypass Rzhava. In their path lay the Sixty Ninth Army and Sixth and Seventh Guards Armies, which would be

Süddeutscher Verlag

▲ The insignia applied to Ju-87s on anti-tank missions.

◀ Stukas of Hans-Ulrich Rudel's tank-busting group

Süddeutscher Verlag

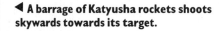

War Stories

O n the eve of a major battle, a group of Russian soldiers took their minds off the forthcoming clash by doing domestic chores and giving their guns a final overhaul. The mood was one of optimism, as they repaired clothes and boots. One youngster felt he ought to dress for the occasion and put on new underwear—but the veterans laughed and asked him if he was getting ready to die. After all, they had a lot of fighting to do before they won, and he would need new underwear when he finally returned home, triumphant.

◀ A barrage of Katyusha rockets shoots skywards towards its target.

Ringier Dokumentationszentrum

the Panthers suffered a high break-down rate. By the critical date of the battle, 12 July, Model had lost half of his tanks.

DEATH RIDE

In the south, where the Germans enjoyed a local tank superiority of approximately 6:1, things initially seemed to go better despite equally stiff resistance. It was, though, the 'death ride' of the panzers.

Manstein had achieved surprise here by 'jumping the gun' and beginning his part of the attack on the afternoon of 4 July, an unusual time of day to start a major offensive. Assault engineers from Army Detachment Kempf went forward to clear lanes through the minefields south-east of Belgorod while the Luftwaffe

▼ German artillery zeroes in as Soviet T-34s go on the offensive.

kept the Russians' heads down. This put the German start line for Kempf's attack firmly astride a long ridge which formed an important tactical feature and gave his artillery observers an excellent position. Then the tanks clattered forward under cover of darkness.

KEMPF FAILS

Daylight brought rain which slowed the advance, and the first Russian defence line behind the Donets lay in heavily wooded country which was not ideal for armoured operation, and also provided superb cover for the Soviet anti-tank guns. As a result, Kempf was unable to break through until the third day of the battle, 8 July.

On his left the three divisions of Hausser's SS Panzer Corps had made much more rapid progress, pushing forward some 15 miles during the first day, breaking through the first defence line as far as Pokrovka. The tanks were deployed in wedge-shaped formation spearheaded by Tigers supported by Panthers on their flanks

Ringier Dokumentationszentrum

while the weaker Mark IIIs and IVs followed in support. Their next objective was Prokhorovka on the Belgorod-Kursk railway line, after which the intent was to force a crossing of the River Psel and attack Kursk from the south-east. After the first day, however, progress was slowed, partly because of the need to wait for flanking army units to catch up, and partly because of the Russians poured seemingly inexhaustible reserves into the line.

SLOW PROGRESS

On the left of the SS Corps, Hoths XLVIII Panzer Corps was heading for Oboyan. Here, Vatutin's defences were particularly strong as he intended to funnel the panzers into a narrow wedge of ground where they would be unable to manoeuvre properly. Moreover, the corps was only able to make slow progress. The rain had swollen a stream across their front into a torrent, and the *Grossdeutschland's* brand-new Panther battalion had the misfortune to run slap into an uncharted minefield. The corps battled its way to the River Pena by the 8th and some units managed to get across before being repelled. Hoth therefore swung the weight of his attack north-westwards, followed on the flank of the SS Panzer Corps, and reached Novoselvka on the 10th. Similarly on the right, Kempf, unable to venture further eastwards, swung north towards Rzhavets.

► A squadron of T-34s charges through one of the many gullies that cut up the Russian plain around Kursk, to close the range with the enemy.

Ringier Dokumentationszentrum

THE LUCY RING

'Lucy' was the code name of a Bavarian anti-Nazi, Rudolf Rössler, living in exile in Switzerland. Together with an Hungarian, Sándor Radó, and an Englishman, Alexander Foote, he supplied Stalin with detailed information on German plans and intentions from 1941 to 1943, claiming to have obtained it from a group of anti-Nazi officers in the German army. In fact, as was only discovered many years later, Foote was actually providing him with ULTRA intercepts from British cryptographers at Bletchley Park, who were regularly deciphering German coded transmissions. The 'Lucy' ring was broken up by the Swiss police in the autumn of 1943 after German army intelligence located their radio transmitters and complained about this transgression of Swiss neutrality.

► A line of Soviet guns in action. 'Lucy's information was vital to the defence of Kursk.

Ringier Dokumentationszentrum

▶ A pair of Russian T-70 tanks drive past a wrecked German vehicle.

▼ Trophy of victory: Soviet soldiers with a knocked-out Panther.

By the time Kempf reached Rzhavets on the 11th, the *Totenkopf* Division had forced a crossing of the Psel – the last natural defensive line in front of Kursk – and three SS divisions were deployed around Prokhorovka and had reached the village of Krasny Oktyabr (Red October). The name recalled another battlefield landmark, of a factory along the Volga River, at Stalingrad. As the battle reached its crucial psychological moment, Vatutin hurled General Pavel Rotmistrov's Fifth Guards Tank Army into the counter-attack. On 12 July some 850 T-34s and KV-1s confronted a total of approximately 700 German tanks. The SS Panzer Corps fought throughout the morning on their own while Hoth drove his XLVIII Panzer Corps to their aid. Kempf's divisions were still some 12 miles (19 km) away and unable to add their weight.

The German tank crews fought with all their customary skill but they were compressed into an area a mere three miles (5 km) square, as Vatutin had planned. Then the T-34s charged them at full speed so as to deny the Tigers with their 88 mm guns and the Panthers with their high velocity 75 mm weapons their usual advantage of range. The Russian tanks swarmed all round the German vehicles, firing into their weaker flanks and rear in distances measured in tens rather than hundreds of yards. Orchards and cornfields were blackened with fire and the wrecks of tanks.

BALL OF FIRE

The experience of the Russian Captain Skripkin, commander of the 2nd Battalion, 181st Tank Brigade, is typical. 'With the order "Forward! Behind me!" the battalion commander headed his tank at the centre of the enemy's defence. With its first round the commander's tank penetrated the armour of one of the Tigers, then turning, set fire with three rounds to another enemy heavy tank. Several Tigers opened fire on Skripkin's tank similtaneously. One enemy shell punctured the side, another wounded the commander. The driver-mechanic and radio operator dragged him out of the tank and hid him in a shell

FATAL DELAY

The purpose of the German attack—to nip out the Kursk salient—was logical, but the execution was poor. If Hitler had not waited for newly designed tanks, his forces might have exploited the disruption caused by Manstein's 'mobile defence' around Kharkov at the beginning of the year, catching the Soviets before they consolidated their new positions. As it was, the delay, coupled with the activities of the 'Lucy' spy-ring, was fatal, enabling Stalin's forces to construct one of the most elaborate defensive systems of the war. When the panzers rolled forward on 5 July, they encountered a 'brick wall' of defences which denied any opportunity to find or exploit lines of least resistance.

▶ The battle of Kursk was fatal to German hopes.

TURNING POINT

Novosti Press Agency

Tass

hole. But one of the Tigers was heading straight for them. The driver-mechanic jumped back into his damaged and burning tank, started the engine and rushed headlong at the enemy. It was as if a ball of fire careered over the battlefield. The Tiger stopped, hesitated, began to turn away. But it was too late. At full speed the burning KV smashed into the German tank. The explosion shook the earth.'

The battle raged for eight hours and at the end of the day honours were about even. Both sides had lost about half their tanks but the power of the panzers had been so weakened

that further advance was impossible.

Moreover, even as the German drive on Prokhorovka was being halted, the Red Army began to probe the Orel salient, permanently halting any German offensive in the north.

On 15 July, Rokossovsky's Central Front struck at the Orel bulge. Orel was liberated on 5 August, and the Germans withdrew to the partly prepared Hagen Line position at the base of the salient.

Meanwhile, to the south of Kursk, the other half of the Red Army's counter-offensive was delayed by the need to reinforce and regroup the forces there. The Russians had also

suffered heavily during *Zitadelle*. Artillery units were taken from fronts further north, while tanks were salvaged from the battlefield and crewed by the lightly wounded.

The Soviet offensive jumped off on 3 August. Belgorod was liberated on the 5th, the same day as Orel. The attack tore a 40-mile (64 km) gap in Army Group South, between Fourth Panzer Army and Army Detachment Kempf. One infantry division divided the Red Army and the Dnieper 100 miles (160 km) to the west.

On 11 August the last battle of Kharkov began. Hitler gave another of his 'stand fast' orders, but on 20 August had to permit the evacuation of Kharkov. At dawn on 23 August the red flag was flying over the city centre. In Moscow, Stalin ordered 224 guns to fire a salute in honour of the victory. The invincible panzers had finally proved fallible.

▲▲ A German bails out of his burning vehicle. The 19th Panzer Division was down to 17 tanks when the attacks finally ended.

▲ Russian tank crewmen are welcomed by the women of a collective farm.

◄ Now it was German prisoners that headed towards the rear. The Red Army had firmly tipped the balance on the Eastern Front in its favour.

Novosti Press Agency

TARAWA

BATTLE DIARY

NOVEMBER 1943

12	First attack groups sail for Gilbert Islands (Operation 'Galvanic')
18–19	Makin and Tarawa 'softened-up' by carrier air strikes and naval bombardment

MAKIN (Butaritari)

20 NOVEMBER

06.10–06.30	Carrier air strike on western ('Red') beaches
06.40–08.30	Naval bombardment of Red beaches
08.32	Assault touch-down on Red beaches
10.00	Red beachhead secure. Progress inland halted
10.15	Destroyer bombardment of lagoon ('Yellow') beaches
10.40	Yellow beach landings commence
pm	Progress bogged down
21–22 NOVEMBER	Intermittent and confused progress

TARAWA (Betio)

20 NOVEMBER

05.10–05.42	Flagship *Maryland* in action against shore batteries
06.10	Dawn air strike arrives (scheduled for 05.45)
06.22–08.55	Area gunfire support from warships
09.13	Assault touch-down commences. Marines confined to beaches
11.54	'We need help. Situation bad'
13.30	'Issue in doubt'

21 NOVEMBER

06.15	Marine reserves arrive
16.00	'We are winning'
22 NOVEMBER	Marines forced back slowly
23 NOVEMBER	'Betio secured'

FEBRUARY 1944

1	Kwaljalein and Roi-Namur assaulted (Operation 'Flintlock')
2 (14.00)	'Roi-Namur secure'
4 (15.30)	'Kwajalein secure'
17	Eniwetok operations commence (Operation 'Catchpole')
22	'Eniwetok secure'

US Library of Congress

ATOLL WAR

Defending to the last man, the Japanese are determined to hold their forward bases, now threatened by a new Allied drive through the central Pacific.

▲▲ **Cap badge of Japanese Imperial Guard.**

▲ **The US Army uses small, flat-bottomed boats to ferry men and supplies in the south-west Pacific.**

By late 1943 the Allies in the Pacific had moved firmly on to the offensive, and the outer limits of Japanese conquest were beginning to be rolled back. Overall Allied strategy was in accordance with that agreed at the Casablanca Conference in the preceding January. Along with much else, this had determined that the war against Germany would have priority and – though an all-out offensive could thus not be mounted against Japan until the European War was satisfactorily concluded – pressure would be exerted in the Pacific theatre to keep Japan fully stretched to deter any further initiatives on her part and to wear her down by attrition.

Like the United Kingdom, Japan was a densely populated island nation with few indigenous natural resources. Having acquired a vast new oceanic empire, Japan had to supply a large number of distant garrisons as well as import the necessary materials to support both population and war effort. Merchant shipping was, therefore, of crucial importance, but she had staked all on a short war and had made virtually no provision for its safeguard.

While the weight of American submarine attacks alone would eventually have defeated Japan economically, the Casablanca Conference called for 'Unconditional Surrender'. Proposed by President Roosevelt and enthusiastically endorsed by Prime Minister Churchill, this policy required the Axis partners to suffer total military defeat and occupation. With military confrontation thus chosen by the Allies, it remained to establish the manner and the means.

The Japanese had conceded defeat on Guadalcanal in February 1943, after a bruising six-month campaign that restored American confidence while costing the enemy dearly in warships that could never be replaced.

In New Guinea the Australians had halted the Japanese juggernaut along the line of the Owen Stanley Range. Being unable to take the southern half of the island, the

TRH Pictures

▲ **Bougainville, largest of the Solomons chain, represented a valuable target due to its strategic harbours and airfields. After their landing in November 1943, US Marines defend their position near Torokina, firing a 75 mm pack Howitzer.**

enemy was deterred from extending himself further to the south-eastward despite his need to realise the strategic objective of severing the line of communication between the United States and Australasia. From this precarious equilibrium was to spring a decisive counter-offensive.

DUAL OBJECTIVES

It had been agreed by the Combined Chiefs of Staff that, besides safeguarding Allied lines of communication and maintaining an offensive on enemy shipping, operations would be conducted along a specific pair of axes that would ultimately threaten Japan itself. One of these was to be a parallel advance through New Guinea and the Solomons chain, with the short-term aim of neutralising the Japanese stronghold of Rabaul in New Britain before progressing to the more distant objective of retaking the Philippines. The other major axis was to be across the central Pacific via the Marshalls, the Carolines and the Marianas, menacing Formosa (present-day Taiwan).

An examination of the map shows immediately that the two campaigns would have to be markedly different in character. That starting in New Guinea involved jungle warfare along a chain of substantial islands separated by occasional stretches of water. The central Pacific, on the other hand, comprised thousands of miles of featureless ocean populated irregularly with atolls.

The area of an atoll was measured only in acres. If it was strategically important, the Japanese would have fortified it, garrisoned it and constructed an airfield for, in the Pacific, he who controlled the air controlled the war. Some islands could be by-passed – some had to be taken. Both American and Japanese knew this. There was little scope for surprise and none for manoeuvre. It required frontal attack — a job for the Marines.

PACIFIC SPLIT

As with any major undertaking, the choice of commanders was crucial to success and, in this respect, the Americans chose well. West of longitude 160 degrees East was the Southwest Pacific Area, the purlieu of the enigmatic General Douglas MacArthur. To the east of this meridian was the vast Pacific Ocean Area, the responsibility of Admiral Chester W Nimitz. It was unfortunate that the boundary intersected the Solomons and that, with little

Topham Picture Library

BATTLE DIARY

OPERATION 'GALVANIC'

NOVEMBER 1943
12 First attack groups sail for Gilbert Islands
18-19 Makin and Tarawa 'softened-up' by naval bombardment

MAKIN – 20 NOVEMBER
6.10-6.30 am Carrier airstrike on western ('Red') beaches
6.40-8.30 am Naval bombardment of Red beaches
8.32 am Marines assault Red beaches
10.00 am Red beachhead secure
10.15 am Destroyer bombardment of lagoon beaches
10.40 am Beach landings commence

23 1.00 pm 'Makin taken'

TARAWA – 20 NOVEMBER
5.10-5.42 am Flagship *Maryland* in action against shore batteries
6.10 am Dawn air strike
6.22-8.55 am Gunfire support from warships
9.13 am Assault touchdown commences
1.30 pm 'Issue in doubt'
21 6.15 am Marine reserves arrive
4 pm 'We are winning'
23 (pm) Betio secured

KWAJALEIN – FEB 1944
1 Operation 'Flintlock'
2 (pm) 'Roi-Namur secure'
4 (pm) 'Kwajalein secure'
17 Operation 'Catchpole'
22 'Eniwetok secure'

WarStories

Imperial War Museum

The US Marines enjoyed fostering a tough image – but it was often hard to keep up. Squashed in a torpedo room of a submarine under fire, on their way to Apemama, 70 marines were thrown about mercilessly as the sub went out of control at a depth of 250 feet. Feeling he should reassure them, the captain arrived. 'You haven't been worried, have you?' Sensing a dig at the marines' nerve, one replied, 'Not in the least. The only thing I've got to say is that this is one hell of a place to have to dig a foxhole.' Touché!

experience of combined operations to draw on, it was not easy to demarcate responsibilities clearly between Army and Navy.

MacArthur himself pushed strongly that his southern thrust should be given priority, on the logical grounds that it would more rapidly deprive the enemy of essential raw materials while allaying lingering Australian anxieties about an invasion of its soil.

The Navy argued that the complementary central Pacific route would prevent the enemy from mounting flank attacks while providing sufficient choices to oblige him to disperse his defending forces widely. A single, overall command was clearly desirable but the personalities involved were simply too powerful to be moved.

COMMAND CHANGES

A further key appointment was that of Vice-Admiral William F Halsey as commander South Pacific in place of the cautious Vice-Admiral Ghormley. Halsey was selected for his aggressiveness (which sometimes got the better of him) and his ability to enthuse the men that he led. His naval assets were termed the Third Fleet, as opposed to the Seventh Fleet under MacArthur.

One last, critically important, personnel change occurred when the Americans, able to decode much of the enemy's signal traffic, intercepted and shot down the aircraft carrying Admiral Isoruku Yamamoto, Commander-in-Chief of the Imperial Japanese Navy's Combined Fleet and architect of the Pearl Harbor attack, on his way to Bougainville on 18 April 1943. Though doubt has been cast since on whether Yamamoto was the genius first assumed, it is not disputed that his successor, Admiral Mineichi Koga, was of a lesser standing.

Observing the 'iron rule' of mounting assaults only within range of fighter cover, Halsey's Third Fleet Amphibious Force, under Rear-Admiral Theodore S

◄ A wartime recruiting poster for the US Marines. Many of the men who invaded Tarawa in November 1943 would have responded to this call in 1941; between the two dates, though, their uniforms and equipment changed quite dramatically.

▼ The main (16 in.) armament of the USS *Maryland* fires towards the island of Tarawa, 20 November 1943. Despite preliminary naval bombardment, Japanese defences survived.

PREPARING THE WAY

To a large extent, the American success in the Pacific depended on effective prebombardment.

Due to their small size, enemy targets suffered little from preliminary carrier air strikes, even though pinpointed by photo reconnaissance. Both landings were supported by battleship bombardment groups, covered by escort carriers.

Makin's garrison had little with which to resist, but Tarawa's guns drew heavy naval gunfire even before first light. The pall thus raised frustrated the planned dawn airstrike, which was ineffective and curtailed. Instead, naval bombardment was resumed and twice extended by 15 minutes due to ship-to-shore delays.

A final airstrike, aimed at covering the moment of touchdown, was 'out of sync' and ahead of Amtracs (amphibious tractors), allowing the defenders to regroup. The need to improve timing of forces was one of the greatest lessons of Tarawa.

TRH/US Navy

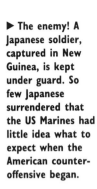

▶ The enemy! A Japanese soldier, captured in New Guinea, is kept under guard. So few Japanese surrendered that the US Marines had little idea what to expect when the American counter-offensive began.

▼ Japanese soldiers practise their signalling skills on Betio, early 1943. The US attack in November would turn the island into a scene of devastation.

Kyodo News Service

Australian Department of Information

Wilkinson, began its moves up the Solomons chain – Rendova in June 1943, New Georgia and Vella Lavella in August. The imporant airfield at Munda (on New Georgia) was taken but that on Vella Lavella was capable of being by-passed economically and an alternative constructed. November saw a landing on Bougainville, from which a hop could be made to the Green Islands, which offered an airfield only 115 miles (185 km) from the enemy's defensive nerve centre at Rabaul.

These advances in the Solomons had been paralleled by MacArthur's leap-frogging progress along New Guinea, from which the offshore diversion to take the Admiralty Islands effectively encircled and isolated Rabaul, which was finally reduced by airpower alone.

OPERATION GALVANIC

These operations fortunately demanded little specialist shipping of which Nimitz, in competition with operations in the Mediterranean, was assembling a vast quantity for his first move in the central Pacific. Operation 'Galvanic'

Supporting and protecting this amphibious force was the newly established Fifth Fleet, under Vice-Admiral Raymond A Spruance. This new-style armada had, as its cutting edge, four separate carrier groups. Able to muster some 700 aircraft between them, such groups could suppress any level of enemy air activity before any amphibious operation commenced. For close air support, escort carriers were, in addition, attached to the amphibious force.

The long, curving arc joining Hawaii and the central Marianas, which marked Nimitz's planned axis, left the Gilberts to the south, apparently a suitable candidate to be by-passed. Powerful garrisons, particularly if based on an airfield such as that on Tarawa, could still, however, pose the threat of flank attack if left to 'wither on the bough'.

TARGET TARAWA

Tarawa was also well within flying range of the Marshalls, Nimitz's first strategic objective. Ignored, it was a menace; taken, it could prove invaluable.

With the nearest US forward airbase 700 miles (1,125 km) distant at Funafuti in the neighbouring Ellice Islands, Tarawa broke the 'iron rule' of fighter support, and only the massive cover afforded by Spruance's carriers made the assault possible. Conspicuous among these were the Essex-class and Independence-class carriers, now in series production. The problems of integrating such enormous agglomerations of power into a force shaped to undertake a specific operation were among the most useful lessons of Tarawa.

General Tojo, the Japanese Prime Minister, was to say after the war that three major factors had caused his nation's defeat – 'leapfrog' strategy, fast carrier operations and the destruction of its merchant marine. In Operation 'Galvanic', these three weapons were all deployed. They were not to be sheathed until 'Unconditional Surrender' became a reality.

▲ Japanese engineers construct an airfield, with Mitsubishi G4M 'Betty' bombers in the background. Projection of airpower into the Pacific was a major concern to both sides.

was to be aimed at the Gilbert Islands and was geared to putting 35,000 personnel ashore within five days on the key islands of Makin, Tarawa and Abemama. It was the first attempt at such an operation and logistics were formidable. Tarawa was about 2,100 miles (3,375 km) from Pearl Harbor and 1,000 miles (1,600 km) from the forward base of Espiritu Santo in the New Hebrides. Over such distances the transport and sustaining of troops in slow beaching craft was out of the question so that, in a time of great shortage, 16 attack transports, four attack cargo ships and two of the new Landing Ships, Dock, had to be assembled.

FORTRESS TARAWA

Less than half a square mile in extent, and with no point more than about 300 yards from a beach, Tarawa's principal island, Betio, was heavily fortified by its Japanese defenders.

Fourteen coast-defence guns ranged in size from 5.5-inch (140 mm) to 8-inch (203 mm) weapons, captured at Singapore. Approaches to beaches were strewn with obstacles to restrict landing craft to lanes swept by 37 mm and 75 mm field pieces. Inshore from the beach ran a continuous coconut-log barricade, pierced for automatic weapons and rifles. Pillboxes, dug-in tanks and anti-aircraft batteries formed a mutually supportive network above a warren of protected bunkers housing personnel, command posts and ammunition dumps.

So sure were they of having created an impregnable fortress that the Japanese commander was noted as saying: 'the Americans cannot take Betio with a million men in a hundred years'. The events were to prove him wrong.

◀ Japanese defences on Tarawa were formidable, as this 'after the battle' shot of a large-scale cannon implies.

DEADLY LAGOON

After struggling ashore in treacherous waters, Tarawa's attackers face death on obstacle-strewn beaches.

Both Pictures: Topham Picture Library

Before the Marshall Islands could be recaptured, it was necessary to neutralise the Gilberts, lying on their flank. Operation 'Galvanic' was thus aimed at taking Tarawa Atoll (with an airfield), Makin Atoll (a seaplane base) and Abemama (suitable for an airfield).

As the first large-scale amphibious operation mounted at so long a range, it demanded an enormous planning effort. About 200 ships were assembled for the transport, support and escort of 27,600 assault troops, 7,600 garrison troops, 6,000 vehicles and 117,000 tons of cargo. Once the Gilberts were taken they were to be used as a springboard against the Marshalls.

During August 1943 the V Amphibious Force ('V Phib') was created in the Fifth Fleet organisation, under Rear-Admiral Richmond K ('Terrible') Turner. To stage two simultaneous assaults on Makin and Tarawa, V Phib was divided into the Northern Attack Force or TF52, and the Southern Attack Force, or TF53, respectively. Turner commanded TF52 as it was the nearer to any expected enemy riposte. Rear-Admiral Harry W Hill commanded TF53.

While all assault troops were under Major-General Holland M ('Howlin' Mad') Smith, USMC, direct control of the 2nd Marine Division, bound for Tarawa, was by Major-General Julian C Smith. The US Army's 165th Regimental Combat Team, slated for Makin, was commanded by Major-General Ralph C Smith.

▲ Grumman F6F Hellcat fighters, equipped with long-range fuel tanks under the fuselage, provide close air support to US forces going ashore on Makin Atoll.

◀ US Marines cross the log seawall on Betio under a hail of fire. Although this offered tempting protection, it was essential to go beyond to destroy the Japanese bunkers.

▶ How the forces – and casualties – compared, Tarawa, 20 November 1943.

BATTLE LINE-UP

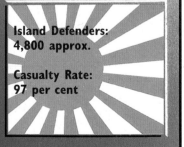

Attack Forces:
16,798 Marines

Casualty Rate:
17 per cent

Island Defenders:
4,800 approx.

Casualty Rate:
97 per cent

'HOWLIN' MAD' SMITH

Holland McTyeire Smith was born of strong Methodist stock in Russell County, Alabama. By 1943 he was a veteran of 61, short-fused and intolerant of sloppiness and ineptitude, which soon earned him the sobriquet of 'Howlin' Mad' Smith. Shortish and bespectacled, he had more the appearance of an irascible small-town schoolmaster than a Marine commander.

But his looks belied him. Devoted to the Corps, he converted the Navy's view of it from a minor defensive force to a fully capable offensive arm of the Fleet itself. Smith pioneered methods of heavy fire support and coordinated combat-loading of transports to deliver equipment in logical sequence, as used in the invasion of Makin and Tarawa so that the right goods became available as they were needed.

As commander of V Amphibious Corps, Smith was teamed in a prickly but effective relationship with Rear-Admiral Richmond ('Terrible') Turner.

Charged with making pre-emptive strikes against the objectives and all enemy airfields in range, before acting in general support to frustrate any counter-attack, was the Fifth Fleet's Fast Carrier Force (TF50). This included six large and five medium-sized carriers, operating in four independent Task Groups.

With Makin and Tarawa only 100 miles (160 km) apart, the two forces sighted each other on 19 November 1943 (D-Day minus one). At first light the following morning the two assaults were launched.

Makin's principal island, Butaritari, was garrisoned by only 800 personnel, many of whom were Korean construction workers. As the atoll was only 200 miles (320 km) from enemy airfields in the Marshalls, however, the Americans were anxious about prolonged exposure of their naval units. For this reason, nearly 6,500 assault troops were committed to guarantee a 24-hour victory.

ATTACK ON MAKIN

Typical of islands on the rim of a coral atoll, Butaritari was long and narrow. At the western end a four-mile (6 km) bar crossed this main axis to form an irregular 'T'. One side of the main axis faced the atoll's central lagoon, the other the sea. The whole island was covered in lofty coconut palms and mangroves.

The American plan was to make an initial assault at the junction of the 'T', then to land artillery at the most southerly point, capable of enfilading the main axis. Once the enemy responded by advancing from his prepared positions to repel the attack, a second assault would take him in the rear.

Following a 20-minute airstrike and a two-hour bombardment from a force including four battleships, the assault went in about 8.30 am. There was minimal opposition and, despite beach congestion, the beachhead was declared secure by 10 am and artillery installed by 12 noon.

Unfortunately, the troops were not combat-hardened (Major-General Holland M Smith, fuming aboard Turner's flagship *Pennsylvania*, described them as 'not too well officered', and 'lacking offensive spirit'). Even supported by tanks they were held up in their hundreds by handfuls of Japanese riflemen.

Neither was the enemy lured from his defensive positions, so that the second assault, in the late morning, was opposed by a hot fire. Far from taking the island in 24 hours, the troops were still bogged down the following day.

Increasingly concerned by reports coming in, Smith, in his best 'Howlin' Mad' tradition, stormed ashore to investigate personally this 'miserable, dilatory performance'. He was to spend one of his worst nights in the Pacific as nervous sentries fired at

▲ **Major-General Holland Smith – the brain behind most of the amphibious landing techniques used in the capture of the Gilberts.**

▼ **With bayonets fixed, US Marines on Red Beach 3 prepare to move towards the Burns Philip pier. The cover on the beach is limited.**

◄ **A US Marine guncrew man a pack howitzer at the height of the fighting for Tarawa Atoll.**

battle-hardened and determined.

American air reconnaissance had mapped the defence to the extent that the garrison's strength had been estimated to within 100 of the correct figure. This was achieved by counting the existing field latrines!

Betio was to be assaulted from the lagoon side on beaches extending from the 'stock' to the 'lock'. Landing was possible on a three-battalion front but necessitated a 6.5 mile passage for landing craft and Amtracs (amphibious tractors) from the transport area. The offshore reef was known to be 500 yards (457 m) wide and covered by very shallow water whose depth was governed by irregular tidal forces. As LCMs (Landing Craft, Mechanised) were thought to be unable to cross it, Amtracs were of vital importance, but

Popperfoto

▲ US Marines on the lookout for Japanese bunkers among shattered palm trees.

Topham

▲ US infantry wade towards their assault beach on Makin Atoll, which was taken after four days of battle.

every sound and 'drilled holes in the command post tent and clipped coconuts off the trees'.

Only at 1 pm on the 23rd, over 76 hours after the initial landing, was Major-General Ralph C Smith able to signal 'Makin taken'. 'Howlin' Mad' subsequently told Nimitz that 'had Ralph Smith been a Marine, I would have relieved him of his command on the spot'.

MUSKET ISLAND

One hundred miles away, at Tarawa Atoll, things were very different. The objective, the island of Betio, was even smaller than Butaritari and shaped, in the official historian's words, like an old-fashioned musket, with 'lock', 'stock' and 'barrel'. Only some 3,500 yards (3.2 km) in length, it was, at the broadest point (the 'lock') only 650 yards (595 m) wide. The 'stock' was criss-crossed by the airfield's runway and taxiways, but except for these areas, the island's natural palm cover had been left undisturbed. Beneath was a competently planned, solidly constructed, interlocking defensive system, manned by about 4,800 personnel, of whom the greater majority were

Topham

US Library of Congress; inset: Topham

▲ A US Marine rifleman poses beside the body of a Japanese defender of Tarawa, 23 November 1943. The bunker to the left gives an idea of the elaborate defences on the atoll.

only Holland M Smith's stern insistence overcame Turner's opposition to using them. Only 125 could be mustered, 60 per cent of which were already worn out.

A total of 18,600 Guadalcanal-tempered Marines were to be put ashore, a 4-to-1 advantage over the heavily entrenched defenders. For two days three of the Fifth Fleet carriers had been giving Betio a 'working over' and, though they inflicted only moderate damage, they obliged the enemy to consume much irreplaceable ammunition.

ASSAULT ON TARAWA

An hour before dawn on 20 November 1943 all minor craft were afloat and preparing for the 'off' when the enemy's big 8-inch guns, far from silenced by carrier attack, began to

lob shells into the transport area. The flagship, *Maryland,* engaged them for an hour with her 16-inch main battery, with two unfortunate results.

Her communications were badly shaken up by the shock of the salvoes, frustrating Admiral Hill's control of the operation to come. The shoot also raised a pall of dust and smoke, defeating the efforts of the planned dawn air strike which, in any case, arrived 25 minutes late. Bombardment was then resumed with the prodigious weight of 2,400 tons of ammunition being expended, at ranges from 15,000 down to only 2,000 yards (13.5 to 1.8 km).

The plan called for over 90 Amtracs to beach between H-Hour and H plus 6 minutes. A long haul, combined with a chop and offshore tidal streams, badly delayed them, however, so that

the landing was postponed from 8.30 am to 8.45 am, then to 9.00 am, finally commencing only at 9.13 am. By then Hill had ceased bombardment for nearly half an hour as there was a real risk of hitting friendly forces in the pall that had been raised. A final strafing by Hellcats was totally mistimed in the confused sequence so that the enemy had 20 undisturbed minutes to collect his wits and reorganise. It was to cost the attackers dear.

DEADLY WATERS

Carrying 20 to 25 Marines apiece, the Amtracs crawled and bounced over the reef, suffering heavily through fire from Japanese strong-points at the western end. Once ashore, they were confined to the beach by a continuous coconut-log

barrier, which was resolutely defended.

None of the follow-up LCVPs (Landing Craft, Vehicle and Personnel) or LCMs meanwhile, was able to cross the reef. Tanks lumbered slowly across the waist-deep water, and marines had to wade up to 700 yards (640 m) through a torrent of fire. Many wounded fell and drowned, unable to rise under the burden of

▲ The aftermath of battle, Red Beach 3, Betio, showing the exposed nature of the US landing area and the devastation caused. On the right, a derelict Amtrac.

▲ ▶ The American flag – 'Old Glory' – flies from a shell-shattered palm on Makin, 20 November 1943. The devastation here is not as widespread as at Tarawa.

LESSONS OF TARAWA

TURNING POINT

As the first strongly opposed landing by the US forces, Tarawa had shortcomings. The preliminary naval bombardment was insufficient, expending 'only' 2,400 tons of shells. It lifted too early and was ill-synchronised with the final airstrike, allowing the defenders to regroup. Enemy defences were proof against fighter strafing with 50-calibre guns. No attempt was made to clear offshore obstacles, so that landing zones were restricted. Radio communications were poor, logistic follow-up inadequate and an over-large contingent of journalists was able to report first-hand on the more sensational aspects of the operation.

▶ An aerial photograph of Betio (Tarawa) gives a clear indication of the ferocity of the fighting.

▲ A B-25 Mitchell bomber makes a low-level pass over a Japanese position in the Marshalls.

▼ US Marines on Roi island watch a pillar of smoke rise from neighbouring Namur, February 1944.

their packs.

With rifles and grenades having little impact on the tenacious defenders, the Marines ashore used flamethrowers and blocks of TNT to scratch a precarious toehold. By 10.00 am the reef was littered with wrecked LVTs and LCMs, many loaded with equipment but crewed by only the dead and the dying, still lashed by remorseless fire. With the close nature of the combat,

bombardment was virtually impossible and air support difficult.

'ISSUE IN DOUBT'

Offshore, in the *Maryland*, Major-General Julian Smith was receiving increasingly alarming messages. At 10.30 am he committed the Regimental reserve, followed almost immediately by half the Divisional reserve, all of which suffered in turn crossing the offshore shallows. By

1.30 pm, Holland M Smith, still off Makin, took the signal 'Issue in doubt' and with the battle still only hours old, had to authorise use of the Corps reserve, the last available.

Of the 5,000 Marines on Betio at the close of this desperate day, a third were estimated to be dead or wounded. The remainder controlled two minuscule bridgeheads, one of about 700 x 300 yards (640 x 275 m) near the 'lock', the other of only one third this area on the 'stock'. It was fortunate that events had also disorganised and fragmented the Japanese, for a determined counter-attack would have succeeded. Nonetheless, they infiltrated snipers and light machine guns to take a deadly toll of reserves arriving at first light on D plus one.

To destroy the Japanese command post, the Marines used bulldozers to earth-up every door and embrasure, poured petrol down the ventilators and incinerated its 300 occupants.

By the close of the second day the airfield and western end of Betio were

two airfields and Eniwetok, which acted as a staging post from the Marianas.

Following the attrition of its carrier air groups in the defence of New Guinea, Admiral Koga's Combined Fleet dared not seek action to challenge the Allied operation. New and improved Amtracs were provided on three times the Tarawa scale. European experience was tapped in the conversion of landing craft for shallow-draught fire-support, while close-support aircraft were converted for rocket firing for the first time.

The initial targets were Kwajalein and Roi-Namur, with a combined garrison of about 9,000. Against this were ranged about 54,000 assault troops, including a floating reserve which, if not committed, would proceed to take Eniwetok.

Already surprised by the Americans' choice of target, the Japanese were then subjected to a deluge of 6,000 tons of explosive, complemented by Marine artillery landed by night on neighbouring islands. On 1 February 1944 the assault went in, to find the defenders still 'punch-drunk', and secured Roi-Namur in just over 26 hours.

Kwajalein took until 4 February, following a defence so desperate that one tank recorded having been attacked by five Japanese officers armed only with swords – only 265 of the enemy garrison survived.

The uncommitted reserve went on to assault Eniwetok Atoll on 17 February 1944. Despite poor cooperation between Army and Marine units, victory was achieved in five days and the way to the Carolines and Marianas was open.

▼ **The charred bodies of Japanese defenders are found in their foxhole on Engebi Island, Eniwetok. In the background are Alligator Amtracs.**

under Marine control with the remaining Japanese confined to the 'barrel' and under heavy fire from destroyers. On 23 November, following 76 hours of carnage, resistance ended. Just 17 Japanese defenders survived out of nearly 5,000.

With Makin also secure, Holland M Smith finally made Tarawa. 'Over the pitted, blasted island hung a miasma of coral dust and death, nauseating and horrifying'. Seeing that over 1,000 of his beloved Marines were dead, their commander was deeply affected, and was adamant – Tarawa was a mistake.

He was wrong, though understandably so. It was the first painful point on a necessary learning curve. Just ten weeks later the Marshalls operations triumphantly applied the experience gained.

NEW MOVES

Admiral Turner, to avoid the chance of their being fortified to the standard of Betio, decided to move directly against Kwajalein and Eniwetok, which meant boldly bypassing the Eastern Marshalls. For days before the planned operations ('Flintlock' and 'Catchpole'), an enhanced Fifth Fleet carrier force (TF58) deployed 750 aircraft to neutralise Kwajalein's

▲ **US Marines shelter from enemy fire while a Grumman F6F Hellcat swoops down to strafe Japanese positions on Eniwetok, February 1944.**

▼ **Victory's human cost: US Marines, caught in the sweep of enemy fire, lie dead on the beach on Parry Island, Eniwetok Atoll.**

CASSINO

BATTLE DIARY

OCTOBER 1943
1	US Fifth Army takes Naples
3	Germans retake Kos
12–15	Fifth Army forces Volturno crossings

NOVEMBER
8–30	Eighth Army crosses River Sangro but unable to make more headway
12–16	Germans retake Leros
20	British evacuate Samos

DECEMBER
2–6	Fifth Army takes Monte Camino
10	Eighth Army crosses River Moro
17	Fifth Army takes Monte Sammucro and San Pietro

JANUARY 1944
12–1	French Expeditionary Corps crosses River Rapido
17–19	X Corps attacks across River Garigliano and takes Minturno
20	II Corps starts first assault on Cassino over River Rapido
22	Anzio landings begin
30	First Anzio breakout attempt

FEBRUARY
2	Anzio attacks called off
7–11	Battle of the 'Factory' at Aprilia
13	Alexander calls off Cassino assault
15	Allied bombing of Benedictine Abbey
16–19	German counter-attack at Anzio repulsed with difficulty

MARCH
15	Allies bomb town of Cassino
15–22	Most of Cassino falls to New Zealanders and Indians

MAY
11–14	French outflank Cassino in south
17	Poles outflank Cassino in north. Kesselring orders retreat
23	Beginning of final Anzio breakout assault

JUNE
2	Germans abandon Rome
4	Allies enter Rome

DEADLOCK AT CASSINO

Süddeutscher Verlag

Having struggled across rivers and flooded valleys, the Allied armies have come to a halt at the formidable German mountain defences around Cassino.

▲▲ **Shoulder flash of US Fifth Army personnel.**

▲ **German paratroopers enjoy a panoramic view from their positions in the hills around Cassino. Any approaching forces are at a major disadvantage.**

O verlooked by the cone of Mount Vesuvius, the ancient port of Naples finally fell to Lieutenant-General Mark Clark's US Fifth Army on 1 October 1943 following a fierce battle during which the city's Italian population had risen in arms against the Germans and suffered heavy casualties. After finally and narrowly breaking out of the Salerno beachhead, the Allied advance up the west coast of Italy had been seriously hindered by a dogged German resistance which had succeeded in its objective of delaying the forward movement so that Field Marshal Albert Kesselring could organise his defences to the north.

The most important feature of these was the Gustav Line which ran across the narrow waist of Italy from near Minturno on the coast of the Tyrrhenian Sea to San

Imperial War Museum

astride Highway 6, dominated by the historic Benedictine monastery atop the 1,693-foot (516 m) massif of Monte Cassino itself. Known as Monastery Hill to the Allies, this was the main obstacle, and it was to delay their advance up through the supposed 'soft underbelly' of Europe by several months. Even before they reached Cassino, though, Mark Clark's troops had other obstacles to overcome.

The first of these was the River Volturno, behind which lay the so-called Barbara and Bernhard Lines. Each of these was a temporary obstacle, not properly fortified or defended in depth but designed as before to delay the Allied advance until preparations in the Gustav Line itself were complete. Behind that, and at the time under command of Field Marshal Erwin Rommel, lay what the Germans called the Green Line, better known as the Gothic Line. This was the 'final frontier', the line

Vito on the Adriatic. Hitler had ordered that the Line should 'mark the end of withdrawals' and Kesselring, generally rated among the top two or three of the *Führer's* generals, was determined to comply if he could.

The Gustav Line utilised the natural defensive features of the rivers Garigliano and Rapido across the coastal plain south-east of Rome, and the river Sangro in the north, opposite General Sir Bernard Montgomery's Eighth Army which was pushing forward from Taranto. The mountainous central spine of Italy rising to over 6,000 feet (1,800 m) was an impossible humpbacked ridge over which to advance, so the Allies were channelled on to the relatively flat coastal zones despite the transverse river lines which would have to be forced. In deteriorating weather which hindered aerial support they slogged onward, fêted one moment by Italian villagers and sniped at the next by German rifles firing from cleverly concealed positions on adjacent hillsides.

▲**Heavy rain added to the difficulties of the Allies' advance: a British Quad artillery tractor, towing a 25 pounder, falls foul of the mud.**

OBSTACLE PATH

If the Gustav Line was the key to halting the Allies' northward advance, the key to the defence of Rome was the little town of Cassino lying on the River Rapido

▼**Major-General Keightley (right), commander of the British 78th ('Battleaxe') Division, confers with Lieutenant-Colonel Hodgson of the Welsh Guards, Cassino, May 1944.**

BATTLE DIARY

OCTOBER 1943
1 US Fifth Army takes Naples
3 Germans retake Kos
12-15 Fifth Army crosses Volturno

NOVEMBER
8-30 Eighth Army crosses River Sangro
12-16 Germans retake Leros
20 British evacuate Samos

DECEMBER
2-6 Fifth Army takes Monte Camino
10 Eighth Army crosses River Moro
17 Fifth army takes Monte Sammucro and San Pietro

JANUARY 1944
12-14 French Expeditionary Corps crosses Rapido
19 X Corps takes Minturno

20 First assault on Cassino
22 Anzio landings begin
30 First Anzio breakout attempt

FEBRUARY
2 Anzio attacks called off
7-11 Battle for 'The Factory', Anzio
15 Allied bombing of monastery

MARCH
15 Bombing of Cassino town

MAY
11-14 French outflank Cassino in south
17 Poles outflank Cassino in north – Kesselring orders retreat
23 Beginning of final Anzio breakout

JUNE
2 Germans abandon Rome
4 Allies enter Rome

Imperial War Museum

Bundesarchiv-Koblenz

beyond which the Allies could not be allowed to pass if the whole of Italy, the Balkans, the Rumanian oilfields and the south of France were not to fall, but on 21 November Rommel was sent to France to oversee the Channel coast defences instead and Kesselring became C-in-C South-West in overall command in Italy. This really put the pressure on him to ensure that the Gustav Line should not fall.

By this time Clark had forced a crossing of the Volturno and broken through the Barbara Line, but his forces had failed to inflict serious damage on the German defenders who used every fold in the rugged ground to lay ambushes and had to be prised out inch by inch. The river was crossed on 13 October despite heavy rain which had swollen it in places to three times its normal five foot (1.5 m) depth but then the advance became hopelessly bogged down. It was not until 5 November that Lieutenant-General Richard McCreery's British X Corps reached Monte Camino, a 3,000-foot (914 m) pinnacle overlooking the River Garigliano and the

entrance to the Liri Valley. Here, and in the surrounding hills, the Germans had laid extensive minefields and set booby traps as well as blasting artillery, mortar and machine-gun positions out of the solid rock.

After several days' savage fighting in the enervating cold and wet, Clark told General Sir Harold Alexander, commander of the Allied ground forces in Italy, that his troops had to be given a rest before trying again. Major-General John P. Lucas' US VI Corps had encountered similar difficulties advancing up the northern bank of the Volturno and his men were just as exhausted as McCreery's, so Alexander agreed. From the middle of November to the beginning of December an uneasy lull thus fell over the battlefield while reinforcements were fed into the line.

NEW ARRIVALS

The new arrivals were Major-General Geoffrey Keyes' US II Corps and General Alphonse Juin's tough Algerian and Moroccan divisions in the French Expeditionary Corps, and it was they who would largely bear the brunt of the fighting over the next couple of months. By this time, though, it was fairly obvious that breaking through the Gustav Line frontally was going to be extremely costly in terms of both time and lives and that there was no chance of reaching Rome by Christmas, so planning began for a new amphibious operation behind the German positions. If this was to be successful, however, pressure had to be kept on the Gustav Line to pin the defenders and prevent Kesselring from transferring troops to contain the beachhead. Unfortunately, Kesselring had already anticipated such an outflanking manoeuvre and had retained reserves near Rome to meet it.

On 2 December the British 56th Division, which had already been badly mauled during the earlier fighting for Monte Camino, launched a new attack and reached the summit under cover of darkness, but it took another four

Imperial War Museum

▲ Founded in 529 by St Benedict, Cassino Monastery had been a focal point of Catholic worship for centuries.

▼ Accompanied by an escort of German officers, 80-year-old Abbot Diamare is led to safety.

days to secure the position completely . At the same time the US II Corps attacked Monte la Difensa – which VI Corps had failed to take despite a ten-day battle at the beginning of November – and Monte Maggiore, while VI Corps now went in around the flank to take Monte Lungo and Monte Sammucro, the last natural obstacles before Cassino itself. An Italian brigade (Italy had declared war on Germany on 13 October) was also badly mauled attacking the tiny village of San Pietro on the 7th and the position did not fall to Lucas' troops until the 17th when the Germans, threatened with encirclement from Monte Lungo, voluntarily withdrew. The weary Allied soldiers stumbled forward the next half dozen miles in a sudden vacuum, and by the end of the year were poised behind the southern bank of the Rapido facing Cassino and the entrance to the Liri valley.

January 1944 was marked by largely abortive attempts to outflank the Cassino position by X Corps on the left and II Corps plus the French Expeditionary Corps on the right while VI Corps was withdrawn from the line to prepare for the amphibious landings around Anzio and Nettuno, a mere 30 miles (48 km) from Rome. The

Bundesarchiv-Koblenz

War Stories

These days, young people are far too ready to write off the elderly as useless – a case in point was Admiral Sir W H Cowan, KCB, MVO. In active service off the coast of Italy, he was Commando Liaison Officer on a reconnaissance raid on the mainland, when he happened upon and rescued a wounded Colonel, risking his life under heavy fire as he did so. For this feat of bravery he was awarded a bar to his existing DSO. The only extraordinary thing was his age – the Admiral was 73.

Imperial War Museum

Popperfoto

▲ **An Allied tank, silhouetted against the dusk, tows a supply truck ashore at Anzio, January 1944. The ease with which the Allied forces carved out a beachhead was not exploited.**

▼**US soldiers inspect a rather crude German human torpedo, captured at Anzio: a torpedo (left), strapped to a detachable driving section, which its on-board pilot cast off after aiming.**

mountain-trained Moroccan and Algerian troops made good headway across the rivers Rapido and Secco and were fighting in the mountains north of Cassino by the time of the Anzio landings on the 22nd, while on the coast the British 5th Division had crossed the Garigliano and captured Minturno. To their right the British 56th Division also got across the river and started heading towards Ausonia, but then Kesselring took the 1st Parachute Division out of reserve and threw its weight behind a counterattack by the 29th Panzergrenadier Division. This stabilised the German right flank but, although McCreery's X Corps was now firmly across the Garigliano on a line stretching from Monte Juga to Monte Natale, in the centre Keyes' II Corps had suffered disaster. The Texan 36th Division tried to force a crossing of the Rapido opposite Sant' Angelo during the night of the 20th but was pinned down by murderous crossfire, many of its boats being holed and others not getting halfway across the river. A pathetically small force established a toehold on the far bank but that was all, and by the 22nd the last 40 or so survivors had been forced to swim back to safety. The proud 36th Division had practically ceased to exist.

Meanwhile, Lucas' VI Corps had stormed ashore on beaches either side of Anzio and Nettuno. General Lucas had not been enthusiastic about the operation from the beginning, remembering the carnage of Salerno, and was astonished to encounter no German resistance. By the end of the day 36,000 men from the British 1st and US 3rd Divisions, accompanied by Commandos and Rangers, had been landed with only 13 casualties from accidents. But Lucas feared a trap and instead of pushing aggressively forward proceeded to consolidate and only slowly expand his beachhead until he considered he had enough manpower and supplies. This inaction gave Kesselring ample time to bring up reserves to cordon off VI Corps and led Prime Minister Winston Churchill to lament that instead of 'hurling a wildcat ashore, all we got was a stranded whale'. The bold plan to cut Kesselring's line of communication between Rome and Cassino and break the stalemate on the Gustav Line had failed.

STRANDED WHALE

It was not until the 30th that Lucas began moving, sending the Rangers ahead of the 3rd Division towards Cisterna and the 1st Division towards Campoleone and Carroceto. For the Rangers it was a disaster. Caught in a crossfire from the guns and tanks of the crack '*Hermann Göring*' Division, the battalion was decimated and only six out of 767 men escaped death or capture.

German counter-attacks over the following few days were concentrated around one of Mussolini's farming communes, Aprilia, which was nicknamed 'The Factory' because of its appearance. On 7 February they launched a concerted assault in the icy rain and two days later the Factory was back in their hands. The British 1st Division made two attempts to retake it on the 11th and 12th but they had suffered such heavy casualties that they were unable to and by the 13th the Allies were back within the original perimeter from which they had sallied forth so confidently a fortnight earlier. The situation was so

Imperial War Museum

◀ A US Army bulldozer clears some of the rubble from the shattered port of Anzio, February 1944. Bombardment of built-up areas always created the problem of subsequent movement.

the Germans were using it as an artillery observation post. In fact they were not, having said all along that they would preserve the ancient abbey's sanctity, but Freyberg persisted and on the 15 February the air strike went in – 229 Allied bombers dropping 600 tons of high explosive. The decision to bomb had not been taken lightly, and there had been urgent discussions in London and Washington before the bombers were despatched. As it turned out, results of the bombing were exactly the opposite to what Freyberg had anticipated, because the Germans did now move into the ruins of the Abbey, the rubble covering cavernous cellars which made it a veritable fortress.

Imperial War Museum

▲ The Allied decision to bomb Monte Cassino was not to their advantage: the rubble provided ample protection for German gunners.

grave that people began talking about a second Dunkirk.

At Cassino, on the night of 5/6 February a regiment of the 34th Division captured Mount Calvary, overlooking the monastery. But Kesselring was pouring reinforcements into the battlefield, including the veteran 1st Parachute Division, who recaptured the peak on the 10th. This marked the whole style of the second battle for Cassino.

Now Fifth Army itself began receiving reinforcements to relieve the exhausted men of II and X Corps. Three fresh divisions – 2nd New Zealand, 4th Indian and 78th British – arrived under the command of Lieutenant-General Bernard Freyberg. And it was Freyberg who insisted that the monastery should be bombed because

Over the 16th and 17th the British, Indians and New Zealanders made several attempts to seize the monastery but they were uncoordinated and all failed. On the 18th General Alexander called a halt to operations. There was also a lull at Anzio, where a determined German attempt to drive the invaders back into the sea had been finally checked by naval and aerial bombardment on the 19th. It was time for both sides to pause and rethink.

AEGEAN DISASTER

The Dodecanese islands, flanked on three sides by Turkey, Greece and Crete, had a strange magnetic attraction for Winston Churchill, who regarded them as a stepping stone to the reconquest of the Balkans. His opinion was not shared by the Americans who regarded any operations here as a risky sideshow – rightly as it turned out. Nevertheless, on 14 September 1943, following the Italian capitulation, men of the elite Special Boat Squadron landed on the island of Kos and used the 5,000 Italian troops on

the island to reinforce its defences. On 3 October the Germans counterattacked with a combined arms force including men of the Brandenburger Regiment – a special commando unit – who kicked the British out and forced the Italians to surrender. It was a similar story on Leros, the second objective on the path to the principal island of Rhodes. Here, the Germans made a parachute drop which came as a surprise to the British who had considered such an operation impossible. A third island, Samos, was abandoned two days later. Although total disaster for Churchill, the Dodecanese campaign was at least the last German victory in the Mediterranean.

Popperfoto

◀ The island of Leros, seen from a German ship, during an attack by Stuka dive bombers.

DEFIANT MONASTERY

Reduced to a pile of rubble by heavy bombing and constant shelling, the ancient monastery still guards the road to Rome.

Imperial War Museum

At eight o'clock on the morning of 15 March 1944 the skies over Cassino reverberated once more to the roar of hundreds of aircraft engines. A mighty fleet of bombers and fighters thundered overhead to drop 1,250 tons of bombs on the already battered town. A war correspondent watching from safety three miles (5 km) away, described the towering pillars of smoke and dust as like 'some dark forest of evil fantasy'. Inside the town the men of the German 3rd Parachute Regiment cowered in their cellars, clinging together 'as if we were one lump of flesh'. Over half of their 2nd Battalion were killed, wounded or buried alive. Then, as the last aircraft departed shortly after midday the artillery opened up, 748 guns pouring shell after shell in a creeping barrage into the town and the monastery. The third battle for Cassino was underway.

General Freyberg had been frustrated by delays in making his assault, codenamed Operation Dickens, because a prerequisite was three days of fine weather to dry out the ground, but for three weeks the weather had refused to cooperate.

Now, at last, he could move. The basic plan was a two-pronged attack from the north, with the 2nd New Zealand Division taking the town of Cassino and Point 193 – Castle Hill – while the 4th Indian Division moved in on their right to take Point 435 – Hangman's Hill – and assault Monastery Hill itself.

MOON CRATERS

As the bombardment ceased, the New Zealanders moved cautiously forward, tanks and infantry side by side. The landscape was cratered like the surface of the moon and dust lay thick in the air, clogging the men's

◀ The aftermath of the Allied bombing – the battered ruins of Castle Hill.

▼ A British 4.2 inch mortar, surrounded by all the trappings of battle, lays down support fire for infantry advancing on Cassino.

Bundesarchiv-Koblenz

noses and throats. Mines and booby traps were a constant hazard, because far from all of them had been set off by the barrage. Moreover, to their surprise, the tough German paras still had plenty of fight in them and emerged from their cellars to contest stubbornly every pile of rubble which had once been a house.

Nevertheless, to begin with the attack seemed to go well, but this was cruelly deceptive because the commander, Major-General Richard Heidrich, had no intention of surrendering his positions. Being on the spot, he was able to direct accurate

▲ A well-armed German paratrooper takes up a defensive position in Cassino, using his 7.92 mm assault gun.

▼ Italian civilians, caught in the trauma of war, wade through the rubble of Cassino town. By the end of the battle, little remained.

BATTLE LOSSES

ALLIED
40,000 approx.

GERMAN
25,000 approx.

US National Archives

Süddeutscher Verlag

Ullstein Bilderdienst

Süddeutscher Verlag

mortar and artillery fire against the New Zealanders, whose supporting tanks were unable to push through the ruins and deep holes in the ground. Nevertheless, by nightfall most of the town was in their hands and Castle Hill had been taken after a fierce firefight.

During the night Gurkhas of the 5th Indian Brigade scaled the rocky heights of Hangman's Hill but were unable to advance any further towards the monastery itself. Victory hung in the balance but the battle-hardened German paras would not give up, having made a veritable fortress of the remains of the Excelsior Hotel which commanded the centre of the town. The 16th March was totally indecisive and, although the New Zealanders managed to capture the railway station on the 17th, a vigorous German counterattack during the night of the 18th/19th almost succeeded in recapturing Castle Hill, leaving the Gurkhas cut off from the rest of the 5th Brigade.

ATTACK HALTED

On the 19th Freyberg sent a company of light tanks by a circuitous route along a road which sappers had laboriously hacked out of the mountainside to attack the monastery from the rear. This created a certain amount of panic among the Germans, who had not expected an armoured

Imperial War Museum

assault over such unsuitable terrain, but they rallied quickly and all 14 tanks were destroyed by fire from the notorious 88 mm guns or by mines. This fiasco marked the real end of the third battle for Cassino but it was not until the 23rd that Alexander called a halt to further offensive operations.

There was a stalemate, too, at Anzio where German reinforcements, including the crack 16th SS Panzergrenadier Division *Reichsführer-SS* had tightened their stranglehold on the beachhead. Even though Lucas had been replaced by the far more aggressive Major-General Lucian Truscott at the end of February, the Allied troops were unable to make any further headway. Both sides dug in and waited at Anzio and Cassino. Kesselring knew that all he had to do was hold on. He fully expected another amphibious landing, north of Rome this time, but of course unknown to him this was impossible because most of the Allied landing craft had been sent back to England in preparation for Operation Overlord — the landings in Normandy planned for the summer.

The next couple of months saw relative inactivity except in the air, where Allied bombers and fighters attacked road and rail targets in northern Italy to disrupt German communications and supplies. The

▲German troops shelter in the ruins of a house in Cassino town, their heavy *Sturmgeschütz* at the ready.

▶ Waiting for the Allies to move, German paratroopers occupy good, mutually supportive fire positions in Cassino town.

▼A Sherman tank noses forward as infantry prepare to advance in streets full of rubble.

Imperial War Museum

Germans in their turn plastered the Anzio position with the 280 mm K5 (E) railway gun 'Leopold' which they concealed inside a tunnel in the Alban Hills. (The Allies nicknamed it 'Anzio Annie' and it now resides in an American museum.) The Germans also made great use of propaganda leaflets showing wives at home with other men and describing the beachhead as a 'death's head'. This crude form of wartime propaganda is usually ineffectual, but many Allied soldiers at Anzio felt they had been more or less abandoned to their fate and morale suffered accordingly.

During April both sides poured reinforcements into position for what each knew would be the decisive struggle for the Gustav Line. The bulk of Eighth Army — now commanded by Lieutenant-General Sir Oliver Leese since Montgomery was back in England for Overlord — was transferred to the Cassino front, just leaving a couple of divisions behind to hold the line on the Adriatic coast. These forces included Major-

General E M Burns' Canadian I Corps, Lieutenant-General Wladislaw Anders' Polish II Corps and Lieutenant-General Sidney Kirkman's British XIII Corps, with Lieutenant-General Sir Richard McCreery's X Corps held in reserve to tie the Germans down. These were welcome reinforcements for Major-General Geoffrey Keyes' US II Corps and General Alphonse Juin's French Ex-peditionary Corps. And it was to Eighth Army that what was supposed to be the final battle for Cassino was entrusted.

PHASE FOUR

On the other side, General Heinrich von Vietinghoff-Scheel's Tenth Army now comprised Lieutenant-General Fridolin von Senger und Etterlin's XIV Panzer Korps and General Valentin Feuerstein's LI Mountain Corps, with Heidrich's 1st Parachute

HERO OF CASSINO

The stubborn and blunt mannered Major-General Richard Heidrich was a hero even before his most famous battle at Cassino. Born in 1896, he served in the small German interwar army after World War I. By 1936 he had become a leading figure in the development of the Third Reich's parachute arm.

After serving in Russia he was promoted from Colonel to Major-General and given command of the 1st Parachute Division in Italy in 1943. With even more medals for his epic defence of Cassino and promoted to Lieutenant-General, he served on the Italian front for the remainder of the war.

Richard Heidrich died in December 1947 at the age of 51, completely worn down by six years of almost continual fighting.

▶ **Major-General Richard Heidrich, the 'defender of Cassino', decides on his next move.**

Süddeutscher Verlag

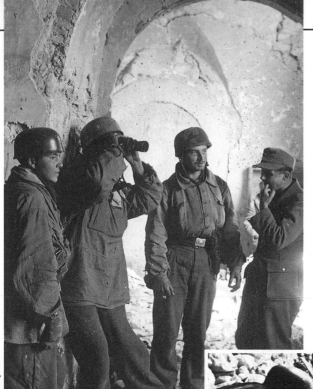

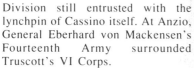
Bundesarchiv-Koblenz/Bruce Quarrie

by surprise. Needless to say, his two subordinates were flown back by the first available plane.

Forty minutes after it had begun the barrage ceased. The men of Kirkman's XIII Corps surged across the River Rapido south of Cassino even though many of their assault boats capsized, throwing their heavily laden occupants into the swollen, swift-flowing water. They rapidly established a bridgehead among the minefields, trenches and barbed wire on the far bank but Anders' Poles on their right to the north of Cassino were less lucky. Hammered by intense

◀ ▼An advantage of holding the high ground is that you can observe enemy preparations for attack, as these German paratroopers have discovered.

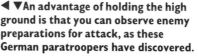
Imperial War Museum

Division still entrusted with the lynchpin of Cassino itself. At Anzio, General Eberhard von Mackensen's Fourteenth Army surrounded Truscott's VI Corps.

The long-awaited battle opened at 11 pm on 11 May with a massive bombardment by over 1,600 artillery pieces along the whole Garigliano-Rapido line. By chance, both Vietinghoff and von Senger und Etterlin were on leave in Germany and Kesselring was taken completely

Imperial War Museum

Bundesarchiv-Koblenz/Bruce Quarrie

PASSAGE TO SAFETY

Lieutenant-Colonel Julius Schlegel was a Viennese officer in the elite *Hermann Göring* Division in 1943. He was also a dedicated art lover and, as the Allies approached Cassino, became increasingly concerned at the damage the monastery treasures might suffer if the building became a battlefield. In October he persuaded the Archabbot, Dom Grigorio Diamare, to allow his men to transport the priceless paintings, manuscripts and sculptures to safety in the Vatican. The Benedictine monks held a special Mass for Schlegel and presented him with an illuminated scroll as a sign of their gratitude.

Unfortunately, the myth that the Germans had looted the monastery persisted after the war and it took no less than General Alexander's direct intervention to release Schlegel from prison.

◀ Some of the abbey's art treasures which survived.

◀ **British infantrymen, their bayonets fixed, make use of every available piece of cover as they advance through Cassino town.**

▲ **At the cost of many casualties in the face of heavy German fire, the Polish troops were crucial in the fight for the monastery.**

German fire as well as slowed down by the steep and rocky mountain slopes covered with thorny bushes, they were unable to make much headway. After suffering nearly 20 per cent losses, they were pulled back 12 hours later to recover.

Despite XIII Corps' initial success, though, their engineers only managed to build two bridges across the river on the first day and a third on the 13th, and it was General Juin's tough, mountain-trained Moroccans and Algerians who won the real laurels in the final analysis. Storming across the Garigliano on the left flank of XIII Corps, by the time their English partners had completed their third

▼ **In the mountains around Cassino, Polish infantrymen throw hand grenades into a German foxhole.**

bridge, the Frenchmen had driven von Senger und Etterlin's 71st Infantry Division back nearly five miles (8 km), causing very heavy German casualties.

By the 16th Kesselring realised that he had no option but to withdraw northwards to the so-called Adolf Hitler Line. Knowing that the Allies would not be held here either, the Field Marshal adroitly changed the name on the maps to the 'Dora' Line so that defeat would not incur quite so much of the *Führer's* wrath!

To begin with, however, Kesselring tried to hang on to Monte Cassino itself and it was not until the unquenchable Poles attacked again on the night of the 16th/17th, threatening to outflank the position from the north, that he ordered Heidrich's valiant but exhausted

paratroopers to evacuate the position. The Polish assault was crucial to the final outcome of the battle. The earlier defeat rankled, and despite their losses, they had kept Heidrich's men bloodshot-eyed from lack of sleep by sending patrols into their positions every night since the 12th, following up with artillery barrages. On this last night they were even more imaginative.

POLISH VICTORY

A patrol succeeded in taking out several of Heidrich's paratroopers' advance posts around Hill 593, overlooking the road along which the tanks had been earlier decimated. Anders swiftly fed a whole battalion into the position. The German paras counterattacked with fury but were unable to dislodge the Poles who, like the French, had a particularly personal reason for wanting to win.

Imperial War Museum

▶ As the heavy fighting takes its toll, Polish soldiers bring down dead comrades from Monte Cassino.

John Watney Photo Library/Interpress

The battle was fought at close range throughout the 17th with bayonet, grenade and submachine gun. As night fell, flares illuminated the ghastly scene. Anders later wrote that 'the critical moment had indeed arrived' and ordered a general assault for the morning of the 18th, but by that time the last of the paras had received the order to retire and the Poles walked astonished into the dusty rubble. At 10.30 in the morning of 18 May the red and white Polish flag at last flew above the dusty ruins.

BREAKOUT AT ANZIO

With the full weight of his Fifth and Eighth Armies now pouring up the Liri valley and the coastal plain, Alexander told Truscott that this was the moment to make a determined effort to break out of the Anzio

◀ With the remains of the monastery towering over them, members of the Polish II Corps attack.

▲ After eight days of bloody fighting, the Polish flag is hoisted in the ruins of Monte Cassino.

THE CRUCIBLE

Cassino was a tough battle in a tough campaign. Fought over the most rugged terrain imaginable and for the most part in miserable winter weather, it drew in soldiers from a host of nationalities and went on relentlessly for more than five months. By the end of it all, over 200,000 soldiers had been killed or wounded. It was a nightmare battle of the sort more usually associated with the trenches of the First World War; even the grand prize of Rome seemed little compensation to the Allies, while the Axis forces, although ultimately defeated, could pride themselves on tying down and wearing down the enemy at a critical stage in the war.

TURNING POINT

▶ Battle-tired and exhausted, German soldiers surrender to the Poles.

▶ After months of arduous fighting, the Allies can finally leave Cassino and advance on the road to Rome.

Top: John Watney Photo Library/Interpress; bottom: US Library of Congres:

beachhead, and head for the Alban Hills, blocking off the retreat of Vietinghoff's Tenth Army.

The attack was launched during the night of the 23rd but the Germans stubbornly held on to Cisterna until the 26th. By this time, though, the Canadian I Corps had breached the Dora Line and Kesselring had to order a further retreat. Mackensen's Fourteenth Army at Anzio held up Truscott's advance just long enough to allow Vietinghoff's Tenth to escape.

On the 25th, advance patrols from II Corps heading north from the Gustav Line bumped into men from VI Corps heading in the opposite direction from Anzio, reuniting Clark's Fifth Army at long last. Then, on the 30th, the Texan 36th Division which had suffered such a mauling earlier in the year, broke through to the east of the German positions in the Alban Hills, threatening to cut them off. Kesselring's lines were crumbling rapidly and on 2 June he asked Hitler's permission to abandon Rome. The *Führer* agreed with surprising grace and Kesselring ordered his forces to evacuate the Eternal City and fall back towards the Gothic Line. Since they had been the first to tackle the Cassino position, it was appropriate that it was soldiers of Mark Clark's Fifth Army who first entered Rome on 4 June.

D-DAY

BATTLE DIARY

6 JUNE 1944

05.30	Bombardment of beaches begins. US troops land on St Marcouf
06.00	German 7th Army HQ informed of bombardment
06.30	H-Hour on Utah and Omaha
07.00	First landing wave pinned down on Omaha. US Rangers begin scaling Pointe du Hoc
07.30	H-Hour on Gold and Sword
07.45	US troops advance inland from Utah. H-Hour on Juno
08.00	US troops on Omaha begin ascending bluffs
09.00	German 84th Corps informed of seaborne landings
09.30	Announcement of Overlord made to press. British troops one mile inland from Gold. British capture Hermanville
10.00	US troops reach clifftops overlooking Omaha
10.30	21st Panzer Division ordered to attack between Caen and Bayeux
11.00	US soldiers enter Vierville
11.15	St Aubin falls to Canadians
12.03	Commandos link up with Airborne troops at Orne bridges
12.15	German tanks reported north of Caen
12.30	British 185 Brigade moves inland from Sword
13.00	US 4th Infantry Division links up with 101st Airborne at Pouppeville
13.30	US troops move inland from Omaha
13.35	German 352nd Division reported to have thrown the enemy back into the sea from Omaha
14.00	Fighting on Periers Ridge overlooking Sword. Hitler holds his first meeting about landings
16.00	British and Germans clash between Villiers-le-Sec and Bazenville. US tanks begin moving inland from Omaha. 12th SS Panzer and Panzer Lehr Divisions released from reserve
16.30	21st Panzer Division attacks Sword beachhead
18.00	British advance on Caen halted
20.00	Colleville-sur-Mer secured by British
20.10	Taillerville captured by Canadians
21.00	Gilders carrying reinforcements land behind Utah and east of the Orne

ALLIED FORTITUDE

Faced with the task of defending a coastline stretching over 3,000 miles, the myth of Hitler's almighty Atlantic Wall soon crumbles.

▲ Spread out thinly along Hitler's illusory Atlantic Wall, German soldiers wait for the enemy. Inset, Insignia of the 21st Army Group.

The *Führer* Directive No. 40, published on 23 March 1942, laid the foundations for the Atlantic Wall, the German Reich's first bastion against the so-called Anglo-Saxon allies, the United States and Britain: 'The coastline of Europe will, in coming months, be exposed to the danger of an enemy landing in force'.

Yet while the German High Command was fully aware of the need to construct defences against a seaborne invasion of Europe, they were still left in a dilemma. Where would the Allies come? The coast to be defended

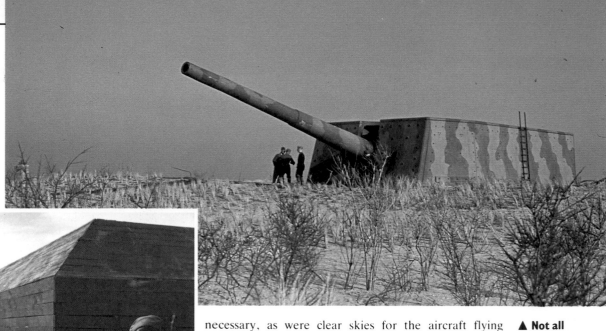

▼ As early as September 1940, the Germans began to build defensive bunkers along the Channel coast. Crude affairs such as this would later be replaced by concrete and steel.

necessary, as were clear skies for the aircraft flying sorties over the invasion area. Finally, a port would be necessary to ensure supply of the invading armies.

ATLANTIC WALL

The last condition was to influence German preparations more than any other. The best concentration of ports in the pinpointed area lay between the mouth of the River Seine and Calais. At Cap Gris Nez, between Calais and Boulogne, the special building unit *Organisation Todt* constructed a massive complex of batteries. There were also smaller such bastions at the mouth of the Seine, in the Channel Islands and around Brest but German propaganda boasting the stoutness of the Atlantic Wall, particularly would be accompanied by photographs of Cap Gris Nez.

The reality in late 1943 was a flimsy balsa screen propped up in one or two places by concrete posts. Most of the fortifications were no more than ordinary field entrenchments – trenches or rifle pits with a few barbed-wire entanglements and a minefield 20-50 yards (18-45 m) deep. On 30 October 1943 a report from the Commander-in-Chief West, Field Marshal Gerd von Rundstedt, appeared on Hitler's desk. It described the shabby situation on the Channel coast.

▲ Not all emplacements were as real as this. Dummies were set up all along the Atlantic Wall, in an attempt to confuse the Allies about the real number of German defence weapons.

▼ Field Marshal Erwin Rommel (second from left) inspects part of the Atlantic Wall, January 1944. He was not impressed with what he saw and insisted on an accelerated construction programme.

was long; German resources were stretched by the demands of fighting the massive Soviet Army.

Military logic easily ruled out serious threats to the Reich from landings in the Balkans, Italy and southern France. Hitler's logic saw a serious threat against Norway, although his generals did not. That left the Atlantic and Channel coasts of France and the Low Countries as the most directly threatened areas. Within this region, more deductions could be made to give certain sectors priority. The Allies were unlikely to attempt a landing beyond the range of aircraft flying from Britain. The efficient use of shipping ruled out beaches that were a lengthy voyage from any British ports. The areas inland would have to be suitable for developing operations on a broad front.

The process of elimination left the Germans with an invasion likely to occur somewhere between St Malo in Brittany and the Scheldt estuary in the Netherlands. The main strength of the German defence would be sited in this stretch of coast, and the first efforts at constructing the Atlantic Wall would take place along it.

The Germans went further, and tried to pick more or less the precise spot and time that the Allies would come. They themselves had experience of planning a large-scale seaborne cross-Channel attack. In devising Operation Sealion, the planned invasion of Britain, the Germans had established four principles for an amphibious attack: the main landing would have to be accompanied by one or more diversionary landings; the assault would have to be made at dawn, and at high tide; calm seas were

Süddeutscher Verlag

The situation was taken in hand. Field Marshal Erwin Rommel was sent by the German High Command to inspect the Atlantic Wall and make a report. Rommel had made a study of Allied invasions at Salerno and Sicily, and he had his own ideas about what must be done to counter seaborne attacks. On 15 January 1944 Rommel was given command of Army Group B, which included all German armies facing Britain.

He soon ordered an energetic effort to construct a real Atlantic Wall. Mines were laid on all the beaches, artillery was dug in and ranged on the assault areas, concrete pillboxes and anti-tank-gun mountings were constructed, and the countryside behind likely invasion beaches inundated by the water of rivers dammed for that purpose. The sand and shingle between low and high water mark was planted with numerous obstacles designed to rip out the hulls of landing craft.

GERMAN UNCERTAINTY

Rommel also sought to have permission to move the six panzer divisions that made up the reserve available in the west to positions close behind the invasion beaches. Von Rundstedt overruled him, preferring to keep a central strategic reserve. The dispute was laid before Hitler for him, Solomon-like, to resolve. On 7 May 1944 the judgement was rendered. Half the panzer divisions were placed in the control of Rommel's Army Group B. The remainder Solomon was to keep for himself, and they were placed directly under the German High Command.

One reason for this compromise solution was the uncertainty over Allied intentions for 1944. The Allies were able to utilise this uncertainty in the elaborate deceptions contrived to confuse the German High Command. These operated on different levels. Phoney radio messages were sent about fictitious units, to be picked up by the alert ears of the German Y Service, their Signals Intelligence unit.

The most effective of the deceptions were the three 'Fortitude' schemes. Fortitude North was carried out almost entirely by phoney radio messages. A fictitious British Fourth Army was established in Edinburgh for a

Robert Hunt Library

► **The propaganda image of the Atlantic Wall – a huge gun is lowered into place in a concrete bunker. The soldier standing on top gives an indication of its size.**

THE FIGUREHEAD

Field Marshal Gerd von Rundstedt was the son of an old Prussian family. He has come to personify the dilemma faced by the old German officers under the Nazi regime. More loyal to the army than the state, his relations with Hitler were coloured by the view that the 'Bohemian corporal' had risen above his station.

In 1938 he retired in protest at Hitler's sacking of the army's commander, but when war was imminent, he was recalled to active duty. He was forcibly retired twice during the war, due to friction with the Führer, but both times his prestige and ability were crucial to the Reich's war effort, and he was recalled.

Von Rundstedt's subordinates were devoted to him, even after his outlook became completely defeatist in July 1944. He died in 1953, aged 78.

► **Rommel and von Rundstedt, main German commanders.**

Bildarchiv Preussischer Kulturbesitz

War Stories

It wasn't just enemy defenders' fire which made some landings hazardous. A Battalion Commander and his HQ staff had boarded their landing craft on the deck of their transport ship and were being lowered into the water. As they reached a point halfway between the rail and the water, the davits jammed and for about 20 minutes they hung just four feet under the sewage outlet from the 'heads'.

As, the Commander recalled, 'the heads were in constant use' (not very surprisingly), 'we received the entire discharge!'

▲ Field Marshal von Rundstedt is shown the defences of La Rochelle, 1944. The Allies had already decided not to mount direct assaults on defended ports – they remembered Dieppe.

▼ German-paid labourers march past the fruits of their work – anti-tank obstacles known as 'Dragon's Teeth' – northern France, 1944.

planned invasion of Norway. Dummy aircraft were also constructed, and the ships that would take part of the invasion force to Normandy were based in Scotland as a decoy to suggest a Norway attack.

Fortitude North picked on a bogeyman that haunted Hitler, the spectre of an Allied invasion of Norway. It was a complete success, and a sizeable German army was stationed there. Fortitude South played on the expectations of the German High Command, by creating the so-called 'First US Army Group', intended to assault across the Pas de Calais, led by Patton, the general held in highest regard by the Germans.

Dummy installations were constructed in Kent and Sussex. Inflatable tanks were placed in fields and surrounded by simulated treadmarks. The *pièce de résistance* was the sending of 21st Army Group's communications to London along a landline from Portsmouth to Kent, and then by wireless to London. Y Service dutifully marked Montgomery's headquarters next to Patton's.

Fortitude South worked as well as Fortitude North. It was capped by Fortitude South II. This only took place after the landings in Normandy had actually happened. It

again used false communications, and it offered the beguiling scenario that the Normandy invasion was a diversion, and that the 'First US Army Group' would soon come storming across the Channel to strike somewhere near Calais. Like its predecessor, it was pretty successful at bamboozling the German leaders.

In May Rommel resumed his demand for control of all the panzer divisions in reserve, but he was refused. He decided that at the first opportunity he would go to Hitler and make a personal appeal. On 24 May the last aerial reconnaissance the German Air Force would make before D-Day revealed no sudden concentration of shipping in the ports of Dover, Folkestone and along the Thames. On 2 June it became apparent that the weather along the Channel was going to worsen. Rommel, who had anticipated a possible attack in early June – if the reports that Allied training had been taking place during low tide were true – chose now to see Hitler. His wife's birthday was on 6 June, so he could combine business with pleasure. The lack of shipping activity and the likelihood of storms and cloudy skies meant it would be safe for the time being.

General Erich Marcks, commanding the LXXXIV Corps defending the area between Caen and Avranches, inspected the fortifications at Arromanches the day before, Thursday 1 June. He said to an Army captain beside him, 'If I know the British, they'll go to church next Sunday one last time and then sail Monday. Army Group B says they're not going to come yet, and that when they do it'll be at Calais. So I think that we'll be

▼ The airborne armada gathers in England — gliders await attachment to towing craft.

Robert Hunt Library

◄ US troops manoeuvre a DUKW amphibian into the well of an LST, in preparation for D-Day. The loading of the myriad ships of the invasion fleet was a complex problem.

▼ Beach defences in Normandy awaiting the invasion.

welcoming them on Tuesday, right here.'

As Rommel was driving back to Germany, the Allied invasion fleet was assembling at its concentration point, 'Piccadilly Circus', in the middle of the Channel. Had German E-boats or patrol planes been on normal routine, they would have spotted the convoy. The anticipated bad weather, however, kept them in port or on the ground.

CHANNEL RENDEZVOUS

In front of the invasion fleet steamed several flotillas of minesweepers, clearing ten channels of German mines. The channels, about half a nautical mile in width, were marked at the edges by floating, lighted buoys. Some of the minesweepers were approaching the Normandy coast in the last hours of daylight, in full view of German batteries. Their sailors were surprised that the guns never fired at them.

In the first wave, nearly 300 combat vessels and over 4,000 landing craft followed the minesweepers. By 5.15 am on 6 June they were in position off the five invasion beaches. Three divisions of airborne troops were already in action, having been dropped during the night. At about 5.30 am the naval bombardment began. First the heavy guns of battleships and monitors hammered away at the batteries of long-range artillery. While they were firing, a trio of E-boats emerged from a smoke screen the Allies had laid in front of Le Havre. They fired their torpedoes, but these missed the big targets, although one struck and sank a Norwegian destroyer.

The next stage in the fireplan was the sustained bombardment of German pillboxes and strongpoints by cruisers. The guns were laid on the beaches between the water and vegetation lines. At the same time the landing craft began their runs into shore.

At 6.30 am, the first landing craft dropped their ramps in front of Utah and Omaha beaches.

▼ With a barrage balloon floating above, part of the vast armada of ships ploughs across the Channel towards the Normandy coast, dawn 6 June 1944.

Imperial War Museum

BATTLE DIARY

HITTING THE BEACHES

6 JUNE 1944
5.30 am Bombardment of US beaches begins

6.30 H-Hour on Utah and Omaha

7 am US Rangers begin scaling Pointe du Hoc

7.25 H-Hour on Gold and Sword

7.45 US troops advance inland from Utah. H-Hour on Juno

8 am US troops on Omaha begin ascending bluffs

9.30 Announcement of Overlord made to press British take Hermanville

10.30 21st Panzer Division ordered to attack between Caen and Bayeux

11 am US soldiers enter Vierville

11.15 St Aubin falls to Canadians

12.03 Commandos link up with Airborne at Orne bridges

12.15 German tanks reported north of Caen

12.30 British 185 Brigade moves inland from Sword

1.30 US troops move inland from Omaha

2 pm Hitler holds first meeting about landings

4 pm British and Germans clash near Bazenville 12th SS Panzer released from reserve

4.30 21st Panzer Division attacks Sword beachhead

6 pm British advance on Caen halted

8 pm Colleville-sur-Mer secured by British

Bildarchiv Preussischer Kulturbesitz

ASSAULT ON THE BEACHES

The most painstakingly planned operation in history is finally unleashed, as thousands of well-trained troops hit the beaches at H-Hour.

Imperial War Museum

Seeing the darkness of the night of 5 June 1944 dispelled by the dawn of 6 June, thousands of men aboard the ships of the Allied invasion fleet looked out over the grey seas of the English Channel and saw long lines of vessels carrying them towards the Continent. To the eyes of some it seemed as if the landing craft, minesweepers, destroyers, cruisers and battleships stretched back to the ports of Britain they had left behind hours ago.

The bombardment of the Normandy coast had already begun. The banging of the ships' guns was accompanied by the roar overhead of medium and heavy bombers of the UK Eighth and Ninth Army Air Forces. To the soldiers in the landing craft plodding steadily forward through the choppy waters, the crashing thunder of the explosions of naval shells and aerial bombs reassured them that the German defenders of the beaches they were about to assault would receive some heavy blows before any Allied soldier stepped ashore.

It was a reassurance gratefully received. The soldiers were having an uncomfortable journey through seas that tossed their small craft viciously. Most of the soldiers and some of the sailors suffered from seasickness that morning, made worse by the hearty breakfasts served to men who would, for the next couple of days, be uncertain of receiving any kind of regular meals.

UTAH BEACH

The landing of the assault waves was timed to coincide with the start of the rising tide. This meant that H-Hour, when the first landing craft were supposed to lower their ramps,

▲ American troops on board LCIs (Landing Craft, Infantry). The calm seas, bright weather and cheerful faces suggest that this is a photograph taken during one of the pre-invasion exercises in England.

BATTLE LINE-UP

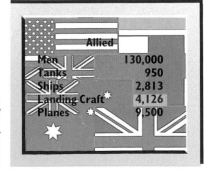

Allied	
Men	130,000
Tanks	950
Ships	2,813
Landing Craft	4,126
Planes	9,500

German	
Men	50,000
Tanks	127
Ships	21
Landing Craft	—
Planes	160

◄◄ On D-Day, things looked different: the first wave of US troops goes ashore on Omaha Beach, in the face of murderous fire.

◄ Opposing forces on 6 June.

Robert Capa/Magnum

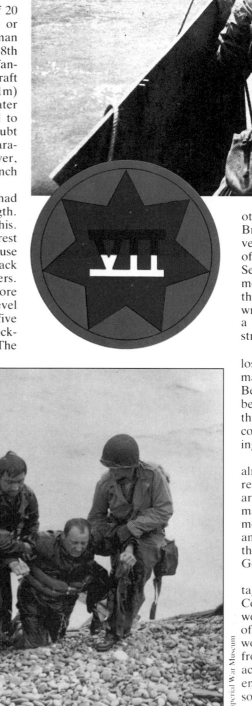

▶ US infantry prepare to land on Omaha Beach from an LCI, preceded by DUKWs and M3 half-tracks. The lack of opposition implies a photo taken late on D-Day.

▶ Insignia of the US VII Corps which landed at Utah Beach.

▼ American soldiers help their less fortunate comrades ashore at Utah Beach, their landing craft having been hit by enemy fire.

would be at different times on the five invasion beaches. The landings at Utah and Omaha, the farthest west of the five, would start about an hour before those at Sword, the farthest east.

The first Allied troops to land on French soil as part of Operation Overlord's seaborne assault were four men of the US Army's 4th Cavalry Squadron. Armed only with knives, they swam on to the Iles St Marcouf, a pair of islets to the north of Utah. The Iles St Marcouf were secured by 5.30 am and the main landing occurred almost precisely on schedule, 6.30 am.

The first wave was made up of 20 LCVPs (Landing Craft, Vehicle or Personnel), each bearing a 30-man assault team drawn from the 8th Infantry Regiment of the 4th Infantry Division. The ramps of the craft went down about 100 yards (91m) offshore; the men jumped into water that was waist-deep, and waded to the beach. One soldier, no doubt relieved that the months of preparation and endless exercises were over, shouted 'Goddam! We're on French soil.'

The anticipated resistance had failed to materialise in any strength. There were two reasons for this. One, the defenders of the nearest German strongpoint, Blockhouse W5, had been stunned by the attack of 276 B-26 Marauder bombers. These had struck in the hour before the landings, and their low-level attack had been devastating. All five artillery pieces arming the blockhouse had been destroyed. The

other reason was soon discovered by Brigadier-General Theodore Roosevelt, Jr., the only Allied general officer to land with the first wave. Searching out landmarks before moving inland, he discovered that the landings had occurred in the wrong place – the Americans were a mile south of Utah beach with its stronger German fortifications.

The reason for the mistake was the loss of one of the control boats that marked the northern edge of Utah Beach for the landing craft. It had been swamped by the high seas, so the incoming vessels navigated their course using the control boat marking the southern end of the beach.

The defenders of Blockhouse W5, already demoralised, put up a feeble resistance that was ended with the arrival of duplex-drive (DD) Sherman tanks, swimming ashore by means of floats and canvas screens, and engaging the blockhouse with their 75 mm guns. By 7.30 am German resistance had ended.

The Americans took full advantage of this piece of good fortune. Combat engineers were soon at work, clearing the gaps in the rows of obstacles so that the landing craft would bring their loads in on a wide frontage. Bulldozers smoothed paths across the sand dunes, while other engineers blew holes in the sea wall so that tanks could drive through.

As the infantry and tanks moved

Imperial War Museum

Robert Hunt Library

Süddeutscher Verlag

◄ By early afternoon, the picture has changed on Omaha Beach — the German coastal defences have been taken and are now manned by US landing troops.

▼ Insignia of First US Army, led by Lt-Gen Omar Bradley.

ahead, they encountered an unexpected difficulty coping with the areas just behind the beaches which had been inundated by the Germans. Laden with their equipment, the Americans now had to wade through a marsh. This slowed their advance considerably. Further delays were caused by traffic congestion on Utah. Two of four roads leading inland had been designated for vehicle use, but one was too close to still active German defenders, so the masses of tanks, trucks and jeeps were confined to a single causeway.

The link with the 101st Airborne Division, dropped by parachute during the night, was made at 1 pm at the village of Pouppeville. By nightfall, the 4th Division's lodgement was far short of its objective line in the north, but to the west and south it was very near. There was a strong pocket of Germans, men of the 6th Parachute Regiment, between Fouville and Turqueville. No link had yet been established with the other division of paratroopers, the 82nd Airborne around Ste Mère-Eglise. On the whole, however, the initial landings at Utah gave Lieutenant-General Omar Bradley, the Commander of the US First Army, cause for satisfaction.

OMAHA BEACH

The same could not be said of Omaha. Unlike its neighbour to the west, the beach is very exposed to the wind and weather, and the seas are far more turbulent. The duplex-drive Shermans could not be launched for fear they would be swamped, while the assault infantry of the 1st and 29th Infantry Divisions suffered badly from seasickness.

To add to their discomfort as they lay drenched in cold salt spray and their own vomit, there was haze and smoke along the shore, which hindered the gunners of the destroyers and cruisers. Naval gunfire support was not as effective. Then, as they neared the shoreline, the full horror of their predicament was realised.

POINTE DU HOC

Pointe du Hoc was an almost sheer cliff towering 100 ft (30 m) high. The Germans had mounted a battery of six 155 mm guns at the top of this rocky promontory, from where they could dominate both Utah and Omaha beaches.

On D-Day, three companies of US Rangers were assigned to assault this crucial position. They shot rope ladders and grappling hooks up the cliff face and scaled to the top. There, they found the casemates were empty. Patrolling the area, they eventually came across the guns which had been moved to an orchard one mile (1.6 km) inland. The unfortunate Rangers would have to hold out against German attacks until 8 June, when they were finally relieved by the advance of US troops from Omaha.

▶ The guns of the battleship USS *Nevada* engage German defensive positions on shore.

They heard the patter of machine-gun bullets on the ramps of the landing craft. The ramps went down, and the last thing many of the front row may have seen was the bullets kicking up water as the Germans fired directly into the mass of men standing in the waist of the vessel, killing and wounding the soldiers before they could even get out.

Men panicked. They hurled themselves over the side into deeper water, or off the ramps trying to get under water for cover. For some, the weight of their equipment dragged them down. Others abandoned packs and weapons to swim towards the beach. Those who got that far faced heavy enfilading fire as they crossed the sand to find the cover of the sea wall.

The second wave suffered almost as heavily as the first. But successive waves had it a little easier, because there were so many targets that the fire of machine guns, rifles and mortars was dispersed.

The agony of Omaha was almost inevitable. It was the only place between the mouth of the river Vire and Arromanches where there were beaches suitable for a landing. It was the only place the Germans needed to fortify, and they were aided by the steep bluffs that dominate the four-mile (6.5 km) crescent of sand. The bombing of Omaha had been very inaccurate, with almost all of the bombs falling far inland. Tank support had either sunk or been knocked out by German anti-tank guns. Radios were soaked in damaging salt water. The defenders were not only a strongly entrenched division, they were battle-hardened veterans of the Eastern Front, the 352nd Infantry Division. The American assaulting force clung wretchedly to the little bit of France they had liberated below the sea wall at Omaha.

At about 12 o'clock Lt-Gen Bradley considered diverting the follow-up troops away from Omaha towards either Utah or the Anglo-Canadian beaches. He chose not to, and it

▲ The insignia of the British I Corps which took part in the landings at Sword and Juno Beaches.

▼ With the initial beachhead secure, supplies are brought ashore direct from the landing ships, Utah Beach, June 1944.

MULBERRY HARBOURS

The Mulberry harbours were probably the most important contribution to the Allies' strategic surprise during Overlord. When the German reconnaissance flights brought back pictures of the massive caissons built along the Thames, they marked them down as anti-aircraft towers. It never crossed their minds that for the invasion of France the Allies might bring their own ports!

The caissons were huge structures of steel and concrete, which would serve as breakwaters. Within this protection lay the spidery network of the floating ports. There were prefabricated piers, docks and quays. The portable harbour was moored to the beaches against it floating away.

On 19 June a force six gale struck the Norman coast, damaging the American harbour off Omaha, but the British one at Arromanches remained a part of the Allied logistics system until the opening of Antwerp.

Complementing the Mulberries was another engineering project, PLUTO (Pipeline under the Ocean). This was used to pump petroleum from Britain to France. At first it came up at Cherbourg, but the joints gave way after only a few weeks. A new line was constructed to Boulogne, but PLUTO did little to prevent the petroleum shortage in September.

Popperfoto

▲ Flexible aluminium piping waits to be coiled on to special drums for the assembly of PLUTO. Inset, right: A convoy of ambulances comes ashore along one of the causeways of the Mulberry Harbour at Arromanches.

Peter Newark's Military Pictures

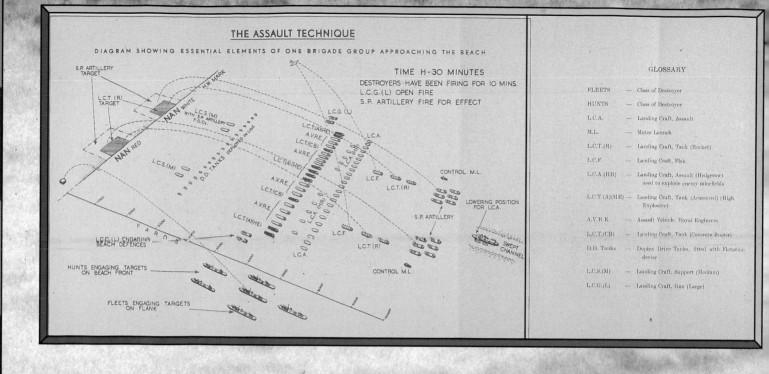

THE ASSAULT TECHNIQUE

DIAGRAM SHOWING ESSENTIAL ELEMENTS OF ONE BRIGADE GROUP APPROACHING THE BEACH

TIME H-30 MINUTES
DESTROYERS HAVE BEEN FIRING FOR 10 MINS.
L.C.G.(L) OPEN FIRE
S.P. ARTILLERY FIRE FOR EFFECT

S.P. ARTILLERY TARGET
L.C.T. (R) TARGET
NAN WHITE
NAN RED
L.C.S.(M) WITH S.P. ARTILLERY F.O.O.I.
L.C.G. (L)
L.C.S. (M)
D.D. TANKS DEPLOYED IN LINE
L.C.T.(A)(HE)
L.C.T.(CB)
A.V.R.E.
L.C.A.
CONTROL M.L.
L.C.T.(A)(HE)
A.V.R.E.
L.C.T.(CB)
L.C.F.
L.C.T. (R)
A.V.R.E.
L.C.A. (HR)
LOWERING POSITION FOR L.C.A.
L.C.G.(L) ENGAGING BEACH DEFENCES
L.C.F.
S.P. ARTILLERY
SWEPT CHANNEL
YARDS
L.C.A.
L.C.T. (R)
HUNTS ENGAGING TARGETS ON BEACH FRONT
CONTROL M.L.
FLEETS ENGAGING TARGETS ON FLANK

GLOSSARY

FLEETS	—	Class of Destroyer
HUNTS	—	Class of Destroyer
L.C.A.	—	Landing Craft, Assault
M.L.	—	Motor Launch
L.C.T.(R)	—	Landing Craft, Tank (Rocket)
L.C.F.	—	Landing Craft, Flak
L.C.A.(HR)	—	Landing Craft, Assault (Hedgerow) used to explode enemy minefields
L.C.T.(A)(H.E.)	—	Landing Craft, Tank (Armoured) (High Explosive)
A.V.R.E.	—	Assault Vehicle, Royal Engineers
L.C.T.(CB)	—	Landing Craft, Tank (Concrete Buster)
D.D. Tanks	—	Duplex Drive Tanks, fitted with Flotation device
L.C.S.(M)	—	Landing Craft, Support (Medium)
L.C.G.(L)	—	Landing Craft, Gun (Large)

CHURCHILL AVRE

Designed to carry and support assault engineers, the Churchill AVRE was fitted with the Petard spigot mortar (firing a 40lbs [18kg] bomb) in place of the standard 57mm gun and was equipped to carry a range of specialised engineering loads. These included fascines, the CIRD mine clearance device and the SBG bridge. 180 Churchill AVRE's were used by the 79th Armoured Division on D-Day

CHURCHILL AVRE

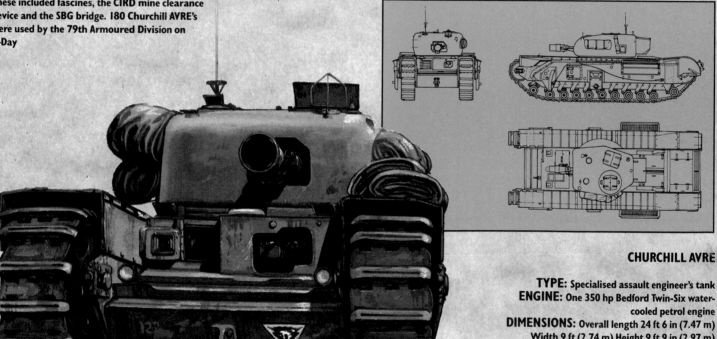

CHURCHILL AVRE

TYPE: Specialised assault engineer's tank
ENGINE: One 350 hp Bedford Twin-Six water-cooled petrol engine
DIMENSIONS: Overall length 24 ft 6 in (7.47 m) Width 9 ft (2.74 m) Height 9 ft 9 in (2.97 m)
WEIGHT: Approx. 80,747 lbs (36,620 kg)
ARMAMENT: One 29 cm Petard spigot mortar and two 7.92 mm Besa machine guns
PERFORMANCE: Maximum road speed 15½ mph (25 km/h) Maximum cross country speed 8 mph (13 km/h) Road radius of action 90 miles (145 km)

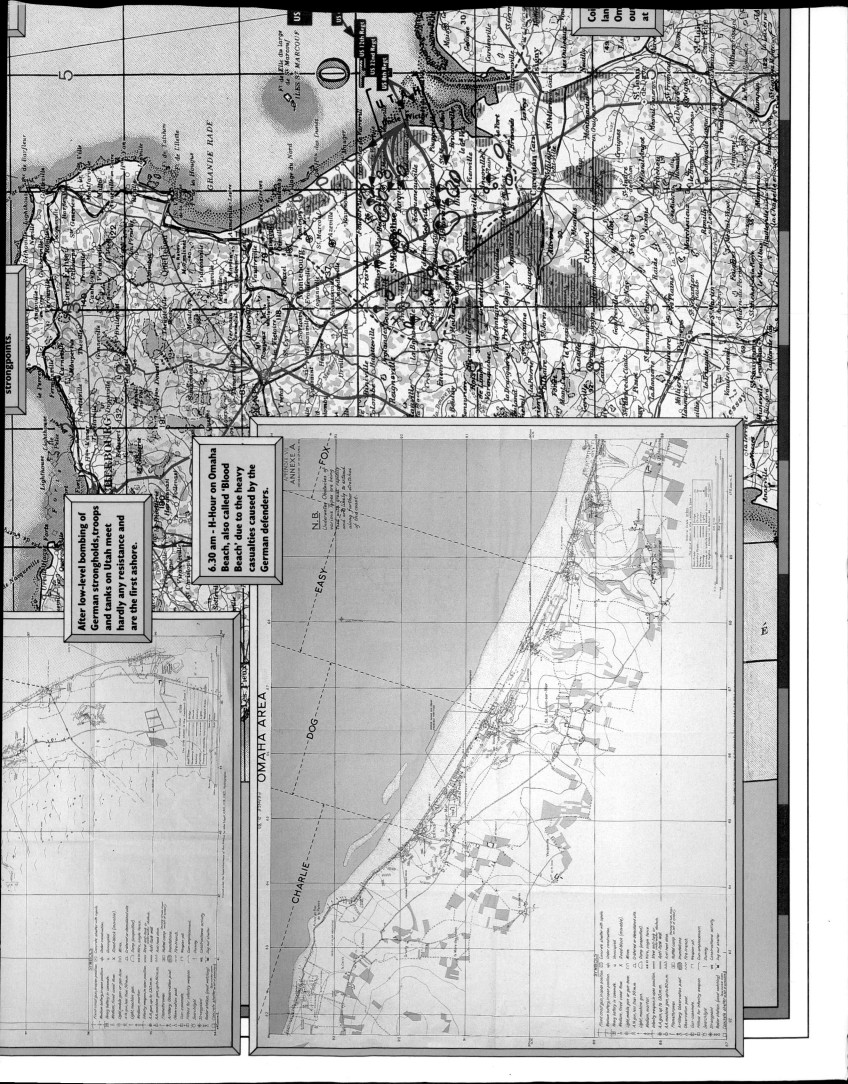

strongpoints.

After low-level bombing of German strongholds, troops and tanks on Utah meet hardly any resistance and are the first ashore.

6.30 am - H-Hour on Omaha Beach, also called 'Blood Beach' due to the heavy casualties caused by the German defenders.

OMAHA AREA

CHARLIE

DOG

EASY

FOX

APPENDIX VII
ANNEXE A.

N.B.
Underwater Obstacles of FOX
various Types are being fixed with great rapidity and will likely to extend during further stretches of that coast.

US 8th Regt
US 22nd Regt
US 12th Regt

UTAH

GRANDE RADE

CHERBOURG

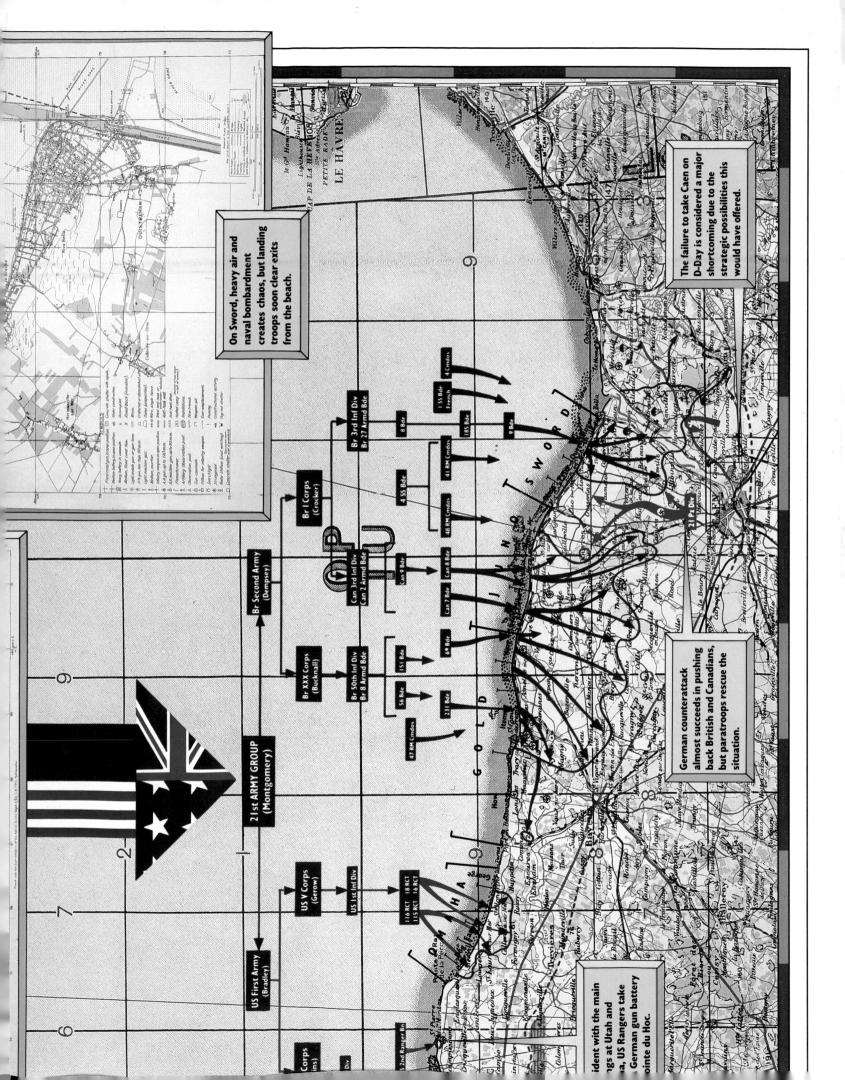

On Sword, heavy air and naval bombardment creates chaos, but landing troops soon clear exits from the beach.

The failure to take Caen on D-Day is considered a major shortcoming due to the strategic possibilities this would have offered.

German counterattack almost succeeds in pushing back British and Canadians, but paratroops rescue the situation.

ident with the main gs at Utah and a, US Rangers take German gun battery ointe du Hoc.

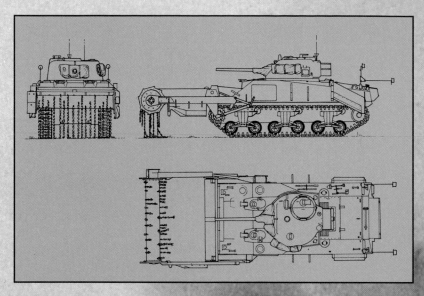

The morning of 6 J
the arrival of Hobar
specialised armou
intended to smas
Normandy beach

SHERMAN CRAB Mk I

The Crab was the most important of a number of mine-clearing versions of the standard Sherman tank. To fit it for the role, the Crab was fitted with a pair of hydraulic lifting arms which carried a 'flail' rotor. Power to drive the rotor was taken from the vehicle's right front sprocket and the mines were exploded by the action of chains on the motor 'flailing' the ground

SHERMAN CRAB Mk I

TYPE: Mine clearance tank
ENGINES: Twin 375 hp General Motors 6-71 diesel engines
DIMENSIONS: Overall length approx. 26 ft 10 in (8.17 m) Width approx. 10 ft 10 in (3.29 m) Height 9 ft (2.74 m)
PERFORMANCE: Mine clearance speed approx. 5 mph (8 km/h)

SHERMAN CRAB

*...ne heralds
...s 'funnies' –
...d vehicles
...open the
...defences*

SHERMAN DD

The Duplex Drive (DD) equipment was designed to enable the Sherman tank to 'swim'. DD conversion involved fitting an inflatable canvas screen around the tank and equipping it with two screw propellers. In water, the DD was steered by swivelling the propellers right or left. On land, the screen was collapsed and stowed whilst the propellers were swivelled upwards

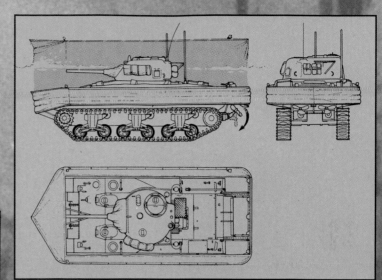

SHERMAN DD

SHERMAN V (DD)

TYPE: Amphibious medium tank with a crew of five

ENGINE: One 370 hp Chrysler 5-line water-cooled engine

DIMENSIONS: Overall length 19 ft 10½ in (6.06 m) Width 8 ft 7 in (2.62 m) Height 9 ft (2.74 m)

WEIGHT: Approx. 73,162 lbs (33,180 kg)

ARMAMENT: One 75 mm cannon, two 0.30 in Browning machine guns plus one optional 0.50 in Browning machine gun

PERFORMANCE: Maximum road speed 25 mph (40 km/h) Maximum cross-country speed 15-20 mph (24-37 km/h) Maximum speed in water approx. 4 knots (7 km/h) Road radius of action 120 miles (193 km)

According to Allied strategy, Bradley's US First Army was to land on Utah and Omaha beaches and, with the help of paratroopers, to cut off the Cotentin peninsula and later take the vital port of Cherbourg. The British were to land on Gold and Sword beaches, and the Canadians on Juno; together, they had the task of rapidly advancing inland, taking the towns of Bayeux and Caen. The inset maps provide a closer look at the five individual beaches which were used by the invading forces.

VERDICT ON D-DAY

> " I have returned many times to honour the valiant men who died . . . every man who set foot on Omaha Beach was a hero. "
>
> **LT-GEN OMAR BRADLEY, US First Army**

> " At the present time, it is still too early to say whether this is a large-scale diversionary attack or the main effort. "
>
> **MORNING REPORT ON 6 JUNE 1944 by the German C-in-C West**

50 YEARS ON

By the end of 6 June 1944, the western Allies could breathe a collective sigh of relief. Although not all the objectives laid down in the D-Day plan had been taken - including the vital town of Caen - all five beaches were in Allied hands, at remarkably little cost. American troops were firmly ashore on Utah and, after a hard morning's fight, had seized Omaha; in the Anglo-Canadian sector all three beaches - Gold, Juno and Sword - were secure, with infantry and armour exploiting inland. It would take time for the beaches to be linked, and the battle for the breakout was going to be hard, but the initial assault could be termed a major success.

Two Canadian brigades hit the beaches of Juno at 7.50 am and, with the help of Shermans, eliminate German strongholds.

JUNO AREA

NAN

MIKE

LOVE

SWORD AREA

PETER

QUEEN

ROGER

OVER
THE SEABOR
TUESDAY 6

As dawn breaks on D-D
is heading for Hitler

The map depicts the area chosen for the Allied landings on D-Day, following a plan devised by the Chiefs-of-Staff for Operation Overlord. Also shown is the allocation of beaches and sub-divisions and the Allied commanders in charge, with General Montgomery in overall command of the Ground Forces. On shore, the main German gun emplacements as well as the extent of the beachheads and German pockets of resistance at the end of D-Day are marked.

KEY

ANGLO-CANADIAN FORCES	**ALLIED OBJECTIVES BY 24.00 HRS ON D-DAY**
AMERICAN FORCES	**AREA HELD BY GERMAN TROOPS AT 24.00 HRS ON D-DAY**
BRITISH 6TH AIRBORNE DIVISION (PARATROOPS)	**GERMAN FORCES**
PARACHUTE DROPS	**GERMAN GUN EMPLACEMENTS**
GLIDER LANDINGS	**FLOODED AREA**
AREA SECURED BY ALLIED TROOPS AT 24.00 HRS ON D-DAY	

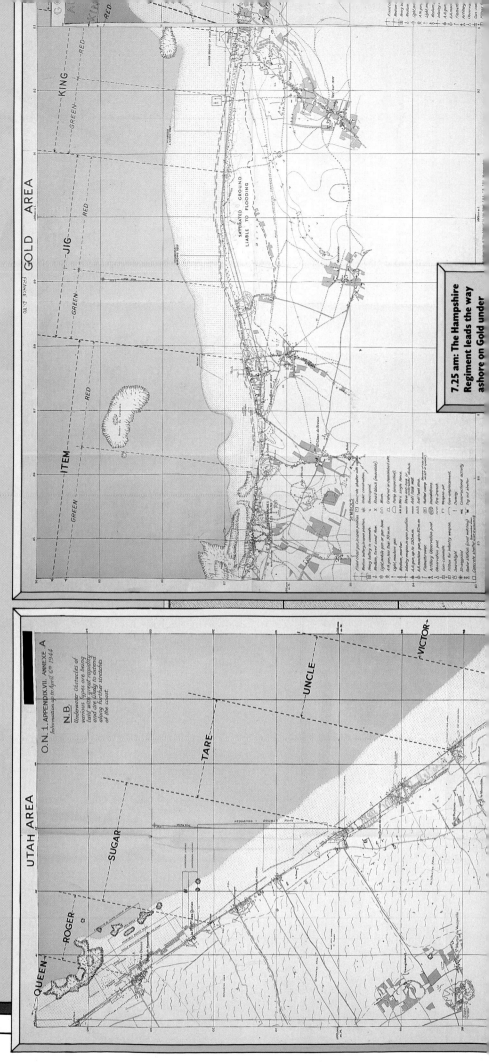

7.25 am: The Hampshire Regiment leads the way ashore on Gold under

GOLD AREA — KING — JIG — ITEM — RED — GREEN

SATURATED GROUND LIABLE TO FLOODING

FRANCE : D.20

SYMBOLS

UTAH AREA — QUEEN — ROGER — SUGAR — TARE — UNCLE — VICTOR

O.N. 1. APPENDIX XVII. ANNEXE A
Information up to April 6th 1944

N.B.
Underwater Obstacles of various types are being laid with great rapidity and are likely to extend along further stretches of the coast.

CAMPAIGN MAP

D-DAY

6 JUNE 1944

BATTLE DIARY

6 JUNE 1944

05.30 Bombardment of beaches begins.
US troops land on St Marcouf

06.00 German Seventh Army HQ informed of bombardment

06.30 H-Hour on Utah and Omaha

07.00 First landing wave pinned down on Omaha. US Rangers begin scaling Pointe du Hoc

07.30 H-Hour on Gold and Sword

07.45 US troops advance inland from Utah. H-Hour on Juno

08.00 US troops on Omaha begin ascending bluffs

09.00 German 84th Corps informed of seaborne landings

09.30 Announcement of Overlord made to press. British troops one mile inland on Gold. British capture Hermanville

10.00 US troops reach clifftops overlooking Omaha

10.30 21st Panzer Division ordered to attack between Caen and Bayeux

11.00 US soldiers enter Vierville

11.15 St. Aubin falls to Canadians

12.03 Commandos link up with Airborne troops at Orne bridges

12.15 German tanks reported north of Caen

12.30 British 185 Brigade moves inland from Sword

13.00 US 4th Infantry Division links up with 101st Airborne at Pouppeville

13.30 US troops move inland from Omaha

13.35 German 352nd Division reported to have thrown the enemy back into the sea from Omaha

14.00 Fighting on Periers Ridge overlooking Sword. Hitler holds his first meeting about landings

16.00 British and Germans clash between Villiers-le-Sec and Bazenville.
German Seventh Army HQ informed of Utah landings.
US tanks begin moving inland from Omaha.
12th SS Panzer and Panzer Lehr Divisions released from reserve

16.30 21st Panzer Division attacks Sword beachhead

18.00 British advance on Caen halted

20.00 Colleville-sur-Mer secured by British

20.10 Taillerville captured by Canadians

21.00 Gliders carrying airborne reinforcements land behind Utah and east of the Orne

BATTLE LEADERS

ALLIED

General Dwight Eisenhower — Supreme Commander, Allied Expeditionary Force

General Sir Bernard Montgomery — Commander, Land Forces

Lieutenant-General Omar Bradley — Commander, US First Army

Lieutenant-General H.D.G. Crerar — Commander, First Canadian Army

GERMAN

Field Marshal Gerd von Rundstedt — Commander-in-Chief West

Field Marshal Erwin Rommel — Commander, Army Group B

Maj-Gen Dr. Hans Speidel — Chief-of-Staff

General Erich Marcks — Commander LXXXIV Corps

...cts the area chosen for the ...s on D-Day, following a pl ...e Chiefs-of-Staff for Opera ...so shown is the allocation ...sub-divisions and the All ...rs in charge, with General ...ry in overall command of ...rces. On shore, the main C ...cements as well as the ex ...heads and German pocket ...e at the end of D-Day are

ALLIED TROOPS
24.00 HRS ON D-DAY

Y

UTAH AREA

O.N. 1. APPENDIX.VII. ANNEXE A
Information up to April 6th 1944

N.B.
Underwater Obstacles of various types are being laid with great rapidity and are likely to extend along further stretches of the coast

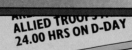

QUEEN

ROGER

SUGAR

ITEM

GREEN

GREEN

RED

crossing the beach and was reduced to platoon strength.

The lynchpin of the German defences was a sanitorium. This large building of several stories had been converted into a substantial blockhouse. Its machine guns turned into a serious threat to the troops on the flanks of Gold.

C Company of the 1st Hampshires, now absorbing the remnants of A Company, advanced on the Germans, but was pinned by mortars

▼ The chaos of a seaborne landing: 30 minutes after H-Hour on Sword Beach, where British soldiers assemble after the landing.

proved a wise decision. At that moment American infantrymen were creeping up the less defended sectors of the bluffs to establish themselves behind the main German positions. Destroyers were sailing in close to shore and firing at German pillboxes.

Slowly and determinedly, the Americans forced a bridgehead, until by nightfall they had established a pair of toeholds. Yet these were

▲ Men of the 48th Royal Marine Commando wade ashore at St Aubin sur Mer on Juno Beach. Their task is to secure the Canadian left flank at Bernières. Note the miniature motorcycle being brought ashore.

precariously perched in enemy territory, and there was no good guarantee that they would be there 24 hours later.

GOLD BEACH

The Anglo-Canadian beaches provided a more balanced picture than either Utah or Omaha. On Gold, the farthest west of them, the 50th (Northumbrian) Division faced enfilading fire from German strongpoints at Le Hamel and La Rivière, yet did not falter as the Americans did at Omaha. The British had better luck getting their tanks ashore.

Excellent cooperation between AVREs (Armoured Vehicle, Royal Engineers) and infantry, combined with support fire from destroyers, enabled the 5th Battalion of the East Yorkshire Regiment to capture La Rivière. Le Hamel was a different matter. The self-propelled artillery firing from landing craft had drifted off target. Those guns assigned to Le Hamel in fact bombarded points further east. So the 1st Battalion of the Hampshire Regiment were attacking without artillery support, and they suffered for it. One company, A, took heavy casualties

and machine guns before it got very far. A flail tank came up to give support, but was knocked out by anti-tank guns before it had a chance to be effective.

Good fortune suddenly came to the aid of the 1st Hampshires. An AVRE in company with some DD Shermans of the Sherwood Rangers Yeomanry advanced on Le Hamel from the east. The AVRE began to shell the sanitorium, and after a few of its large mortar bombs had blasted the building, German resistance was broken. Le Hamel was cleared and the 1st Hampshires pushed on to take Arromanches.

All of 50th Division was ashore by 1 pm, and throughout the afternoon British troops were pushing inland. About 4 pm 69 Brigade made contact with a strong German force in the area between Villiers-le-Sec and Bazenville. This was made up of a battalion of the 915th Regiment, the 352nd Fusilier Battalion and a couple of anti-tank batteries. After a stiff fight the Germans were driven across the river Seulles.

As on Utah, the advance inland was slowed by the congestion of traffic trying to get off the beach.

▼ Formation badge of the British Second Army, whose C-in-C was Lieutenant-General Sir Miles Dempsey.

▶ The first German prisoners are marched into captivity, watched by Canadian troops on Juno Beach, June 1944. Many of the German soldiers were inexperienced 'volunteers' from Eastern Europe.

ALLIED INVASION

TURNING POINT

The D-Day invasion of northern France on 6 June 1944 was an enormous operation, fraught with danger and risk. Every aspect of the planning, from the choice of landing area to the creation of an invasion fleet, had to be meticulous, while at the same time ensuring that the enemy was not alerted to Allied intentions. On D-Day itself, all the elements of a combined Allied force had to be brought together and used in harmony – air forces to weaken the enemy response, warships to protect the transport fleet, airborne divisions to secure the flanks and, of course, infantry and armour to carve out the toehold from which the liberation of western Europe would begin. The fact that it all worked is a lasting tribute to all the people involved.

Bildarchiv Preussischer Kulturbesitz

▼ A fully-laden M3AI half-track leads a miscellany of trucks off Omaha Beach, 7 June 1944. In the background may be seen part of the invasion fleet.

Imperial War Museum

Beach-masters and engineers with their bulldozers desperately moved tanks and troops along as fast as possible, but in this case the delay was due to the choppy tide being blown in by the wind faster than the planners had allowed for. Clearing of the beach obstacles was delayed, and landing craft had slowly to negotiate a few narrow gaps to get their loads ashore. By nightfall 50th Division was just short of its D-Day objective, the town of Bayeux.

JUNO BEACH

The 7 Brigade of the 3rd Canadian Division hit the beaches of Juno at about 7.50 am, and its neighbour, the 8 Brigade, ten minutes later. The two brigades had divided the objectives found on Juno. 7 Brigade struck at the village of Courseulles, while 8 landed opposite a strongpoint in the village of Bernières.

Of all the landings, the Canadians at Juno got closest to their planned objectives. Once the strongpoints had been eliminated, the Canadians moved rapidly inland. A party of tanks reached the Caen-Bayeux road but withdrew when they found no supporting infantry had kept pace.

SWORD BEACH

On Sword the British 3rd Infantry Division landed on the narrowest front of all the invasion beaches in an attempt to provide a sufficiently concentrated force to punch through the German defences to Caen. The British soldiers were fortunate that the beach was narrow. They could get across the short distance to cover, and be exposed to German shooting for only a short time. The Germans occupied well-fortified positions, however, with strong pillbox complexes in Ouistreham, Lion-sur-Mer and at La Brèche.

The fight for La Brèche took three hours, and cost the 1st South Lancashires and 2nd East Yorkshires heavy casualties. The East Yorkshires also attacked Ouistreham. A probe by the 1st South Lancashires in the direction of Périers Ridge was forced back into Hermanville when German anti-tank guns knocked out

defenders still held out, but they retreated after seeing gliders pass overhead in the direction of a landing zone near Ranville.

At nightfall, the commanders of the Allied Expeditionary Forces could feel relieved. All the 30 landings had succeeded in establishing bridgeheads. At Utah, Gold and Juno they were deep.

Omaha was the shallowest and weakest, while Sword faced strong armoured opposition. The battle to open a Second Front was far from over, though. Strong German counterattacks could still destroy the separated Allied forces in detail and drive them back into the Channel. But the hardest part of the assault had been accomplished – the Allies had fought their way ashore.

THIS IS THE YEAR !

IT'S UP TO US TO LET 'EM HAVE IT !

▲ ◄ **American soldiers gather a motley collection of prisoners. They are probably** *Organisation Todt* **labourers, recruited from all over occupied Europe. Inset, left: Pre-invasion propaganda.**

▶ **British Commandos push inland from Sword Beach. They are advancing towards an enemy gun emplacement, under sniper fire.**

several of the accompanying tanks.

The 1st Special Service Brigade landed at mid-morning, and moved inland very quickly to relieve the airborne troops holding the Orne bridges. Its leading elements, including the brigade commander Lord Lovat, arrived at the bridges at 12.03 pm. Most of the commmandos continued on over the Orne and took up defensive positions on the eastern flank of the Sword bridgehead.

The capture of Caen was the mission of 185 Brigade. This was ashore and formed up by 11 am, but traffic jams kept them from advancing until 12.30 pm. Then, the 2nd King's Shropshire Light Infantry went forward even though their tank support had not turned up. They had cleared most of Périers Ridge by 2 pm, and began moving down the road from Hermanville to Caen.

From mid-morning onwards, 3rd Division's headquarters had received reports of tanks assembling to the north and west of Caen. The German response to the landing had been delayed by the local corps commander, General Erich Marcks, who had hoped to get the 12th SS Panzer Division for a counterattack as well as the 21st. The German

High Command refused to release the 12th SS, and the 21st Panzer had to be redeployed from east of the Orne to face the more critical situation in the west. As a result, its attack did not go in before 4.30 pm.

Its tanks probed the British defensive perimeter around Biéville, while a blocking force was put in place at Lébisey, between Sword and Caen. The Biéville attack was beaten back by a squadron of the Staffordshire Yeomanry. The Germans then tried to find a chink in the defence on Périers Ridge, but again had to wheel away in the face of accurate fire from tanks and anti-tank guns.

A third attempt was made at Point 61, to the north of Périers, but this was also rebuffed. A few tanks of the 21st Panzer managed to reach the coast at Luc-sur-Mer, where some

War Stories

The German Navy did not distinguish itself on D-Day. Just three E-boats put in a chance appearance and, as the mist cleared, their commander found himself surrounded. However, before turning tail, he ordered his boats to launch all their torpedoes in the general direction of the enemy. The torpedoes sailed through the entire fleet until, on the far side, the Combined Ops HQ Ship, HMS *Largs*, had to go astern smartly to avoid them. Finally, one sank an unlucky destroyer – but the rest of the fleet escaped scot free.

THE MARIANAS

BATTLE DIARY

DECEMBER 1943
26   MacArthur invades New Britain

FEBRUARY 1944
5   MacArthur takes Kwajalein in the Marshall Islands
10–18   US carriers launch attack on Truk in the Carolines. Japanese abandon Truk as fleet base
21   Nimitz' forces takes Eniwetok (Marshall Islands)

APRIL
3   After February attack, MacArthur takes Admiralty Islands
26   MacArthur takes Hollandia (New Guinea)

MAY
27   MacArthur invades Biak Island, which is reinforced by the Japanese

JUNE
3–9   US carrier-based aircraft attack Japanese bases on Palau, Peleliu, Truk and Yap
11–13   US carriers attack Guam, Saipan and Tinian in the Marianas
13   Ozawa sails from Borneo and Ugaki from Bataan and rendezvous in the Philippine Sea
15   Nimitz invades Saipan
19–20   Battle of the Philippine Sea

JULY
9   Saipan taken

AUGUST
1   Tinian taken by Nimitz
10   Nimitz advances and takes Guam

RING OF FIRE

The headlong American drive to liberate Japanese-held islands in the Pacific reaches the strategic Marianas – but first, a massive naval air battle is brewing.

▲ A first wave of US Marines comes ashore on the island of Saipan, their way cleared by the Underwater Demolition Teams, 15 June 1944. Inset: the insignia of the US Eastern Defense Command.

The rim of the Pacific Ocean is known as 'The Ring of Fire' because of its numerous volcanoes, both extinct and active, the result of mighty earth movements. Its western edge in particular consists of long chains of volcanic islands whose slopes rise dramatically from the ocean. Such islands are in complete contrast to the coral atolls which characterise much of the central Pacific and where most of the fighting up to 1944 had taken place. From the point of view of the Americans, these island chains were essential stepping stones to Japan. Already, in late 1943, the US war machine had turned its massive resources to routing the Japanese in the scattered Marshall and Gilbert Islands. Despite massive loss of life on both sides, relentless US amphibious and aerial attacks and

All pictures: US National Archives

naval bombardment had finally reclaimed the Japanese strongpoints of Tarawa, Kwajalein and Eniwetok.

Now, to keep up the momentum of the headlong American progress, General Douglas MacArthur pushed grimly along the northern coast of New Guinea, ever closer to his goal of the Philippines, while Admiral Chester Nimitz's Central Pacific forces were concentrating for their assault on the Marianas.

LOGICAL PROGRESS

Why choose the Marianas rather than the Carolines, the next stepping stone in line? From their major bases in the Carolines, notably Truk and Ponape, the Japanese were able to menace both axes of the American advance. But air power from both MacArthur and Nimitz was using every airstrip to pound the enemy remorselessly. With the taking of key islands in the Marshalls in February 1944, their airfields had been added to others stretching in a 14,000-mile (22,400 km) arc from Eniwetok to New Guinea. So effective were the results that Nimitz decided to bypass the Carolines, allowing their Japanese garrisons to 'wither on the vine', and make straight for the Marianas.

The advantage of this was that it brought US forces much closer to Japan in one hop, while still wearing away at Japanese air power and preventing it from harassing the US forces.

The Marianas were a prime objective. These 15 major islands, set in a 400-mile (640 km) string, once taken, would change the axis of Nimitz's advance from east-west to south-north, aiming directly at Tokyo. And they were within B-29 Superfortress bombing range of Japan itself.

In March 1944, when the decision was taken to move against the Marianas, Nimitz had already lost many of his forces to the D-Day preparations in Europe. The three Marine and two Army divisions that he retained were still more than sufficient, however, for assaulting on the narrow front offered by the island terrain. But now he would have to break the 'iron rule' by operating beyond the range of land-based air support. Carriers had proved their ability to work in this capacity, and large numbers

◄ Preparing for the invasion of Saipan, SBD Dauntless dive-bombers line the deck of Vice Admiral Mitscher's carrier, Lexington, 15 June 1944. With Hellcat fighters and Avenger torpedo-bombers, the US air strength totalled an amazing 865.

◄ In the Battle of the Philippine Sea, the massive resources of the US Navy muster against an outnumbered enemy. Sailors on board USS *Mexico* load a seemingly endless supply of 14-inch shells in preparation for the Guam invasion.

of them were being brought into service.

Only the four southernmost islands of the Marianas – Guam, Rota, Tinian and Saipan – had a strategic value. In contrast to low-lying coral atolls, here Nimitz's forces would have to fight on mountainous and heavily wooded volcanic islands. Furthermore, on three of them the garrisons would be assisted by a large Japanese civil population.

Operation Forager was conceived on a breathtaking scale. The Fifth Fleet commander, Admiral Raymond A Spruance, had overall responsibility for the experienced Admiral Richmond K Turner's Joint Expeditionary Force (TF51). This comprised three groups – the Northern Attack Force (TF52) under Turner himself and Lieutenant-General Holland M ('Howlin' Mad') Smith, United States Marine Corps, which carried the 2nd and 4th Marine Divisions for Saipan; the Southern Attack

Force (TF53) under Rear Admiral Richard L Conolly and Major-General Roy S Geiger, carrying the III Amphibious Corps for Guam; and a Floating Reserve (TG51.1) under Rear Admiral William H Blandy and Major-General Ralph Smith, carrying the US Army's 27th Infantry Division. Dedicated bombardment groups were attached to both TF52 and 53, as well as escort carriers to provide on-call, pinpoint air support. With the involvement of 535 craft and 127,000 troops it was necessary to send TF53 from the Solomons and the others from Hawaii.

Covering the armada was Vice Admiral Marc Mitscher's fast carrier force (TF58) with seven attack carriers and eight light carriers, divided evenly over four task groups (TF58.1 to 58.4). Between them they could muster 229 SB2C Helldiver and SBD Dauntless dive-bombers, 443 F6F Hellcat fighters and 193 TBF/TBM Avenger torpedo bombers. In addition to each task group's close escort, there was Vice Admiral William Lee's TG58.7 – a self-contained battle group, built around seven modern battleships.

THE TRAP IS SET

It was Spruance's aim to trail his coat just sufficiently to encourage the Japanese to attack his carriers, so giving the assault force a free run. But a fight was inevitable anyway, as Admiral Soemu Toyoda, the new Commander-in-Chief of the Japanese Combined Fleet, had already devised a plan to bring about the long-sought fleet action. This plan, *A-Go*, was to be initiated by any American attempt to breach a nominal defensive perimeter running from the Marianas, via the Palaus to western New Guinea. As the Americans now enjoyed overwhelming strength in every category, it would seem that Japanese aggression got the better of Japanese wisdom, as the time for set-piece actions was long past.

The trigger came on the afternoon of 11 June, when over 200 US aircraft, working at maximum range, hit airfields on Saipan and Tinian. This signalled a general churning-up of grass strips throughout the Marianas and islands to the north in order to reduce land-based Japanese air support during the coming landings and to prevent rapid reinforcement from that direction.

The attack came as an unpleasant surprise to the Japanese, who had hoped for the 'decisive battle' to be

NAVAL OPTIMIST

Vice Admiral Jisaburo Ozawa was not strictly a 'carrier admiral' — but he possessed an able intellect, ever ready to exploit new ideas.

Aged 54 at the outbreak of the war, he adopted enthusiastically the fluid form of naval war demonstrated by Vice Admiral Nagumo.

After Nagumo's defeat at Midway, Ozawa was appointed in his stead, and in the new First Mobile Fleet, Ozawa commanded about 90 per cent of Japan's naval strength. He alone carried the responsibility which on the American side was shared by Spruance and Mitscher. It was surely this solitary command and his unflagging optimism which conspired to bring about his defeat in the Philippine Sea.

Although he offered to resign, he was placed in command of the northern force of the Japanese fleet and continued to serve, playing a decoy role in the Battle of Leyte Gulf, until the Japanese surrender.

Imperial War Museum

Let's give him Enough and On Time

▲ A US war production poster emphasises the need for efficient supply to the front line – the people's war effort translates so directly to the fighting.

fought farther to the south-west, near the Palaus. This was because the activities of American submarines had created a desperate shortage of refined bunker fuel, obliging the ships to burn unprocessed Borneo crude which contained damaging impurities. This in turn meant that Japanese carriers could not move very far or very fast without risking damage to their engines. Furthermore, the Japanese could only counter the immense superiority in American carrier-based air strength by using land-based air to the greatest possible extent.

Commanding the First Mobile Fleet (equivalent roughly to an American Task Force) was Vice Admiral Jisaburo Ozawa. He saw that, if he reacted swiftly, he could still capitalise on certain advantages in his own favour. He knew that American carrier aircraft could strike with full loads at only about 200 miles (320 km) from their decks. His own aircraft could attack at ranges up to 300 miles (480 km), allowing his carriers to remain out of US range. In addition, the island airstrips permitted not only land-based airstrikes, but also allowed his carrier aircraft to attack, fly on to refuel and rearm, and then hit the Americans again on the return

flight. These airstrips, however, were only beaten earth, and therefore very vulnerable to air strikes.

By early June, an estimated 540 Japanese aircraft were placed to support *A-Go*, but little account had been taken of the large number which had been despatched south in reaction to MacArthur's recent landing on Biak.

From the 12th to the 15th, Mitscher's aircraft battered the airstrips incessantly, his Combat Air Patrols (CAPs) demolishing any attempts at aerial counterattack. Japanese pride concealed the extent of these losses from Ozawa, who was also fed with inflated reports of damage suffered by the American carriers.

▲ Ashore – but still not out of the wet – US Marines come under fire as they land on a Saipan beach, their arrival supported by the 75 mm guns of an LVTA in the background shallows.

UNSUNG HEROES

Seldom making the headlines, US submarines, mounting their long, arduous patrols into the Pacific from Australia, had a commanding influence on Japan's wartime fortunes. Japan depended totally on her merchantmen to sustain garrisons, supply the battle fronts and deliver raw materials.

So it was that, alone or in groups, such as 'Blair's Blasters' or 'Park's Pirates', US submarines provided vital intelligence and stalked the hated merchantmen, sinking so many tankers that, by June 1944, the Japanese fleet's movements were already hobbled by an acute shortage of fuel.

With Saipan as a base, the submarines continued in their disruptive role — one as effective as that of the U-Boat 'Wolf Packs' in the Atlantic.

▶ An officer in an American submarine, scans the Pacific for signs of Japanese activity.

right angles to the prevailing wind, and Lee's battle-line, covered by the weakest carrier group, TG58.4, was stationed between the American carriers and the Japanese fleet, ready to fight off Ugaki's battleships if they intervened in the coming battle.

Spruance's overall battle-plan was to destroy Ozawa's carriers first, then progress to the battleships and cruisers. Lee, after fulfilling his defensive role, would be available to mop up damaged and straggling ships left behind by the fleeing Japanese fleet.

The forthcoming naval action would be history by the time Saipan fell. Of the 67,500 American troops committed to the island, 3,400 would be dead and of the defenders, just 1,780 would survive. The writing was on the wall for the Japanese Empire.

BATTLE OF THE PHILIPPINE SEA

19 JUNE 1944
4.15 am Spruance traces Ozawa's radio message and heads away from Japanese positions
8.16 US submarine *Albacore* stalks Japanese Force A
8.30 Van Force launches 69 aircraft which Spruance detects. Spruance attacks Guam airfields – aerial battles last until about 10.00, with a loss of 35 Japanese aircraft
9.00 Force A of 128 aircraft launched against Mitscher, but 97 are destroyed
9.09 *Albacore* cripples the carrier *Taiho*
10.00 Ozawa's Force B of 47 aircraft launched, but is attacked and scattered by 12.00
12.20 pm US submarine *Cavalla* cripples *Shokaku*

2.32 *Taiho* explodes
2.00–3.00 Minor Japanese attack on Mitscher deflected
2.50 49 Japanese aircraft try to land on Guam – most are destroyed, the rest crash land and break up
3.00 *Shokaku* explodes

20 JUNE
3.40 pm US Avenger finds Japanese carriers
4.20 Mitscher launches 216 aircraft and follows them with carriers to reduce the range of their return
6.40 US aircraft attack Japanese carriers
7.00 *Hiyo* sunk. *Ryuho, Chiyoda, Zuikaku* damaged. Twenty US aircraft lost
10.52 Last US stragglers land back on carriers, remainder deemed lost

FEROCIOUS FIGHTING

The opening shots of the invasion of Saipan were fired on 13 and 14 June by ships of TG58.7. While effective, this still left Japanese strongpoints on the beaches, which were subsequently strengthened now that it was obvious where the attack would come. For just such attacks as this, the Americans had created a new force of Underwater Demolition Teams (UDT), which used the preliminary bombardment as cover for surveying and making ready the approaches to the landing beaches by blasting openings in the reefs where necessary.

Armed with UDT intelligence and plans, the Saipan assault began at first light on 15 June when an initial wave of 96 Amtracs went in. Within the space of 20 minutes, over 8,000 Marines went ashore – but the 30,000 defenders had improvised well. Their artillery was plentiful, well-dispersed and obviously pre-calibrated on to likely targets, and successive waves of US invaders had to fight from the moment they crossed the reef. It took them three days of ferocious fighting to reach their first-day objectives.

Mitscher, meanwhile, was deploying to meet a full-scale threat from the Japanese fleet. Ozawa's carrier force had left its Borneo anchorage on the 13th. At the same time the main Japanese surface fleet under Vice Admiral Matome Ugaki was rushing up from New Guinea, where it had been supporting the Japanese invaders of Biak island. By the evening of the 17th, Ozawa had a good idea of American strength and dispositions and was some 450 miles (720 km) to their west.

Appreciating that a major action was brewing, Spruance postponed the Guam landing. All four US carrier groups were refuelled and concentrated some 180 miles (290 km) west of Tinian by noon on 18 June. The three strongest groups were set on a north-south axis, at

▼ Japanese supply lines are blocked by marauding US aircraft and submarines — a cargo ship comes under air attack. Inset: Mitscher's Task Force 58.

TURKEY SHOOT

An ambitious Japanese plan is afoot to destroy the US Pacific Fleet with a force less than half its size. It would be a battle of grim determination against quick wits and huge resources.

T he islands that make up the Marianas chain point like an arrow at the heart of Japan. So when American forces landed on Saipan on 15 June 1944, the stage was set for a major sea battle in the Philippine Sea. However, Admiral Jisaburo Ozawa, in command of the First Mobile Fleet, did not have a defensive battle in mind. Having watched the build-up of American strength in the Pacific, the Japanese plan known as *A-Go* was designed to wear it down again by bringing about a major sea battle. Strangely enough, the possibility of defeat by the Americans does not seem to have entered into the Japanese calculations, although their fleet was half the size of the American one and their Zero fighters were sitting ducks when up against the American Hellcats. Clearly they were still suffering from the 'victory disease' that had infected the Japanese after Pearl Harbor and for this, the only cure was abject defeat.

FINDING THE ENEMY

Meanwhile Vice Admiral Mitscher's Task Force, TF58, was positioned 180 miles (290 km) west of the Marianas by the early afternoon of the 18th. Ozawa's position was unknown to the Americans but as an aggressive 'carrier admiral', Mitscher's natural instinct was to head west, fight a night surface action and mop up the next morning with carrier aircraft. This plan was vetoed by Spruance, who felt that the confusion of a night engagement handed the Japanese an unnecessary advantage as they were highly experienced at this type of battle. From the Japanese standpoint, Spruance's position close to the island airfields was ideal for Operation *A-Go*. A land-based air search failed to pinpoint TF58 during the morning of the 18th so Ozawa sent out carrier

aircraft. These sighted various American groups at 3.14 pm and about 4.00 pm at a range exceeding 400 miles (640 km), well beyond the range of American search aircraft.

Ozawa intended, during the night of 18/19 June, to keep the Main Body of his fleet (incorporating his six largest carriers in two groups) about 400 miles (640 km) from the Americans and his separate Van Force (three groups, each built around one, smaller carrier) some 300 miles (480 km) distant. He was beyond Mitscher's reach while, some 200 miles (320 km) beyond his enemy, lay the supporting airfields on Guam and Saipan. Ozawa felt confident of victory.

Remembering that delay in earlier actions had cost them dear, Vice

▲ The pilot of an Avenger torpedo bomber takes a well-earned drink, after the night pursuit of the Japanese at the end of the battle. The message on the blackboard sums up the tactics used by both sides.

◄ How the forces compared, 19 June 1944.

◄◄ On the deck of USS *Hornet*, the fire crew assist the pilot of a Curtiss SB2-C Helldiver to safety. Meanwhile another party of men get ready to push the wreckage into the sea to clear the deck for later arrivals.

BATTLE LINE-UP

USA aircraft 865   JAPAN aircraft 540

USA		JAPAN
15	aircraft carriers	9
7	battleships	5
22	cruisers	12
62	destroyers	22
25	submarines	—

► Resting his navigation computer and oxygen mask on the wing, Lieutenant Andy Vraciu signs for the condition of his plane after returning from a combat mission. Vraciu flew from the 'Big Lex' and made 19 kills in the course of the battle.

▲ Shoulder insignia of the Headquarters of the Pacific Air Wing, US Marine Corps.

Admiral Takeo Kurita, commanding the Van Force, decided to mount a 67-strong airstrike on his own initiative. This would have taken Mitscher by surprise, out of the setting sun. The aircraft would then fly rearmed and fueled for the rerun the next day but, fearing that his initiative contravened his commander's wishes, Kurita cancelled the move as the aircraft took off.

To prepare for an extreme-range strike at first light on the 19th, Ozawa divided his forces. By 4.15 am, everything was ready but he broke radio silence to request simultaneous land-based air support. The commander on Saipan, Rear Admiral Kakujo Kakuta, probably for no better reason than to 'save face', at no stage warned that the 500 aircraft on which *A-Go* depended were, in reality, nearer 50, and these were

needed to defend the airfields, which were being systematically ploughed-up by American air attack.

Monitored by American listeners, Ozawa's radio message warned Spruance that the enemy were about 300 miles (480 km) to his west. The American admiral, clear that his primary duty was to protect the Saipan landings, decided to move closer to the invasion beaches to prevent the Japanese from attacking from the other direction. Spruance made the Japanese fleet come to him, although the 'carrier admirals' wanted to get their aircraft into action as soon as possible.

During the early hours of the decisive 19 June, the Americans were thus steaming away from Ozawa but, heading into wind, could mount a rapid response. At a time when the Japanese had still not been

▼ A twin-engined Japanese bomber goes down in flames over the USS *Kitkun Bay*. Lacking armour and self-sealing tanks in their aircraft, the Japanese were easy prey for a flak barrage as at far right.

THE FEROCIOUS GNOME

Vice Admiral Marc A Mitscher's greatest talent was his ability to create a unified fighting machine by welding together the many units of his carrier force. His record — he was never defeated — is a tribute to his competence and authoritative command.

Although the same age as his adversary, Jisaburo Ozawa, Mitscher looked older. His slight frame and wizened features (inevitably crowned by a lobsterman's cap) combined with his aggressive approach to battle earned him the affectionate nickname of 'the Ferocious Gnome'.

Having earned his pilot's wings in 1915, he served continuously in US naval aviation, commanding the carrier USS *Hornet* from 1941, launching Doolittle's raiders towards Tokyo and assisting at Midway.

Never one to enjoy the limelight, he shunned publicity — but his taciturn manner covered a deep concern for his men, who rewarded him with immense loyalty and affection.

All pictures: US National Archives

sighted. TF58 was dogged by enemy reconnaissance aircraft.

The day dawned clear and bright. Ozawa, believing that Spruance was being harried by the land-based air-strike that he had ordered earlier, prepared his own. At 8.30 am, even as the blips representing Japanese aerial activity showed on his radar plots, Spruance had a last crack at the Japanese airfields, damaging them further and destroying 35 enemy aircraft over Guam.

EMERGENCY CALL

While the Japanese planes were still 150 miles (240 km) away, the sheer size of the approaching Japanese airstrike was obvious. The American fighter controllers issued a 'Hey, Rube' emergency call, bringing back all their fighters to cover the carriers, while launching reinforcements. From Kurita's Van Force, the enemy comprised 45 bomb-armed Mitsu-bishi A6M Zeros, eight Nakajima B6N 'Jill' torpedo-bombers and an escort of 16 Zero fighters. These

▲ Zero fighters, carrying belly tanks for long range, line up for take-off from a Japanese carrier. Sandbags are piled on the deck to form a bomb shelter. This picture was captured during the war.

▲ Japanese arm badge indicating bomber crews.

orbited over the carriers for 10 minutes to regroup, and so gave Mitscher adequate time to organise CAPs – Combat Air Patrols – on a rotating schedule and to store his attack aircraft below.

While the Hellcats were often considerably outnumbered by Kurita's aircraft, they found that the Japanese had no idea of how to defend themselves. The bombers simply scattered and the fighters concentrated on survival.

Those attackers evading the CAP then had to cross Rear Admiral William Lee's 'battle line'. This was composed of battleships and cruisers, each bristling with anti-aircraft guns, positioned so that they could protect each other. Using proximity-fused ammunition for the first time, their fire was particularly destructive because they exploded on a 'near

▶ Helldiver dive bombers and Avenger torpedo bombers off Saipan. These aircraft were the spearhead of the American carriers.

▼ Avengers take off to bomb Tinian from USS *Monterey*. Though single-engined, these were large, heavy aircraft and putting one down on a carrier was a test of flying skill.

All pictures: US National Archives

complete ignorance of the fate of his men, Ozawa then launched a third, 47-plane, strike between 10 and 10.15 am. Due to an error in interpreting a signal from a search aircraft, this group was routed too far to the north, bypassing Lee and approaching Mitscher from an unexpected direction. Again, the radar detected them at 100 miles (160 km) and the formation was jumped by 40

miss' as well as a 'hit'. Lee's units incurred only superficial damage but the Japanese attack broke up, leaving Mitscher's carriers unmolested. The second strike, mounted from Ozawa's carriers, followed about half an hour later. Detected at 115 miles (185 km) range at 11.07 am, it was a mix of 128 aircraft.

The American fighter controllers watched the raid on radar and also eavesdropped on radio transmissions, using Japanese-speakers to give an immediate translation. They intercepted with Hellcats at 50 miles (80 km) range. Some 20 attackers evaded the F6Fs which had to look

on as Lee's battle line engaged them in a furious 10-minute anti-aircraft barrage at about noon. Except for the damage caused by one Japanese aircraft crashing into the battleship *Indiana*, the damage inflicted was negligible.

Two small groups of Yokosuka D4Y 'Judy' and Nakajima B6N 'Jill' bombers succeeded in breaking through to the carriers, causing a few anxious moments before succumbing to the carriers' own AA guns. A staggering 97 of the 128 attackers were destroyed, but Ozawa was not perturbed by their non-return to the carriers until the following day. In

War Stories

Staff Sergeant Victor Pizzuto, a ball-turret gunner in a Liberator bomber based in the Marshall Islands, was astonished when his strafing fire on what he took to be a Japanese power station at Jaluit, suddenly blew it sky high in a spectacular explosion. At first he thought some other aircraft had bombed the building – but it turned out that he had hit the jackpot. With a few well-aimed rounds of machine-gun fire, he had single-handedly taken out a massive, high-powered ammunition and explosives dump!

hastily assembled Hellcats. The Japanese showed their inexperience once more for, having lost only seven of their number, the majority failed to find any targets on an ocean littered with ships.

Mitscher, still unaware of the Japanese fleet's position, launched more search aircraft but, as 300 miles (480 km) still separated the rapidly manoeuvring carrier groups, they found nothing. Ozawa now launched a further airstrike. This was definitely his last throw. It was a ragbag of his surviving aircraft – 82 in all – from four decks. These, too, were poorly directed and, finding nothing, they split into two groups.

The smaller of these again bypassed the outer American defences by sheer good fortune and sighted Task Group 58.2. The carriers here were very vulnerable because they were recovering aircraft and their CAP was at high altitude. The radar

◄ **Douglas SBD Dauntless dive bomber on a hunt-killer mission as the sun sets. By June 1944, American pilots were more skilled than the Japanese and could operate in worse conditions.**

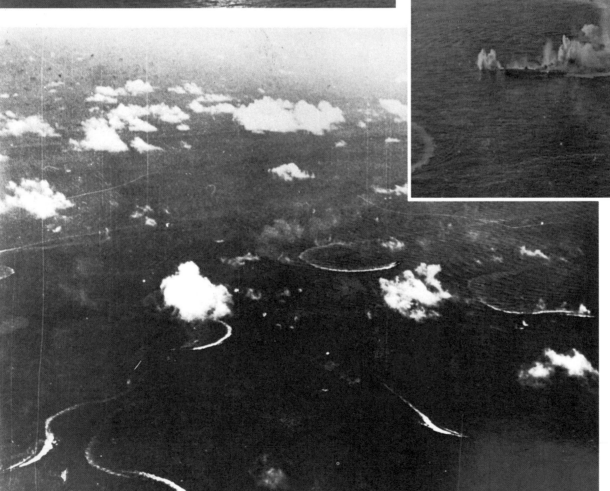

▲ **A large** *Shokaku-***class carrier, already burning, bracketed by bombs dropped by aircraft from Task Force 58. The destroyer escorts are manoeuvring wildly to avoid sharing her fate.**

◄ **Under aerial attack, the Japanese ships either steam in a circle or steer S-turns to confuse the attackers.**

US National Archives

DON'T BE A JERK—DON'T GET A MOSQUITO BAYONET IN YOUR.

KEEP COVERED, FROM SUNDOWN TO SUNRISE AND— USE YOUR REPELLENT

FIGHT THE PERIL BEHIND THE LINES

▲ **Marines push on towards a Japanese oil dump, set on fire by the 37 mm cannon mounted on an Amtrac. Preliminary bombardment has stripped the trees.**

▲ **Malaria is a major problem on islands like Saipan and Guam, where there are plenty of pools for mosquitoes to breed in. Repellents do not really work.**

▶ **Seebees (Construction Battalions) repair the runway of Aslito airfield on Saipan on 30 June 1944. The open framework is a hangar in course of construction while the camouflaged control tower is in the background.**

US National Archives; inset: Imperial War Museum

gave less than 15 minutes' warning but a combination of a hastily-organised air defence and brisk manoeuvring by the ships saw them through with no more than a few near misses.

The second group, 49-strong, flew straight on to Guam, arriving at about 2.50 pm. Here they jettisoned their bombs and prepared to land.

Hellcats patrolling the island accounted for 30 of the Japanese planes orbiting the airfield, although their effort was largely superfluous, for the surface of Guam's Orote Field was so bad that each surviving aircraft, on landing, was damaged beyond repair.

In the course of these four frantic hours, soon nicknamed the 'Great Marianas Turkey Shoot', the Japanese had lost well over 300 aircraft. To rub in the defeat, several American submarines were stationed across Ozawa's projected route and even as his flagship *Taiho* was flying-off her 42-plane contribution to the second strike, she was being stalked by the USS *Albacore*. The torpedo computer on *Albacore* failed but Captain Blanchard fired a six-torpedo spread. Only one hit and her captain was disappointed to see the enemy's largest carrier proceed unchecked.

SUBMARINE ATTACK

Three hours later, the same group of carriers encountered the US submarine *Cavalla* which was able to get within 1000 yards (915 m) of the *Shokaku*. At 12.20 pm, this veteran of the Pearl Harbor raid staggered as

▲ GIs sweat while they keep a 4.2 in (100 mm) mortar pounding away at the Japanese lines.

carriers, but was not Radio Tokyo confirming that the enemy had already lost eleven?

Then at last, at 3.40 pm an Avenger from the US carrier *Enterprise* found the Japanese. The initial assessment of 220 miles (354 km) range was soon modified to 275 (442 km), but now Mitscher had the chance he wanted and had 216 aircraft aloft in an incredibly short 10 minutes. It was 4.20 pm, sunset was at 7.00 pm; they could not get back

▼ Mountainous Saipan has many caves which give refuge to the Japanese civilian settlers – but snipers also use this type of cover.

three torpedoes found their mark. The American submariners had to sit out three hours of depth-charging which ended abruptly at about 3 pm as the escorts withdrew, and the *Shokaku* sank. *Taiho* suffered a similar fate. Her single injury had ruptured the seals in the fuel stowage and distribution system, allowing aviation gas vapour to collect in the ship. She exploded and sank with many of her crew, though Ozawa was able to transfer his flag and, most important, the Emperor's portrait, to a cruiser.

By about this time, the cautious Spruance began to consider an attack but Mitscher, whose afternoon searches had been unsuccessful, was unwilling to mount night searches, even with his radar-equipped Avengers. Flying-boats were equally unlucky.

A fine dawn on 20 June found Spruance still looking for his enemy, but increasingly convinced that he had quit. Ozawa, however, still blind to his disaster, sought Spruance. Boarding the carrier *Zuikaku* at about 1.00 pm, the Japanese admiral took stock. He still had 102 aircraft embarked. Together with those he believed were ashore, he could finish the Americans. He had lost two

SUPPLYING FORAGER

The assault on the Marianas, involved 535 combatant and auxiliary aircraft and 127,000 troops. It was the US's most ambitious operation so far. The planning, completed in three months, was complicated by distances – over 1,000 miles (1,600 km) from Eniwetok and 3,500 miles (5,600 km) from Pearl Harbor.

Shipping involved would be tied up for three months – and while a 5,000 ton freighter could feed 90,000 men for 30 days, food perished rapidly in the heat, so planning was crucial. Nearly 50 tankers shipped a total of 4.5 million barrels of bunker fuel, 275,000 of diesel oil and 400,000 of avgas.

Up to the landing on Guam, Forager consumed an astounding 6,378 rounds of 14- and 16-inch ammunition, 19,230 of 6- and 8-inch and 140,000 of 5-inch.

▶ Lt-Gen Holland M. Smith, left, Admiral Raymond Spruance, right, with a Marine Major-General.

SPRINGBOARD

TURNING POINT

In the American drive across the Pacific, naval and air power were crucial. The US Marines were becoming expert at the techniques of amphibious assault, but this required the movement of men and supplies, in convoy, across immense tracts of ocean. If the Japanese could locate the convoys and strike at them with carrier-borne aircraft, US losses could climb so high that the Pacific war would become a stand-off. However, by June 1944, American carriers far-outnumbered the Japanese and the Hellcat fighter could blast the Zero and its inexperienced pilots out of the sky. The Battle of the Philippine Sea was therefore decisive: the Imperial Navy could no longer make an effective challenge to the American amphibious assaults and the way was open for the B-29s to carry the war to the Japanese home islands.

◄ **Battleship main armament consisting of 14 in (350 mm) guns fire in support of the landings on Guam.**

All pictures: US National Archives

to the carriers before dark. Though TF58 followed its own aircraft at top speed, to shorten the round trip, Ozawa himself was steaming away. Some aircraft had an outward leg of 330 miles (530 km) to the Japanese carriers, far beyond normal range.

At 6.40 pm, as the dying sun neared the horizon, the Americans attacked at last. The Japanese carriers were in three groups, their vital oil tankers trailing some 40 miles (65 km) astern.

Faced by 75 Japanese fighters and a curtain of multi-coloured flak from the capital ships, and with one eye on their fuel gauges, the attackers did not hesitate. In a confusing 20 minutes, the carrier *Hiyo* was torpedoed twice, later sinking by fire and explosion. Carriers *Ryoho*, *Chiyoda* and *Zuikaku* were all damaged by dive-bombers, the *Zuikaku* very seriously. Understandably, in the gloom and confusion, the fliers overestimated their success but a pair of oil tankers were also disabled, later being scuttled.

noon of the 22nd, the Japanese fleet anchored off Okinawa, in good shape except that the aircraft carriers lacked aircraft.

On 8 July, resistance ended on Saipan. Tinian was safely in American hands by 7 August and Guam surrendered on 10 August. The final American move in this theatre was a thrust to the Vulcana Islands by TG58.1. Yet more Japanese aircraft were destroyed and the airfields put out of action.

▲ A Japanese prisoner awaits questioning by one of the hastily-trained Japanese-speaking officers in the Intelligence Corps.

Twenty attackers were shot down, the remainder settling down to coax their aircraft home. They had 240 to 300 miles (385 km to 480 km) to go and the night was dark and overcast with a thunderstorm. Mitscher kept his carriers well separated to act independently and at 8.45 pm, they turned into the wind to help the pilots land. Deck lights and search-lights were turned on and starshells were fired to mark their position. One Avenger, piloted by Lieutenant Commander Evan O Aurand, was sent up to shepherd some of the last sheep home. With dry tanks, aircraft ditched or put down on the first available deck while two pilots managed to land simultaneously on one carrier. Almost half the aircraft landed on the 'wrong' carriers. At 10.52 pm, all that could returned were deemed to have returned, formation was re-established and the task commenced of recovering ditched aircrew, whose markers strewed the sea like a 'June meadow full of fireflies'. Exactly 100 aircraft were lost, but fewer than 50 crewmen.

Spruance pursued the enemy until the next day, but without hope of overhauling Ozawa. On the after-

▲ Marines jump into the surf, after their Amtrac grounds on the coral reef at Tinian.

▶ A small patrol of Marines goes after a still smaller group of Japanese troops hiding out in the hills and jungles of Tinian. This is one of the rare occasions that a pistol is a really useful weapon.

BATTLE DIARY

1	Eisenhower takes command of Allied ground forces. Montgomery promoted to Field Marshal
3	Brussels liberated
4	Antwerp liberated: Montgomery proposes 'full-blooded thrust' to Eisenhower
10	Montgomery and Eisenhower meet in Burssels. Market Garden is given go-ahead. US troops cross German border
17	Air borne landings take place around Arnhem, Nijmegen and Eindhoven. British XXX Corps attacks towards Eindhoven. 2 Para captures north end of Arnhem bridge
18	XXX Corps links up with 101st Airborne Division near Eindhoven
19	XXX Corps and 82nd Airborne link up at Nijmegen
20	Bridge at Nijmegen captured
21	2 Para surrenders north end of Arnhem bridge. Attempt by XXX Corps to break out from Nijmegen fails. 1st Airborne pinned by Germans around Oosterbeek
22	Polish tropps dropped around Driel. German counter-attack cuts off road to Arnhem north of Veghel
23	Attempt by Poles and XXX Corps to cross Lower Rhine and reinforce 1st Airborne fails
24	Second attempt to reach 1st Airborne fails
25	British 1st Airborne withdraws over Lower Rhine

A BOLD PLAN

Poppperfoto

In the wake of their recent successes, the Allies agree on a bold and imaginative plan to catapult their armies on to Germany's doorstep.

▲ Montgomery's hope: a major parachute drop and glider landing to capture the bridges over the Lower Rhine.

▲ ▲ Shoulder patch for members of the SHAEF staff.

The Supreme Allied Commander interrupted his subordinate's speech: 'Steady, Monty, you can't talk to me like that. I'm your boss.' Dwight D. Eisenhower, the American general in charge of a fractious coalition army including French, Canadian and Polish units in addition to its substantial majority of American and British troops, was being remarkably restrained. He had heard British Field Marshal Bernard Montgomery describe a series of cables sent to him from Supreme Headquarters, and penned by Eisenhower himself, as 'balls'. Montgomery, now reminded of his proper place in the chain of command, apologised to the American. The meeting, being held in a C-47 transport plane at Brussels on 10 September 1944, then got down to its real business.

Imperial War Museum

▲ **Field Marshal Montgomery, mastermind of the operation, talking to Brigadier Hackett (centre), commander of 4th Para Brigade, and Major-General Urquhart, commander of the 1st Airborne, in the hectic days before the assault.**

Montgomery's outburst came at a tricky time for inter-Allied cooperation. His role during Operation Overlord as ground commander of the armies fighting the Germans in north-west Europe had just come to an end. Now he was merely the commander of 21st Army Group, on a level equal to General Omar Bradley and General Jacob Devers, the American commanders of the other two Allied army groups in France. Montgomery had led his men to a great victory in Normandy, liberated Paris and Belgium, and now pursued what seemed to be mere remnants of the enemy's forces back to the German border. The very day of Montgomery's meeting with Eisenhower, Allied soldiers crossed into the Reich – men of Bradley's all-American 12th Army Group.

Further to the south, Lieutenant-General George S. Patton's US Third Army was pressing forward as relentlessly as possible, entering the region of Lorraine, formerly part of France though annexed by Hitler in 1940. On all fronts the Allies were advancing, hindered more by the difficulties of keeping their own men supplied than by any resistance from the Germans.

Yet it was this advance on all fronts that Montgomery believed constituted the Achilles heel of the overall Allied strategy. His anger over what he saw as operational incompetence at the highest level had precipitated his outburst.

FULL-BLOODED THRUST

On 4 September 1944, Montgomery had sent a message to Eisenhower saying, 'One really powerful and full-blooded thrust towards Berlin is likely to get there and end the war'. It was maintained, correctly, that the overall supply situation was unable to sustain two such thrusts. Eisenhower did not agree, but neither did he formally disagree. Montgomery saw a chance to influence the direction of the campaign, and asked Eisenhower to come to Brussels, 21st Army Group's advanced headquarters.

Thus he was bringing to a head one of the last debates on a major strategic issue the Allies would face in their long battle against Hitler: whether to attack into German territory on a broad or narrow front. The Allied commanders divided into two groups on the issue, the supporters of a broad front being mainly American (though including the British General Frederick Morgan), and those of the narrow front being mainly British (though paradoxically including Montgomery's great rival Patton).

The debate had opened at a conference at Tourniers in France on 19–20 August. At it Eisenhower had overruled Montgomery's scheme for an advance on a narrow front, a position he maintained throughout the next three

Gas Oorthuys Archives

DUTCH COURAGE

Dutch Resistance groups were formed almost immediately after the country's defeat in 1940. Like other groups in occupied Europe, the Dutch organised sabotage acts against the despised *Moffen*, their nickname for the Germans. Their most valuable service to the Allied cause was in providing information on German troop movements.

However, in one of their intelligence coups in 1941, the Germans captured radio transmitters and codes from Dutch SOE operators and kept up regular fake transmissions, with disastrous results for the Allies. Agents and supplies were sent from London straight into the hands of the enemy.

This made British Intelligence suspicious of any information from Dutch sources, with fatal consequences. Despite warnings from the Dutch Resistance concerning German armoured divisions near Arnhem, the drops went ahead, and landed paratroopers right in the midst of the enemy.

◄ **Dutch Resistance men learn to assemble a Sten gun.**

Bundesarchiv-Koblenz

◄ **German troops in the streets of Arnhem show no signs of apprehension about their task of holding back the Allied airborne invasion.**

weeks in the face of steady, sniping arguments from Montgomery, from the British chiefs of staff in London, and from some of his own subordinates.

Montgomery, however, would not let it go. The Joint Intelligence Committee, an Anglo-American staff that analysed and evaluated intelligence gathered from all sources, thought that organised resistance by the Germans would not continue beyond 1 December 1944. Furthermore, the German generals' attempt to overthrow Hitler on 20 July 1944 revealed a dissension in the enemy's high command that might once more come to the aid of the Allies.

OPERATION MARKET GARDEN

On 3 September, at a meeting with Bradley, Montgomery hinted at trying an operation to seize the bridges over the Lower Rhine (Dutch: *Neder Rijn*) at Arnhem for an armoured thrust to follow up. The plan, Operation Market Garden, was finally revealed and approved at the 10 September meeting in Brussels. The Anglo-US First Airborne Army would be dropped at points along the road from Eindhoven to Arnhem. The British XXX Corps would at the same time launch an attack along this road, relieving the airborne forces and capturing the bridges at Arnhem. If successful, Hitler's *Westwall* defences would be outflanked and the Rhine would be crossed. It would also leave Montgomery's army group in an excellent position for conducting that 'single bold thrust' further east into Germany in the late autumn, threatening the industrial heart of the Ruhr. It would be difficult for Eisenhower to refuse to fuel his British subordinate's success.

The operation was scheduled for 17 September, cutting planning down to a mere week. This was not the handicap it might seem, for Operation Market (the

airborne aspect of the plan) was only another in a series of proposed airborne assaults. The most recent, code-named Comet, had been cancelled on the same day that Montgomery proposed Market Garden. Comet had envisaged dropping the British 1st Airborne Division, with the Polish Parachute Brigade Group, around the Dutch towns of Grave, Nijmegen and Arnhem. Market was to be a much more powerful version of this, to the relief of the men who were detailed to carry out the Comet assault. The Polish commander, Major-General

Bundesarchiv-Koblenz

▼ **Lt-Gen Bittrich (centre), of II SS Panzer Corps, confers with his C-in-C, Field Marshal Model. Bittrich's units around Arnhem were far stronger than expected.**

BACKGROUND

Stanislav Sosabowski, on hearing of this reckless Comet scheme, could only say in amazement, 'But the Germans, General, the Germans. This mission cannot possibly succeed!' Market inspired only a little more confidence. Lieutenant-General Frederick 'Boy' Browning, commander of the British I Airborne Corps, is said to have uttered his famous response about '(maybe) going a bridge too far' upon being told of Market.

HIGH SPIRITS

Yet pessimism could not survive in the atmosphere of confidence that gripped circles of the Allied high command that glorious late summer of 1944. For air support of Market Garden, the planning staffs could speak in terms of 1,000 transports, 1,000 bombers and 1,000 fighters. There were 150,000 men in 14 divisions committed to Market Garden – a mammoth force equivalent to the US Third and First Armies combined!

The road to Arnhem was 64 miles (103 km) long, and was punctuated by five major river or canal crossings. There were also several more minor bridges that had to be captured in the operation. The US 101st Airborne Division would be dropped at the southern end of the corridor. Its major targets were the bridges between Eindhoven and Veghel. To the north, the US 82nd Airborne Division would grab the crossings around Grave and Nijmegen. At Arnhem, the British 1st Airborne Division, with the Polish Brigade attached, would seize the bridges over the Rhine, on which hinged the success of the Allied thrust into Germany.

The Garden part of the plan was made up of a single thrust by a division of XXX Corps up the main highway. A pair of divisions, one each from VIII and XII Corps, would make subsidiary attacks on its flanks.

It was decided that the drops would take place in daylight. Speed being the imperative element of Market Garden, it was vital that the airborne troops' landing should be accurate, and that the organisation of the scattered battalions should proceed rapidly.

▼ On the morning of 17 September, gliders and their tugs prepare for take-off at fields across England.

The commander of the 1st Airborne Division, Major-General Robert 'Roy' Urquhart, and his staff put together their plan for Market in two days. Five landing zones were selected to the north-west of Arnhem, most on the north bank of the Rhine. Urquhart had wanted to land troops immediately to the south of the bridges, a little to the east of where the Poles would come down, which would give his men a good chance of grabbing them before the Germans could react. The RAF had rejected this notion, expressing doubts about the suitability of the terrain and fears about the concentration of anti-aircraft guns in the area.

FIVE-HOUR MARCH

So Urquhart had to be satisfied with landing and drop zones that were no closer than six miles (9.6km) to his objective – a five-hour march. Urquhart also had to compromise on the number of troops and the amount of equipment he would be able to take over. Ideally, the whole airborne division, plus the Poles, should have been carried over in one lift, but there were not enough transports to accomplish this. Browning did not help matters by insisting that his airborne corps headquarters, which would be the combat headquarters for the whole Market operation, should be landed at Nijmegen on the first day. Another 36 aircraft had to be allocated to this. Consequently, Urquhart would only be able to land six of his battalions on the first day of Market; the rest of his division would have to follow on the second day, with the Poles arriving even later than that.

The Market plan relied on a large amount of luck. The weather would have to be good for the initial landings, and for at least two days after, to land all of Urquhart's force. A serious deterioration in the weather would leave the airborne bridgehead, dependent on airborne re-supply, without the ammunition and medicines it would need to fight. The long march from the landing zones to

the objectives required the Germans to respond slowly to the attack. Their resistance to the Garden thrust would also have to be feeble to ensure its rapid advance.

With a plan built on so many contingencies, the last thing it needed was a Cassandra's voice warning of impending disaster. Yet, as in Greek tragedy, a voice was raised demanding the reconsideration of the whole operation. The Intelligence officer of the I British Airborne Corps, Major Brian Urquhart (of no relation to the general), regarded the operation as unsound. He read a 21st Army Group Intelligence report indicating

that the II SS Panzer Corps might be refitting in the Arnhem area. This report was confirmed by intelligence received from the Dutch Resistance, and consolidated by oblique-angle photographs taken by reconnaissance aircraft at Major Urquhart's request. Major Urquhart vociferously put his case for at least a postponement, if not cancellation, to General Browning, waving the photographs of camouflaged German vehicles under the nose of the dapper general. Instead of his requested postponement, Major Urquhart received a visit from the corps' medical officer. He was diagnosed as on the verge of a nervous breakdown and sent on sick leave.

Market Garden would go ahead without him. After the war Brian Urquhart wrote, 'Once a group of powerful people have made up their minds on something, it develops a life and momentum of its own that is almost impervious to reason or argument. This is particularly true when personal ambition or bravado are involved.'

◄ The first Allied drops meet with limited resistance, but the German troops on the ground are quick to react. Here, infantry gather in the woods around Arnhem to oppose Allied movements.

Imperial War Museum

▲ In the war-damaged streets, a German StuG III assault gun lies in wait for the Allied attack.

BATTLE DIARY
MARKET GARDEN

Bundesarchiv-Koblenz

SEPTEMBER 1944

1 Eisenhower takes command of Allied ground forces; Montgomery promoted to Field Marshal
3 Brussels liberated
4 Antwerp liberated
10 Market Garden is given go-ahead; US troops cross German border
17 Airborne landings take place; British XXX Corps attacks towards Eindhoven; 2 Para captures north end of Arnhem bridge
18 XXX Corps links up with 101st Airborne
19 XXX Corps and 82nd Airborne link up at Nijmegen

20 Bridge at Nijmegen captured
21 2 Para surrenders north end of Arnhem bridge; attempt by XXX Corps to break out from Nijmegen fails; 1st Airborne pinned around Oosterbeek
22 Polish troops dropped around Driel; German counterattack cuts road to Arnhem
23 Attempt by Poles and XXX Corps to cross Lower Rhine fails
24 Second attempt to reach 1st Airborne fails
25 British 1st Airborne withdraws over Lower Rhine.

◄ German soldiers, alerted to the oncoming assault, gaze skyward for signs of the enemy.

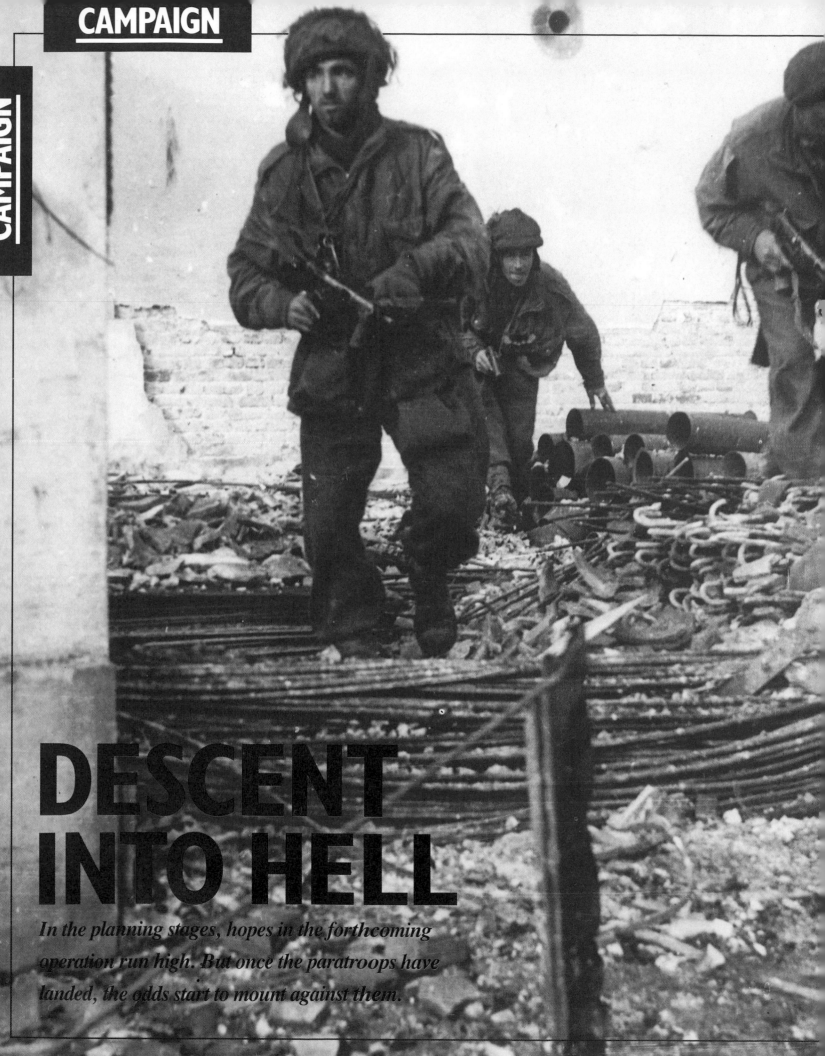

DESCENT INTO HELL

In the planning stages, hopes in the forthcoming operation run high. But once the paratroops have landed, the odds start to mount against them.

Sunday, 17 September 1944, was a fine late-summer's day. The sky was clear, the temperature just right. It was perfect flying weather. By mid morning, 1,500 transport aircraft and glider-tug combinations were airborne over England. The people who looked up from the towns and villages saw a stream of aeroplanes that took an hour to pass overhead. Soon these civilians would hear on their radios of the new Allied offensive, a battle in Holland.

PRE-BATTLE TENSION

The airborne assault troops inside the transports were resigned to an unpleasant flight. Each was loaded down with around half his weight in equipment, and any position assumed in this bulky cocoon – sitting, standing, or kneeling – was uncomfortable.

The troops had squeezed their way into C-47 transports or gliders and were packed tightly together, about 20 or so per Dakota. All were nervous and afraid. Some turned to the Sunday papers to relieve their anxieties, others to books or to thoughts of home and family, and many prayed. A few secretly took to drink, the soldier's traditional remedy for pre-battle tension.

The aerial convoys flew along two routes to the Continent. Those on the northern route were destined for drop zones (DZs) and landing zones (LZs) around Arnhem and Nijmegen; those on the southern route for Eindhoven. As the long streams of aircraft crossed into Holland, they came under fire from German anti-aircraft guns, mostly 88 mm or 20 mm in calibre. The shells burst in the air around the aircraft formations, the fragments of shrapnel pattering on the side of the aeroplanes like pebbles.

The Number Ones, the leading jumpers, were soon on their feet as the transports neared the drop zones. Each aeroplane's door was opened and the Number One stood there, waiting for the green 'go' light, while the slipstream's breeze pulled at the camouflage netting of his helmet. The men behind stood up as well, fingering the heavy kitbags of equipment that would accompany them on the descent. A little before 14.00 hours the 1st Parachute Brigade began its jumps over DZ 'X', west of Arnhem.

The glider-borne troops faced a different experience. Their fates were even more in the hands of their pilots, who manoeuvred the gliders through the air to find an open space on the assigned landing zone. Even a good landing ended in a shuddering, bone-jarring crash as the glider hit the deck, its wheels coming up through the fuselage.

Once on the ground, the troops of the British 1st Airborne Division, commanded by Major-General Roy Urquhart, rallied to their assembly

▲ **Setting off from their bases all over England on D-Day, 17 September, British paratroopers display every sign of confidence in their mission.**

◀ **Once on the ground, despite prebombardment of key areas by the RAF, the paratroopers' task of clearing houses is made difficult by German snipers.**

BATTLE LINE-UP

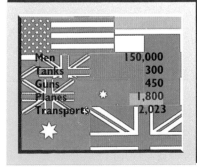

Men	150,000
Tanks	300
Guns	450
Planes	1,800
Transports	2,023

Men	89,000
Tanks	145
Guns	300
Planes	150
Transports	—

◀ **The combined ground and airlanding forces which took part in Operation Market Garden.**

Both pictures: Imperial War Museum

◀ The skies over Arnhem fill with parachutes, as Market, one of the biggest Allied airborne operations of all time, gets under way.

▼ An Allied landing zone covered with gliders, which leave behind visible tracks on the ground. Gliders could airlift a great number of troops into one spot.

▲ Arm-badge showing Pegasus, symbol of the British Airborne Forces.

▲ The eagle emblem of the US 101st Airborne Division.

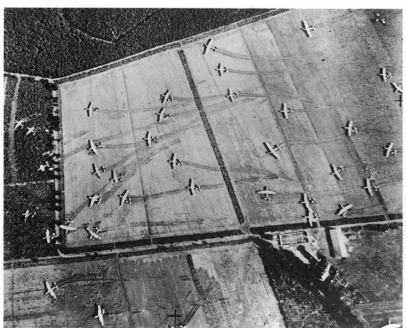

points. For most it was a coloured smoke-marker, but the 7th King's Own Scottish Borderers (KOSB) were summoned by the skirl of bag-pipes, while the 2nd Parachute Battalion gathered to the sound of a hunting horn belonging to their idiosyncratic commander, Lieutenant-Colonel John Frost.

At about the same time as the British paratroops were descending near Arnhem, Garden got under way. The Guards Armoured Division launched the attack, advancing behind a rolling barrage. German defenders put up a stout defence, and had to be winkled out by infantry. After hard fighting the Guards could only get as far as the village of Valkenswaard, a bare seven miles (11 km) from the front line, before the advance was halted for the day.

Such slow, stuttering progress was characteristic throughout the Garden operation, which had expected to reach Arnhem in two days.

The American drop was near perfect, perhaps the best the planners could reasonably expect. The US 101st Airborne Division captured four minor bridges around the town of Veghel quite easily, the Germans hardly bothering to put up a fight. At Son, however, to the north of Eindhoven, the bridge over the Wilhelmina Canal was blown up in the faces of the American paratroops. A timber bridge was thrown across the canal so the Americans could advance on Eindhoven, but an important break had been made by the Germans along the British path of advance.

The commander of the 82nd Air-

borne, Brigadier-General James Gavin, described his drop as 'better than had ever been experienced'. It was just as well because his division had to take and hold three objectives in an area with a 25-mile perimeter. The main objective was the long highway bridge over the Waal at Nijmegen. The whole of Gavin's area was commanded by the Groesbeek Heights which, in enemy hands, would provide an excellent platform for artillery observation. The bridge over the Maas at Grave was the third objective.

At Grave the bridge was captured by putting a company down at the south end, while rushing reinforcements from the nearest DZ to seize the north end. This stage of the operation went without a hitch. The Groesbeek Heights were also taken with ease. But an attempt by a battalion to seize the Nijmegen bridge was halted when it encountered heavy German resistance.

THE PRIZE

The main prize of Market, the bridges at Arnhem, was to be taken by Brigadier Gerald Lathbury's 1st Parachute Brigade (the 1st, 2nd and 3rd Parachute Battalions), with the help of the 1st Airborne Reconnaissance Squadron. The reconnaissance troops would rush forward in their jeeps as soon as they were ready,

Bundesarchiv-Koblenz

Frost's battalion, 2 Para, was the first of the parachutists to move off, and advanced down to the Lower Rhine and then, for the most part following the main road along the bank, into Arnhem. The railway bridge was demolished by the Germans just as the paratroopers reached it. A pontoon bridge nearer Arnhem's centre had been partially dismantled. Frost's men continued their advance, all their hopes set on the bridge ahead.

After a seven-hour march, the forward elements of 2 Para reached the highway bridge. It was nearly night. When Frost himself arrived shortly after 8 pm, a brisk battle with

the small German garrison guarding the bridge left his command in control of the north end, but the Germans held the south. 2 Para occupied several of the buildings around the highway ramp, and awaited reinforcements.

These were still some distance away. 1 and 3 Para had moved out for Arnhem only a little time after Frost's men. But the Germans had already begun to organise their defences. While Frost had been able to slip through a gap already closing between the German resistance line and the river, the other paratroop battalions, marching along more northerly routes, ran into many

◀ A camouflaged German anti-aircraft gun waits for the second Allied airlift after plans for the drops have fallen into their hands.

while the parachutists followed up on foot. The 1st Airlanding Brigade (1st Border Regiment, 7th KOSB and 2nd South Staffordshires) was to guard the DZs and LZs north of Wolfheze for the rest of the division, scheduled to arrive the next day.

Despite something of a hold-up due to the loss of 22 of their vehicles, the Reconnaissance Squadron drove off towards Arnhem, only to run into an ambush just beyond Wolfheze.

snipers. Accurate German mortar fire and a few tanks slowed the advance right down. By nightfall, the bulk of 1st Parachute Brigade was still in Oosterbeek.

CAUGHT BY SURPRISE

The prompt response of the Germans owed much to the presence of II SS Panzer Corps (9th and 10th SS Panzer Divisions). Market Garden caught the German commanders completely by surprise. While they were certain that a major offensive would happen soon, their attention was focused to the south, around Roermond, or to the north-west, along the Dutch coast.

Once the Allies had revealed their hand, however, it was quite easy to guess their plan. Reinforcements were soon being rushed to the Arnhem area, and to points further

▲ Men of the 1st Airborne Division's Artillery Regiment unload signal equipment from the first gliders to land near Arnhem.

◀ British paratroopers take cover next to their smashed glider, which broke up during the landing.

Left and above: Robert Hunt Library

Robert Hunt Library

▲ **A column of 2 Para, 1st Parachute Brigade, laden down with their guns and equipment, on the long march into Arnhem.**

▲▶ **German troops on their advance towards Oosterbeek, scene of some of the heaviest fighting. In the background, a German StuG III assault gun.**

south along the Meuse-Escaut Canal. The Germans were greatly assisted by the recovery of a copy of the Market Garden plan from a crashed glider and were able to deny the British most of their supply DZs, keeping Urquhart's men short of food, medicines and ammunition.

German attacks ceased with the coming of dawn on 18 September. 1 Para and 3 Para resumed their attempts to reach Frost, but faced a German opposition that had been steadily reinforced in the night, while the paratroopers' numbers shrank as they took more casualties. Attempting to match the successes of 2 Para, 1 and 3 Para shifted their advance south, nearer the river. In the course of this fighting General Urquhart, in the thick of the action, found himself trapped in a house

behind German lines. Later on 18 September, Brigadier Hackett's 4th Parachute Brigade arrived, encountering heavy ground fire before being committed to the battle around Arnhem.

Starting at 9.30 am, Frost's men had to contend with a major German attempt to push them out of their position. The commander of 9th SS Panzer Division's reconnaissance

unit had imperfect knowledge of the situation around the bridge, and used part of his force to perform what he thought would be a simple mopping-up operation.

The column drove into a firestorm. 2 Para did not have sufficiently heavy weapons to knock out the four armoured cars leading the column, but the half-tracks were subjected to a hail of PIAT rounds,

Imperial War Museum

MAJOR-GENERAL URQUHART

Major-General Robert 'Roy' Urquhart was born in 1901, the son of a doctor. He passed out from Sandhurst in 1920 and, in the early days of war, held a succession of staff appointments, culminating in the post of commander of the 231st Infantry Brigade.

In January 1944, back in Britain, Urquhart was put in command of 1st Airborne Division. He was not made entirely welcome at first, the airborne troops being suspicious of a commander plucked from the infantry arm. Urquhart's tendency to air sickness and total inexperience of both parachuting and gliding did not assist his cause. But he approached his duties with an assured attitude, showed a willingness to learn and treated his soldiers with a respect and sensitivity which won him the devotion of his men and the confidence of his officers.

◀ **Urquhart outside his HQ at the Hartenstein Hotel.**

normal high-explosive ones, and some of the buildings caught fire. At night, the paratroopers felt as if they were caught up in some inferno, with the flickering glow of the fires lighting the now-ruined town centre.

DISASTER STRIKES

On Tuesday, 19 September, Frost's men were subjected to a programmed bombardment, the din of which was terrifying. In the lulls, they could plainly hear the sound of tank tracks, as the SS men manoeuvred their vehicles around the wreckage of the street fighting. Soon

self-propelled guns came up to blast to smithereens selected houses held by the paratroopers. Slowly and steadily, Frost's command was being eliminated.

Their comrades were trying to get to them, but the task, once difficult, was now near impossible. Two battalions, and the remnants of two more, were pressing from the 1st Airborne Division's concentration around Oosterbeek towards Frost and his men. They had been bogged down around St Elisabeth's Hospital, on the outskirts of Arnhem, for two days now.

▼ Soldiers of the 1st Para Battalion take cover in a shell hole in the perimeter around the Hartenstein Hotel, into which they have been gradually squeezed by the Germans.

sub-machine gun and Bren-gun fire, mortar rounds and grenades.

Beginning in the afternoon of 18 September, the British pocket at Arnhem bridge was subjected to a sustained bombardment by artillery and mortars that steadily increased in intensity. German snipers also infiltrated the area and made any movement by the British risky, if not fatal. In the barrage, phosphorus shells were fired along with the

◄ Abandoned trams and dead bodies litter the streets as the Germans move their tanks towards Oosterbeek, 20 September 1944, leading up to the bitter fighting at St. Elisabeth's Hospital.

War Stories

P inned down at Arnhem, Urquhart was moved by the enormous bravery and courage shown by the men in the house-to-house fighting. It had its funny side, however. In one bombardment a soldier remarked, 'Well, they've thrown everything but the kitchen stove'. As he spoke, an explosion rocked the building, showering the men with plaster, laths and, incredibly, a cooker. Picking himself out of the debris, he added, 'I knew the bastards were close – but I didn't think they could *hear* us'.

▼ An armoured column crosses the bridge over the Waal at Nijmegen. Attempting to relieve the airborne troops at Arnhem, the ground forces meet heavy resistance.

Right: Airborne Forces Museum; all other pictures: Imperial War Museum

When they attempted one more push, they were met by a hail of shot and shell. From across the river, anti-aircraft cannon ripped into the airborne soldiers' advance, shooting shells that could tear a man in half. The British were halted once again, the only success of the attack being the release of Urquhart from his temporary captivity, and his return to headquarters.

The 1st Airborne Division was now truly isolated. Bad weather over England had kept the third and final instalment of reinforcements from reaching them. The glider-borne elements of the Polish brigade landed on 19 September, but the Germans, aware of the plans, gave them a very hot reception and caused heavy casualties. To the south, the Garden thrust was crawling along the road, having got as far as Nijmegen, where the bridge was still in German hands.

▲ The wild boar emblem of the British XXX Corps which, at the time of Market Garden, was under the command of Lt-Gen Brian Horrocks.

THE GAMBLE

Operation Market Garden was a gamble. If it had paid off, the dividends would have been high – Allied forces would have thrust a thin finger across the myriad waterways of southern Holland, crossed the Lower Rhine and threatened the approaches to the Ruhr. But these advantages were not gained. The ultimate failure to consolidate the gains made by the paras north of the Lower Rhine at Arnhem largely negated the advances further south, for the finger of opportunity rapidly became a salient of vulnerability. Important bridges may have been seized and advances made, but without success at Arnhem, the operation as a whole was of limited value.

▶ The casualty rate of Operation Market Garden is high.

TURNING POINT

around the village of Driel, on the south bank of the Lower Rhine. But this was now just reinforcing failure. Sosabowski was unable to link up with Urquhart, and went over to a defensive position around Driel.

On 22 September, elements of the 43rd (Wessex) Division, making an end-run around the German defences on the Arnhem road, established a fragile corridor joining the Poles at Driel to Nijmegen. An attempt to reinforce Urquhart on the night of 22/23 September failed when the Germans spotted a makeshift ferry. Another attempt was made on 24/25 September, by the 4th Battalion, Dorsetshire Regiment, of the 43rd Division, but this time the strong current carried the boats away

To capture the Nijmegen bridge, a battalion of the 82nd Airborne carried out a daring river assault in broad daylight simultaneously with an attack by Guards and other 82nd Airborne troops along the road. Once on the other side, though, the Guards found that the Germans were there in strength. Only a small bridgehead could be established on the other side of the Waal.

The troops the Guards encountered had been rushed south from Arnhem over the road bridge. Both ends were now in German hands. Frost's command, reduced to about 140 men, all wounded and without ammunition, had finally given up early on 21 September when faced with German tanks that shelled the buildings at point-blank range.

END IN SIGHT

Though Frost's valorous struggle had ended in defeat, the rest of the 1st Airborne Division hung grimly on, defending a steadily shrinking perimeter around the Hartenstein Hotel in the suburb of Oosterbeek. As a unit, Urquhart's command had shot its bolt. Offensive action against the

Germans was out of the question. They could only cling to their position and hope for relief.

Relief was still at Nijmegen. The Germans, with the Arnhem bridge secured, turned their attention away from the British airborne troops and towards the Guards. The SS men who had overwhelmed Frost now moved south and blocked the highway. Meanwhile, Urquhart's command was subjected to the same constant and heavy shelling that Frost's had, and also to sustained local attacks that gradually wore away 1st Airborne Division's defences.

The bad weather over England lifted briefly on 21 September, enabling Stanislar Sosabowski's Polish troops to make a partial drop

from Urquhart's command, isolating them both from the Airborne Division and their own.

On 25 September, eight days after Urquhart's men had landed in Holland, they were ordered to withdraw across the Rhine. That night – a rainy, blustery one – Canadian engineers piloted storm boats powered by outboard motors back and forth across the Rhine, guided by periodic bursts of tracer fire to mark the limits of the safe channel. Of the 10,000 men who had gone in, they brought back 2,163 men of the 1st Airborne Division, 160 Poles and 75 men of the Dorsetshire Regiment. They left behind 1,200 dead and 6,642 wounded or missing. Market Garden was finished. Montgomery's gamble had failed.

▲ On 25 September, after their 8-day ordeal, the evacuation of paratroopers across the Lower Rhine begins. About 2,000 of the men are lucky enough to make it to the other side, despite constant shelling by the Germans.

BATTLE OF THE BULGE

BATTLE DIARY

AUGUST 1944

19	Hitler first conceives plan for autumn counter-offensive

SEPTEMBER

4	Allies capture Antwerp
5	US forces cross the Meuse
13	Beginning of operation to clear Scheldt estuary
17–25	Operation 'Market Garden'
27	Third Army commences attack on Metz

OCTOBER

2	Renewal of First Army offensive at Aachen
6	Beginning of battle for the Breskens pocket
21	Fall of Aachen
27–29	Battle of Beveland

NOVEMBER

1	Commandos land on Walcheren island
2	Allies capture Zeebrugge. End of the battle for the Breskens pocket
8	Walcheren garrison surrenders
22	Fall of Metz

DECEMBER

3	Third Army establishes bridgeheads over the Saar
16	Start of German Ardennes offensive
17	Malmedy massacre
18	Kampfgruppe Peiper captures Stavemont
23	Allies pull back from St Vith
24	Peiper orders retreat. 2nd Panzer Division reaches the Meuse
26	Siege of Bastogne lifted

JANUARY 1945

16	US First and Third Armies meet at Houffalize
23	St Vith recaptured
31	End of 'Battle of the Bulge'

TO THE GERMAN BORDER

Associated Press/Topham

Though hundreds of miles on from Normandy, the Allies have still not captured a large port. As a result, lack of supplies for the fighting men is the major limitation on offensive operations.

▲▲ **Commando badge, showing the commando dagger.**

▲ **Casualties evacuated from Flushing are brought ashore at Breskens beach on 2 November 1944.**

At the very moment in mid August 1944 when the crack panzer divisions in Normandy were desperately struggling to escape from the Falaise Pocket, Adolf Hitler issued a secret order calling for the creation of a new Army Group to launch a counterattack in November. With his forces retreating over the Seine in disarray, Hitler realised that France and Belgium were lost.

German strategy over the next three months was reduced to buying time in which to conscript and train every man between the ages of 16 and 60 who was not already in uniform to form *Volksgrenadier* battalions for the defence of the Fatherland. In the interim, German forces in the west were to fall back as slowly as possible to the West Wall (the Siegfried Line) behind which they could regroup for the counterstroke.

When the Allies broke out of Normandy, General Sir Bernard Montgomery's 21st Army Group raced for

▲ The dyke which keeps the sea back from Walcheren Island comes under bombardment from an offshore naval group, prior to a commando attack.

Robert Hunt Library

forced to base their decisions on the availability of supplies rather than any other factor. The rate of advance slowed, giving Hitler the breathing space he so desperately needed.

Even the fall of the great Belgian port of Antwerp on 4 September failed to help the Allied supply situation because General Gustav von Zangen's Fifteenth Army still controlled both banks of the Scheldt estuary leading to the port. Clearing the Scheldt and making Antwerp accessible therefore assumed the highest priority. It would solve the supply problem at a stroke. But strangely, Montgomery seems to have missed the significance of Antwerp and had to be pressurised by Eisenhower before he would allocate sufficient forces to the problem.

The River Scheldt flows into the North Sea via a wide waterway, flanked on the north by South Beveland. This in turn is attached by a road and rail causeway to Walcheren Island, which was defended by strong coastal gun batteries. German forces also occupied the southern shore of the estuary from Zeebrugge to the Braakman inlet and had established defensive lines on two canals, the Leopold and the Dérivation de Lys.

This position constituted a major problem for the Allies, made worse by the destruction of the dykes which allowed the sea to flood all the land below sea level. In this waterlogged terrain, criss-crossed with canals and

Brussels and Antwerp with the Ruhr as its target. General Omar N. Bradley's American 12th Army Group steered towards Aachen, Metz and the Saar, with reinforcements steadily moving up to join them from the invasion of the south of France. The German armies retreated steadily, but in orderly fashion.

As the Germans still held all Channel ports except Dieppe and Cherbourg, most Allied supplies were still being unloaded by hand over the beaches and taken up to the front line in trucks. As Allied troops plunged hundreds of miles north and east into Holland and towards the German border, acute shortages of petrol and ammunition set in at the front. Allied generals were

▲ Troops laden down with kit walk ashore across the mud near Flushing. Their landing craft are beached at the water's edge.

◄ Forces take cover in the anti-tank obstacles round Walcheren as the barrage comes down safely ahead of them.

Robert Hunt Library

Associated Press/Topham

Imperial War Museum

▲▲ A Liberty ship from the first Allied convoy to enter the Scheldt is towed up the river towards Antwerp on 27 November 1944.

soaked by autumn rains, armour was of no use – it was a job for the 'poor bloody infantry'.

Nevertheless it was a vital job. To let von Zangen's Fifteenth and General Kurt Student's First Parachute Armies remain contained in northern Holland would have left a very real threat to the advancing Allies.

General Henry Crerar's Canadian First Army eliminated the German position on the south bank of the Scheldt from Antwerp west to the Braakman inlet by 20 September and forced a crossing of the Albert Canal to the east. Further progress then slowed due to the terrain and dogged German resistance, until the infantry divisions, freed by the end of German resistance in France, began arriving at the end of the month. By 6 October the Canadians had pushed north to within three miles (5 km) of Woensdrecht, at the neck of the Beveland peninsula, but were unable to make further headway until reinforced a fortnight later.

ESTUARY BATTLES

On the same day, an infantry brigade from II Canadian Corps established a bridgehead over the Leopold Canal. On 9 October, two more regiments crossed the Braakman in amphibious vehicles to land in the rear of the German 64th Infantry Division, defending the remaining pocket on the south bank of the estuary. The Germans, taken by surprise, fell back and patrols from the two bridgeheads linked up on 14 October. Within a fortnight they had captured the town of Breskens, opposite Flushing on the southern tip of Walcheren. On 22 October, they launched an attack against Fort Frederik Hendriks, close to the mouth of the Scheldt, opposite Flushing. The Fort fell after three days' heavy fighting and the final German strongholds in the Channel ports of Knokke-sur-Mer and Zeebrugge surrendered on 1 and 2 November respectively.

To the east, the reinforced British I Corps renewed the attack on Woensdrecht on 23 October and at last succeeded in forcing Student's paras to retreat. They were prevented from crossing on to South Beveland by flooding and heavy defences on the western bank of the ship canal which cuts across the neck of land connecting with the mainland. On 27 October the defenders were forced to fall back and by the 29th, South and North Beveland had both fallen. Only the fortress of Walcheren was left in German hands.

Walcheren Island is formed like a dish with steep sand dunes forming the rim and the interior lying below sea level. British and American bombers had made repeated attacks on the coastal positions since 3 October, breaching the dyke and flooding the interior – but the German fortifications were barely touched.

Brigadier B W 'Jumbo' Leicester's 4th Special Service Brigade (41, 47 and 48 Royal Marine Commandos) embarked in landing craft at Ostend on 31 October. Having crossed 30 miles (48 km) of open sea, they landed

War Stories

Given the choice between a Bren gun and a Sten gun, there would be no doubt in the average British infantryman's mind. Give him a Bren any day. The Sten gun was a notoriously unpredictable weapon – as Private Alfred Jenkins discovered as his company tried to break into a locked out-building on their way through Holland. Somebody called for the corporal to come and shoot out the lock with the Sten gun. The company braced itself for the report – but there was silence. As he squeezed the trigger, all that came out was a jet of water.

in a thick sea mist on the western tip of Walcheren on 1 November. Simultaneously, 4 Army Commando took the shorter route across the Scheldt from Breskens to Flushing. At Westkapelle, artillery support from the battleship HMS *Warspite* and the gunboats *Erebus* and *Roberts* failed to silence the coastal batteries which caused heavy casualties among the naval task force and the Commandos as they stormed ashore. In Flushing, 4 Army Commando scrambled up the sea wall, hacked through the barbed wire on the waterfront and by nightfall had secured most of the town.

WALCHEREN FALLS

The two Commando forces linked up outside Flushing on 3 November, the same day that the Canadians reached Middelburg in the centre of the island, and the German garrison gave up on 8 November. But it was another three weeks before minesweepers cleared the estuary and opened the port of Antwerp for Allied shipping.

These developments encouraged Hitler to press ahead with his plans for a counter-offensive, despite his generals' opposition. And while Montgomery's 21st Army Group was pushing on into Holland, Lieutenant-General Courtney Hodges' US First Army was advancing north east, on the British right flank towards Luxembourg and the German town of Aachen. On Hodges' own right flank, Lieutenant-General George S. Patton's US Third Army was advancing east, towards Metz and the Saar. Both advances were stalled by the fuel crisis and so it was

Popperfoto

Robert Hunt Library

▲ Aachen, where the early Emperors were crowned, is defended fiercely. German snipers are cleared from the buildings by bringing the walls down with artillery fire.

◄ A jeep crosses the outer defences of the West Wall.

not until 5 September that the first American troops crossed the River Meuse. But the two American armies were advancing in different directions, opening a gap of some 100 miles (160 km) between them – and in this gap lay the mountains and forests of the Ardennes. On 4 September, Hitler recalled Field Marshal Gerd von Rundstedt from retirement and appointed him C-in-C West, replacing Field Marshal Walther Model. Model, noted for his creative improvisations, was to command Army Group B, which would carry out the counteroffensive.

By the middle of September, Hodges' men had crossed the German frontier west of Aachen, causing a degree of civilian panic, but Patton was stalled in front of the heavily defended fortress of Metz in eastern France.

SHREWD VETERAN

Although a close comrade of Hitler's, SS-General 'Sepp' Dietrich bore no illusions. Asked to support opposition to the Ardennes offensive, he remarked, 'If I ever want to get shot, that's how I'll go about it'. A former Sergeant-Major in the Kaiser's army, he helped establish Hitler's take-over by organising the 'Night of the Long Knives' in 1934. He was rewarded with command of the *Leibstandarte*, but took over the I SS-Panzer Corps in June 1944. After the Ardennes retreat, he performed a masterly delaying action against the Russians from Hungary into Austria, but Hitler, unimpressed, stripped him of his medals – which he reputedly sent back in a chamber pot. Although lacking academic and military education, he was an immensely resourceful and daring general, and was idolised by his men. Sentenced to life imprisonment for war crimes, he was actually released in 1955, dying a free man in 1966.

Popperfoto

There was then a lull while Allied supplies and hopes were devoted to the Arnhem operation. After the failure there, the general offensive started up again on 2 October and Hodges broke through the West Wall on 3 October. V Corps held off determined counterattacks over the next few days. The Aachen garrison held out until 21 October, after the city had been totally surrounded. It was the first German city to fall in the west and opened the way to the Ruhr and Rhine crossings.

The battle to clear the Hürtgen Forest, beyond Aachen, was so bloody that the shattered survivors were sent to recuperate in the Ardennes, the 'quiet' sector of the front. V Corps remained in the line to the south of Aachen while Lieutenant-General William H. Simpson's newly arrived Ninth Army moved in on their left.

Patton's drive on Metz was still held up around Bruyères and St Dié: it was not until 18 November that the first GIs entered Metz itself and 22 November before the German garrison laid down its arms. This cleared the way to Saarbrucken, the largest town of Germany's second most important industrial area. On 3 December, despite torrential rain and knee-deep mud in what Patton called 'this nasty country', his men secured crossings over the River Saar and by the middle of the month had established a strong bridgehead, ready to advance across southern Germany.

It was under these circumstances that Hitler finalised his plans for the Ardennes operation codenamed *Wacht am Rhein* ('Watch on the Rhine'). Even he had to admit

► **Field Marshal Gerd von Rundstedt, Commander-in-Chief of German forces in the West during the Battle of the Bulge.**

►► **Field Marshal Walther Model. Pushed back to the Ruhr at the end of the war, he shot himself to avoid the disgrace of captivity.**

Imperial War Museum

to the commander of the Fifth Panzer Army, Lieutenant-General Hasso von Manteuffel, that he was putting everything 'on one throw of the dice'.

By the time Patton had established bridgeheads over the Saar, a German strike force totalling 25 divisions had been assembled without alerting the Americans. Many of these formations were inexperienced and understrength, but they were faced only by some six divisions of Major-General Troy H Middleton's III and Major-General Leonard Gerow's V Corps. The pieces were in place; the game was about to begin.

▼ **M10 tank destroyers of the US First Army advance up one of the few tracks through the Hürtgen Forest.**

WATCH ON THE RHINE

Aachen has fallen to the Americans, the first large German town to do so. But the Führer has a long-nurtured plan to throw the Allies back into the sea.

It was a bitterly cold night and the shivering sentries blew into their gloves trying to keep warm. Suddenly, at 5.30 am, shattering the silence, the eastern horizon erupted in a blaze of light followed by a wave of sound as nearly 2,000 German artillery pieces opened up. All along the 85-mile (136 km) Ardennes front between Monschau in the north, on the German borders, and Echternach in the south, in Luxembourg, sleepy GIs tried to work out what was going on. This was called the 'Ghost Front', because nothing ever happened, but over the next few days the phrase would come to have a more macabre meaning.

Petrified American soldiers, many of them fresh from home, others recovering from the physical and psychological mauling they had received during the battles for Aachen and the Hürtgen Forest, scrambled out of sleeping bags to man their foxholes. Landing in dense forest, the German shells were particularly effective, with splinters from the trees added to the shell fragments and causing dozens of casualties. Cries rang out for stretcher bearers as company and battalion commanders tried to find out what was happening in their sector and on the rest of the front.

THE ALLIED RESPONSE

In the next few days, the Germans managed to make a substantial dent in the American lines, but the 'bulge' never went so deep as to disrupt the movement of Allied reserves. And though Montgomery had to order a few local withdrawals in the north, the Allies stabilised the front by Christmas Day, using their reserves in a coordinated plan rather than a piecemeal panic.

Some of the attacking German divisions had recently emerged, shattered, from the battles in France and

Imperial War Museum

had been rebuilt. The bulk of these were assigned to Field Marshal Walther Model's Army Group B, and were assembled in great secrecy to the east of the 'Ghost Front'. Many of the remaining formations were *Volksgrenadier* units formed by scraping the bottom of the barrel of the male German population. Trained in six weeks especially for Operation Watch on the Rhine, these men were like lambs sent to the slaughter.

Troops and tanks had moved up to assembly areas in the Eifel Mountains by night, to prevent detection by Allied aircraft. They were hidden under camouflage in the snow-covered woods during the day. Likewise, supply trains were concealed in railway tunnels and new code names were given to headquarters units to

▲ An SS machine-gun section, equipped with an MG 42 on a bipod mounting, stop for a smoke in this scene from a German propaganda film.

◄ American GIs trudge through the snow behind a Sherman. Though they are well-equipped with winter clothing, it is still difficult to imagine worse conditions in which to conduct a defensive battle.

BATTLE LINE-UP

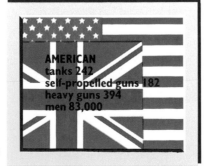

AMERICAN
tanks 242
self-propelled guns 182
heavy guns 394
men 83,000

Popperfoto

GERMAN
tanks 950
self-propelled guns 1,900
men 275,000

◄ Though the Germans have numbers on their side on 16 December 1944, Allied reserves soon make up for this.

▲ Lieutenant-Colonel Otto Skorzeny, ordered to disrupt opposition to the *Wacht am Rhein* operation.

▼ The crew of a King Tiger watch over a column of American POWs trudging rearward.

now renamed *Herbstnebel* ('Autumn Mist') – was rescheduled for mid December to give time for the forces to be assembled. There was also the hope that wintry weather would prevent the dreaded Allied rocket-firing 'Jabo' fighter-bombers operating against the German armour.

Hitler's plan, which he refused to let his generals modify except in matters of detail, was to burst through the Ardennes to the deep valley of the Meuse, then sweep north-west towards Brussels, Antwerp and the sea, cutting the Allied forces in two. This would cause such disruption to Allied plans, Hitler believed that the Western Allies would ditch the Russians and negotiate a separate peace. This would free German forces to tackle the rapidly deteriorating situation on the Eastern Front.

WILD OPTIMISM

It was a pure pipedream, of course, because Britain, the USA and Russia had already agreed to insist on Germany's unconditional surrender. Nothing less would do. Moreover, most of Hitler's generals – including Rundstedt – felt they would be lucky to reach the Meuse, let alone Antwerp. But Hitler, more dictatorial than ever since the July bomb plot, was adamant, and few people were ready to stand up to him. So the grandiose but doomed scheme went ahead.

The assault in the north was to be led by SS-General 'Sepp' Dietrich's Sixth Panzer Army with four SS panzer, one panzergrenadier, one parachute and four *Volksgrenadier*

conceal their real function. Radio traffic was kept to a minimum. So although Lieutenant-General George Patton had detected the withdrawal of General Hasso von Manteuffel's Fifth Panzer Army from the Lorraine front in eastern France, and it was later reported in the Aachen area, the Allies expected it to be thrown into this section of the German defences to prevent a breakthrough to Cologne.

Although originally planned for November, the German offensive –

(infantry) divisions. To Dietrich's left, Manteuffel's Fifth Panzer Army consisted of four panzer, one panzer grenadier and four *Volksgrenadier* divisions. Finally, in the south, General Erich Brandenberger's Seventh Army was ordered to establish a blocking position or hard shoulder to prevent any intervention by Patton's Third Army. He had only one parachute, one infantry and three *Volksgrenadier* divisions and a panzer brigade with which to do this.

In addition, Otto Skorzeny's so-called 150th Panzer Brigade, dressed in American uniforms and driving American vehicles, would spread alarming rumours and sow confusion behind Allied lines. A parachute battalion would also be dropped ahead of Dietrich's force to secure the important road junction at Malmédy, vital for control of the road to Liège and Antwerp. Even though only the SS panzer divisions were up to strength in tanks, the combined strike force was stronger than that assembled for the invasion of France and the Low Countries in 1940.

WINTER SETBACKS

Luckily for the Allies, several factors would prevent Hitler's offensive building up the necessary momentum. The main one was the combination of weather and terrain. The narrow, winding roads through the

US National Archives

objective of Antwerp was north-west of the German start line, so the panzers had to advance against the grain of the hills. On top of this, the Germans were desperately short of petrol and would have to rely on capturing American fuel dumps to keep going. Finally, the *Führer* underestimated the stubbornness with which the outnumbered GIs would fight, in order to buy time for their reinforcements to arrive.

When the artillery barrage lifted, early on 16 December searchlights stabbed the sky, reflecting off the low clouds to create 'artificial moonlight' – a trick the Germans had learnt from Montgomery! Then the men of Dietrich's *Volksgrenadier* and parachute divisions moved forward, many clad in white and invisible in the snow, to clear the path for the panzers and establish a hard shoulder on the northern flank of the 'bulge', while Manteuffel's panzers

◄ In a propaganda shot taken at Poteau, to the north-east of St Vith, SS soldiers go into action across a road, all for the benefit of national morale.

Imperial War Museum

Ardennes were only wide enough for tanks in single file even in the summer. Snow and ice would make a quick advance even more difficult, and the wooded countryside was too steep and broken for the armour to advance across country.

Moreover, the main roads of the Ardennes, by which the panzers had brought Blitzkrieg to Europe in 1940, led in a generally south-westerly direction. But the main

► A *Kübelwagen* (amphibious Volkswagen jeep) at one of the crucial crossroads. St Vith is second only in importance to Bastogne as a road junction.

THE MALMÉDY MASSACRE

On 17 December 1944, men of Lieutenant-Colonel Joachim Peiper's Group picked up prisoners from Battery B of the US 285th Field Artillery Observation Battalion near Malmédy. After making them lay down their arms, they herded the Americans into a field and killed 85 by machine-gun fire. Testimony at the war crimes trial varied. Senior Private Georg Fleps, identified by 1st Lieutenant Virgil Lary as a ringleader in the massacre, claimed that he only began to fire after some men tried to escape, although Lary denied it. Fleps was sentenced to death and Peiper, although absent at the time, was indicted and jailed as the CO responsible for the group. Only in 1975 did vengeance catch up with Peiper in Traves, France, where he was supposedly killed by anonymous raiders.

◄ GIs set about the grisly task of recovering the bodies of their comrades-in-arms.

► Three of Skorzeny's men are shot by firing squad, condemned to death as spies for operating behind the lines in American uniforms. Skorzeny himself was acquitted of the same charge after the war.

▲ Badge of Major-General James Gavin's 82nd Airborne Division.

moved up supported by the infantry. Right from the beginning, though, things started to go wrong.

MIXED FORTUNES

In the north, Dietrich's grenadiers met unexpectedly stubborn resistance from the US 2nd and 99th Infantry Divisions and were unable to get on to the Elsenborn Ridge. This left the advance to Malmédy open to counterattack and artillery bombardment by Major-General Leonard Gerow's V Corps. But to their left, things seemed to be more promising for the Germans.

The leading 4,000-man battlegroup of Sixth Panzer Army, *Kampfgruppe* Peiper – named after its commander, SS-Lieutenant-Colonel Joachim Peiper – surged through the

gap which had opened up between the US V and VIII Corps at Losheim. This led to the head of the Amblève valley and was a dangerous development for the Allies because Peiper's route lay via Stavelot, bypassing Malmédy and leading straight to Liège on the Meuse or west through Werbomont towards Namur.

By 10am on 17 December, Peiper's force had reached Honsfeld, and captured an American fuel dump at Büllingen. Shortly afterwards they captured a group of American artillerymen. There is no way that an armoured column can cope with passengers, so these men were left in a field near Malmédy, where many of them were subsequently shot in cold blood. Meanwhile, the para-

troopers dropped ahead of Peiper had suffered a disaster. Weather delayed their take-off by 24 hours, and when they dropped on 17 December, they were scattered all over the countryside by strong winds. The survivors hid from the US 1st Infantry Division which was rushing to reinforce the defenders on Elsen-

THE 82nd AIRBORNE

Already blooded on D-Day and at Nijmegen bridge, the 82nd Airborne, commanded by Major-General James 'Slim Jim' Gavin (deemed by many the best airborne leader of the war), played a vital role during the Battle of the Bulge by blocking the advance of Peiper Force down the Amblève valley. Though facing a column of fully equipped panzers, the lightly armed paratroopers, along with the 30th Infantry Division, held their ground with determination.

When Montgomery took command of the American forces on the north side of the Bulge on 20 December 1944, one of his first moves was to 'tidy the battlefield' and the 82nd were later ordered to withdraw as part of the same process of shortening the Allied front line. This was too much for Gavin, who protested that his division had never withdrawn in its history – but Montgomery's military logic was irresistible and the 82nd complied.

born Ridge and after four days, the paras split up to make their weary way back to German lines.

Peiper captured Stavelot on 18 December after some delay because, the previous evening, he had halted when his lead tank was ambushed. At 11.15 am a few miles further on, Peiper watched as the bridges at Trois Ponts were blown up by US combat engineers. Unable to find fresh fuel – even though there was actually a large dump only a couple of miles north of Stavelot, had he but known it – Peiper turned north and tried again to cross the Amblève at Habiemont beyond La Gleize. But as the leading tanks came in sight of the bridge, combat engineers again fired the demolition charges. He then went on to the defensive, holding Stoumont and La Gleize against the US 30th Division until Christmas Eve. Then, abandoning his surviving vehicles, he ordered his men to break out and retreat. Only 800 survived.

The remainder of Sixth Panzer

▼ **A detail from an American armoured infantry battalion clear away jerry cans, emptied to prevent fuel falling into German hands.**

Robert Hunt Library

Camera Press

Army had been unable to exploit Peiper's original success because of the threat to their flank caused by the arrival of the 1st Infantry Division to reinforce the 2nd and 99th on Elsenborn Ridge. Accordingly, Hitler switched the weight of the attack from Dietrich to Manteuffel, who had surrounded and decimated the green 106th Division in the Schnee Eifel, right in the middle of the developing 'bulge'. He had only

▲ **A King Tiger at the side of the road at Villers-la-Bonne-Eau is examined by curious GIs. The tank is as likely to have run out of fuel as to have been hit by air strikes.**

WarStories

Having delivered his now famous retort, 'Nuts', in response to the German ultimatum to surrender, General McAuliffe and his men were under devastating fire by the evening of 22 December. Short of supplies, cold and hungry, 101st Airborne were, however, much boosted by their leader's reply. Their resolve was summed up as one paratrooper peered out of his foxhole to take in food and ammunition. Told that the Germans had them surrounded, he responded 'So, they've got us surrounded, the poor bastards . . .'

▶ Major-General Maxwell Taylor (right), commander of the 101st Airborne, was in Washington when the Battle of the Bulge started. Having flown the Atlantic and 'hitchhiked' into Bastogne with one of the relieving columns, he shakes hands all around.

CLASH OF EGOS

The aims of Hitler's Ardennes offensive were over-ambitious but in one respect at least, that of disrupting Anglo-American co-operation at the highest level, they came close to success. Relations between Eisenhower as Supreme Commander and Montgomery as Commander of 21st Army group had always been strained, and after Ike ordered Omar Bradley to hand over command of American troops north of the Bulge to Montgomery, the British Field Marshal claimed publicly that he had 'saved the day' for the Americans. Though Patton, Bedell Smith and other American generals hated Monty's guts, it is to Eisenhower's eternal credit that personal feelings were not allowed to destroy Allied cohesion. It was during this time that the British and the Americans came closest to achieving cooperation as Allies.

TURNING POINT

BASTOGNE
BASTION
OF
THE BATTERED
BASTARDS
OF THE 101ST

Robert Hunt Library

▼ By the end of the battle at Bastogne, the defenders are devastated by battle weariness.

been stopped in front of the important road junction of St Vith by the timely arrival of first the 7th Armored Division, linked to the 82nd Airborne on the shoulder.

Similarly, further south, Manteuffel's main armoured spearhead had cleared the ridge known as Skyline Drive, crossed the rivers Our and Clerf, and was racing towards the vital road junction at Bastogne. As it happened, they lost the race because the US 101st Airborne and elements of the 10th Armored Division reached the town in the nick of time.

Instead of trying to fight his way through, Manteuffel directed the 2nd and 9th Panzer Divisions to bypass the obstacle and head for the Meuse, bringing the 116th and *Panzer Lehr* Divisions in on their flanks to help. Bastogne itself was surrounded by the 15th Panzergrenadier and 26th *Volksgrenadier* Divisions. On 22 December, General Heinrich von Lüttwitz sent a party out under a white flag to ask the Americans to surrender. Brigadier-General Anthony McAuliffe replied only 'Nuts' and his men prepared to die in their shrinking perimeter.

ALLIED REINFORCEMENTS

The 2nd Panzer Division reached Celles, overlooking the Meuse, on Christmas Eve. This was the deepest German penetration into Allied lines but the climax of the battle took place on Christmas Day. At Bastogne, men who had shaken hands the night before, believing they would not live through another day, held out against all odds.

Next day, leading elements of Patton's 4th Armored Division, roaring up from the south, broke

A la population de BASTOGNE

Robert Hunt Library

Associated Press Topham

through Brandenberger's Seventh Army and into Bastogne. Patton's men had travelled the 160 miles (260 km) in 36 hours, moving the axis of their advance through 90° in the process. For the first time, Allied rocket-firing aircraft joined the battle as the weather had lifted a little.

Meanwhile, even though St Vith had been evacuated on 23 December after Hitler diverted the 2nd and 9th SS Panzer Divisions from Dietrich's to Manteuffel's command, elements of the British XXX Corps began to arrive from reserve positions in Belgium and Holland to bolster the northern and central sectors of 'the bulge'. The 29th Armoured Brigade drove 2nd Panzer Division out of Celles on 27 December.

Despite their personal differences Montgomery and Patton managed to work together during this crisis. American soldiers on the north of the bulge lost contact with their corps and army HQ, so were placed under British command. Montgomery positioned his XXX Corps as a longstop on the other side of the Meuse, as soon as the scale of the German operation became clear, la-

ter using them to reinforce the American counterattack. However, it was really Patton's relief of Bastogne which did the trick.

At the turn of the year, deteriorating weather set in again, hampering air operations, but it was obvious that the German offensive had failed. Most of Dietrich's Sixth Panzer Army was taken out of the line, leaving Manteuffel's and Brandenberger's men in a shrinking pocket. In early January 1945 Hitler tried to divert Patton's attention by a new offensive codenamed *Nordwind* ('North Wind') in Alsace to the south, and the US Seventh and French First Armies found themselves in difficulty around Strasbourg and Bitche. However, the 'Battle of the Bulge' was effectively over. Units of Hodges' First and Patton's Third US Armies finally linked up at Houffalize, north of Bastogne, on 16 January 1945. A week later St Vith was recaptured.

By the end of January the Germans were back behind their start lines and the Allies were pushing towards the Rhine. Anglo-American casualties in dead, wounded, captured and missing totalled about 75,000 but German losses were closer to 120,000 – and at this stage of the war, these German losses could never be replaced. Hitler's last throw of the dice had not given the double six he had gambled on.

▲ Shermans of the US 40th Tank Battalion, 7th Armored Division, line up ready to commence firing on enemy positions on the far side of St Vith. The date is 22 December 1944, during the 'horseshoe' defence.

◀ After the battle, a soft-topped US supply truck lies in a Bastogne street, victim of the German shells which also devastated the street.

LEYTE GULF

BATTLE DIARY

OCTOBER 1944
20 Leyte Gulf landings

NOVEMBER
2   Carigara taken
5–15 Battle of Breakneck Ridge on Leyte

DECEMBER
15 Invasion of Mindoro
22 Ormoc Valley secured (Leyte)

JANUARY 1945
9   Lingayen Gulf landing, central Luzon

FEBRUARY
3   Battle of Manila begins
28 Invasion of Palaawan

MARCH
2   Corregidor recaptured
3   Manila secured
31 US capture Zamboanga peninsula on Mindanao

APRIL
28 Central Visayan islands cleared of Japanese

MAY
1   First Australian landings on Borneo

JUNE
15 Sulu Archipelago secured
30 Eastern Mindanao secured

AUGUST
15 Japanese surrender

LANDING AT LEYTE

US Library of Congress

The large size of many of the Philippine islands permits the Japanese to make a switch to defence in depth. They will be dislodged only with difficulty.

▲▲ **The six-pointed star of the Sixth Army. Many US Army units have symbolic designs for their patches.**

▲ **US troops dig in while a soldier mounts guard with a water-cooled Browning .30 machine gun. A Springfield rifle is within easy reach nearby.**

After General Douglas MacArthur had been chased by the Japanese from the Philippine Islands in March 1942, he provided one of World War II's famous quotes: 'I shall return'. This promise loomed large in deciding American strategy in 1944 when the tables were turned and it was the Americans' turn to do the chasing.

But MacArthur's bold claim was not the only factor influencing US President Roosevelt at a conference at Pearl Harbor on 26–27 July 1944. The Americans felt strong loyalty to the unfortunate Filipinos, who had been under Japanese subjugation since the US retreat.

The alternative was to push singlemindedly for Japan, via Formosa, between the Philippines and Japan. This was the preference of US chief of Naval Operations

Hulton-Deutsch Collection

Admiral Ernest J King and others, who believed that the Philippines could safely be bypassed. But, in the end, Roosevelt settled for an invasion of the Philippines.

Such an invasion was not a surprise to the Japanese themselves. The question that concerned them most was where the invasion would land. The Philippines comprise numerous islands, mostly irregularly shaped, jungle-covered and mountainous. The capital, Manila, is on the largest island, Luzon, the target for the 1942 Japanese invasion. But for an American seaborne landing, the smaller island of Leyte, well to the south east of Luzon, was a prime candidate. Leyte Gulf is large and sheltered and faces the US-held Marianas. The island itself, some 125 miles (200 km) across, has a convenient flat coastal strip, and was a good jumping-off point for the whole Philippines operation.

Although the Japanese High Command envisaged the 'decisive battle' of the Pacific War being fought on Luzon, Southern Army Command, responsible for defending the Philippines, believed that the initial American attack would come on Leyte. Initially, only the Japanese 16th Division, 21,700 men strong, held the island, but reinforcements could be quickly ferried in from elsewhere in the Philippines. Overall, there were about 432,000 Japanese combatants in the Philippines.

THE LANDINGS BEGIN

True to expectations, Lieutenant-General Walter Krueger's Sixth Army landed in Leyte Gulf on 20 October 1944. To begin with, the Japanese observed the new 'defence-in-depth' philosophy which had worked well on Peleliu, allowing the US 1st Cavalry Division to come ashore with minimal loss. This was fortuitous for the US troops, as between an excellent beach and the mile-distant highway that ran parallel to it, was a strip of

▲ **A Filipino soldier holds a marker panel on a beach on Leyte Island during landings in November 1944.**

▶ **LSTs (Landing Ship Tank) unload at bulldozed piers near Tacloban Airstrip. The LSTs are loaded with stores, vehicles and ammunition.**

▶ **US 155 mm guns are readied for a fire mission from behind their improvised protection of palm trees and earth. The relatively exposed position indicates that there is no danger from counter-battery fire.**

Right: Hulton-Deutsch Collection; inset: US National Archives

swamp, a 'morass . . . often waist deep, in places even up to the armpits . . .' Three crossing places were required to ferry all the equipment across, but the low-level opposition allowed the Cavalry to take their primary objective of the Tacloban airstrip without delay.

Further south, the 24th Infantry Division, like the 1st Cavalry part of X Corps, had to contend with a stream, widened and deepened into a tank trap and covered by strongly constructed pillboxes connected by tunnels. Shallow water offshore had hampered their approach, the Japanese cannily allowing the initial waves ashore before isolating the subsequent waves with heavy mortar fire. Infantrymen had to assault the Japanese strong-points with bazookas and flamethrowers as no heavy weapons were available.

There followed a brisk fight to capture Hill 552, a small feature commanding both beach and the town of Palo. The commanding officer of the 24th stated that the 14 lives that this cost saved 1,000. Close behind the assault wave came General MacArthur himself, wading ashore at Palo in a tropical downpour accompanied by his staff and the Philippines President-in-exile, Sergio Osmeña, who had left with MacArthur in 1942. Over a portable transmitter, hoarse with emotion, the general announced: 'This is the Voice of Freedom, General MacArthur speaking . . . I have returned . . .'

US National Archives

TYPHOONS

Around Dulag, some ten miles (16 km) to the south, XXIV Corps was also well established, having achieved most of its objectives. With only 49 dead in its initial assault, Sixth Army was well placed to consolidate and advance northward along the flat and populous Leyte Valley. However, the invasion had been brought forward two months from the planned date. As a result, it coincided with the start of the wet season. Rain, storms

▲ Bogged in the mud of Tacloban, a US truck churns to a halt despite its chains and four-wheel drive.

and even typhoons battered the island.

The 200,000 Americans had the advantage over the Japanese of being concentrated at one spot, but only Tacloban and Dulag airstrips were available and by now most of the aircraft carriers had been drawn away by the naval battle of 24–26 October. A large number of minor Japanese air raids failed to inflict decisive damage but ensured that few GIs enjoyed any rest in their foxholes.

In addition, American airstrip building went slowly. Almost two months were wasted trying 'to improve strips that were unimprovable . . . It was a real-estate problem and the real-estate agents failed badly'.

Following up Southern Command's decision to fight the decisive battle on Leyte, the Japanese Navy started running a series of reinforcement convoys to Ormoc, on Leyte's west coast. Known as the *TA* Operation, this repeat of the 'Tokyo Express' that had worked so well at Guadalcanal was equally effective, tripling Japanese strength by 12 November and putting ashore 45,000 troops and 10,000 tons of supplies.

By the end of October, the Sixth Army had advanced into Leyte Valley, after a stiff encounter at the well-defended Catmon Hill, which had initially been by-passed. Battle reports refer to the difficulties of coping with dense foliage, man-high cogon grass, swamps and heat exhaustion.

On 2 November, X Corps took the coastal town of Carigara at the head of the Leyte Valley. Part of XXIV Corps had already penetrated to the west coast south of Ormoc, so the Americans could now advance on the town from two directions, thereby cutting the enemy reinforcement route. X Corps advanced south on Highway 2, which climbed rapidly from the coast, zigzagging around a series of heavily wooded interlocking spurs.

This was a naturally strong defensive position controlled by the Japanese 1st Division. With artillery hidden on the far slopes of the hills, hidden trenches and foxholes and concealed machine guns, the Japanese were ready to fight the bloodiest battle of the Leyte campaign. Endless downpours turned the grass that covered the

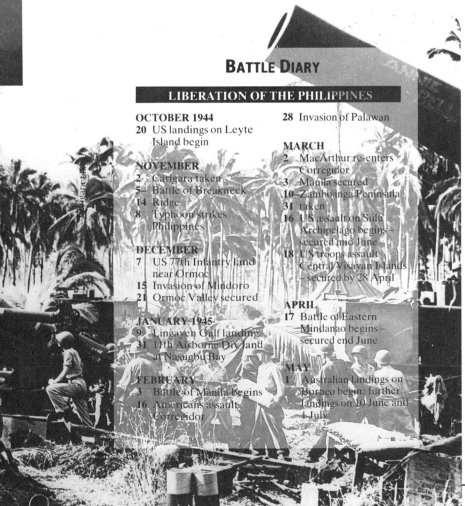

BATTLE DIARY

LIBERATION OF THE PHILIPPINES

OCTOBER 1944
20 US landings on Leyte Island begin

NOVEMBER
2   Carigara taken
5– Battle of Breakneck
14 Ridge
8   Typhoon strikes Philippines

DECEMBER
7   US 77th Infantry land near Ormoc
15 Invasion of Mindoro
21 Ormoc Valley secured

JANUARY 1945
9   Lingayen Gulf landing
31 11th Airborne Div land at Nasugbu Bay

FEBRUARY
3   Battle of Manila begins
16 Americans assault Corregidor

28 Invasion of Palawan

MARCH
2   MacArthur re-enters Corregidor
3   Manila secured
10 Zamboanga Peninsula
31 taken
16 US assault on Sulu Archipelago begins – secured mid June
18 US troops assault Central Visayan Islands – secured by 28 April

APRIL
17 Battle of Eastern Mindanao begins – secured end June

MAY
1   Australian landings on Borneo begin: further landings on 10 June and 1 July

storm, the fronds flattened like streamers of wet silk . . . the howling of the wind was like a thousandfold plaint of the unburied dead . . .'

Soaked, begrimed and weary men fought without quarter for yards of unnamed and vertiginous slopes. The issue was only finally resolved when the ridge was outflanked east and west in battalion strength, cutting Highway 2 to the rear of the defenders. Breakneck was

in American hands on 14 November, but two further days were spent driving the Japanese off the neighbouring heights that commanded the road. The battle cost the 21st Infantry Regiment over 760 casualties.

As the Japanese were proving impossible to eject from the wilderness of hills in western Leyte, MacArthur postponed the invasion of the next island for ten days and broke the deadlock with a surprise amphibious landing. The newly arrived 77th Infantry Division landed near Ormoc on 7 December: it was what the Americans called an end run. The devastated port fell three days later.

On 6 December, in response to growing American air superiority, the enemy made a series of desperate attacks on the American airstrips using infantry, paratroops and crash-landed demolition groups. For four days, US engineers and supply troops fought for their lives before order was restored.

SUICIDE ORDERS

Although the Ormoc Valley was fully secure by 21 December, the battle for Leyte bogged down into a sodden exercise in logistics. Weather and terrain often loomed larger than the enemy, hands that had once held weapons now groped for a hand-hold on the vegetation of each anonymous, knife-edged ridge. The only consolation to the Americans in their misery was that the enemy was even worse off. Desertion was common among the Japanese and lack of facilities to treat the wounded so widespread that '. . . commanders employing persuasive language frequently requested seriously wounded soldiers at the front to commit suicide . . . the majority died willingly . . .'

On 30 December 'with tears of remorse' Lieutenant-General Tomoyuki Yamashita, commander of the Four-teenth Area Army, speaking from Manila, told the defenders of Leyte that they would henceforth subsist on their own resources . . .' 'They say it is harder to live than

already treacherous slopes into a muddy slick that made climbing very dangerous, earning this feature the name of 'Breakneck Ridge'.

It was small-scale deadly combat with the enemy rarely seen. Then on 8 November conditions were made even more impossible by a typhoon of astonishing ferocity. 'From the angry immensity of the heavens, floods raced in almost horizontal·sheets. Palms bent low under the

▲ **Death from above – a Japanese destroyer (inset) is pounded to destruction by B-25 bombers off Leyte. The USAAF escort fighters shoot down the Japanese fighters which attempt to intervene.**

◀ **A sand-bag and timber bridge is built by US Army engineers over a stream in a swamp on Leyte.**

War Stories

Even though the Japanese on the Philippines had their backs to the wall, their determination to fight to the death was unshaken. Unsuspecting US troops at Buri airstrip were caught in a Japanese grenade and bayonet attack – but the myth of the ruthless efficiency of the Japanese infantryman was deflated as the Japs ran up and down in the chaos, shouting their few essential English phrases: 'Hello! Hello! Where are your machine guns?' and, even more compelling, 'Surrender! Surrender! Everything is resistless!'

to die . . . be patient enough to endure the hardships of life . . . and be ready to meet your death calmly for our beloved country . . .' Throughout January 1945, however, increasing numbers of Japanese soldiers were crossing over to the neighbouring islands of Cebu and Negros to escape starvation.

In March Major-General Sosaku Suzuki, commander of the Thirty-Fifth Army on Leyte, himself departed, his tenacity being ill rewarded when the ship carrying him was attacked from the air and he was killed. Organised resistance on Leyte was at an end, but the defence had cost the Japanese the bulk of their remaining fleet and between 40,000 and 60,000 dead ashore.

By November 1944 it was apparent to Yamashita ('Tiger of Malaya' and 'Victor of Singapore') that Leyte could not be held. He estimated that by mid December MacArthur would feel strong enough to make his next move, which he guessed would be the invasion of Luzon. This was beyond fighter range from Leyte, so Yamashita forecast that an intermediate island would also be seized to establish airfields.

However, it was only on 3 October that the American Joint Chiefs of Staff (JCS) themselves finally named Luzon as the next objective rather than Formosa. Admiral King retained his 'adamantine devotion' to the latter but lost Nimitz's support when it was realised that too few troops would be available. MacArthur had them and was keeping them for the 'holy grail' of Manila. Luzon was undeniably less risky than Formosa and the vital fast carrier groups would be committed to support of the invasion for a far shorter period.

Implicit in the plan was that General Krueger's Sixth Army would break the back of resistance on Luzon and then hand over to General Eichelberger's Eighth Army, which was mopping up on Leyte. The final clearance of the Philippines was to be undertaken by Filipino guerrillas or the reconstituted National Army, while the Netherlands East Indies and British possessions would be recovered by Anglo-Australian forces.

▼ **US soldiers examine the entrance of a Japanese bunker. In the foreground the corpse of a defender bears mute testimony to the savagery of the fighting.**

Hulton-Deutsch Collection

US National Archives

SOLDIER'S SOLDIER

A German-born child immigrant Walter Krueger was self-made and self-educated, a hard man who had worked up from 'buck private' to three-star general. A soldier's soldier, he was a superb tactician.

General MacArthur specifically asked for Krueger to command the Sixth Army in February 1943. This army was scattered 'from hell to breakfast' throughout Australia and New Guinea and he led them on a 30-month slog to Japan.

MacArthur stated after the war that history had not accorded Krueger his due, and assessed him thus: 'Swift and sure in attack; tenacious and determined in defence; modest and restrained in victory – I don't know what he would have been in defeat because he was never defeated . . . The great mantle of Stonewall Jackson would certainly fit his ample frame.' Krueger retired from the Army in 1946 and died in 1967.

MACARTHUR'S RETURN

Driven out of Manila in 1942, MacArthur promises to return – and so he does, but by the time Manila is back in American hands, the city is in ruins.

◀ **The first wave of US troops wade across a stream on Luzon Island as the advance begins on San Fabian. They are armed with M1 Garand rifles and carry spare ammunition and entrenching tools. Sleeves are worn rolled down as protection against insects and sunburn.**

First base for the liberation of Luzon was the island of Mindoro, separated from Luzon by just a narrow channel. Airfields on Mindoro would allow land-based fighters to cover the main invasion. The wet weather had seriously delayed airfield construction back on Leyte, however, so D-Day for Mindoro was put back from 5 December to 15 December 1944. Six of the Seventh Fleet escort carriers were detailed off to provide cover against the *kamikazes* in place of planned land-based Army Air Force units.

While the Third Fleet carriers bombed Luzon as a distraction, the assault force, with two Regimental Combat Teams (RCTs), made the three-day passage from Leyte to Mindoro. *Kamikazes* had learnt how to evade the Combat Air Patrols (CAPs), by flying low or using the terrain, and scored several hits. The worst was on the bridge of the fleet flagship *Nashville*. Among the 133 dead were two Chiefs of Staff.

In contrast, the actual landing was unopposed. Within five days one airstrip had been built from scratch, and another was ready in 13 days, but for the next fortnight *kamikazes* continued to exact a toll on offshore shipping. Some 200 *kamikazes* were launched against the invasion fleet alone, one in four hitting its target. Mindoro's airfields would not guarantee the Luzon assault force a free run but 'probably saved that bloody passage from becoming a mass slaughter'. Lingayen Gulf, its chosen objective, was 750 miles (1,200 km) from Leyte and with *kamikazes* as numerous and virulent as hornets, the passage would not want for excitement.

The 164-ship support, under Vice-

▲ **PBY Catalina flying boats of the Seventh Fleet air-sea rescue squadron fly over Lingayen Gulf. Below them the invasion fleet masses for the assault landings.**

▼ **Opposing forces as at 9 January 1945, giving US forces landing at Lingayen Gulf and Japanese troops present on Luzon.**

BATTLE LINE-UP

45,000–50,000 men Reserve	262,000 men (this includes
Armoured Group	Tank Division)
Regimental Combat Team	
Infantry Division	
Airborne Division	

US Library of Congress

▲ **US soldiers climb down the scrambling nets to board landing craft in Lingayen Gulf. In heavy seas this can be a very hazardous operation for men loaded with weapons and ammunition.**

Admiral Jesse B Oldendorf, sailed for Lingayen Gulf on 2 January 1945. Comprising vessels as disparate as battleships, minesweepers and 'Elsie Items' (LCI gunboats), they were not due at Lingayen until 6 January. Twelve escort carriers with fighter strength worked in cooperation with the AAF to maintain a 40-strong CAP but the unconventional tactics of the *kamikazes* enabled many to strike home before they were spotted.

The *Ommaney Bay*, for instance, was fatally struck by a twin-engined aircraft that 'seemed to drop plumb out of the sky', defying radar and lookouts alike. Such lightly built escort carriers had no armour and both aircraft and bombload penetrated deeply before exploding. With large stores of aviation fuel and ordnance aboard, the situation rapidly became uncontrollable, the ship having to be abandoned and scuttled within 40 minutes.

LOW-LEVEL ATTACK

Against the escort carrier *Manila Bay*, two wave-lapping Zeros used different tactics: fast-weaving to avoid AA fire, they approached to within 1,000 yards (900 m) before pulling up into steep climbing turns, rolling over on their backs and plunging at the ship. One hit and one near-missed but the ship was saved by well-trained damage control parties. Oldendorf commenced his pre-assault bombardment of Lingayen on 6 January but was seriously de-

layed by *kamikaze* attacks. The battleship *New Mexico* took a hit that killed the captain and a British Army liaison officer. Rear Admiral Chandler died from being drenched in flaming gasoline when his cruiser, *Louisville* (the 'Lady Lou'), was hit a second time. On that dreadful first day, one ship was sunk and 11 damaged.

Four days behind Oldendorf came the main assault convoy, carrying I and XIV Corps of the US Army and MacArthur himself on the cruiser *Boise*. The narrow channels between the islands meant that ships were strung out over 40 miles (65 km), complicating the air defence. Suppression strikes by Vice Admiral William Halsey's Third Fleet carriers reduced the *kamikaze* threat and the assault went in on time on 9 January, unopposed and over the same beaches used by the invading Japanese three years previously.

BIRTHDAY TREAT?

It was MacArthur's opinion that General Yamashita would not fight a defensive battle for Manila, which he therefore expected to be liberated in about a fortnight. The Sixth Army commander, General Walter Krueger, hoped to have MacArthur entering the capital in a procession on 26 January, his 65th birthday. However, American progress was decided not by the level of enemy opposition but by stretched logistics and a shortage of bridging materials for dealing with the many water-

Below and right: US National Archives

◀ **Crewmen duck as the blazing remains of a *kamikaze* crash down on the deck of the USS *Marcus Island* in the Sulu Sea, 15 December 1944. The aircraft has been hit by AA fire and exploded before hitting the carrier.**

▶ **US troops land on Luzon — in the background the huge volume of invasion shipping can be seen. The striped panel in the sand is a guide for landing craft crews.**

◄ A Zero explodes in fire and smoke over the USS *Intrepid*, 25 November 1944. US Navy AA crews aim to shoot *kamikazes* out of the sky — even badly damaged Japanese aircraft will attempt to crash on warships.

War Stories

More unbelievable than humorous is the tale of the Japanese Red Cross nurse, Tai Kubota, who survived near starvation and hideous conditions before the Japanese surrender on the Philippines. A POW with the US Army, her verminous clothes were burned and she was well treated before being returned to Japan late in 1945. To her astonishment, the first thing she was asked on returning to the Japanese Red Cross was, 'What happened to your mess-tin and water bottle?' A wretched welcome indeed!

would defend the mountainous bulk of Luzon to the north and east of Lingayen. The *Shimbu* group with 80,000 men was responsible for the area east of Manila and the wild Bicol Peninsula in the south, while the 30,000 troops of the *Kembu* group were anchored in the Zambales Mountains from where they could menace XIV Corps' right flank as it drove southward, besides denying use of the Clark airbase.

Pressured by MacArthur to take the all-weather Clark airstrips before the rains arrived, Krueger was forced to alter his plans. With better going on the right, XIV Corps would press on, with I Corps, guarding its left and rear. By the end of January, Clark airbase was in American hands following reduction of the *Kembu* group in their powerful defensive positions. On their right, in a typical MacArthur move, XI Corps were put ashore south of Zambales without opposition (except for one man who was savaged by a Filipino carabao, a sort of wild ox and a beast of uncertain and vile temper). XI Corps was ordered to link up with XIV Corps, having sealed off the neck of the Bataan Peninsula which formed the west side of Manila Bay. Though deeply symbolic to the Americans, Bataan was regarded by the Japanese as a defensive dead-end

courses of the narrow coastal strips.

Yamashita did indeed draw back, but withdrawal was forced on him. After the futile fight on Leyte, he was short of men and stores. The skies and seas belonged to his enemies and there was no prospect of further reinforcement. His supply dumps and communications were being sabotaged by the increasingly capable and confident Filipino guerrillas. Finally, he was blessed with a complex command structure which gave him no control over the naval infantry units in Manila, commanded by Rear Admiral Sanji Iwabuchi.

In addition, the 100-mile (160 km) Lingayen-Manila axis was difficult to defend so, despite the effect on morale, Yamashita decided to yield the capital as forecast.

Yamashita then reorganised his troops into three groups. Of these, the 152,000 strong *Shobu* group

▲ The remains of a Japanese Ki-46 'Dinah' reconnaissance aircraft is examined by US troops.

and it was only lightly held.

The only practical highway, however, was constricted as a defile known as Zigzag Pass, above Olongapo (the Pacific Fleet's favourite 'run ashore' in happier times). It cost XI Corps 250 dead in a fortnight of bitter fighting necessary to overcome the Japanese forces. By the time XI Corps had swung into Bataan to flush out survivors, the battle for Manila was in full swing.

FIGHT TO THE DEATH

But as Yamashita, unwilling to feed Manila's million inhabitants, started to pull out, some 16,000 Japanese naval troops moved in. By the time High Command reacted and ordered them out it was too late. Surrounded, they refused to yield without a fight.

Manila sprawls for ten miles (16 km) around the bay, evenly bisected by the Pasig River which flows through the heart of the city. The Japanese were concentrated to the south of the river, with Admiral Iwabuchi personally commanding

◄ The striking unit patch of the 1st Cavalry. The 'First Team' were proud to be the liberators of Manila.

► US soldiers fire a 37 mm anti-tank gun at Japanese positions in Intramuros, the old walled centre of Manila.

5,000 diehards, in the old Intramuros district and the Government buildings. Strongly built in stone, the latter had been extensively fortified and interconnected by tunnels.

Beyond the southern outskirts lay Fort McKinley and Nichols Field, strongly held by 5,000 more naval

troops. A Japanese army detachment defended the highways running up from the south, the direction from which the Americans were originally expected to come.

MacArthur, anxious for the many prisoners and interned Filipinos held in the city, ordered the 1st Cavalry and 37th Divisions to mount separate thrusts from the north, and a race for Manila developed, with units advancing at speeds of up to 50 mph (80 km/h).

DEVASTATION

Entering the city on 3 February the US troops had by the following day released those incarcerated in the Santo Tomas University and the nearby prison. Though not in any great strength, north of the river the Japanese caused great difficulties to American troops fresh from months of jungle warfare and unaccustomed to dealing with barricaded streets and fortified buildings. Falling back, the enemy blew the Pasig bridges, having demolished anything of value and causing an uncontrollable fire that destroyed more of Manila than any other Allied capital apart from Warsaw.

In assault boats and LVTs the

CORREGIDOR REGAINED

The seizure by the Japanese of the fortress island of Corregidor in May 1942 had stung the US badly.

Early on 16 February 1945, the attention of the 5,000-strong Japanese garrison on Corregidor focused on a fleet of American LCMs approaching from nearby Bataan. Suddenly, a group of low-flying C-47s appeared, dropping 1,000 paratroops on top of the plateau and seizing the ruined barracks there. Distracted, the Japanese attacked the paratroops, allowing the amphibious troops to land almost unopposed.

Close combat for Corregidor's caves, ravines, ruins and tunnels lasted until 26 February. Only 20 Japanese were captured and few escaped, but the operation cost 210 American lives.

▶ **US paratroopers make a unique airborne assault on one of the smallest landing zones of World War II.**

All pictures: US National Archives

◀ **A stretcher party carries a wounded soldier after the heavy fighting in Manila. All street fighting is tough, but the Japanese make Manila a savage battleground.**

▶ **A flamethrower fires a 'dry' shot into a Japanese position in Intramuros. US flamethrowers could fire unignited 'wet' fuel and then follow it with a burning 'dry' shot.**

148th US Infantry stormed across the river on 7 February. A priority objective was the city's electrical power station on Provisor Island but, after four days vicious building-to-building fighting, the recaptured plant was beyond repair. XIV Corps crossed the Pasig in strength upstream on 10 February and, driving clear to the coast, isolated the district.

On 31 January, elements of the 11th US Airborne Division came ashore at Nasugbu Bay, some 50 miles (80 km) south of the city and opposite Bataan at the mouth of Manila Bay. By 5 February, despite a brisk engagement crossing the Paranaque River, they faced the garrison at Nichols Field. Well provided with automatic and medium

calibre guns salvaged from wrecked naval craft, the Japanese naval troops poured a hail of fire over the 11th, prompting the radio message 'Tell Halsey to stop looking for the Jap Fleet. It's dug in on Nichols Field'. Finally, bombed by Marine aircraft and chewed up by artillery concentrations, the unusable airfield was taken on 12 February.

Iwabuchi's men were slowly, remorselessly compressed into the old city. Without hope, and becoming more fanatical in the face of defeat, they began to commit excesses against both people and property. One of the toughest struggles was at

the hospital and adjacent University of the Philippines, fortified (against all conventions) and housing 7,000 civilians, held virtual hostage.

MacArthur would allow no bombing of historic Intramuros, so artillery was used with great precision to breach the ancient 40-foot (12.5 m) thick walls. Through the gaps, and from across the river, infantry assaulted the fortified zone on 23 February. Only 25 of the remaining 2,000 defenders were taken prisoner but, in the dungeons below Fort Santiago, American troops discovered almost the whole male population of the quarter, who had

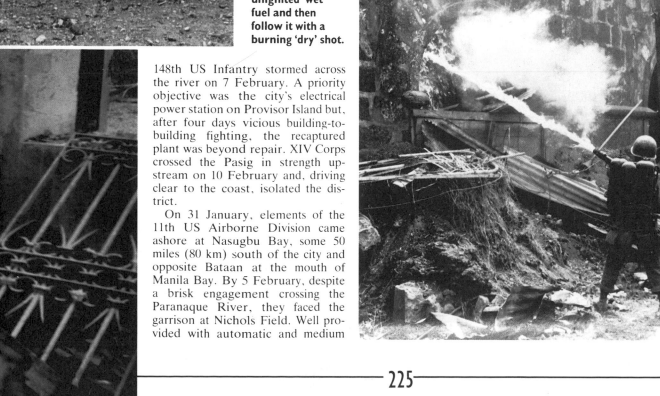

been murdered in cold blood.

On 3 March, the Finance Building was cleared and, with it, organised resistance in Manila ended.

MacArthur had liberated the city in fulfilment of his sacred pledge, but only at the cost of its destruction. The month-long battle cost XIV Corps 1,010 dead, the Japanese 12,500.

DESPERATE RESISTANCE

But on Luzon 170,000 Japanese troops were still alive and kicking. The southern *Shimbu* group was harried into trackless wastes. Filipino guerrilla groups gradually took over the clearing-up operations from the Sixth Army, which was progressively pulled out to retrain for the invasion of Japan itself.

In northern Luzon, the Sixth Army, having lost 8,297 killed on the island, handed over to the Eighth. The *Shobu* group had been driven back into strategically unimportant areas and 50,000 survived to surrender at the war's end.

The Eighth Army, not required for the pending Iwo Jima operation, was used by MacArthur to retake the central and southern Philippines. Beyond moral obligations to the Filipinos who had resisted the Japanese so courageously, the General cited the need for airfields. Japanese communications in the South China Sea could be severed

All pictures: US National Archives

STRATEGIC VICTORY

General Douglas MacArthur's insistence on a US liberation of the Philippines, made against the advice of strategic planners in Washington, involved the Americans in hard and costly fighting. Indeed, the war in the myriad islands was not yet over when the atomic bombs were dropped on Hiroshima and Nagasaki, and Japan surrendered, in August 1945. But MacArthur had his reasons. Some were purely personal – as the commander of defeated Filipino and US forces in 1942, he felt obliged to lead the liberation – but others were political and strategic. The Philippines had for long been the jewel in the crown of US influence in the Western Pacific and, although the islands were already on the way to independence, that influence was likely to be important once the war was over.

TURNING POINT

▲ Under fire on Cebu, men of 3rd Bn 132nd Infantry hug the shore of Cebu Island. In the background Amtracs have started to move towards the treeline.

◄ The political and military victor of the Philippines, General Douglas MacArthur 'returns' to the islands. He was adamant that US forces should liberate them to save the Filipinos from Japanese occupation.

▶ Sherman tanks offer cover to men of A Coy 1st Bn 185th Infantry as they advance under small arms fire on Panay Island. The US Army photographer who took the picture was moments later wounded in action.

Much the same story applied to the Sulu Archipelago and the major islands of the Visayas – Panay, Negros, Cebu and Bohol. By August 1945, organised Japanese resistance had virtually ceased, although tens of thousands of emaciated survivors remained to surrender. The way to Borneo and the East Indies was open.

▼ The Stars and Stripes fly over the observation post of 1st Bn 151 Regimental Combat Team on Carabao Island, April 1945.

▲ The unit patch of the US Eighth Army. Today they boast the proud motto 'Pacific Victors'.

◀ T Sgt Wilburn L Kirksey of the 25th Infantry Division on the lookout in the Luzon Hills near Balete Pass.

and air superiority could be exerted over oil-rich Borneo. Speed was essential to beat the onset of the rains.

Palawan is a long, narrow island stretching between the Philippines and Borneo. It was assaulted by the Eighth's 41st Division on 28 February. With terrain causing more trouble than the 1,750-strong garrison, the 270 mile (430 km) long island was taken at the cost of only ten American dead.

Poor subsoil made it impossible to build an airfield on Palawan in time to cover the assault on the Zamboango peninsula of Mindanao. But the guerrillas not only controlled an airfield on Mindanao, they also guided in the amphibious landing. The 9,000 Japanese defenders retreated to the high ground but were eventually obliged, 6,400 fewer, to retreat into eastern Mindanao.

BERLIN

BATTLE DIARY

OCTOBER 1944

6	Russians renew Hungarian offensive
16	Horthy abdicates
19	Fall of Belgrade

JANUARY 1945

12	Beginning of Russian drive to the Oder
17	Fall of Warsaw

FEBRUARY

13	Last Germans capitulate in Budapest

MARCH

6	Final German counter-attack in Hungary

APRIL

16	Beginning of final drive on Berlin
18	Russians break through the Oder-Neisse line
22	First Soviet troops reach outskirts of Berlin
24	Berlin surrounded
26	Beginning of the battle of Berlin
28	Mussolini executed
30	Hitler and Eva Braun commit suicide

MAY

2	Fighting ends in Berlin
4	Ceasefire signed at Lüneburg Heath
7	Germany surrenders unconditionally
8	VE day

CLEARING THE BALKANS

Camera Press

Hitler's Eastern realm is crumbling away, and he can stage little more than futile attempts to stem the Russian tide.

▲▲ Insignia of the 3rd SS Panzer Division. Previously in Poland, it was transferred to Hungary in early 1945.

▲ With Hitler's fortunes on the decline and the Red Army moving steadily west, joyous scenes of liberation are witnessed all over Eastern Europe.

The Polish Home Army was still battling valiantly for the liberation of Warsaw from its Nazi occupiers, when the Germans suddenly found themselves in more trouble further south, in the Balkans. On 20 August 1944, the Russian Marshals Rodion Malinovsky and Fedor Tolbukhin threw the full weight of their 2nd and 3rd Ukrainian Fronts against General Johannes Friessner's Army Group South Ukraine in Rumania. Almost half of Friessner's front line was held by Rumanian troops of unreliable loyalty, and the Rumanian Third Army on the lower Dniester collapsed almost immediately, opening the road to the Danube. The German Sixth Army on the Rumanians' left flank was now in an untenable position. Friessner tried to pull back to a new line behind the River Prut but it was an impossible task for, even as Tolbukhin's tanks were sweeping round the southern flank, Malinovsky's had broken through the Rumanian Fourth Army at Iasi and were racing to encircle from the north. The two pincers met near Husi and the best part of over 12 German divisions went into 'the bag'. Within a week of fighting, Army Group South Ukraine had virtually ceased to exist.

CHANGING SIDES

Meanwhile, on 23 August, Rumania's King Michael I had ordered the arrest of the pro-Nazi dictator Ion Antonescu and announced his acceptance of Allied armistice terms. Friessner responded on Hitler's orders by sending his last 6,000 reserves into Bucharest. Loyal Rumanian troops held and then surrounded them, so Hitler ordered the *Luftwaffe* to bomb the city. King Michael retaliated on the 25th by declaring war on his former ally. On the 31st, Soviet troops entered Bucharest; on 13 September, Malinovsky signed an armistice agreement with King Michael's new government. Friessner's remaining forces in Rumania retired into the Transylvanian Alps.

Meanwhile, on 26 August, the Regency Council of the infant King Simon II of Bulgaria announced its wish to withdraw from the war and become neutral. Despite the fact that Bulgaria had only been at war with Britain and America and that no Bulgarian units had fought in Russia, Stalin refused to accept this plea. On 5 Septem-

ber he declared war on Bulgaria. Three days later Tolbukhin's troops crossed the frontier and the panic-stricken Regents desperately declared war on Germany. Even this made no difference to Stalin, and Russian troops quickly overran the country, encountering no resistance. An armistice was signed on 28 October and a new communist régime established.

The loss of Rumania and Bulgaria to the Russians left the German forces in Greece and Yugoslavia in an unenviable situation, and the moment he heard the news of Rumania's surrender, General Alexander Löhr, commanding Army Group E in southern Greece, ordered a

▲ **Russian troops parade through the streets of Belgrade in October 1944, when – after three years of occupation – Yugoslavia's partisans linked up with the 3rd Ukrainian Front.**

retreat of all his forces to join up with Field Marshal Maximilian Freiherr von Weichs' Army Group F in northern Greece and Yugoslavia. Although the majority were evacuated by sea and air, Löhr was forced to leave about 20,000 men behind on various Greek islands, including Crete. German forces in Yugoslavia had already suffered a great deal of trouble from Tito's well-organised partisan brigades and, with Soviet and Bulgarian forces massing on Yugoslavia's border and a new British expeditionary force about to arrive in Greece, the guerrilla leader intensified his efforts.

BELGRADE FALLS

Tolbukhin, however, did not seem to be in a hurry and it was not until 22 September that his leading divisions began crossing the Danube near Turnu Severin. They met strong opposition from the tough Alpine and SS troops under Weichs' command, but by 4 October had reached Pancevo only 10 miles (16 km) from Belgrade. The Russians at this time were more concerned with the situation in Hungary than with the liberation of Yugoslavia, giving Weichs invaluable time. Nevertheless, within ten days armoured columns had cut the valley of the River Morava south of the capital, forcing the German troops still retreating from the south to take a more westerly route around Sarajevo, harassed at every point by the partisans. On the 14th Tolbukhin's troops linked up with Tito's in the outskirts of Belgrade, and after holding on for five days to give his remaining forces time to fight their way through towards Vukovar, Weichs abandoned the city.

Even while the frontiers of the Third Reich were being so steadily eroded, Hitler had to contend with communist guerrillas in the Czech province of Slovakia, who now

Bildarchiv Preussischer Kulturbesitz

▲ Bucharest is liberated by the Russians on 31 August 1944, after they have crushed the remaining German and Rumanian resistance.

Marshal Ivan Koniev's 1st Ukrainian Front commenced moving towards Czechoslovakia through the Carpathians on 8 September, followed by General I E Petrov's 4th Ukrainian Front on the 14th, but by this time the Germans held the whip hand in Slovakia: the insurgents had been forced to withdraw into the Tatra Mountains and revert to guerrilla warfare instead of open battle. Although abortive, the Slovak rebellion had had the significant effect of drawing desperately needed German troops out of Poland and Hungary, where the last critical battles before the final drive on Berlin were now taking place.

DRIVE INTO HUNGARY

On 6 October, four days after the Polish Home Army surrendered, the Russians renewed their offensive into Hungary. Malinovsky struck with five full armies, one of them armoured, plus two mechanised brigade groups. The advance went well to begin with, but was halted outside Debrecen in a furious two-day battle from the 10th to the 12th by the surviving divisions of Friessner's renamed Army Group South. After a pause to allow supplies to catch up – the railway gauges in Rumania and Hungary were different to the Russian standard – Malinovsky returned to the attack.

However, in the interim, the Hungarian Regent, Admiral Miklos Horthy, had been conducting secret negotiations for an armistice with Stalin. Hitler found out about these and forced Horthy to abdicate. He also sent five fresh divisions to reinforce Friessner, and on the 20th the Germans counterattacked around Debrecen.

FORTRESS BUDAPEST

After a furious battle lasting three days, Sixth Army managed to surround the best part of three of Malinovsky's corps. The last survivors to escape from the pocket on the 29th were forced to abandon all their tanks and artillery. But the Germans had only secured a temporary reprieve, because on the same day Malinovsky's Sixth Guards Tank Army smashed through the Hungarian Third Army and on 15 November was within 30 miles (48 km) of Budapest. By this time, too, with Belgrade secured, Malinovsky was able to call on reinforcements from Tolbukhin, and their combined forces converged on the Hungarian capital, which Hitler

intensified their efforts to throw off the Nazi yoke. By late August Hitler was sufficiently worried about the situation to send seven divisions of German troops in to occupy the province and disarm the Slovak Army. The first clashes occurred on 29 August and next day Slovak Radio broadcast a call for a national uprising. Partisans and regular army units began operating together to throw out the invaders while, like the Poles in Warsaw, they waited for the arrival of the Red Army.

DIVERSE INTERESTS

With the end of the war in Europe clearly in sight in the autumn of 1944, it was imperative that the 'Big Three' – Churchill, Roosevelt and Stalin – settle a variety of issues which would shape the future. They agreed on a conference to be held at Yalta in the Crimea in February 1945 with the key question of Germany itself being discussed. Partition was agreed as the best way of preventing a resurgent Fourth Reich, with each of the Allies (France being belatedly admitted) to control a zone. During the conference, Stalin made the prophetic remark that it was easy for the Allies to maintain unity during a war, but that 'the difficult task came afterwards when diverse interests tended to divide them.' Could this have been an indication of the Cold War that developed in the years to come?

► The 'Big Three' at Yalta – Prime Minister Churchill, President Roosevelt and Russian Premier, Stalin.

Bildarchiv Preussischer Kulturbesitz

had declared a 'fortress' to be held at all costs. His obsession would draw troops away from Poland, where they would be sorely missed when the Red Army renewed its offensive across the Vistula in January 1945.

Before that, on 30 November 1944, Malinovsky and Tolbukhin, having recovered from the setback at Debrecen, began pressing in on Budapest from north and south and by 7 December had reached Lake Balaton. On Christmas Eve, while world attention was focused on the 'Battle of the Bulge' in the Ardennes, the first Russian troops entered the city suburbs; by the end of the year Budapest was completely surrounded and its 100,000-strong garrison (principally IX SS Corps) was under siege.

HITLER'S LAST ATTACK

With the situation in Warsaw seemingly stabilised as winter approached, Hitler had also withdrawn the 3rd and 5th SS Panzer Divisions (IV SS Panzer Corps) from Poland and sent them to Hungary to try to break through to the relief of Budapest. They began their attack north of Lake Balaton on 18 January and punched a 40-mile (64-km) salient into the Russian line, getting to within 15 miles (24 km) of the city before their advance was brought to a halt on the 27th. At the same time, realising his Ardennes offensive had failed, Hitler pulled 'Sepp' Dietrich's Sixth SS Panzer Army out of the line in the West on 22 January with the intention – despite protests from his generals – of sending it to Hungary as well. It was too late. By this time Soviet troops occupied roughly half of Budapest and on 13 February the final German survivors capitulated.

The *Führer* was still insanely determined to retake the city, and four days later Dietrich's freshly arrived I SS Corps (1st and 12th SS Panzer Divisions) counter-attacked against the bridgehead Malinovsky had established over the River Hron, threatening Vienna. Their approach, conducted under the tightest possible security, had been undetected and they took Malinovsky completely by surprise, smashing Seventh Guards Army and, after a week's furious action, forcing the Russians to withdraw behind the river. This set the scene for the last major German offensive of the war, codenamed *Frühlingserwachen* (Spring Awakening), which was de-

▲ **With Russian troops pouring into the Reich during the last winter of the war, Germans flee westwards, hoping to reach safe haven with the Allies.**

▶ **Taking advantage of a lull in the fierce fighting for Hitler's 'fortress' Budapest, a Waffen-SS soldier chats to his Hungarian colleague.**

War Stories

One of the most famous photographs of the war, the raising of the Red Flag over the *Reichstag*, was, in fact a reconstruction of a scene which took place by night. Knowing the moment would be re-enacted, an outstanding Soviet war photographer got permission from Marshal Zhukov to shoot the scene from the air, then, unauthorised, flew on to Moscow. The next day he flew back to Berlin, bearing an armful of copies of the newspaper, *Pravda*. For him, the crowning glory was his photo on the cover – a wartime photo scoop!

▲ Hungary's capital, Budapest, bears the scars of the intense fighting which developed between its beleaguered German garrison and the Red Army from late December 1944. But the city held out against all odds until 13 February.

signed to recapture Budapest.

On 6 March, Dietrich's Sixth SS Panzer Army (five Panzer, two infantry and two cavalry divisions), aided by General Hermann Balck's Sixth Army which also had five panzer divisions, again attacked north of Lake Balaton, while Löhr's Second Panzer Army (which had some armour but no actual panzer divisions) pushed east from south of the lake as a diversion. Forewarned of the operation by deserters, Tolbukhin had prepared his defences in depth and by the 10th, slowed by thick mud and lack of fuel, the Panzers had only managed to advance 20 miles (32 km).

Then, on the 16th, Malinovsky and Tolbukhin went over to the attack themselves. Although the remnants of Army Group South continued to fight back vigorously, their efforts were doomed. Within days the Russians were up to the Austrian border and drove straight on to Vienna, which, after several days of hectic street fighting, fell on 13 April.

PUSH TO THE ODER

On 12 January, after gathering massive resources, the Russian 'steamroller' went into action on the Vistula front. At 10.30 am, after a massive artillery bombardment, infantry and tanks of Marshal Koniev's 1st Ukrainian Front smashed out of their bridgehead some 200 miles (320 km) south of Warsaw, and within five days had driven a hole 100 miles (160 km) deep into General Josef Harpe's Army Group A, which only had six panzer divisions left. Warsaw fell on 17 January and Harpe was relieved of his command by an irate *Führer*, who replaced him with General Ferdinand Schörner.

On the 14th further attacks had been mounted north and south of Warsaw by Marshal Georgi Zhukov's 1st and Marshal Konstantin Rokossovky's 2nd Belorussian Fronts, the former paralleling Koniev's westward drive while the latter, quickly gaining ground, swung north to converge on General Georg-Hans Reinhardt's Army Group Centre in East Prussia. Already under pressure from General Ivan Chernyakovsky's 3rd Belorussian Front on the Baltic, Reinhardt's troops were completely surrounded in a pocket backing on to the Gulf of Danzig by the beginning of February. By this time too, Zhukov and Koniev had crossed the prewar German frontier and reached the River Oder, the final natural defensive line before the very gates of Berlin. With only 50 miles (80 km) to go, the final act was about to begin.

BATTLE DIARY

RUSSIAN BREAKTHROUGH

OCTOBER 1944
6 Russians renew Hungarian offensive
16 Horthy abdicates
19 Fall of Belgrade

JANUARY 1945
12 Russian drive to the Oder
17 Fall of Warsaw

FEBRUARY
13 Last Germans capitulate in Budapest

MARCH
6 Final German counter-attack in Hungary

APRIL
16 Final Soviet drive on Berlin starts
18 Russians break through Oder-Neisse line
22 First Soviet troops reach outskirts of Berlin
24 Berlin surrounded
26 Beginning of final battle of Berlin
28 Mussolini executed
30 Hitler and Eva Braun commit suicide

MAY
2 Fighting ends in Berlin
4 Ceasefire signed at Lüneburg Heath
7 Germany surrenders unconditionally
8 VE Day

THE FINAL CHAPTER

Deprived of its glory as the capital of the Third Reich, the city of Berlin has become a battleground from which only the luckiest emerge alive.

On 1 April 1945, Soviet supremo Josef Stalin summoned his two ablest marshals, Georgi Zhukov and Ivan Koniev, to Moscow. In his study in the Kremlin, he told them that General Dwight D Eisenhower was planning a joint Anglo-American operation under the command of Field Marshal Sir Bernard Montgomery to capture Berlin. Both Soviety military leaders were indignant at the thought that, after all their men's efforts since the previous October, and with their forces poised on the Oder only some 50 miles (80 km) from the German capital, the biggest prize of the war would go to the Western Allies. They went away to prepare their plans, knowing that, with the final collapse of the Reich at stake, the Germans would put everything into the defence of Berlin and that the operation would be nothing like the headlong rush through Poland in January and February.

RACE TO BERLIN

Two days later, they returned to Stalin with their plans. Both men were highly competitive, although their rivalry lacked the animosity which existed between Montgomery and General George S Patton. Each wanted Berlin for himself, but Koniev's forces were still partially tied down fighting to the south in Silesia, and it would take too long to get reinforcements to them from the Baltic, so, in the end, the main assault across the heavily defended Seelow Heights, to the east of Berlin, was entrusted to Zhukov's 1st Belorussian Front, while Koniev's 1st Ukrainian Front was to provide support on its left and drive to the River Elbe.

Almost simultaneously, Marshal Konstantin Rokossovsky's 2nd Belorussian Front would resume its advance in the north, while the 3rd

◄ Berlin, 30 April 1945: the Red Flag reaches the top of the *Reichstag*, the Red Army's target. It took two more days of heavy fighting before the German defenders inside the building laid down their weapons.

► Once the inexorable Soviet 'steamroller' gets going, all defences put up around Berlin give way, while natural barriers, such as rivers and canals, prove puny obstacles.

SCR Library

Suddeutscher Verlag

▲ By 24 April, the Russians have reached some of the city's suburbs, firing their 'Stalin's organs' in the general direction of the *Reichstag*.

Belorussian Front – commanded by Marshal Alexander Vasilevsky since Chernyakovsky's death in action in February – would complete the subjugation of the German forces in East Prussia. The date for the start of the last battle was set for 16 April, to give Zhukov and Koniev time to assemble and prepare their forces.

Zhukov had the First and Second Guards Tank Armies and nine mechanised armies, while Koniev had the Third and Fourth Guards Tank Armies, plus six mechanised armies; each of their Fronts now included a Polish army, which had been formed early in the year from

◄ A comparison of German and Soviet forces at the start of the Battle of Berlin.

BATTLE LINE-UP

GERMAN
Men 1,000,000
Guns 10,400
Tanks 1,500
Aircraft 3,300

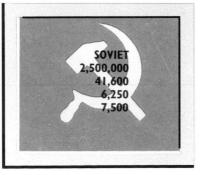

SOVIET
2,500,000
41,600
6,250
7,500

Ullstein Bilderdienst

spite all the efforts of one of Germany's most competent surviving generals, Gotthard Heinrici.

Heinrici's casual attitude towards sartorial elegance and his frank contempt of ceremony belied an extremely tough and often unorthodox character. He had been chosen to replace *Reichsführer-SS* Heinrich Himmler, whose appointment to command the new Army Group Vistula in January had merely underlined his military incompetence. Despite the fact that Hitler had sacked, executed or forced to suicide most of his competent and experienced senior commanders, he had in Heinrici and the CO of the recently renamed Army Group Centre, Ferdinand Schörner, two of the most capable of the survivors.

Their resources, however, were too limited to stem the Soviet tide. Heinrici had the Third Panzer Army, north of Berlin, and Ninth Army, directly to its east, as the principal blocking forces, with LVI Panzer Corps as a mobile reserve, while to their south was Schörner's Fourth Panzer Army. Into the fray would also be thrown Twelfth Army which, at the beginning of April, was still holding the Americans on the Elbe east of Magdeburg.

THE LAST RESORT

Finally, in Berlin itself were some 90,000 teenagers and grandfathers of the *Volkssturm*, or 'People's Army'. The older men, cynical and disillusioned veterans of World War I, had military experience, but most of the

Polish volunteers eager to exact revenge. Rokossovsky only had five armies, none of them fully armoured, but even these would prove sufficient to drive west to Stralsund, Rostock and Wismar, de-

▲ **Members of the *Volkssturm* head for the Berlin suburbs in a final effort to fend off the Russians.**

▼ **The link-up of Soviet and US forces at Torgau heralds the end of the war in Europe.**

Bundesarchiv-Koblenz

Süddeutscher Verlag

▲ **Clutching their last possessions, swarms of refugees wander aimlessly through a city reduced mainly to rubble by the day and night Allied bombing.**

youngsters had received little more than basic weapons' training in the Hitler Youth. Yet, when the Russian assault began, Hitler, buoyed up by astrological predictions of victory, was sufficiently deluded to believe these could turn back the Soviet tide.

Just before dawn, at 5 am on 16 April, the attack began with a massive artillery bombardment

Left and below: Bildarchiv Preussischer Kulturbesitz

against Ninth Army's positions. Then Zhukov borrowed a trick from Montgomery and switched on all his searchlights, pointing them at the low-lying clouds to illuminate the way for the infantry and tanks. But the Germans fought back with suicidal determination, throwing four reserve divisions into the fray, and when darkness fell, Zhukov had failed to breach the Seelow Heights. He ordered the attack to continue during the night, bringing up more tanks and artillery, and by nightfall on the 17th he was through. However, he had only gained seven or eight miles (11–13 km), far less than originally planned.

▲ Soviet tanks ferry in soldiers of the victorious Red Army now that the *Reichstag* has fallen and only little resistance remains.

▼ A last-minute casualty, as Berlin's defenders, harassed by fanatical leaders, keep up the resistance.

Bildarchiv Preussischer Kulturbesitz

Meanwhile, at 6.15 am, Koniev had launched his own assault against Fourth Panzer Army, sending his infantry across the River Neisse around Triebel in assault boats, covered by an artillery barrage and smokescreen; then the sappers hastily erected pontoon bridges for the tanks. However, his advance was also slow, and it took him until late on the 17th to break through the first

▲ Leaving the warren to surrender: fighting did not only take place at street level – the city's extensive Underground network was also used during its defence.

Ullstein Bilderdienst

Novosti Press Agency

two lines of defence. Fourth Panzer Army, ably commanded by Lieutenant-General Fritz Gräser, now dug itself into the third and last line behind the River Spree.

Dismayed by Zhukov's lack of progress, Stalin ordered Koniev to achieve a breakthrough and swing his two tank armies northwards towards Berlin. The assault was resumed on the 18th, and Zhukov at

▲ Russian troops have reached the Brandenburg Gate, May 1945.

▼► After their surrender, German soldiers are marched into captivity; many, never to return.

Ullstein Bilderdienst

last cleared the remaining pockets of resistance on the Seelow Heights. With totally inadequate reserves, the German line was now breaking up in several places – even the cream of the remaining SS Panzer Divisions, acting in their accustomed role as a 'fire brigade', were unable to stop the remorseless advance. Koniev swept across the Spree at Spremberg on the 18th, and the Third and Fourth Guards Tank Armies spurred on towards Berlin. Fourth Panzer Army was cut off from its line of

retreat and eliminated piecemeal by Koniev's infantry and artillery, supported from the air.

Ninth Army was similarly encircled by the 22nd, by which time both Zhukov's and Koniev's tanks were in the outskirts of Berlin, while Rokossovsky, who had started his own attack across the Oder on the 20th, had similarly cut Third Panzer Army off from Berlin.

On 20 April, Adolf Hitler celebrated his 56th birthday in the *Führerbunker* beneath the Chancel-

Bildarchiv Preussischer Kulturbesitz

▲ The end of the fighting in Berlin: the famous *Unter den Linden* avenue becomes a first-aid centre.

▼ Hitler makes one of his last public appearances, to decorate members of his Hitler Youth.

lery, just to the south of the Brandenburg Gate. Nazi Party officials broke off their preparations to flee the doomed city in order to pay their last respects. Hitler was morose, despite the arrival of his mistress, Eva Braun, who declared she was going to stay with him to the end. His entourage tried to persuade him to leave Berlin, but after the inevitable failure of a counterattack on the 21st, led by SS-General Felix Steiner, the *Führer* announced his

determination to stick it out with the two million people who still lived in the battered city.

By the 24th, Berlin was completely surrounded and Rokossovsky had Third Panzer Army on the run, despite difficult terrain which hampered armoured operations. The next day, leading elements of Koniev's troops met up with men of the American First Army at Torgau, on the river Elbe. Then, on the 26th, the final battle for Berlin began.

ARMAGGEDON

In Berlin – the largest city of World War II to become the scene of a pitched battle – all the most terrifying elements of an all-out war were magnified beyond belief. To the Russian soldiery, it was retribution for the people of Kharkov, Kiev,

Leningrad, Stalingrad and hundreds of smaller towns. To the inhabitants of Berlin, it was the worst nightmare come true. No woman was safe from rape. No man, especially if he wore the hated uniform of the SS, was immune from a vicious beating at best or a bayonet or bullet at worst. Knowing their fate, the people of Berlin fought with animal ferocity through this final week of the war in Europe.

STREET FIGHTING

Homes already reduced to rubble by Anglo-American bombing were further pummelled by the Red Air Force, while Zhukov's and Koniev's artillery and tanks slowly slogged their way from house to house and street to debris-strewn street. The Russian squeeze tightened inexor-

War Stories

After almost six years of war, the end of hostilities came, not only as a relief, but also as a shock. John Leopard, on a slow, northbound convoy to disband the German Army in Bremerhaven, remembered passing an equally long, slow German column, going south under British escort. To his surprise, a guitar came to life – instruments in both columns picked up the tune and everyone in earshot sang along. Absurdly, men who had tried to kill each other the previous day were united in a common anthem – *Lili Marlene*!

Right: Novosti Press Agency; below Süddeutscher Verlag

HITLER'S DEATH

The rapidly failing physical and mental powers of the man who had once mesmerised half the world were dealt a mortal blow on 28 April 1945, when he received news of the execution of his old ally, Benito Mussolini. It may well have been this which hastened Hitler's decisions to marry his mistress and commit suicide – but no-one knows for certain. It is generally acknowledged that, on 30 April, after a final conference with remaining staff, he called Eva and they retired to their suite in the bunker. Several silent minutes passed, then a single shot rang out. Hitler's body was on the floor, Eva Braun's unmarked body lay nearby. Wrapped in blankets, the two bodies were carried into the Chancellery garden, soaked in petrol and set alight.

◀ The bunker entrance lies in ruins.

▲ After taking Berlin, Marshal Koniev's troops march into Prague, the capital of Czechoslovakia, on 9 May 1945. Earlier, the citizens had staged a revolt to free themselves from German occupation, but by the time the Red Army arrived, the fighting was over.

ably from the suburbs inward towards the central symbols of the Nazi power structure – the R*.ichstag* (Parliament building) and the Chancellery. Young boys shivered in cold, damp holes in the mud and masonry, armed with *Panzerfausts* almost as big as themselves, waiting in the hope of destroying just one Russian tank. On the other side were hardened veterans of dozens of battles, intent only on vengeance.

Water, electricity, gas and sanitation were things of the past and food was virtually unobtainable, even on the black market. And still the shells crashed, machine guns and rifles stuttered, grenades splattered bodies with lethal shrapnel. Living in his dreamworld, safe in the bunker, Hitler listened to the death of all his hopes and ambitions, pouring out his hatred of the Jews and Bolsheviks to any who would still listen.

By 27 April, Soviet forces had taken Templehof airfield, and the fighting was concentrated in the Spandau and Grunewald areas. By the next day, Koniev's men had virtually cleared the Potsdamer

FALL OF BERLIN

Berlin was the ultimate prize in the European war. Once the city had been captured by the Allies, the centre of the Nazi empire would be smashed, and although some residual resistance might have to be dealt with elsewhere, the fighting would be virtually over. In this sense, it did not matter who seized Berlin – the Anglo-Americans from the west or the Soviets from the east – for the priorities had to be to stop the killing and impose the peace. At the time, it seemed fitting to allow Stalin to exact his revenge for four years of unremitting war and take the prize; only in retrospect were the strategic and political consequences fully recognised. The Battle for Berlin laid the foundations of a new hostility which was to characterise the postwar world.

▲ By the time Russian tanks have reached the historic centre of Berlin, the war is practically over.

Strasse and Russian troops were within a mile of the Chancellery and the *Reichstag*, spurred on by Stalin's explicit wish that the Soviet flag should fly there in time for the May Day celebrations.

On the 29th, further gains were made in the Moabit and Wilmersdorf areas. The same day, Adolf Hitler married Eva Braun underneath the rubble of his Thousand Year Reich. In the early hours of the next morning, the *Gestapo* headquarters on Prinz Albrechtstrasse fell after a battle against hardened SS troops which lasted all day, and shortly afterwards Soviet troops were pouring fire at the *Reichstag*.

REICHSTAG FALLS

At 3.30 pm the newlyweds retired to the privacy of their own room and committed suicide. That evening, the Red Flag flew over the *Reichstag*. On 1 May Hitler's confidant Martin Bormann disappeared, and Joseph Goebbels and his wife, Magda, also committed suicide, after giving their children cyanide. Hermann Göring and Heinrich Himmler

would follow suit. Admiral Karl Dönitz, appointed *Führer* in Hitler's last will and testament, broadcast an appeal to the nation to continue the struggle against Bolshevism. With greater wisdom, the commander of what was left of the Berlin garrison, General Karl Weidling, surrendered, and by 3 pm on 2 May, all fighting had stopped, apart from isolated clashes.

On 3 May, Dönitz sent messengers to Montgomery's headquarters on Lüneburg Heath and arranged the surrender of all remaining German forces in northern Germany, Holland and Denmark the following day. Then German representatives, including chief of staff Alfred Jodl, were taken to Eisenhower's headquarters at Reims in France to complete the negotiations. The Germans contested them every inch of the way, only to capitulate fully at 2.41 am on 7 May. The troops in Kurland, East Prussia, and in Prague continued to fight on until the next day, when they too, utterly exhausted, laid down their arms.

The German unconditional surrender document was ratified in Berlin on the 9th, but 8 May has entered history as VE Day. Hitler's war was over and reconstruction could begin.

▶ One of its few surviving defenders resigns himself to his fate, as the *Reichstag* blazes in the background.

IWO JIMA

BATTLE DIARY

FEBRUARY 1945
19	Landings on Iwo Jima – Operation Detachment
20	No 1 Airfield taken
23	Flag raised over Mount Suribachi
27	No 2 Airfield taken

MARCH
3	No 3 Airfield taken
4	First B-29 lands
6	P-51s and P-61s of USAAF 15th Fighter Group arrive
16	Iwo declared secure
26	Last Japanese survivors stage suicide attack
26–29	Kerama Retto seized

APRIL
1	Landings on Okinawa – Operation Iceberg
9–12	First assault on Shuri Line
12–13	Japanese counter-attack
16–18	Taking of Motobu Peninsula
16–24	Taking of Ie Shima
18–24	Outer Shuri defences taken

MAY
4–5	Japanese counter-offensive. Major kamikaze attack on fleet
8	Americans open attacks on Inner Shuri defences
31	Shuri town occupied

JUNE
4–11	Final battles at Oroku and Yaeju-Dake
18	General Buckner killed
22	US flag raised over Okinawa

SANDS OF IWO JIMA

The US landing at Iwo Jima is a costly one – but the prize is a vital way-station for the ultimate goal, Japan itself.

▶ 23 February 1945 – four days after the landing on Iwo Jima – a detachment of Marines raises the American flag on top of Mount Suribachi, but the island is far from being taken.

I n terms of bombs dropped per unit area, few targets of World War II could match the ordeal of Japanese-held Iwo Jima. As the American assault on the island was predictable, it was felt that surprise would hardly be compromised by sustained pre-bombardment. Sporadic raids began in August 1944 but, for the 74 days preceding the landing on 19 February 1945, Marianas-based B-24 Liberators of the US Seventh Air Force bombed the Volcano and Bonin Islands daily, paying Iwo Jima particular attention. By night, radar-equipped B-25 Mitchells disrupted the shipping on which the Japanese garrison depended. At this stage of the war the Allied Joint Chiefs of Staff (JCS) were still planning for the eventual necessity of invading and conquering Japan itself. A sustained bombing offensive, therefore, had to be mounted to reduce the will to resist. This was possible only after taking Saipan, but since it was 1,300 miles (2,000 km) away from Tokyo, this meant that B-29s had

US National Archives

All pictures: US National Archives

▲ A Grumman TBM Avenger over the extinct crater of Mount Suribachi, Iwo Jima, after the island was secured at the end of March 1945.

bombers and as a base for the P-51 Mustang long-range fighter.

Admiral Chester W Nimitz, C-in-C Pacific, had the draft plan for Operation Detachment, the taking of Iwo, ready in four days, but delays to General Douglas MacArthur's forces in Luzon necessitated its postponement until mid-February. Overall command for the attack would be with Admiral Raymond A Spruance, Commander Fifth Fleet. The experienced team of Vice-Admiral Richmond K Turner and Lieutenant-General Holland M Smith, US Marine Corps, would have the operational command. Major-General Harry Schmidt's V Amphibious Corps – the assault force – comprised the 3rd, 4th and 5th Marine Divisions. In support, as ever, was Vice-Admiral Marc A Mitscher's Fast Carrier Force (TF 58).

INHOSPITABLE IWO

Iwo's bulkier northern end consists of a low plateau with rocky shores unsuitable for landings. The tapering neck, protruding to the south, terminates in the 550-foot (168-m) cone of Mount Suribachi. While adjacent beaches were suitable for landings, they were dominated from the volcano's slopes and covered to a considerable depth with a fine ash that made walking difficult and running impossible. Even tracked vehicles needed steel matting to run on. Inhospitable, Iwo was described even by the Japanese as '. . . only an island of sulphur; no water, no sparrow and no swallow . . .'

During 1944 the Japanese had evacuated nearly 1,000 inhabitants who had eked out a precarious living producing sulphur. After the fall of Saipan, the island was strongly reinforced by both army and navy units. The army commander, Lieutenant-General Tadamichi Kuribayashi, was held in sufficient esteem to have been honoured by an audience with the Emperor. A naval aviator, Rear-Admiral Toshinosuke Ichimaru, commanded naval personnel and there were three more or less autonomous headquarters on the island.

Due to the split command, there existed a composite system of shoreline defences and defence-in-depth. Deeply-emplaced artillery dominated the low-lying

to fly with reduced bomb loads.

About midway between Saipan and Tokyo, in the volcanic outcrops of the Nansei Shòto archipelago, is the pear-shaped island of Iwo Jima. Only 4½ × 2½ miles (7.25 × 4 km) in extent, the largest of the group, it had two airfields and a third under construction. As a halfway house, it would act as a refuge for damaged

isthmus from both Suribachi and the plateau. Pillboxes covered the beaches, while one minor and two major defence lines crossed the plateau from coast to coast. Behind 50 feet (15 m) of sand there was up to four feet (1.2 m) of concrete wall. Dispersal, concealment and camouflage of all defence positions were stressed. Caves were given multiple entrances, each with a gun position. Mortar pits were flush with the ground, enclosed and near-invisible. Each artillery position was ready to fire at all the key points on the island.

Limited by geography, the Americans planned to land the 4th and 5th Marine Divisions simultaneously on the isthmus, moving left to take Suribachi and right to advance along the axis of the island. The reserve 3rd Division would land later and be deployed as required.

Iwo's sustained aerial bombardment was not matched by that of the Navy. Where the Marines had requested ten days of shelling, Spruance gave them only three. Experience had shown that 90 per cent of damage was inflicted within the first three days, while to prolong the bombardment would to be invite mass *kamikaze* attacks. Spruance later drew heavy criticism for his decision, but it remained a fact that Iwo, just one-fifteenth the area of Saipan, still received 30 per cent more weight of ordnance, some 10,650 tons.

SOFT LANDING

As D-Day, 19 February, dawned, the tiny island paled into insignificance among the armada of 450 ships that enveloped it. Seven battleships and seven cruisers, later joined by ten destroyers, opened fire at 6.40 am. By 7.45 am no less than 482 LVTs were waterborne, the eight battalions of Marines embarked in them studying the mounting pall of dust and smoke for the first sign of the Japanese. The screaming ceiling of shellfire ceased temporarily at 8.05 am as 120 aircraft blasted the

▲ Burning F4U Corsairs litter the deck of USS *Saratoga*, which has come under attack by several *kamikazes* off Iwo Jima, February 1945.

▼ The Marines have landed but the ordeal is far from over – raked by enemy fire, they have to overcome the 15-ft (4.5-m) wall of treacherous volcanic ash.

BATTLE DIARY

IWO JIMA & OKINAWA

FEBRUARY 1945
19 Landings on Iwo Jima – Operation Detachment
20 No 1 Airfield taken
23 Flag raised over Mount Suribachi
27 No 2 Airfield taken

MARCH
3 No 3 Airfield taken
4 First B-29 lands
6 P-51s and P-61s of USAAF 15th Fighter Group arrive
16 Iwo declared secure
26 Last Japanese survivors stage suicide attack
26/29 Kerama Retto seized

APRIL
1 Landings on Okinawa Operation Iceberg
9/12 First assault on Shuri Line

12/13 Japanese counterattack
16/18 Motobu Peninsula taken
16/24 Taking of Ie Shima
18/24 Outer Shuri defences taken
25 Stalemate of Shuri

MAY
4/5 Japanese counter-offensive. Major *kamikaze* attack on fleet
8 Americans open attack on Inner Shuri defences
31 Shuri town occupied

JUNE
4/ Final battles at
11 Oroku and Jaeju-Dake
18 General Buckner killed
22 US flag raised over Okinawa

defenders with napalm, rockets, and cannon.

As the first wave approached the beach a dozen Support Landing Craft each released a salvo of 120 4.5in rockets on points immediately beyond the beaches. On schedule, at 9 am, the first Marines touched down. They met little opposition – Kuribayashi had ordered the garrison to weather the storm of fire deep underground.

Once landed, the assault troops found themselves faced with a 15-foot (4.5-m) high wall of soft volcanic ash. This caused much congestion on the beach as they could only advance where shellfire had blown gaps. Heavily-laden Marines attempting to dash inland lumbered instead through ankle-deep ash, finding themselves suddenly raked by fire. Support ships closed into shoal water to assist, but many landing craft broached or were swamped by the swell on the steep-to beach. Tanks, landed by 9.45 am, themselves bogged down and became targets, while air support could do little but keep the skies clear of the enemy.

The advancing Marines found themselves attacked from the rear by the enemy who were emerging from subterranean positions. By nightfall the situation became clearer. Marines had tenuously isolated Suribachi and had advanced 500 yards (457 m) to the perimeter of No 1 Airfield. Each dug in where he was.

NIGHTMARE

Dawn revealed the first day's nightmare. 'Whether the dead were Japs or Americans, they had died with the greatest possible violence . . . Only legs were easy to identify; they were Japanese if wrapped in khaki puttees, American if covered by canvas leggings.' Ammunition for mortars was in particularly short supply so, again, it was up to each individual's courage, the flamethrower and the grenade. Mount Suribachi malevolently dominated the efforts of the invaders. Despite being blasted by naval gunfire on every face, its slopes spewed a deadly fire on anything that moved. The able Kuribayashi,

▲ Supplies are brought ashore now that the Marines have gained a foothold, in spite of many casualties.

aware that invasion would divide the island's defences, had made each end self-sufficient.

A Regimental Combat Team (RCT) of three battalions began the task of taking Suribachi on D plus 1. Paths had all been demolished by naval gunfire. The few tanks available proved of little use in the broken ground. The Marines made about 200 yards (183 m) on the first day, for over 160 casualties, spending a first sleepless

▼ Iwo Jima claimed one of the highest tolls of casualties in the history of the Marines.

PRIZE FIGHTING

As the Americans edged closer to the Japanese home islands in early 1945, they faced hardening opposition which augured ill for the final attacks on Japan itself. If these were to be made easier, it was apparent that airfields closer than the Marianas would be needed, initially to provide fighter escorts for the B-29s as they hammered Japanese industry and morale, then as bases for the bombers themselves. It had to be accepted that losses among the assault forces would be high, but the attacks on Iwo Jima and Okinawa were vital prerequisites of victory. Operations Detachment and Iceberg were going to be tough assignments for the Americans.

▶ Marines make inland for Mount Suribachi, ducking behind volcanic sand rises for protection.

TURNING POINT

night under intermittent mortar fire and the cold glare of flares. For three days progress was marked in scores of yards and casualties. Finally on D plus 4, a detachment won the crater edge after a brief shoot-out and at 10.20 am the Marines below were cheered by the sight of 'Old Glory' streaming from an improvised pole. The battle for this insignificant rise had cost the Americans 895 casualties compared with the Japanese's 2,000.

Advancing along Iwo's axis, the invaders discovered most Japanese strongpoints yet unscathed. 'Again it was tragically apparent . . . that human flesh would have to succeed where heavy armament (had) failed.' By D plus 5 the Marines controlled No 1 Airfield but they and the landing beaches were swept by interlocking fire from the plateau. Losses among battalion and company commanders were high.

Isolated and previously unnamed heights, such as 'Charlie-Dog Rise', the 'Amphitheater' and 'Peter/Oboe Hills' were disputed for days. 'Peter', near No 2 Airfield, attracted a 20-minute bombardment from a battleship and two cruisers of 1,200 artillery rounds and 500-lb bombs. Yet, even with the help of 26 tanks, the Marines had to fight for two days to subdue it.

From 26 February, observation planes were able to use No 1 Airfield while, on 4 March, a damaged B-29 made the first emergency landing. The suffering began to look worthwhile. Airpower was also used to evacuate the injured and supply ammunition.

FINAL PHASE

Slow progress continued across the broken, jumbled wilderness, where, to survive, one 'kept low and kept moving'. By 4 March the Japanese had been blasted from most of the higher ground and a week later the 'final phase' began. This was against resistance around Kitano Point, in the island's extreme north, and a nearby ridge, dubbed 'Cushman Pocket'.

With the fall of the pocket on 16 March, Iwo was declared 'secured'. In that its airstrips could be repaired and utilised, this was true, but the remaining Japanese, as the official history records, 'did not simply hole up and die'. On the 26th, there came a last gasp attack by 300 defenders, many of them officers wielding swords and possibly including General Kuribayashi himself. Most were killed – some were even in American uniform. Twenty-five days after the flag-raising on Suribachi, the Stars and Stripes also waved over Kitano Point.

▶ **A Japanese dug-out is cleared cautiously by a Marine – often the wounded Japanese concealed grenades or other troops still left in the shelter.**

War Stories

The words of Admiral Chester Nimitz on the bravery of those who fought at Iwo Jima have become famous: 'Among the Americans who served on Iwo Island, uncommon valour was a common virtue.' Undoubtedly this was a well-deserved tribute. Less well known were the words of a US Marine wounded in the battle. 'I hope to God that we don't have to go on any more of these screwy islands.' As those who continued the fight on Okinawa were soon to learn, the Marine didn't get his wish.

Including those slaughtered in this final attack, the official Japanese death-toll on Iwo Jima numbered 20,703, only 216 having been taken prisoner. However, pockets of resistance still remained. Their clearance during April and May accounted for 1,600 more Japanese dead. From all causes the Americans lost over 6,800 of their men.

By the end of the war, 2,251 B-29s had used Iwo's facilities. Several had made emergency landings on more than one occasion. 'If you had wounded aboard, you held out for Iwo. If you had to bail out, air-sea rescue units were sent from Iwo. Even if you never used Iwo as an emergency base it was a psychological benefit. It was there to fall back on.'

All pictures: US National Archives

THE LAST BATTLE

The first Okinawa assault is strangely unopposed. The landing forces can only wonder apprehensively when the action will start.

The men of Lieutenant-General Simon Bolivar Buckner Jr's Tenth Army, disembarking from their LVTs over Okinawa's Hagushi beaches on 1 April 1945, had seen combat on Guadalcanal and New Guinea, on Bougainville, Guam and Leyte. Each encounter had exacted a

Both pictures: US National Archives

◄ **Flame-throwing tanks come into action as the troops moving inland suddenly face dogged resistance.**

▲ **A battleship fires salvoes into the beaches on Okinawa just before the amphibious landings take place.**

act as a further base from which to bomb Japan and to support China. The need to cut Japan off from its raw materials was already being met by the reconquest of Luzon.

Far smaller than Formosa, Okinawa would be easier to take and was closer to Japan itself. Already short of resources, King agreed. Operation Iceberg was on.

Largest of the Ryukyus, Okinawa is irregular in shape, some 60 miles (97 km) in length and from two to 18 miles (3.2 to 28 km) wide. The island is effectively divided by the Ishikawa isthmus into a mountainous northern two thirds and a smaller, fertile southern region.

In the latter lived three quarters of the 460,000 native Okinawan population, whose comparative poverty and lack of interest in the

code of *Bushido* was despised by the Japanese occupiers. Here also were the major airfields and, in Nakagusuku Bay, an anchorage large enough for the fleet.

THE PLAN

Air superiority for Iceberg would be established strategically by bombers from the Marianas and China pounding Japanese airfields. Tactically, Vice-Admiral Marc A Mitscher's Fast Carrier Force (TF 58) would, for the first time, be reinforced by the Royal Navy's TF 57. The latter's four fleet carriers would act as a buffer between the Americans around Okinawa and the Japanese airfields on Formosa and neighbouring islands.

Following Leyte Gulf, the Japanese fleet was considered a

high price for victory, and the imminent final battle for Japan was expected to be tough.

Although Admiral Ernest J King, C-in-C US Fleet, had favoured Formosa, the Commanding Generals, Pacific Ocean Area, had argued convincingly that Okinawa would equally well satisfy requirements to

▶ **The manpower figures for Operation Iceberg show the amazing American superiority needed to take this last bastion before mainland Japan.**

BATTLE LINE-UP

182,821 men	77,199 men

spent force, but it was yet not to be ignored. Carrier-based operations by the US Fleet after 19 March were met by a coordinated plan, *Ten-Go*, which combined conventional bombing with *kamikaze* attacks, using both aircraft and the new piloted suicide bomb, the *Ohka*. American losses and damage began to mount alarmingly.

The Iceberg schedule called for the Tenth Army to advance from the Hagushi beaches to seize the nearby airfields of Yontan and Kadena by L plus 3. Ishikawa isthmus was to be taken by L plus 15, isolating the north to allow ground forces to secure the southern end by between L plus 30 and L plus 60.

Buckner's army comprised Major-General Roy S Geiger's III Amphibious Corps (Marine), made up of the 1st and 6th Marine Divisions, and Major-General John R Hodge's XXIV Army Corps with the 7th and 96th Infantry Divisions. In reserve were the 2nd Marine and the 27th

US National Archives

◄ **Badge of the 1st Marine Division, part of Buckner's assault troops, which saw previous action at Guadalcanal.**

and 77th Infantry Divisions.

On this fine Easter Sunday morning, the objective was to win an island which was close enough and large enough to act as a springboard for a modern Armageddon. But, if the Americans appreciated the immense strategic significance of Okinawa, why did the Japanese apparently not?

As the assault troops fanned out through the drifting pall that marked the recent pre-assault bombardment, there seemed to be no reaction. In

place of fanatical defence at the water's edge came a few desultory mortar and artillery shells. 'The absence of any but the most trivial opposition, so contrary to expectation, struck the men as ominous . . .' One infantryman who, with his comrades, simply walked to his initial objective, expressed a commonly-felt emotion, 'I've already lived longer than I thought I would'.

WELL PREPARED

His apprehension was well-founded. The latest intelligence reports had estimated 56,000 Japanese combatants to be on Okinawa. In fact, the defending Thirty-Second Army comprised 39,000 infantry and 38,000 men in other units. About 10,000 naval personnel were available to act as ground troops and 20,000 Okinawans had been conscripted. Though weak in armour, the army was well above establishment in artillery and lighter weapons. Its commander, Lieutenant-General Mitsuru Ushijima, was highly regarded and enjoyed total loyalty. Together with his senior staff officer in charge of operations, Colonel Hiromichi Yahara, he had appreciated American intentions very accurately.

Ushijima was realistic enough to recognise defeat, and based his defence on making the Americans' victory as costly as possible. Only the

◄ **These Marines taking a ride on a Sherman tank still have reason to be cheerful – their landing on 1 April went virtually unopposed. However, very soon, the situation would change.**

► **Lt-Gen Simon Buckner (left) meets with Major-General Roy Geiger (right), who succeeded him as commander of Tenth Army after Buckner was killed on 18 June 1945.**

▼ **Seeking cover among the gravestones, US Marines move in to take Cemetery Ridge, one of the heavily contested Japanese strongholds.**

US National Archives

US National Archives

E. W. W. Fowler

◄ **A deceptively calm landing for the Marines on one of the beaches of Okinawa.**

E. W. W. Fowler

BOLD LEADER

As the son of a Confederate Army general, Lt-Gen Simon Bolivar Buckner Jr (left in picture) was well prepared for a lifetime spent in the army. Commanding the Alaskan defences in the prewar period, he was later responsible for the 1943 assault on the North Pacific islands of Attu and Kiska – the first US territories to be regained from the Japanese.

A stern disciplinarian, he appeared to be the archetypal career soldier. Described as a dynamic and inspirational leader, he was not afraid to lead his men from the front. When he was appointed commander of the Tenth Army for the invasion of Okinawa, he earned the respect of his subordinates by frequently visiting the front-line troops. During a visit to one of his favourite Marine regiments on 18 June 1945, he was killed when a shell exploded over his observation post, hurling a splinter of coral into his chest.

south was to be strongly contested. Assault troops were to be allowed ashore in numbers sufficient to prevent rapid evacuation, whereupon an all-out aerial and fleet attack on their shipping would isolate them.

To survive, they would then be obliged to fight Ushijima on his chosen ground, a five-mile (8-km) fortified line running across from coast to coast through the old capital of Shuri. This so-called 'Shuri Line' comprised an interlocking system of caves, blockhouses and pillboxes, skilfully employing and adapting the terrain's natural ruggedness.

US National Archives

▲ Advancing towards the capital of Naha in southern Okinawa, Marines pass the body of a Japanese defender.

No assault enjoyed a heavier preliminary bombardment. Within three hours 44,825 medium- and heavy-calibre shells, 33,000 rockets and 22,500 mortar shells were expended, overlaid with napalm. A feint attack was staged on the opposite coast. By nightfall on 1 April 60,000 men were ashore with armour and artillery. Both airfields had been taken. The lack of opposition (Ushi-

All pictures: US National Archives

▲ **To support their desperate ground defence, the Japanese prepare to send up 1,900 *kamikazes*.**

Kakazu Ridge and Item Pocket, remained contested. Conventional techniques worked badly. In one operation, for instance, the Americans recorded that 19,000 artillery shells accounted for just 190 Japanese. As combat was usually conducted at close range, Buckner's men developed 'Blowtorch and Corkscrew' methods. The first employed mobile armoured flame-throwers or even the pumping of gasoline through a hose, for ignition

▶ **The *Yamato* goes down on her suicide mission to wreak havoc among the invasion forces.**

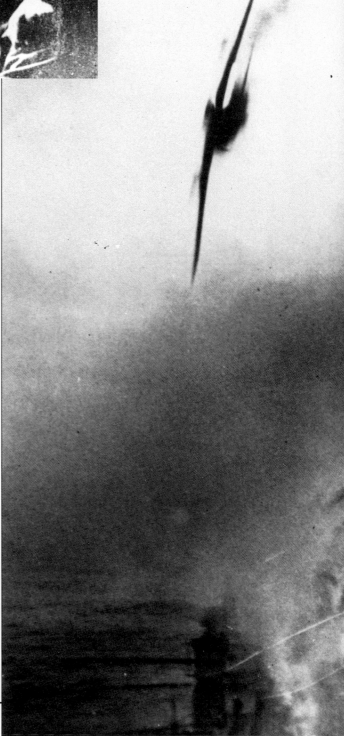

jima had even forbidden his artillery to betray its presence by firing) made the operation seem 'like a manoeuvre'.

By the evening of L plus 2 the Americans had cut clear across the island, the isthmus was in sight and XXIV Corps was heading south for Shuri. Meeting only nominal resistance, units began to take risks and their advance lost cohesion. Then, on 4 April (L plus 3), three tanks were rapidly knocked out by a single well concealed 47 mm anti-tank gun.

The invaders had contacted the outposts of the Shuri Line and the following day the advance slowed to a crawl under heavy fire. Small features were contested which now acquired distinctive names – Cactus Ridge, Tombstone Ridge, Tomb Hill. The Pinnacle, a 477-ft (145-m) hill surmounted by a stone tower, harboured two Japanese rifle platoons. They were well entrenched behind minefields, covering the approaches with machine guns and mortars.

FLYING BOXCARS

A new experience on Cactus Ridge was bombardment by the enemy's 320 mm spigot mortars. The projectiles were so large that they were dubbed 'Flying Boxcars', capable of exploding with a terrific concussive effect. Japanese infantry would allow attacking armour to pass through their concealed positions

before cutting down their supporting troops with flank fire. The tanks would then be attacked with satchel charges and flaming rags. Crews eventually had to defend themselves with sidearms and grenades but, on bailing out, were bayoneted.

Stalemate developed on 12 April. In miserable weather XXIV Corps found it could control Kakazu Ridge, but Japanese defences on the reverse slope prevented them advancing beyond the crest. With the Americans now in contact with the Shuri Line, the defenders adopted a mass overnight infiltration attack. Loaded with 110-lb (50-kg) packs, the Japanese advanced deeply, and desperate hand-to-hand fighting developed. One staff sergeant won a Medal of Honor by holding up an enemy file with grenades. When these were exhausted, he threw activated mortar bombs. In all sectors the Japanese persisted until their dead 'were stacked up like cordwood'.

A massive artillery, naval and aerial bombardment preceded a general American counterattack on 19 April. Despite local successes, it failed to penetrate. Head-on assaults of Japanese positions proved expensive, but outflanking manoeuvres also tended to fail for, as one battalion commander remarked, 'You can't bypass a Jap because a Jap doesn't know when he is bypassed.'

Nonetheless, five days of dogged endeavour saw the outer Shuri Line pierced in so many places that Ushijima was obliged to pull back, though key positions, such as

Late on 6 April 1945 the world's largest battleship, the 68,000-ton *Yamato*, weighed anchor in the Inland Sea. She was bound for Okinawa to destroy those amphibious ships that had survived a planned *kamikaze* onslaught. There would be no return, for sufficient fuel remained only for a one-way trip.

Reported by an American submarine almost immediately, the Japanese were contacted by the first carrier reconnaissance aircraft early on 7 April. Taking no chances, the Americans placed six battleships between the *Yamato* force and Okinawa but, by 10 am, about 280 carrier strike aircraft were airborne. Lacking air cover the *Yamato* even used her 18-inch guns to deter her attackers, but to no avail. Between 12.41 and 2.17 pm she absorbed ten torpedoes and 23 heavy bombs. At 2.23 pm the ship erupted in a towering mushroom of smoke, sinking with 2,498 of her crew.

with a phosphorous grenade. If the Japanese were particularly deeply entrenched, Corkscrew teams blew their cave entrances with explosive charges.

So daunting was the prospect of attacking the inner Shuri Line that Buckner was urged to consider a second amphibious landing to outflank it. Geography was against the proposal (indeed, Ushijima fully expected it) and the commander rejected the idea as 'another Anzio, only worse'.

Fortunately, the 6th Marine and 77th Infantry Divisions had experienced a lighter task in northern Okinawa. The Marines had needed to fight hard for the precipitous, pine-clad ridges around Yae Take in the Motobu Peninsula, but a stiffer fight faced the 77th for the offshore island of Ie Shima. Its sizeable airfield and the neighbouring town were held with suicidal fanaticism by both military and civilians. Individuals would readily run at the Americans with satchel charges or

◄ **A narrow escape for USS *Sangamon*, as a *kamikaze* plane plummets into the sea close by.**

▼ ***Kamikaze* attack on USS *Bunker Hill*: these suicide missions were the greatest threat to the US fleet.**

live mortar bombs.

Having renewed his more depleted divisions, Buckner attacked the Shuri defences again in the rain and mud of late April. They appeared impregnable. Reverse slopes became 'forbidden land', so strongly were they held and covered. Any knob or feature was riddled with shot. At 'Needle Rock', for instance, phosphorus shells fired into a cave caused smoke to issue from 30 other apertures, many previously unsuspected.

COUNTERATTACK

Again, on 4 May, the Americans were surprised by a Japanese counterattack. The secure judgement of Colonel Yahara had been overridden by the aggressiveness of Ushijima and his Chief-of-Staff, General Isamu Cho ('Each soldier will kill at least one American devil'). To support the offensive, Japanese artillery was obliged to be brought into the open, suffering from counter-battery fire.

Amateurish Japanese attempts at amphibious landings along either coast were easily dealt with, but the coordinated *kamikaze* blitz on the fleet offshore was a more serious matter. Within 24 hours, for the loss of 131 aircraft, the Japanese sank or damaged 17 American ships and inflicted 682 casualties.

On land, only the central Tanabaru Escarpment saw the attackers make a significant salient, but by 7 May this had been nipped out at the cost of 500 Japanese dead. Ushijima is reported to have apologised to Yahara, while Cho, considered to be 'the incarnation of the fighting will of the Japanese Army', now conceded defeat to be only a matter of time.

Reverting to the earlier attritional tactics that had served them so well, the Japanese skilfully re-allocated personnel to maintain balanced unit levels. Continuing naval losses, particularly in the vulnerable line of early warning radar picket ships, made an American attack imperative. This began on 11 May, the intention being to engage the centre of the Shuri Line with a holding

War Stories

As the Americans reached Okinawa, news got to the folks back home of mass suicides among the Japanese people on the islands of the Kerama chain. Convinced by Japanese propaganda that death was better than a ghastly fate at the hands of the American barbarians, at least 200 people killed themselves, some even attempting self-strangulation! Had they anticipated the generosity and fairness shown to the surviving civilians by the 'barbarians', they would probably have simply been kicking themselves for jumping to conclusions!

attack while enveloping either end. Stubborn strongpoints were to be contained for later reduction.

A quick assembly of a Bailey bridge saw Marines across the Asa River in the west, but attempts to

◄ Three Marines are pinned down by enemy fire in the bombed-out Okinawan capital of Naha. Although the Shuri Line was beginning to crumble, isolated pockets of resistance remained everywhere, to be cleared out at the cost of many casualties. The town fell on 27 May 1945.

▼ Celebrations are called for by 1st and 7th Division Marines on Hill 89, after Lt-Gen Ushijima's suicide put an end to organised Japanese resistance on 22 June. Apart from a few mopping-up operations, the battle of Okinawa was over.

take the Sugar Loaf position, east of the capital Naha, were heavily hampered by artillery fire from the heights around Shuri town. On 14 May, 50 Marines failed to take the Sugar Loaf, just ten returning. Two platoons took it later, but only 20 survived, their defences being almost immediately overrun.

BITTER FIGHTING

Sugar Loaf, like others of Yahara's defences, was covered by neighbouring hills, in this case, Horseshoe and Crescent. The eventual reduction of these comparatively insignificant features saw some of Okinawa's bitterest fighting: 2,662 Marine casualties and 1,289 cases of combat fatigue.

The weary trail continued – Dakeshi Ridge, Chocolate Drop Hill, Wart, Charlie and Flat Top. Intelligence noted the undiminished 'Japanese . . . willingness to suffer annihilation rather than to sacrifice ground . . .'

The Shuri Line was finally turned at its far eastern end. Conical Hill took so many naval shells that it was dubbed 'Million Dollar Hill' before being taken, which allowed the 7th Division to advance down the coast road toward Yonabaru in the southeast of the island.

It started to rain unremittingly, causing tracked vehicles to bog down. Ammunition and wounded were moved by men. Yellow clay clogged every weapon. In the foxholes mere existence was more important than attack.

By the end of May, Shuri town was nearly enveloped. With between

All pictures: US National Archives

▲ The ground fighting on Okinawa claimed over 100,000 Japanese lives. With certain defeat staring them in the face, only a few of the troops surrendered.

◄ During the clearing operations flame-throwing tanks are used to get to the enemy still holding out in the defence system of caves in the southern parts of the island.

50,000 and 70,000 of their best troops dead, Japanese resistance began to weaken. Surprisingly and skilfully, Ushijima extricated his remaining force from the Shuri pocket in order to prolong the struggle further south.

When the rains ceased in early June, the Marines surrounded and destroyed the enemy's naval troops in the Oroku Peninsula and, with increasing mobility, XXIV Corps penned up Ushijima and 30,000 men in the craggy massif of Yaeju-Dake.

Not until 2 July was Okinawa declared secure. Of 12,520 Americans killed or missing, 4,907 were Navy personnel, a testimony of the ferocity of the *kamikaze* war offshore. About 110,000 Japanese were lost in all, but the final irony was that the island never acted as an invasion springboard. The war ended in August 1945. Okinawa had been the last American battle.

THE ATOM BOMB

BATTLE DIARY

1931 to 1941

1931   British scientists Cockcroft and Walton split the atom

1932   James Chadwick discovers the neutron

1934   Frenchman Frederic Joliot-Curie discovers that bombarding unranium with neutrons produces artificial radioactive products such as plutonium. Enrico Fermi refines this work during the same year

1938   The first paper describing atomic fission is published

1939   Joliot-Curie confirms the chain reaction. Following Einstein's letter to him, US President Roosevelt sets up the Uranium Committee to oversee the development of an atomic weapon

1941   The basis for a practical atomic weapon is established

SEPTEMBER 1942

16   General Groves is placed in charge of the logistics of the bomb programme. Grove appoints J Robert Oppenheimer as scientific director

MARCH 1943

The Los Alamos research centre becomes operational. Scientist Seth Neddermeyer suggests the implosion method of detonation

1944

Throughout the year, technical difficulties suggest that it might not be feasible to produce a practical atomic bomb at all

JULY 1945

16   The Trinity implosion device is exploded successfully at the Alamogordo bombing range in New Mexico

AUGUST

6   The 'Little Boy' uranium gun-type weapon is dropped on Hiroshima

9   The 'Fat Man' plutonium implosion weapon is dropped on Nagasaki

BUILDING THE BOMB

Scientists in various countries have been working on nuclear physics. But in America secret research is being pushed towards a practical application – the ultimate weapon.

American interest in building an atomic device can be traced back to April 1939 when the expatriate Hungarian scientist Leo Szilard read a paper written by the Frenchman Frédéric Joliot-Curie, which proved beyond doubt that a weapon based on atomic fission was possible. This confirmed work which Szilard himself had done. In June, the German Siegfried Flugg published a further paper outlining the state of nuclear physics in Germany. Ironically, Flugg's intention was to try and keep the research international and peaceful, but the political situation of the day set off alarm bells when it was realised how advanced Germany was in the field.

Fearing that Germany was well on the way to building an atomic bomb, Szilard enlisted the help of German physicist Albert Einstein in drawing President Roosevelt's attention to the threat and starting an American weapons programme. Einstein wrote his famous letter to Roosevelt (which he was to regret bitterly in later life) on 2 August 1939 and provoked a response which was to set in motion a development programme that culminated in the mushroom clouds over Hiroshima six years later, almost to the day.

Initially the programme was placed in the hands of the Bureau of Standards' Uranium Committee, under the chairmanship of Lyman Biggs. Biggs was an unhappy choice, as he was ill and obsessed with secrecy. So slow was progress that the British tried to speed things up in July 1941 by sending across a group of atomic scientists

◄ Heralding the dawn of the Atomic Age, a gigantic explosion lights up the night sky over the New Mexico desert in the early hours of 16 July 1945.

Associated Press/Topham

Courtesy of Franklin D. Roosevelt Library

▲ **Albert Einstein takes the oath of US citizenship in 1940. He was one of the many learned and distinguished people who left their country for political reasons. Einstein addressed a letter to President Roosevelt, below, urging him to speed up America's own development of the bomb.**

led by the Australian, Marcus Oliphant, who had been working on a British weapon since 1940. Oliphant quickly realised that he was not going to get very far with Biggs. Despondently, he turned to an old friend in America's scientific community, Ernest Lawrence, in order to impress on the Americans how urgent the threat of a German atomic bomb really was.

Lawrence needed little convincing and began a quiet campaign to outflank the Uranium Committee. He buttonholed James Conant, the Committee's chief scientist, and represented the British evidence. This time it received a more sympathetic hearing and Conant began to organise an investigative mission to Britain. He also presented the case at a meeting with Roosevelt on 9 October 1941. This resulted in the President's scientific adviser, Vannevar Bush, being charged with expediting the development of an atomic bomb in every way possible.

Lawrence returned to his laboratory in Berkeley, California, and began work on converting his cyclotron (a device for accelerating particles, such as protons, for research purposes) into a machine for extracting the fissionable uranium 235 from the naturally found material

which normally comprises about 99.3 per cent uranium 238 and about 0.7 per cent uranium 235. At the same time, he began a study of Oliphant's work. To help him, he recruited an old student of his, J Robert Oppenheimer, who was assigned the task of calculating just how much uranium 235 would be needed for a workable bomb. This was Oppenheimer's first involvement with 'the bomb' and he was one of those responsible for what was essentially the blueprint for the weapon which came out of a meeting held on 21 October 1941. The idea developed was, like the physics, simple. To generate a chain reaction, Oppenheimer calculated that about 220 lb (100 kg) of uranium 235 would be sufficient to create a critical mass in which fission would start and continue. Creating this critical mass would be achieved by using two 110-lb (50-kg) 'sub-critical' pieces, which would be brought together to create the critical mass at the appropriate moment. The meeting's report also calculated that such a bomb would generate an explosive energy equivalent to several thousand tons of conventional explosive.

BLUEPRINT FOR THE BOMB

Oppenheimer began working full-time on the project in January 1942 and by the following May was in sole charge of the development of the actual bomb mechanism. Throughout the year, he continued to refine the bomb specification, a process which was aided by a galaxy of scientific talent, including the Swiss physicist Felix Bloch, the future Nobel Laureate John van Vleck, Germany's Hans Bethe and the Hungarian Edward Teller, who went on to create the thermonuclear bomb.

While progress was now greater than it had been in Biggs' day, work on the bomb was still relatively fragmentary. This was all to change in September 1942 with the appointment of Colonel Leslie R Groves to run the practical aspects of the programme, by now known as the 'Manhattan Project' after the Manhattan Military

District under which it nominally came.

Never one to let the grass grow under his feet, Groves immediately embarked on a tour of his empire. He was not pleased by what he saw. At Pittsburgh he viewed a technique of extracting uranium 235 by centrifugal force. He felt that the method was not producing results and that the work-force was not showing enough zeal. Pittsburgh closed down. Columbia University fared better with Groves showing interest in their gaseous diffusion technique. At Chicago he was again impressed with the work being done – but less so with an air of indecision pervading the laboratory. At Berkeley, Lawrence showed him the electromagnetic separation process but had to admit that it had still not yet produced worthwhile quantities of fissionable uranium.

OPPENHEIMER MADE BOSS

Following a meeting in late October 1942, Groves decided that Oppenheimer was his man to run the research and that his suggestion of a unified laboratory should be taken up. The site eventually settled on for the new laboratory was one of Oppenheimer's boyhood haunts, Los Alamos in New Mexico. Just about accessible from Santa Fe, Los Alamos offered the security of being in a sparsely inhabited area. For the 30 or so scientists Oppenheimer initially envisaged as being needed for the job, Los Alamos would just about do; for the hundreds of people who were eventually to work there, its basic facilities were to become a source of constant friction.

Oppenheimer's Berkeley team moved out to Santa Fe in March 1943 to find Los Alamos in a state of total confusion. Facilities were not ready, arguments between the Army engineers building the place and the scientists who were to work there were rife and the whole heady mess was capped by the influx of wives and children the civilian personnel brought with them. While confusion reigned in New Mexico, Groves was driving ahead with

two huge uranium plants at Oak Ridge in Tennessee: without fissionable material there could be no bomb. Alongside these, a plutonium plant was being constructed at Hanford, Washington. The scale of the effort involved can be grasped from the no less than 45,000 construction workers being drafted in to build Hanford.

Back at Los Alamos a somewhat inarticulate young scientist, Seth Neddermeyer, threw a spanner into the works by suggesting another way of starting the necessary chain reaction. Up until then, work had proceeded along the lines of the 'gun method', that is, firing one sub-critical mass into another to create the appropriate critical mass. Neddermeyer suggested what has become known as the 'implosion method'. In this technique, because the fissionable material was to be formed into a hollow sphere surrounded by explosive, it would implode, rather than explode, creating a solid sphere sufficiently dense to go critical.

The road to an implosion bomb was by no means smooth. Neddermeyer arranged to create the symmetrical detonation necessary to create the critical mass and failed. Oppenheimer, increasingly exhausted by the fear of failure, arguments with other scientists and the ever-looming Groves, turned on Neddermeyer and brought in other explosive experts (notably, the Englishman James Tuck and the White Russian chemist George Kistiakovsky) over his head. Some comfort was gained at the end of 1943 when it was confirmed that uranium 235 would work in a gun-type bomb.

BATTLE OF ALAMOGORDO

While the scientists at Los Alamos struggled with implosion, Oppenheimer set out to find a place to test such a bomb. In the late spring of 1944, a location within the USAAF's Alamogordo bombing range (again in New Mexico) had been selected. Codenamed Trinity, the first problem for the test team was to get rid of the ranchers in the area, a process which involved the US Army shooting

▲ Scientists of the University of Chicago Research Group. The Italian Nobel Prize winner Enrico Fermi can be seen in the front row, second from right. Much depended on the outcome of his crucial experiment on 2 December 1942, to create the world's first nuclear chain reaction.

US National Archives

▶ Robert Oppenheimer in conversation with Albert Einstein (left). Despite his crucial role in the development of the bomb, Oppenheimer remained a controversial figure throughout his career in the eyes of the US Secret Services.

DARK STAR

J Robert Oppenheimer was born on 22 April 1904, the son of New York businessman Julius Oppenheimer and his art teacher wife, Ella. In 1925 he came to England to work at the Cavendish Laboratory under Ernest Rutherford. During this period, he got involved in what we now know as quantum physics.

In the autumn of 1929, Oppenheimer took up an assistant professorship at the University of California at Berkeley. Here, he made a friend of the physicist Ernest Lawrence and had his first brush with communism. During 1941 Lawrence co-opted Oppenheimer to work on the development of the atomic bomb, and, within the Manhattan Project, he became director of the Los Alamos research centre.

Throughout his work on the bomb, Oppenheimer was under a security cloud because of his earlier left-wing associations. This finally brought him to the point where, in April 1954, he was virtually put on trial for treason. His political rehabilitation came in 1962, and in 1963 he received the Atomic Energy Commission's prestigious Fermi Award. Diagnosed as having throat cancer, he died on 18 February 1967, one of the most enigmatic figures to have come out of the crucible of the 1939–45 scientific effort.

▲ Oppenheimer and Groves (right) view the remains of the tower from which the Trinity device was exploded.

hopes were dashed during the following month due to a lack of reliability in the available explosive detonators and the non-availability of the necessary firing circuitry. Out at Alamogordo, conditions for those building the test facilities were far from good. Daytime temperatures of 100°F (38°C) were the norm and many personnel fell victim to skin complaints and dysentery brought on by the gypsum in the available water.

Despite everything, by June 1945 construction of the tower which would house the test device was under way. Among the many last-minute preparations was a decision about what to do if things went wrong and it became necessary to evacuate towns, such as San Antonio, Bingham, Carrizozo and Alamogordo itself. Having to take account of possible civilian casualties seems to have genuinely annoyed Groves, but he nonetheless made arrangements with the Governor of New Mexico to declare martial law and evacuate the local population if necessary.

LAST-MINUTE TENSIONS

On 30 June, Oppenheimer fixed the date for the Trinity test: 16 July 1945 at 4 o'clock in the morning. Things were still not going well with the implosion problem. Oppenheimer insisted on a facsimile device which would be exploded 24 hours before the actual test as a final check that the explosive content would work as proposed. This started problems between 'Oppy' (as Oppenheimer was universally known) and Kistiakovsky, a situation not made easier by the discovery that the moulds to be used for forming the explosive shell were cracked and pitted.

On 11 July, Los Alamos personnel collected the fissionable plutonium core of the Trinity device for its journey to the test site. Work on the bomb itself began the next morning. More frights occurred when it was discovered that the firing mechanism had failed under test. Investigation revealed that it had been tested so

up water tanks as the only way to force some of the diehards off their land. By early 1945, the military had won the 'Battle of Alamogordo' and began preparing the site.

The early months of 1945 must have been agonising for Oppenheimer and his staff. In April, the problem of symmetrical implosion seemed to have been solved, but

BOFFINS AND BOMBS

The atomic bomb can be traced back to John Dalton's Modern Atomic Theory of 1808 – the idea that small particles (atoms) form the building blocks of all matter. Henri Becquerel in 1895 explained radioactivity as the energy given off by the decomposition of unstable atoms – and their main component, the nucleus. Important leaps forward were the man-made disintegration, and then the splitting, of the atom by Ernest Rutherford in 1919 and John Cockcroft and Ernest Walton in 1932. James Chadwick's 1932 identification of the neutron allowed Frédéric Joliot-Curie to produce plutonium by bombarding uranium atoms with neutrons. In 1938 Enrico Fermi (far left) won a Nobel Prize for controlling the speed of nuclear reactions. That year Otto Hahn (below right) discovered the crucial fission process by neutron-bombarding uranium nuclei, releasing a chain reaction of energy and more neutrons. Soon afterwards, nuclear scientists everywhere realised that a measured amount of uranium in a bomb could create a chain reaction large enough to destroy a city. In 1939, Niels Bohr (above right) showed that the isotope uranium 235 – far faster and more efficient in chain reactions than the more common uranium 238 – was better suited to forming the bomb.

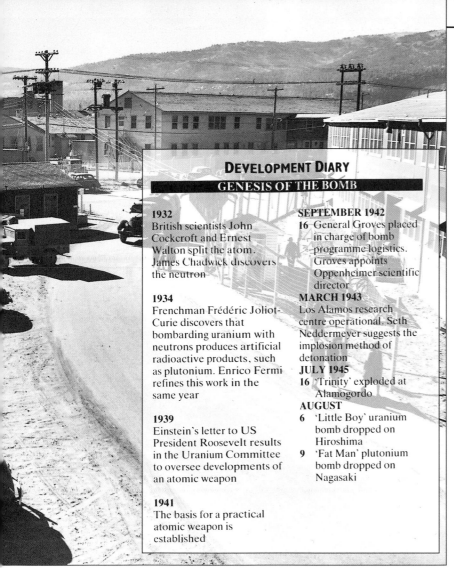

DEVELOPMENT DIARY
GENESIS OF THE BOMB

1932
British scientists John Cockcroft and Ernest Walton split the atom. James Chadwick discovers the neutron

1934
Frenchman Frédéric Joliot-Curie discovers that bombarding uranium with neutrons produces artificial radioactive products, such as plutonium. Enrico Fermi refines this work in the same year

1939
Einstein's letter to US President Roosevelt results in the Uranium Committee to oversee developments of an atomic weapon

1941
The basis for a practical atomic weapon is established

SEPTEMBER 1942
16 General Groves placed in charge of bomb programme logistics. Groves appoints Oppenheimer scientific director

MARCH 1943
Los Alamos research centre operational. Seth Neddermeyer suggests the implosion method of detonation

JULY 1945
16 'Trinity' exploded at Alamogordo

AUGUST
6 'Little Boy' uranium bomb dropped on Hiroshima
9 'Fat Man' plutonium bomb dropped on Nagasaki

◄ Produced at a cost of two million dollars, the Trinity device looks like nothing more than a giant football on skis. With the cream of the world's scientists watching from a distance of 5 miles (8 km), it was detonated successfully on 16 July 1945.

was still too bright to look at. I kept blinking and trying to take looks, and after ten seconds or so it had grown and dimmed into something more like a huge oil fire with a structure that made it look a bit like a strawberry. It was slowly rising into the sky from the ground, with which it remained connected by a lengthening stem of swirling dust. Then, as the cloud of hot gas cooled and became less red, one could see a blue glow surrounding it, a glow of ionised air. It was an awesome spectacle; anybody who has seen an atomic explosion will never forget it. And all in complete silence: the bang came minutes later, quite loud, though I plugged my ears, and followed by a long rumble like heavy traffic very far away. I can still hear it.'

SHATTERER OF WORLDS

Trinity had exploded with a power equivalent to 20,000 tons of TNT. Oppenheimer was to recall later, 'There floated through my mind a line from the *Bhagavad-Gita* in which Krishna is trying to persuade the Prince that he should do his duty: "I am become death, the shatterer of worlds".'

many times that it had overheated and melted a number of solder joints. Worse was to come when the facsimile device failed to produce a symmetrical shock wave when it was exploded on 14 July. To cap everything, the weather began to deteriorate.

Oppenheimer was now close to breaking point: he was constantly chain smoking, his six-foot (1.80-m) frame down to a weight of 115 lbs (52 kg). A little light came into his darkness on the 15th, when Hans Bethe told him that the results from the facsimile test were meaningless because of a fault in the way the experiment had been organised. But just knowing that the real thing might yet work cheered Oppenheimer enormously.

TEST EXPLOSION

By midnight on the 15th, Trinity was shrouded in rain, and further storms were forecast as moving towards the test site. Groves and Oppenheimer agreed to postpone for a couple of hours to give the weather a chance to improve. By 4 am on the 16th, the rain stopped and, after consultation with the meteorological team, the decision was taken to explode the device at 5.30 am.

What happened next is best described by Otto Frisch: one of those who saw it:

'Without a sound the sun was shining – or so it looked. The sand dunes at the edge of the desert were shimmering in a very bright light, almost colourless and shapeless. This light did not seem to change for a couple of seconds and then began to dim. I turned round [the observers were instructed to stand with their backs to the blast] but that object on the horizon which looked like a small sun

▲ Laboratory buildings at Los Alamos, a remote and inhospitable desert location in New Mexico, which was to become the temporary home for hundreds of workers attached to the development of the bomb.

► Two months after the blast at the Alamogordo site, scientists (among them Dr Oppenheimer, with hat), measure the fall-out using a radio-activity meter.

Associated Press/Topham

THE BIG BANG

Rushed from prototype to production, the
A-bomb is dropped on Hiroshima and Nagasaki.
The horrifying outcome stuns the world – and
forces Japan into submission.

◄ ◄ **A last wave from the cockpit of _Enola Gay_ before Colonel Tibbets sets off with his fateful cargo on 6 August 1945. Among the crew of the now famous B-29 were bombardier Ferebee (left) and navigator Van Kirk (right).**

▲ ▼ **In President Truman's hands lay the awesome responsibility of deploying the first atomic bomb. By 24 July 1945 possible targets had been specified in a secret memorandum (below).**

A s the scientists at Los Alamos struggled to get the atomic bomb to work, the military was already making preparations for its use. It was never truly doubted that the bomb would be put to use, the real question was how and against what. The original target, Germany, had surrendered by May 1945, so the obvious choice was Japan.

There were good reasons for this, as at the turn of the year, it seemed likely that the Pacific War could only be ended by the invasion of the Japanese Home Islands. Even the most conservative estimates suggested that such an operation would cost many thousands of Allied lives. An atomic explosion might just tip the balance and force Japan to surrender without an invasion.

From 1943 onwards there had been considerable debate within the scientific community on the morality of using an atomic weapon (always assuming that it could be made to work). This prompted suggestions that the atomic bomb should be 'demonstrated' to the Japanese – an idea which involved notifying Japan that such a bomb would be exploded at a particular site in the Pacific, and, having seen its effects, if the country still did not choose to surrender, the next one would be used for 'real'. This policy was eventually discounted because it was felt that with prior notice the Japanese might try to move prisoners of war into the target area and that in any case, the Japanese were fanatical enough to carry on fighting – even having seen what such a weapon could do. Accordingly, it was decided to notify the Japanese that if they would not surrender, a weapon of 'unimaginable power' would be used.

As reasonable as the thinking behind the decision to use the atomic bomb against Japan might have seemed under the circumstances, there may have been a darker purpose behind it. American policymakers were already looking hard at the post-war world. One of their greatest concerns was the Soviet Union. In the short term, the major unanswered question was whether or not Russia would support its Allies in the Pacific by declaring war on Japan after the defeat of Germany. Equally unclear was what, in the longer term, would Stalin do with the huge war machine he had created to defeat Germany. Would he try to expand Soviet power in both Western Europe and the Far East in direct opposition to American interests?

The new US President, Harry Truman (Roosevelt had died on 12 April 1945) saw 'the bomb' as an ace card with which to intimidate – or at least restrain – Stalin's ambitions. A practical demonstration of its power could only enhance the effect. Truman began playing this hand at the Potsdam Conference where, having received the news of the successful Trinity test, he informed Stalin of the American atomic programme.

Stalin showed little surprise at the information – a somewhat puzzling response for the American nego-tiators who believed that the Russians knew nothing about the programme. In fact, they knew quite a lot through the work of spies, such as Klaus Fuchs, David Greenglass and Julius and Ethel Rosenberg. Stalin had already begun his own atomic programme which was to culminate in a successful test explosion on 14 July 1949.

A practical delivery system for the new American weapon was already

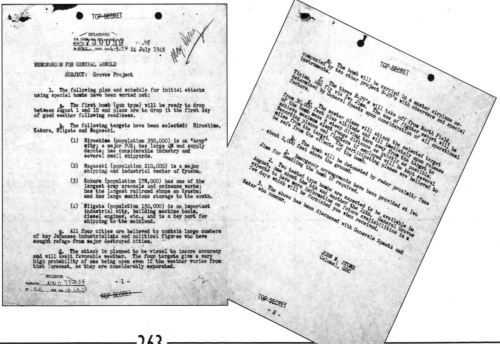

Right: Popperfoto, inset: US National Archives

◄▲▼ The crew that flew the mission to Hiroshima (left). Euphemistically nick-named 'Little Boy', the bomb (above) weighed 9,000 lbs (4,082 kg) and packed the explosive power of 20,000 tons of high explosive – enough to devastate an area more than 1½ miles (2½ km) from the point of impact, as marked by the outer circle (below) on this aerial view of the city after the explosion.

being developed as early as 1944 when consideration was being given to which aircraft was to carry it. At this stage, the most likely practical weapon was a gun-type plutonium bomb requiring a 'barrel' some 17 ft (5.18 m) long. Of America's warplanes, only the B-29 could carry something that big – and then only by joining its two bomb bays together. (Because of this, the British Avro Lancaster was also seriously considered as the carrier aircraft).

TEST BOMBS

The development of the implosion concept meant that there were two types of bomb available. The gun-type was codenamed 'Thin Man' and the implosion type 'Fat Man'. Test drops of dummies of these, known as 'shapes', began at Mirror Lake in March 1944. The last release in the series severely damaged the test aircraft, which was unavailable again until June. By this time, it had been decided that, while a gun-type plutonium bomb would not work, a uranium 235 variant would. Thus was born 'Little Boy', which was compatible with the carriage in the standard B-29 bomb bay.

On 17 December 1944 – the 41st anniversary of the Wright brothers' first flight – the Twentieth Air Force's 509th Composite Group was activated to operate the atomic bom-

bers. Based at Wendover Field, Utah, and under the command of Colonel Paul W Tibbets Jr, the crews of the Group's flying squadron, the 393rd, had no real idea of what they were training for as they flew some rather unusual flight profiles, ending in the release of single bombs from very high altitude. Indeed, Tibbets was the only man in the unit who knew exactly what the mission was.

While the 509th practised, work proceeded to refine the fusing technique with a series of test-device drops over the Salton Sea range facility. Other trials involved the delivery of 'pumpkins' – the 'Fat Man' casing without the atomic material installed – over the USN's Inyokern rocket range. The 'pumpkin' bombs were produced by a special team at the Californian Institute of Technology who, under the codename 'Camel Project', were also responsible for the bomb assembly mechanisms and the combat delivery of the operational devices to the bases in the Pacific.

As the 509th got used to the mission, it too began dropping 'pumpkins'. The early training flights revealed many problems with the B-29 'specials', so much so, that a second batch of modified aircraft had to be acquired. On 26 April 1945, the Group began its deployment to the Pacific, with its adv-

AP INDICATES AIMING POINT

STATUTE MILE

Popperfoto

anced air echelon arriving at North Field, Tinian, on 18 May. The unit's ground echelon reached the island on 18 May with the first B-29 touching down on 11 June.

By the end of the month, the Group began combat-flight training with a series of practice missions against Rota or Truk by formations of up to nine aircraft. As is the way in all service communities, the other B-29 fliers at North Field soon got wind that the 509th was something special and, equally quickly, began to give its crews a hard time as they scoffed at their lack of involvement in 'real' combat.

'PUMPKIN MISSIONS'

The group had brought with it a number of 'pumpkins' which were now filled with high explosives and dropped on Japanese targets from 20 July onwards. Going out in small formations of up to six aircraft and dropping single 'blockbuster' bombs did little to stem the tide of ribaldry concerning the unit's combat prowess. Much more important for Tibbets was the knowledge that at least one of the weapons he was to take into combat actually worked: if Trinity exploded, so would 'Fat Man'.

Twelve 'pumpkin' missions were flown (20, 24, 26 and 29 July), while on Tinian work proceeded on assembling 'Little Boy' and 'Fat

Man'. Because a sea route had been chosen, getting the parts from America was somewhat fraught as there was always the possibility of submarine attack *en route*.

Once ashore, work began in conditions of great secrecy, with the first bomb, 'Little Boy', being completed on 31 July 1945. Seven days earlier, the order had been issued for the 509th to drop the first of its 'special'

bombs, as soon as weather permitted after 3 August 1945, on any one of four targets: Hiroshima, Kokura, Niigata or Nagasaki.

By 5 August 1945, the Twentieth Air Force's meteorological service predicted good visual bombing weather over the four targets, and on the following day, the order was given for the 509th's 13th mission – the first atomic attack. The order

▲▲▶ Charred corpses litter Hiroshima. The heat from the blast has stripped the paint off a gas main 1¼ miles (2 km) away (above right), leaving a 'shadow' of the spindle in front.

AGE OF THE BOMB

The world changed irrevocably just after 8.14am on 6 August 1945. Up to that point, man's capacity to wage war had been awesome enough – the loss of more than 20 million Russian lives in four years of conventional war bore witness to that – but it had been a time-consuming and costly business. Hiroshima was different: for the first time destruction could be guaranteed and instantaneous, using a single bomber carrying a single bomb. Gone were the days (and nights) of devastating a city street by street, presuming that the bombers could find their targets and concentrate their bomb-loads; now, in a flash of blinding light, entire urban complexes could literally disappear. It was an image and a reality that would not go away. We live with it still.

US Navy

A-BOMB CASUALTIES

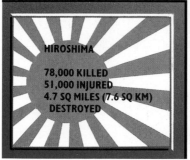

HIROSHIMA

78,000 KILLED
51,000 INJURED
4.7 SQ MILES (7.6 SQ KM)
DESTROYED

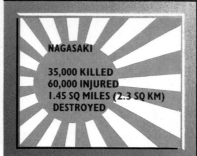

NAGASAKI

35,000 KILLED
60,000 INJURED
1.45 SQ MILES (2.3 SQ KM)
DESTROYED

specified the urban/industrial area of Hiroshima as the primary target, with Kokura and Nagasaki as backups. The bomb was only to be released if the target area could be clearly seen. Bombing altitude was specified at between 28,000 and 30,000 ft (8,534 and 9,144 m) at an airspeed of 200 mph (322 km/h).

TAKE-OFF

At midnight local time, the crews were briefed and at 1.37 am three F-13A 'Photoforts', piloted by Major Claude Eatherly (in *Straight Flush*), Major Ralph Taylor (in *Full House*) and Major John Wilson (in *Jabbitt III*) launched from Tinian to reconnoitre the weather over Hiroshima, Nagasaki and Kokura respectively.

At 2.45 am Colonel Tibbets released the brakes on his aircraft (nicknamed *Enola Gay*) and lumbered down one of North Field's four runways under the weight of 'Little Boy'. *Enola Gay* was accompanied by Major Charles Sweeney's *The Great Artiste* and Captain

▼ **Exhausted Japanese troops – now truly defeated – wait in the ripped-out shell of a railway station in Hiroshima.**

▲ **Unaware of the perils of radiation, a stunned Japanese surveys the bleak landscape of Hiroshima: even the stark trees seem to throw up their 'hands' in despair.**

US National Archives

Maarquardt's unnamed B–29 which were to act as instrumentation/observation platforms.

At 6.05 am the small formation crossed over Iwo Jima and turned north-east towards the target area. This was the signal for USN Captain William 'Deak' Parsons to crawl into the cramped bomb-bay and arm the bomb. This done, Tibbets began to climb towards bombing altitude at 7.41 am and reached 32,700 ft (9,967 m) by 8.38 am. Hiroshima was spotted 31 minutes later and at 8.14 am Hiroshima time, Major Thomas Ferebee released 'Little Boy'. Relieved of its load, *Enola Gay* lurched upwards as Tibbets puts his plane into a hard banking turn to exit as fast as possible.

sion horror, it is hard to imagine or express what happened that day in Hiroshima. Worse (if that is possible) was to come in the form of radiation sickness afterwards. One woman recalled:

'My daughter, she had no burns and only minor external wounds. She was quite all right for a while but on the 4th September (four weeks and one day after the attack) she suddenly became sick. She had spots all over her body. Her hair began to fall out. She vomited small clumps of blood many times. I felt this was a very strange and horrible disease. We were all afraid of it and even the doctor didn't know what it was. After ten days of agony and torture, she died on September 14th.'

JAPAN STUNNED

At first, the Japanese government could not comprehend what had happened. The news of the Hiroshima attack reached Tokyo on the 7th and it seemed so incredible that an investigation team was sent out to discover the truth. Actually, some members of the Japanese government had been trying to make peace since late July but were prevented from gaining the upper hand by the Allies' determination to remove the Emperor. On 8 August, the Japanese Ambassador in Moscow went to see the Soviet Foreign Minister, Vyacheslav Molotov, in an attempt to enlist Russian help in mediating between his country and the British and American governments. For his pains, Ambassador Naotake Sato was informed that a state of war now existed between Russia and Japan. The two events combined to make the argument for surrender overwhelming.

In Hiroshima on that fateful morning, the air raid sirens had sounded three times by 7.00 am local time. At 7.30 am the all clear was sounded and the morning rush hour began. Shortly after 8.00 am the 509th formation was spotted but no additional alert was sounded, as the aircraft were considered to be a reconnaissance flight and therefore of no danger to the city. At 8.14 am and 43 seconds, 'Little Boy' detonated at about 1,900 ft (579 m) above the town.

Within the next few seconds at least 78,000 people (25 per cent of Hiroshima's daytime population) died, another 51,000 were injured to a greater or lesser extent, at least 70,000 buildings were destroyed and

Hiroshima had, to all intents and purposes, ceased to exist. In the aircraft, Tibbets' crew felt two distinct shock waves as the bomb detonated, followed by a single 'My God!' from one of the crew members (probably the tail gunner) as he watched the mushroom cloud rising above the city. Fifteen minutes after release, Parsons transmitted the message 'Clear cut results, exceeding TR [Trinity] test in visible effects, and in all respects successful. Normal conditions continued in aircraft after delivery was accomplished'. Satisfied, Tibbets flew back to Tinian.

The dead were the lucky ones. The blast and thermal injuries were horrific. Even in our age of televi-

▲ ▶ **Handing over the baton. Major Sweeney (left) is bid godspeed, before he sets off to drop the second atomic bomb on Nagasaki, by Col Tibbets, now a veteran of the process.**

US National Archives

◄ The ominous mushroom cloud rises once more over Japan (left), as Nagasaki is bombed on 9 August 1945.

▼◄ Hapless women and children flee with meagre belongings from the carnage around them, their cloth masks scant protection against the stench of death and destruction.

The Japanese government's indecision about accepting the Allied surrender terms signed Nagasaki's death warrant. Hearing nothing after the Hiroshima attack, the Americans went ahead with preparations to drop 'Fat Man'. Amazingly, the timing of the attack was left to the Field Commander on Tinian.

Originally scheduled for 11 August 1945, the 'Fat Man' attack was actually executed on the 9th. At about 3 am Tinian time, Major Charles Sweeney lifted off in *Bockscar* and headed for the mission's primary target, Kokura. Over Japan, Sweeney hit bad weather and lost contact with one of the two observation aircraft accompanying him. Over Kokura, Sweeney made three bombing runs without being able to see the target. Following the 'no see, no bomb' ruling, he diverted to Nagasaki. This too was 'socked in' and it was only by chance that a hole opened in the cloud cover long enough for a successful bomb run.

SECOND CHOICE

At around 11am Japanese time, Nagasaki vanished under the still novel mushroom cloud as 'Fat Man' killed 35,000 and injured another 60,000. The lower casualty figures were no indication of the superiority

War Stories

One of the major factors which decided America in favour of dropping the atom bomb was that, if it came to an invasion of Japan by US forces, the losses would be huge. The condition of the US Pacific veterans bore witness to the strains of continual combat. People wanting to justify the bombing might consider the words of one such vet: 'Take it from the voice of experience. If my company makes one more invasion, you had better tell the medical corps to have 42 straitjackets – for there are 42 of us left.'

of one bomb type over the other but rather an accident of geography: Hiroshima was surrounded by hills which contained and magnified the effect. Nagasaki was more open.

The diversion had left Sweeney very low on fuel and he only just made it back to Iwo Jima. As *Bockscar* touched down, the Pacific War was all but over. In the wake of the two atomic attacks, an intense de-

▼ **All that is left of the historic and prosperous port of Nagasaki is rubble and ruin. The ultimate application of science finally ended the war.**

bate started (and, indeed, continues) about the morality of using such weapons. At this remove, we can see why the Americans went ahead with the attacks and that they did indeed save both Allied *and* Japanese lives which would otherwise have been lost in an invasion of the Home Islands. Equally, many thought (and still think) that the bombs were just retribution for the bestial behaviour the Japanese armed forces had shown towards those they conquered and captured.

Whatever the rights and wrongs of such thoughts, we do well to remember Hiroshima and Nagasaki as a terrible lesson as to what we can do to ourselves and the planet which sustains us.

JAPANESE SURRENDER

After the destruction of Hiroshima and the Soviet declaration of war on Japan, the peace faction in the Japanese Imperial Council was presented with the 'supreme opportunity to turn the tide against the die-hards and to shake the government loose from the yoke of military oppression under which it had been lumbering for too long'. Following the Nagasaki raid, the Japanese Foreign Minister, Shigenori Togo, informed both London and Washington that Japan was ready to capitulate providing the Emperor's future as head of state could be guaranteed. On 11 August the Allies replied that a restriction of the Emperor's power, a democratically elected government and occupation by Allied forces would satisfy them.

On the 14th, Emperor Hirohito finally managed to get the Imperial Council to accept the Allies' terms. The next day Hirohito broadcast to his people: 'Indeed we declared war on America and Britain out of our sincere desire to ensure Japan's self-preservation and the stabilisation of East Asia, it being far from our thoughts either to infringe upon the sovereignty of other nations or to embark upon territorial aggrandisement. But now the war has lasted for nearly four years. In spite of the best that has been done by everybody – the gallant fighting of the military and naval forces, the diligence and assiduity of our servants of the State and the devoted service of our 100,000,000 people – the war situation has developed not necessarily to Japan's advantage, while the general trends of the world have all turned against her interests. The enemy, moreover, has begun to employ a new and most cruel bomb, the power of which to do damage is indeed incalculable, taking toll of many innocent lives. Should we continue to fight, it would not only result in the ultimate collapse and obliteration of the Japanese nation but would lead to the total extinction of human civilisation.'

▼ **The momentous signing of the surrender documents aboard the *Missouri* on 2 September 1945.**

Robert Hunt Library

INDEX